"In this riveting first cut of history, Yonah Jeremy Bob and Elliot Kaufman take readers behind the scenes to learn how Israeli leaders directed a multi-front war, took risks, often defied Washington, and delivered crushing blows to their enemies. *In the War Room* is the book to read to understand the beginning of a new era in the histories of Israel and the Middle East."

Lt. Gen. H. R. McMaster, US Army, (Ret.),
former US national security advisor and bestselling author of *At War with Ourselves*, *Battlegrounds*, and *Dereliction of Duty*.

"*In the War Room* is a gripping narrative that tells the inside story of the bitter infighting and strategic calculations that led Israel to victory in the longest and bloodiest war in its history. With extraordinary access to officials across the Israeli political and military establishments, Yonah Jeremy Bob and Elliot Kaufman offer readers a clear and coherent narrative and the closest look yet at a war whose repercussions continue to shake the world."

Prof. Walter Russell Mead, Global View columnist for *The Wall Street Journal* and author of *The Arc of a Covenant: The United States, Israel, and the Fate of the Jewish People.*

"With gripping detail, this is the story of how Israel's leaders fought back from the catastrophe of October 7 to decimate Hamas, Hezbollah, and Iran—and change the face of the Middle East."

Elliott Abrams, former US special envoy for Iran, National Security Council senior director, deputy national security advisor, and author of *Tested by Zion.*

IN THE WAR ROOM

IN THE WAR ROOM

The Inside Story of Israel's Fight Against Hamas and the Iranian Axis

YONAH JEREMY BOB
AND ELLIOT KAUFMAN

WICKED SON

A WICKED SON BOOK
An Imprint of Post Hill Press

ISBN: 979-8-89565-480-4
ISBN (eBook): 979-8-89565-481-1

In the War Room:
The Inside Story of Israel's Fight Against Hamas and the Iranian Axis

Cover Design by Jim Villaflores

Post Hill Press
New York • Nashville
wickedsonbooks.com
posthillpress.com

Published in the United States of America
1 2 3 4 5 6 7 8 9 10

TABLE OF CONTENTS

PREFACE

The future of the region hung in the balance. Israeli Prime Minister Benjamin Netanyahu was on a plane from Tel Aviv to New York to give a major speech at the United Nations, but who could spare a thought for words? The next few days would be all about deeds.

He received a call from his war-room partners, Defense Minister Yoav Gallant and Army Chief of Staff Herzi Halevi. It was late September 2024, and the three men were about to decide whether to assassinate Hassan Nasrallah, the terrorist leader of Hezbollah in Lebanon for the past thirty-two years. Geopolitically, Hezbollah was the elder brother of Hamas in Gaza. Nasrallah had also become the top adviser to Iran's supreme leader, Ayatollah Ali Khamenei. In the world of Shia Islamic politics, violence, and jihad, Nasrallah was a legend.

Missing from the debate that followed was Benny Gantz, the Israeli opposition leader who had helped Netanyahu and Gallant run the war from when he joined a unity government in October 2023 until he resigned in June 2024. Gantz shared in all the fateful early decisions that set the course of Israel's fight against Hamas, Hezbollah, and Iran.

Netanyahu was pleased that Gantz was now out of the way. He might have tried to restrain the prime minister. While Gantz had been more aggressive than Netanyahu at the start of the war, by the time Gantz quit the war room, the prime minister felt he had been holding back critical, if audacious, military moves. Netanyahu further begrudged Gantz for having helped oust him from power a few years prior.

Gallant also resented Gantz, who had become chief of staff of the Israel Defense Forces (IDF) in 2011 after Gallant's nomination for the post had been sunk in a highly politicized process. But the two had more recently found themselves in agreement. Both supported cutting a deal with Hamas to return the Israeli hostages held in Gaza, even at the cost of ending the war.

Neither trusted Netanyahu, who had tried to fire Gallant before the war and had reneged in a previous coalition government on a deal to rotate in the prime minister's chair with Gantz. The three leaders tolerated one another only because they had a war to wage in Israel's defense.

Netanyahu banged on the table to get the assassination moving. He hit it loudly enough for Gallant and Halevi to hear over the phone back at military headquarters in Tel Aviv. After some wrangling, Halevi convinced the prime minister to accept the Air Force's recommendation on timing—when to drop the more than eighty large bombs on Nasrallah. Yet the IDF chief and Gallant would lose the argument over whether to inform the US in advance of the operation. Believing this would endanger the mission, Netanyahu would not hear of it. The Biden administration would be looped in only once Israeli planes were on the way to Lebanon and could not be stopped. This would lead to one of the tensest exchanges of the war between the two allies.

At 6:30 p.m. on September 27, as the sun was starting to set, the Israeli Air Force hit Nasrallah's secret underground lair so hard that the terrorist leader and many other top Hezbollah officials were not only killed, but crushed. This was the day the Iranian axis began to crumble.

All the men involved in the critical phone call of the airborne war room realized that Israel had finally turned a corner. The war that started on October 7, 2023, with the proportional equivalent of "fifteen 9/11s," as President Joe Biden had put it, would not end until Israel had reordered the military map of the Middle East.

* * *

After Hamas stunned Israel on October 7, slaughtering nearly twelve hundred people and taking over swaths of the southern part of the country, Israel's counterattack proceeded in stages. For the first eleven months, the Gaza front was primary. Israel fought from Gaza City in the northern Gaza Strip down to Khan Yunis and then Rafah, with interludes for a hostage and ceasefire deal, debates with the Biden team over next steps, and a direct military exchange with Iran. Hezbollah joined the war against Israel on October 8 and fired rockets for these eleven months, yet this fight was kept on a lower burn. Gaza was Israel's focus.

From September 2024 until a ceasefire at the end of November 2024, Israel took the fight to Hezbollah. The Lebanon front was primary, again with a spectacular Iranian interlude. Israel would defeat Hezbollah soundly, and in its wake came the fall of Bashar al-Assad's regime in Syria. President Donald Trump returned to office in January 2025 with a second Gaza hostage deal that quieted the war until spring 2025.

In June 2025, Israel attacked Iran, targeting its most valuable nuclear and conventional capabilities with total aerial supremacy. Though Israelis paid a price on the home front, they saw their greatest military achievements in over fifty years. Trump and the US Air Force joined for one devastating mission to top it off.

By that point, Israel had smashed Hamas and Hezbollah, killing their leaders, destroying their arsenals, and setting them back by many years. This meant Israel indirectly, yet substantially, aided the Syrian rebels in toppling the Assad regime. From these blows, the anti-Israel and anti-America proxy axis that Iran spent decades building might never recover. With the destruction of so much of the Iranian nuclear and ballistic-missile programs, the balance of power in the Middle East had shifted dramatically.

From July 2025 until the final Gaza hostage deal and ceasefire of October 2025, however, Israel struggled on the diplomatic front. The death, destruction, and suffering in Gaza caused by the war had been a deep ethical and diplomatic challenge throughout, but now the threat of starvation began to overshadow Israel's military accomplishments. After a failed, aggressive Israeli airstrike against Hamas officials in Qatar, President Trump seized the moment to impose a ceasefire on both sides. He called it peace.

* * *

All the while, Israel's war room was dynamic, which is a polite way to say that it was fractious and unstable, deeply divided on matters of principle and strategy, and torn by political interest and personal animosity. It was also dynamic in the physical sense that meetings were held in different parts of Tel Aviv and Jerusalem, with different officials—the prime minister, the defense minister, and the IDF chief—each playing host and trying to influence the direction of debate by the setting and the attendees. Though critics often framed Israel as a single-minded enemy, there was rarely one "Israeli" view, not even among the leaders running the war.

Whom to fight first? How to fight? When to make peace? How much to concede for the hostages' safety? These questions and their answers from Israel's leaders—on the phone with an alternately angry or indulgent White House—would shape the war, for better and for worse.

On October 9, 2023, when Israel was a wreck, its government was in disarray, and 251 hostages had just been taken to Gaza, we were told something astonishing. It came by way of Netanyahu's foreign-policy adviser Ophir Falk, a counterterrorism PhD who still speaks English with the Canadian accent of his youth. "This war started out worse than even the Yom Kippur War" of 1973, "and with even less early warning," he began. "But if we get this right, it could end better than even the Six-Day War" of 1967, "and with an even greater chance for peace."

In the months that followed, the critical decisions made by Netanyahu, Gallant, and Gantz helped Israel come back from the failures of October 7 to achieve stunning gains against its enemies. Military victories, especially over Iran and Hezbollah, left Israel in a stronger and safer position than before the war. Some of these victories will likely translate into longer-term diplomatic gains, even if it did not seem that way in the heat of the propaganda war. It is easy to forget, but in strategic terms, Gaza may have been Israel's least important front.

At the same time, Israel has already paid a steep diplomatic price for its failures in Gaza. Part of this stems from the world's double standards for Israel; its enemies begin wars of annihilation, but when Israel fights back, observers accuse it of wanton aggression. Part of it, however, stems from Israel's own decisions. Some of these belong to the entire war room. Others belong to the Israeli military and Shin Bet intelligence agency. Still others belong to Prime Minister Netanyahu alone.

Keeping the war alive for two years, with all that the devastation meant for Gazan civilians, was a choice. The costs of that choice have been to make Israel a punching bag even in allied nations. Support for Israel tanked in the US, in particular among American liberals, who are likely to call the shots in Washington about half the time in the pendulum of US politics.

Blocking humanitarian aid to Gaza for two months in 2025 was an unforced error that failed to squeeze Hamas. Instead, it led to substantial food insecurity in Gaza—even if it was exaggerated by critics and if United Nations aid distribution was partly to blame. The policy succeeded only in delegitimizing the Jewish state in many quarters, including some in which support had held until then.

On October 7, 2023, some six thousand fighters from Hamas and its allies were able to penetrate Israel in around 119 locations, conquering villages, intersections, and even the forward operating base of the IDF's Southern Command. Israel failed in every way possible. Yet not even a year later, on September 17, 2024, Israel appeared hypercompetent, wounding some three thousand five hundred Hezbollah fighters in a matter of seconds in the coordinated explosion of the terrorist organization's pagers.

How could the same Israel be beaten so badly on October 7 by Hamas, find itself largely unable to rescue the hostages, and then pull off the pagers operation against Hezbollah? Or Operation Rising Lion on June 13, 2025, when Israel shocked Iran by hitting its nuclear program, ballistic-missile sites, military leadership, and nuclear scientists? How could the same war room that gave a master class when it turned its gaze to Hezbollah and Iran be so plodding and unimaginative when it focused on Gaza?

One answer is that Israel's options are always worse with the Palestinians than with other Middle Eastern foes, and that its strategic aims and moral case in fighting the Palestinians are more disputed, even among Israelis.

Another is that Hamas held hostages. Still a third is that Israel succeeded when it was prepared. Its campaigns against Hezbollah and then Iran were rolled out in exquisite sequences, one strike leading to the next, leaving its enemies gasping for air and unable to respond as anticipated. Once Israel began to fight Hezbollah and Iran in earnest, the results were spectacular and decisive, and came at shockingly little diplomatic cost.

In Gaza, by contrast, Israel was caught unprepared, and not only on October 7. Israel's war room and military always seemed to be improvising in Gaza, stopping and starting, questioning their next move and whether there should even be one. The fighting would drag on and achieve much more mixed results at a great cost in human life and global opinion.

This shook Israel's relationship with the US to its foundations during the Biden administration. The Trump administration subsequently presented new opportunities for Israel, but Netanyahu did not always seem to know what to do with them.

Where he did know what to do was Iran. In twelve days that shook the world in June 2025, Israel's Air Force and elite spy agency, the Mossad, humiliated the Iranian regime. Netanyahu and his right-hand man Ron Dermer then convinced President Trump to drop the "Midnight Hammer," as the Pentagon called it, smashing three Iranian nuclear sites with thirty-thousand-pound bunker-buster bombs and Tomahawk missiles to finish the job. The single greatest threat to Israel, and one of the largest threats to world peace, was neutralized as effectively as Jerusalem could have hoped.

The events of this war were historic, and *In the War Room* provides the most detailed, inside account of it available anywhere, shedding new light on the twists and turns. How did Israel come back from its darkest hour to crush the Iranian proxy axis and own the skies over Tehran? Why did Israel struggle, at great diplomatic cost, to bring the war in Gaza to an end, even as it defeated Hamas militarily? This story of Israel's war room contains the answers to these questions and more. We now reveal the untold saga of how three political enemies, Netanyahu, Gallant, and Gantz, debated and made the critical decisions that shaped the war.

NOTE ON SOURCES

This book is based on around two years of private interviews, briefings, and trips to combat zones on four fronts: Gaza, Lebanon, Syria, and the West Bank. This accounts for the overwhelming majority of the book's material, forming its core.

Between us, we interviewed Israeli Prime Minister Benjamin Netanyahu, Defense Minister Yoav Gallant, War Minister (and later opposition figure) Benny Gantz, all of the top Israeli military and intelligence officials—some of whom cannot yet be named—and various other top political officials. We have also interviewed top Biden and Trump administration officials in the US State Department and US Defense Department, former US National Security Advisor Jake Sullivan, Trump administration envoy to the Middle East Steve Witkoff, and others. In addition, we spoke to and received briefings from over one hundred senior Israeli military officials, including nearly every critical member of the IDF high command. Some of these officials also presented the authors with real-time documentation to back up their narratives.

Some of the contents of this book we published previously in our respective outlets, *The Jerusalem Post* and *The Wall Street Journal*, which we note here as a broader recognition, without citing specifics as we do with other sources. Much of the material, however, is being revealed for the first time.

The interviewees in the book cover a broad political spectrum of Israeli and US officials with different views of Netanyahu, Biden, and

Trump. The book homes in on some of the spirited arguments between the decision-makers involved and tries to give a fair hearing to multiple sides of those debates.

Obtaining information from some of the above officials, especially Mossad and some Israeli military officials on controversial security and political topics, was challenging. Sometimes, we secured their cooperation only by promising anonymity or partial anonymity. There are areas in which we had to avoid revealing when and how we learned certain information. Citations, then, would have presented challenges in any scenario. Since Yonah lives in Israel, this book comes under the jurisdiction of the Israeli censorship regulations. We succeeded in many battles with the censor, but there were small portions of the book that we were required to cut. In other instances, we had to make reference to foreign sources rather than our independent Israeli sources to sidestep censorship barriers, provided the information from foreign sources was also accurate.

For these reasons and more, a joint decision was made with the publisher not to cite our own interviews, which we mention here. We use citations instead for other authors' works.

CAST OF CHARACTERS

The Israeli War Cabinet

Prime Minister Benjamin "Bibi" Netanyahu. Israel's longest-serving prime minister, with the scars and enemies to prove it.

Defense Minister Yoav Gallant. Tough, old-school retired general. Fought with Netanyahu over both domestic and national security policies, despite being in the same party. Fired by Netanyahu on November 5, 2024, and not for the first time.

War Minister Benny Gantz. Tall, stoic former defense minister and IDF chief. Had a power-sharing agreement in 2020 that Netanyahu reneged on. Became the Israeli opposition's great hope to moderate or replace Netanyahu for much of the war. Joined the unity government on October 11, 2023, and resigned over wartime disagreements on June 9, 2024.

Strategic Affairs Minister Ron Dermer. Netanyahu's right-hand man. Miami-born former Israeli ambassador to the US who never fully gave up the job. Nonvoting war cabinet observer. Stepped down on November 11, 2025.

War Minister Gadi Eisenkot. Former IDF chief and the dove of the war cabinet. He joined the unity government on October 11, 2023, as Gantz's partner, and resigned on June 9, 2024. Nonvoting war cabinet observer.

Shas Party Leader Aryeh Deri. Sephardic ultraorthodox politician and key coalition partner for Netanyahu. Nonvoting war cabinet observer.

The Israeli Security Services

IDF Chief of Staff Herzi Halevi. Modest, but aggressive. In charge on October 7, 2023, he would recover to lead Israel's counteroffensives in Gaza and Lebanon and the push into Syria. Resigned on March 5, 2025.

Mossad Director David "Dadi" Barnea. A "gadget-loving killing machine" who would lead explosive clandestine operations in Lebanon and Iran and emerge from the shadows for hostage negotiations in Qatar.

IDF Chief of Staff Eyal Zamir. Rose from Israel's periphery and armored corps to lead the military after March 5, 2025, on a new Gaza offensive. He would leave his legacy by defeating Iran in Operation Rising Lion.

Shin Bet Director Ronen Bar. Also in charge on October 7, 2023, he would lead counterterror operations in Gaza and Lebanon. After Netanyahu tried to fire him, he resigned on June 15, 2025.

Military Intelligence Chief Aharon Haliva. On vacation on October 7. Resigned in mid-2024, after underestimating Iran's retaliation to an Israeli assassination. Left office on August 21, 2024.

Southern Command Chief Yaron Finkelman. Three months into the job, he did not react strongly enough to the warning signs on October 7, but then led the defeat of Hamas's twenty-four Gaza battalions. Resigned on March 6, 2025.

Division 98 Commander Dan Goldfus. The general who broke Hamas's tunnel strategy in Khan Yunis in southern Gaza.

The Iranian Axis

Supreme Leader Ayatollah Ali Khamenei. Ruled Iran with an iron hand since 1989. Worked for decades to destroy Israel by surrounding it with an axis of proxies known as the "ring of fire." Refused, even at great cost, to give up his nuclear program.

Iranian Foreign Minister Abbas Araghchi. Held to Khamenei's line on uranium enrichment as time ran out on President Trump's deadline for nuclear negotiations.

Quds Force Unit 1800 Commander Mohammad Reza Zahedi. Led Iran's Islamic Revolutionary Guard Corps operations for Lebanon and Syria. Assassinated by Israel in Damascus on April 1, 2024, leading to the first of three major rounds of fighting between Tehran and Jerusalem.

Hezbollah Secretary General Hassan Nasrallah. Led the Hezbollah terrorist group in Lebanon from strength to strength for thirty-two years. He had become "the axis of the Iranian axis." Joined Hamas's war on Israel on October 8, 2023. Assassinated by Israel in Beirut on September 27, 2024.

Hezbollah Military Chief of Staff Fuad Shukr. The primary architect of Hezbollah's military strategy. Responsible for smuggling Iranian weapons and amassing the most fearsome nonstate arsenal in the world. Assassinated by Israel in Beirut on July 30, 2024.

Hamas Gaza Chief Yahya Sinwar. The mastermind of October 7. A fanatic willing to sacrifice Gaza in his attempt to destroy Israel and reverse the diplomatic marginalization of the Palestinians. Killed by Israel in Rafah, Gaza, on October 16, 2024.

Hamas al-Qassam Brigades Commander Mohammed Deif. The military brains behind the October 7 attack's success. Legendary for surviving more than half a dozen Israeli assassination attempts. Assassinated by Israel in al-Mawasi humanitarian zone in Gaza on July 13, 2024.

Hamas Political Bureau Chairman Ismail Haniyeh. Former Gaza terrorist leader and Palestinian prime minister who made it out to live the good life in Qatari luxury hotels. Led hostage negotiations for Hamas. Assassinated by Israel in Tehran on July 31, 2024.

Syrian President Bashar al-Assad. London ophthalmologist turned brutal dictator who picked up in Syria where his father had left off. Reduced his country to an Iranian proxy to defend his rule. Overthrown on December 8, 2024.

Hayat Tahrir al-Sham Rebel Commander (later Syrian President) Ahmed al-Sharaa. Al-Qaeda commander who broke away to lead the Turkish-backed Islamist rebel alliance that overthrew Assad. A jihadist or a statesman? "Distrust and verify," said Israeli leaders.

The Key US Officials

President Joseph R. Biden. "The most pro-Israel person in his own government." Backed the Israeli war effort from the start, yet tried to restrain it almost as soon. Bent but did not break in the face of anti-Israel political pressure. Served from January 20, 2021, to January 20, 2025.

Defense Secretary Lloyd Austin. A steady hand who helped Biden influence Israeli policy through his strong ties to Gallant and sometimes Gantz. He came to believe that Israel was spiraling out of control and into a larger regional war.

National Security Advisor Jake Sullivan. The architect of President Biden's de-escalation strategy. One of the president's primary interlocutors and day-to-day messengers to the Netanyahu government.

Secretary of State Antony Blinken. Perpetually frustrated with Netanyahu. Led Biden's push for a more limited Israeli war, a Saudi deal, and a revitalized Palestinian Authority to run Gaza.

Central Command Chief Erik Kurilla. The US general considered toughest on Iran. One of main US interlocutors with Gallant, Halevi, and Zamir regarding key war decisions.

Ambassador to Israel Jack Lew. Biden's man on the ground to improve the humanitarian situation for the Palestinians and push for Saudi normalization with Israel.

President Donald J. Trump. Threatened Hamas with "hell to pay" to extract a hostage deal. Gave Netanyahu room to run in Gaza and delivered the last blow to Iran's nuclear program. Brought Israel and Hamas to a final deal in October 2025. Took office on January 20, 2025.

Special Envoy to the Middle East Steve Witkoff. Trump's go-to deal-maker from the real-estate world who had Israelis on edge during nuclear negotiations with Iran. But his "term sheet" was never good enough for the ayatollah. Worked with Jared Kushner to develop Trump's Gaza peace plan.

CHAPTER ONE

INSIDE THE WAR ROOM

Yoav Gallant could not sleep on the night of October 10, 2023. This was not, as one might expect, because of the shock of Hamas's invasion three days earlier. At 6:29 a.m. on October 7, Hamas, the jihadist ruler of Gaza, had sent its death squads across the border into Israel. As they took over twenty-two villages and went on a rampage, slaughtering civilians en masse, they also dragged 251 men, women, and children to Gaza as hostages.

Strange as it may seem, it was not Hamas that roiled the mind of Israel's defense minister on the night of October 10. It was another, even more potent threat to Israel: Hezbollah. What to do about the Iran-backed terrorists in Lebanon, and when? Should Israel, a nation and military still in disbelief, only beginning to bury its dead, now take a new and unforced risk big enough to stun its enemies and transform the war in its infancy?

Gallant was a Shayetet 13 commando, the Israeli equivalent of a Navy SEAL. Over the years, he earned a reputation as a tough, old-school general and helped rebuild the IDF into a serious fighting force from 2006 to 2008. Gruff, sometimes short-tempered, and tall with a penetrating stare, Gallant became defense minister in early 2023 with the goal of neutralizing the Iranian nuclear threat that loomed over Israel like a sword of Damocles.

As chief of the IDF's Southern Command during the 2008–2009 war with Hamas, Gallant had history in Gaza. Just when he said he "had Hamas on the ropes" and was ready to invade the stronghold of Rafah, Gallant was ordered on January 19, 2009 by then–Prime Minister Ehud Olmert to stand down. With President Barack Obama on the way in, the war was brought to a close—prematurely, Gallant felt.

The events since had only confirmed Gallant's judgment. Hamas would recover to strike Israel harder than it had ever anticipated. Militarily, the October 7 invasion was the most devastating blow Israel had received in five decades. That the attack took place at all was the greatest failure of Israel's government to protect its people, badly tarnishing the image of Israeli intelligence as an all-seeing, all-knowing, omnicompetent machine. Israel's leaders—political, military, and intelligence—never saw the Hamas attack coming.

The resulting war gave Gallant the chance to do what he had been prevented from doing fifteen years earlier, namely, to "fix" Israel's mistake, as he put it, and "take care of business" with Hamas in Rafah. This is the critical city on Egypt's border with Gaza through which Hamas had smuggled many of its weapons.

In the days after October 7, however, Gallant mainly was trying to decide—and then convince a notoriously hard-to-pin-down prime minister and cabinet—what Israel's policy should be against Hezbollah. Armed by Iran with an extraordinary missile arsenal, the US-designated terrorist group had long cowed the Lebanese Armed Forces and shared Hamas's goal of destroying the Jewish state. In support of Hamas's invasion, Hezbollah started shooting rockets at northern Israel the very next day, on October 8. Gallant still believed, as he did before the war, that Hezbollah, not Hamas, posed the larger, perhaps existential threat to Israel. During his sleepless night, he came to two conclusions.

First, Israel needed to execute a devastating strike against Hezbollah right away. A combination of intelligence, sabotage, artillery, and air power could cripple the terrorist group before it could use its well-trained troops and tens of thousands of sophisticated missiles to follow up Hamas's attack with a far more powerful assault of its own. This would allow Israel to regain the initiative, shock the Iranian terror axis, and isolate Hamas in Gaza.

Second, Gallant concluded that Netanyahu, his Likud party leader and boss in Israel's coalition government, though renowned for his hawkishness, would be dead set against his proposal.

Netanyahu talked tough in public about "total victory." Early on, he said, "We're continuing until the end, until victory, until Hamas is annihilated. I say this in the face of great pain, but also in the face of international pressures. Nothing will stop us." But within the defense establishment, the prime minister was viewed as hesitant and even paranoid about the potential of military conflicts to spiral out of control.

Netanyahu had long viewed himself as conservative in the use of military force—resolute in defense of Israel's security while treasuring the life of each Israeli soldier. His own elder brother, Yoni, the pride of his family and the bearer of his father's political ambitions, was killed while leading Israel's 1976 hostage-rescue mission at Entebbe, Uganda. Netanyahu himself had been wounded in combat multiple times. Gallant sensed that this innate caution, combined with worry about a negative American reaction to a full-scale attack on Hezbollah, would lead Netanyahu to refuse what he, Gallant, deeply believed to be the necessary first step.

The US could also be counted on to oppose Gallant's plan. In the Middle East, as in Ukraine, the Biden administration's overriding impulse was de-escalation. In a Foreign Affairs essay that went to print just before the October 7 attack and arrived in subscribers' mailboxes later in the month, US National Security Advisor Jake Sullivan boasted that Biden policies had made the Middle East "quieter than it has been for decades. The progress is fragile, to be sure. But it is also not an accident." In particular, Sullivan wrote, "We have de-escalated crises in Gaza and restored direct diplomacy between the parties after years of its absence" and "enhanced deterrence, combined with diplomacy, to discourage further [Iranian] aggression."

The online version of the essay, published after October 7, deleted many of the lines above.[1] While the Biden administration understood that Israel was going to act against Hamas after the group's invasion, it held tight to the de-escalation doctrine regarding other Iranian proxies. Yet there was one element favorable to Gallant's position.

The day after Hamas invaded southern Israel, while the Israeli military was still desperately trying to oust Hamas gunmen from its territory—it would take four to five days to do so—Hezbollah's infantry had started firing rockets on Israel's north, putting some eighty thousand Israeli civilians in mortal danger. While Hezbollah's attacks were unprovoked, lethal, and far more than symbolic, they also represented only a tiny fraction of the harm the terror group could have inflicted had it been "all in" against Israel. Hezbollah was firing hundreds of rockets on small, nearby border towns, not using its juggernaut one hundred fifty thousand–rocket arsenal to blanket Israel's main population centers, such as Tel Aviv and Haifa.

How to respond was the most important question facing the war cabinet on October 11. Gallant came prepared to shoot down all other options. One was to continue engaging in low-key, proportionate responses to Hezbollah, attacking merely the sources of the rocket fire. This tit-for-tat approach was designed to avoid a larger confrontation with Hezbollah while Israel focused on Hamas. Another option was to intensify retaliatory attacks on Hezbollah, but in a measured way, mainly via heavier strikes on Hezbollah's launch sites and against its forces near the border.

Gallant knew the arguments in favor of these more moderate options. What horrified him and some of the senior officers in the IDF far more than a general escalation of the conflict—more than objections from the Biden administration, and more than the devastation and death that Lebanese civilians would suffer—was what would happen to Israel if it let Hezbollah strike hard first. Even with Israel's air-power advantage and world-class, three-tier air-defense system of the Arrow, David's Sling, and the Iron Dome, Hezbollah's missiles could easily kill five thousand Israelis within hours, dwarfing the twelve hundred already killed by Hamas.

Even if only 10 percent of the rockets penetrated Israel's air defenses—and the Iron Dome's best performance was around a 90 percent shoot-down rate—Hezbollah could destroy dozens of multistory buildings in Tel Aviv, damage large swaths of Ben Gurion International Airport, reduce the capacity of Israel's electrical grid by 33 percent, decimate Israel's northern border villages, and level around a third of Haifa, home to the country's crucial maritime port. Hezbollah had that power. It all would depend on who struck first on a large scale.

Gallant saw an escalation by Hezbollah as a clear and present danger, one that Israel could not risk. To avoid it, he had in mind a devastating preemptive attack on Hezbollah's missiles, launchers, and leaders—one even harsher and more rapid than what Israel would carry out nearly a year later.

It would have started early in the morning of October 12, when Hezbollah's short-range rocket assets, antiaircraft defenses, command centers, tunnels, and other strategic assets in a dozen southern Lebanese villages would come under a hail of munitions, all at the same time. Within minutes of that first strike would follow a set of attacks on sites much farther from the border, in Beirut, Baalbek, and the Bekaa Valley, where Hezbollah kept its long-range, precision, strategic missiles. Within twenty-four hours, Gallant proposed, the Israeli Air Force would strike Hezbollah more than one thousand times with a variety of five-thousand-pound American GBU-72 bombs, two thousand–pound bombs, one thousand–pound bombs, and other munitions.

Operating in waves, the IDF could destroy between 70 percent and 80 percent of Hezbollah's high-value weapons in the first thirty minutes, Gallant estimated, and then bring down hellfire on the wider Hezbollah apparatus in southern Lebanon and beyond. The IDF's US-supplied F-35 stealth fighters, F-15 Eagles, F-16 Fighting Falcons, Apache helicopters, Blackhawks, Sikorsky CH-53 Sea Stallions, C-130s, Gulfstreams G550s, and other aircraft would be used in this assault, which would be like nothing Lebanon had ever seen before.

The effect would be devastating. Most of Beirut's 2.5 million people would quickly leave and be made homeless. This would be tragic, but Hezbollah would not be able to use them as human shields the way Hamas used Gazan civilians. In worst-case scenarios, more than twenty-five thousand Lebanese would be killed, perhaps only half of them Hezbollah fighters, in only the opening days of the operation. (In the actual operation, nearly a year later, Israel succeeded beyond expectations in keeping the civilian casualties in Lebanon to a low level.) Among the dead, presumably, would be Hassan Nasrallah, Hezbollah's leader with vast amounts of Lebanese, Syrian, Israeli, and American blood on his hands.

The death and destruction in Lebanon would no doubt be condemned in much of the world, including the US, but Gallant believed it was a price that Israel would need to pay in exchange for the tremendous strategic advantage. Israel could finally defeat Iran's most important proxy army, which sat on the Jewish state's northern border. The north of Israel, and the country's heartland as well, could be made safe again.

* * *

Gallant's plan started to form three days earlier, on October 8, when he assembled a "Red Team" of former top Israeli intelligence and defense officials headed by Tamir Hayman, the chief of Israeli military intelligence from 2018 to 2021. This team's job was to answer an important question as fast as it could: "Is there coordination between Hezbollah and Hamas, and what is the nature of any such coordination?"

The question was not theoretical. Nor was it merely retrospective. Gallant told Hayman there was a clear risk of an imminent Hezbollah invasion, using the more than six thousand elite fighters of Hezbollah's Radwan Force deployed by the border with Israel. That would be a much more dangerous invasion force than even Hamas had mustered, with better-trained fighters backed by Hezbollah's huge rocket-and-mortar arsenal. Despite Hezbollah's low-level involvement since October 8, Gallant was concerned that the two Iranian proxies were still coordinating closely. "Hezbollah is waiting until Israel is busy, and has committed most of its forces to fighting Hamas, to then launch a full invasion," Gallant said.

The October 8 Red Team analyzed the issue and returned to Gallant that same day with a surprising answer: There had been no direct Hezbollah–Hamas coordination for the day of October 7—though Israel would later learn that Hezbollah and Iran had been involved in earlier stages of the planning. More pressing, the Red Team found no information to support Gallant's theory that the Lebanese terror group was waiting to pounce on Israel with an all-out attack. The team believed that Nasrallah wanted to keep the conflict at a low simmer; he did not want to provoke an Israeli reaction that would put Hezbollah's standing in Lebanon at risk.

But what if the intelligence were wrong? Israel had missed Hamas's October 7 attack entirely. One day later, could it trust the same intelligence establishment to predict Hezbollah's next move with any certainty?

That logic, however, could also be used to poke holes in Gallant's plan. What if the IDF did not know the full extent of Hezbollah's arsenal or preparations? Israel could be provoking a retaliation from Hezbollah that would cause nearly as much damage as the first strike Gallant so feared. Everything would hinge on the accuracy of Israeli intelligence and the trust Israeli leaders would place in it.

Despite the Red Team's findings, Gallant issued a standing order to the IDF on October 8 that it should make sure to strike Hezbollah first if there were any indications that the terror group was on the verge of a major attack. This, he hoped, would allow Israel to retain some element of surprise.

We now reveal for the first time a series of dramatic insider moments and twists leading to the fateful decisions regarding Hezbollah that day. In the early morning of October 11, Gallant reviewed all the relevant intelligence on his own. By 9:45 a.m., he was at Air Force headquarters in Tel Aviv to survey the potential plans for attacking Hezbollah. He spoke with a half dozen IDF chiefs, asking them whether they were for or against a massive first strike. When Gallant walked into different meetings with these top officers to debate his Hezbollah attack plans, he was confronted with a wide range of reactions. Some commanders were invigorated by the plan. Other meeting rooms were filled with doubt and a deep desire to avoid unnecessary risks that could not be meticulously calibrated.

The IDF intelligence analysis chief was especially circumspect about rolling the dice against such a dangerous foe, when he and his team had been caught off guard by Hezbollah's much weaker partner, Hamas. Likewise, Gallant's top Defense Ministry appointee, who ran the ministry's day-to-day affairs, while normally known as a high-risk roller, was adamantly opposed to gambling everything against Hezbollah at this precarious moment. Still in shock from October 7, the defense chiefs were terrified of possibly losing US support by attacking Hezbollah, right when American assistance would be most crucial for toppling Hamas.

At 11:15 a.m., Gallant discussed the critical issues with the IDF Chief of Staff Herzi Halevi. Even taller than Gallant, Halevi towered over most people, and had worked his way up the ranks after starting his military career in the IDF's special forces, the Sayeret Matkal. He was one of Gallant's top officers during the 2008–2009 Gaza war, building a long-standing relationship that would leave little daylight between the two during the October 7 war. Halevi later became IDF southern commander, responsible for all of Gaza, then chief of IDF intelligence, deputy IDF chief and, finally, IDF chief in January 2023. He had reached the pinnacle. On one hand, Halevi could be daring, fierce, and creative. On the other hand, he was far more cerebral and intellectual than a typical Israeli general, preferring nuance and longer-winded literary references in his presentations, where many of his colleagues' styles were crisp and down to earth.

Gallant and Halevi had talked often in the past few days. If it were up to them, they would have attacked Hezbollah on October 9 or 10, but Gallant knew they would need some time to convince Netanyahu. In their past discussions, Halevi had asked tough questions about Gallant's plan. By this point, however, he wholeheartedly supported a major strike. "If there are two enemies," Halevi said, "you go after the stronger one first." This was accepted doctrine, derived from one of the fathers of modern warfare, Carl von Clausewitz. Otherwise, the stronger of the two enemies is likely to catch you by surprise or when your forces are depleted.

The defense minister called Netanyahu. He was unable, however, to get through to the prime minister. Netanyahu does not have a personal cell phone and can only be reached through top aides. This time, the aides were all throwing up obstacles. Gallant called several more times, trying to move the process forward. Still, the prime minister was refusing to take his calls. This, amid a war and crisis, was not a good sign. But Gallant was not known for backing down.

He marched from his office on the fourteenth floor of the Defense Ministry across the campus to the prime minister's office. The walk was only a few hundred meters, but between the long elevator ride and the security check, it could be around thirty minutes of travel time that the defense minister did not have to spare.

Inexplicably, Gallant still could not get in to see Netanyahu. Instead, Ron Dermer came out to meet him. Dermer, born and raised in Miami Beach, had been advising Netanyahu in one capacity or another since 2000, and over time became his closest ally. A born talker, Dermer could provide an unending stream of words in Israel's defense—fluid, coherent and usually compelling—whether in a meeting or on CNN in prime time. Aligned with the prime minister in long viewing Iran as the existential threat to Israel and American evangelical Christians as Israel's chief ally, he served as Israeli ambassador to the US from 2013 to 2021. In December 2022, he became Israel's strategic affairs minister, a nondescript title that gave him great range and power as Netanyahu's top diplomat and trusted lieutenant.

Gallant got right to the point. He told Dermer that he had to inform Netanyahu that a major attack on Hezbollah must go forward right away and could no longer be delayed. Of course, Netanyahu already knew that Gallant wanted to attack Hezbollah. The prime minister's unavailability, even over the phone, was a way to avoid the subject altogether. That would be easier than saying no, which could be used against him should it leak. And in Israel, everything leaks eventually.

Netanyahu did not realize that Gallant had concluded, based on real-time intelligence, that the window for such a move against Hezbollah was rapidly closing. These kinds of granular developments in the field were a defense minister's arena. Prime ministers usually do not get down into the military details unless they are about to affect strategic choices. Gallant wanted to tell Netanyahu: Delaying further could mean losing the option to attack.

Dermer listened, then turned back to his office, leaving Gallant in the reception area. Rather than call Netanyahu, however, Dermer called Jake Sullivan, the US national security advisor.

According to Gallant, the very act of calling Sullivan at this juncture was an error. There was no way the US would endorse a strike to expand the conflict. But Dermer's call was an early hint to Gallant that Netanyahu wanted the US to "force" him not to attack Hezbollah. That way, he did not need to reject the option himself and look weak doing so.

Dermer and Sullivan had an initial talk, which quickly led to a direct call between Biden and Netanyahu. When Netanyahu raised the idea of a major Israeli strike on Hezbollah, Biden pushed back full throttle: "Do not do this," the president said, to nobody's surprise. "You know me. We have known each other a long time. This is a mistake. Do not go down this road."[2]

Netanyahu responded, "I hear you. You've been very clear. But I also want to be clear that we're going to make our own decision, and while this conversation will inform it, it will not decide it."[3]

* * *

Gallant tried to call Dermer many additional times during this period, but Gallant could no longer reach his fellow minister, let alone Netanyahu. Then, at 1:15 p.m., Gallant got through to Dermer again. Finally, at 1:20 p.m., Gallant spoke to Netanyahu himself in the prime minister's office at Israel's military headquarters after two hours of delay.

When Gallant entered, the two men eyed each other suspiciously. Their mutual trust had already blown up in March 2023 when Gallant publicly lambasted Netanyahu's controversial proposal to reduce the power of Israel's Supreme Court. The effort had produced some of the biggest protests in Israel's history. Gallant would now either press Netanyahu into a major strategic attack that the prime minister was not ready to undertake or put him on the record as being against military action after Israel had suffered its worst massacre. "Afraid" is how it would be leaked. It was the worst kind of meeting that Netanyahu could imagine. Though the prime minister tried to put on a confident face, he looked like a deer caught in the headlights.

As ever, Gallant got right to the point. He recounted to Netanyahu the argument made by Halevi, about taking down the stronger enemy first. Gallant also added arguments of his own: that a first strike would be the best way to get ready for the inevitable escalation of Hezbollah rocket attacks against Israel's home front, and that once Hezbollah did launch such an attack, it would dwarf the power that Hamas could bring to bear after October 7.

Only two days earlier, in a private meeting between Netanyahu and Gallant, the two, along with Dermer, were starting to formulate the decision that they expected to hand down to the war cabinet. At that time, Gallant had felt that Netanyahu was in favor of attacking Hezbollah. The two had discussed some of the strategy and tactical details that such an operation would entail, and the prime minister certainly had not shot it down. But by 1:20 p.m. on October 11, a shift had taken place. Gallant felt he was not speaking to the same person as he had two days before.

"Listen, it's complicated," Netanyahu now told Gallant. "What will the Americans say?"

"What is correct for the State of Israel is all that matters," Gallant responded. He added that Israel needed to fight the Iranian axis, of which Hezbollah was a major part, not merely fight the leading enemy of the moment, Hamas.

Netanyahu replied, "We also need a national unity government immediately, and we cannot carry out consultations for that at the same time that we would be initiating a massive conflict with Hezbollah."

"OK, go form a unity government," Gallant countered.

For Netanyahu, who was governing with a narrow majority in the Israeli Knesset, including Israel's unpopular ultra-Orthodox and hard-right parties, it was essential to form a broader emergency coalition to gain trust from the other half of the country. On October 11, that was his main priority, and, unbeknownst at the time to Gallant, it was what he had been busy negotiating all day.

Israel is a parliamentary democracy, which means that its prime minister stays in power only so long as a majority in the parliament, called the Knesset, declines to bring him down and force an election. Due to Israel's many fissures and system of proportional representation, its government is usually an unstable coalition of four to six smaller political parties. No one party, not even Netanyahu's Likud, is even nearly large enough to form a government by itself. Unlike a US president, who is guaranteed a four-year term, this means that Israeli prime ministers usually do not serve out their full four years. Early elections typically ensue between the third and fourth year, when some coalition partners—who are also rivals—decide to topple the government.

Netanyahu's parliamentary majority, starting in January 2023, had been thin: His bloc commanded sixty-four seats in the 120-seat Knesset. It also included a hard-right party, led by Itamar Ben-Gvir, that he held in low regard. He needed Ben-Gvir and also the right-wing National Religious Party leader Bezalel Smotrich to form a government, but he much preferred a wider coalition with more respected, centrist figures such as Benny Gantz and Gadi Eisenkot.

Although Defense Minister Gallant technically aligned with Netanyahu's Likud, he had started politics in a different party and joined the Likud in part for tactical reasons. He was much more of an independent actor than the prime minister would have liked, but this is common with defense ministers in Israeli coalitions. Moreover, even as top Israeli generals in the end salute the prime minister, according to Israeli culture and traditions, the IDF chief and top generals also will sometimes publicize their disagreements with the prime minister on security policy. In that sense, the defense minister, IDF chief, and top generals have far more power to disagree with and challenge Israeli prime ministers than

Westerners might assume. Sensitive to the elevated political risk, prime ministers also tend to be reluctant to overrule them.

In the end, Gallant's plan depended on a cabinet meeting that was tentatively set for later in the afternoon on October 11. He expected to have substantial support from the IDF and intelligence services, putting Netanyahu in a difficult spot. Behind the scenes, however, the prime minister was trying to bring Gantz, his main opponent, into a unity government before the meeting. This way, Gantz could weigh in on his side on a variety of issues, including Hezbollah. It was at this meeting that Gallant would make his key pitch to take out Hezbollah right away, gaining the element of surprise while everyone expected Israel to focus its retaliation on Hamas, the perpetrator of the October 7 atrocity.

* * *

Entering the cabinet meeting room, Gallant was met right away with surprises.

The first was that Benny Gantz was already present, along with his closest ally, Gadi Eisenkot. Both men were former IDF chiefs of staff and Netanyahu's political rivals. Gantz especially was formidable at this time, considered the leading political figure to challenge Netanyahu as prime minister. Gantz is also likely the physically tallest figure in the history of Israeli politics, looming even over other tall generals. He had been defense minister (2020–2022) and IDF chief (2011–2015), the latter after a political ambush had shoved Gallant out of the race for the job. That wound never fully healed.

While Gantz had been called naive when he entered politics in 2019, five years of political combat against Netanyahu had hardened him. Even so, his self-deprecating instinct was still to be congenial, low key, and to seek common ground, not plunge into conflict. His and Eisenkot's presence in the room signaled to Gallant that, though no unity government had been announced, one effectively had already been formed. It did not bode well for Gallant, he knew, if Gantz and Eisenkot were already weighing in on the critical decisions of war and peace.

Gantz and Eisenkot were known for being more cautious about committing to major operations, and certainly more cautious than Gallant. But the debate reached much further. All the key members of the war cabinet had been yanked from their complacency regarding Hamas into a mood of existential crisis of the sort not faced since the Yom Kippur War fifty years earlier. Yet the men retained their political rivalries and tangled personal histories from earlier Israeli conflicts.

Besides the three key decision-makers, Eisenkot and Dermer were also part of every small war cabinet gathering. Formally, they were non-voting "observers," but they played active and influential roles. Aryeh Deri, leader of the ultra-Orthodox Shas party, was often also present as an observer. A canny politician and Netanyahu ally, he was typically a moderating influence on security issues. In larger meetings, other coalition partners such as Smotrich and Ben-Gvir, and legal officials such as Justice Minister Yariv Levin and Attorney General Gali Baharav-Miara, were often present. Depending on the topic at hand, a range of IDF officials might be present, as well as Mossad Director David Barnea and Shin Bet Director Ronen Bar. All played a part and had varying levels of influence. Yet when the war room made its most important decisions, only Netanyahu, Gallant, and Gantz would vote.

When they met on October 11, the room was thick with tension, conflicting analyses, and personal and political feuds—never mind that none of those present had slept much during the past five days. All of them bore varying forms of responsibility for the October 7 disaster, and all had a deep-seated fear that they would go down in history as the leaders who failed Israel against Hamas, regardless of their decades of accomplishments.

Wearing all black, both pants and shirt, Gallant was sitting near Netanyahu. When he argued with the prime minister, Gallant waved his right hand with his thumb and pointer finger extended, for emphasis. He was not audibly growling, but his facial expression was fierce, his eyes lit up with a rare fire. When he wasn't speaking, his lips were pressed with determination.

Netanyahu was wearing a dark suit with a blue tie to match his shirt. His arms were crossed, right on top of left. He was quieter than his voluble public persona would lead one to expect, listening intently and staring so hard at whoever was speaking as to make him feel truly on a hot seat. The feeling from Netanyahu's stare was somehow intensified by his glasses, which he was always careful to remove in public.

Like Gallant, Gantz was also wearing all black. His hands folded, Gantz had neither as ferocious an expression as Gallant nor one as blank as Halevi, who was still showing some of the shock of that dreadful first week. Calm, Gantz seemed to know he would be the one to shape the turn of events.

There was not one physical war room, but several: the prime minister's office in Jerusalem, a separate prime minister's office in Tel Aviv at military headquarters, and the IDF high command's underground situation room, also at military headquarters in Tel Aviv. Many key deals or fateful debates and decisions were hashed out in those rooms. Others were reached with only two or three members of the political echelon or defense establishment present in side talks in their individual offices before joining the larger group to push through what had been decided elsewhere. Netanyahu was usually part of these side talks, but sometimes Gallant and Halevi or one of them and Gantz worked privately on an issue to get Netanyahu off the fence.

The long table at which they convened in the underground situation room on October 11 was light on technology. Pads, pencils and water bottles were its only adornments. No cell phones were allowed, to avoid leaks and recordings, though sometimes the principals would provide after-the-fact leaks from memory. All of them sat in high-backed black swivel chairs. Nearby walls offered video screens, providing updates from the field alongside the insignia of the State of Israel. One screen showed a photo of the Israeli Air Force bombing Hamas command centers in Gaza, with the name of the new operation, Swords of Iron, flashing across in white.

* * *

Gallant, Halevi, and other IDF officials led parts of the meeting, describing what a major strike on Hezbollah would look like and how soon it could start. They explained how many aircraft would be involved and how many active-duty and reserve forces would be ready to invade southern Lebanon and maintain a defensive line in northern Israel. They discussed the different elements of Israel's multitier air-defense system that might need to come into play, including where they would place the various air-defense batteries, given that not every area could be shielded. This was a grim topic, prioritizing the defense of population centers, military power centers, and other classified locations at the expense of the rest of the country. Such trade-offs underscored how much was at stake.

But even as this technical discussion was taking place, there was, besides the presence of Gantz and Eisenkot, a second surprise for Gallant. Netanyahu seemed to be portraying himself as a supporter of the bold attack that Gallant had become convinced the prime minister really opposed. Netanyahu sounded off about how hard he wanted to hit Hezbollah and how strong Israel's response would be to the terror group's unprovoked rocket attacks. He seemed determined to make Hezbollah's Nasrallah regret piling on Israel while it was down.

Both Halevi and Gallant, each of whom had spent years observing Netanyahu, perceived that the prime minister was acting in a sophisticated way that actually undermined the case for attacking Hezbollah. While Netanyahu talked about a tough response, he wove into his comments the need to weigh the views of the US and of Gantz. In turn, Gantz, supported by Eisenkot, did not conceal his opposition to a major strike on Hezbollah at this stage. For him, the risks of a larger Lebanon war outweighed the benefits of an early move. When Netanyahu said they should further consult the Americans, Gallant responded the way he had earlier in the day: "We should not ask the US. That would be like asking for a veto." It would be a point that Netanyahu would later come to make himself, and against Gallant, but for now, the prime minister ignored it. He ordered Dermer to call Sullivan a second time. Netanyahu paused the cabinet meeting and said they would reconvene a few hours later after this latest call to Washington.

Dermer and Sullivan spoke midafternoon Israel-time. Dermer told Sullivan that "the debate is shifting in the direction of a preemptive strike." Sullivan warned in response that an attack on Hezbollah would lead to a massive regional war. "What you are thinking about doing is dangerous. It's irrational.... Do not go ahead with it."[4] Next, Sullivan set up what some top Israeli defense officials saw as a kind of ambush by looping in virtually the entire White House team. Biden's top intelligence, military, and national security advisers, including Secretary of State Antony Blinken, Defense Secretary Lloyd Austin, CIA Director William Burns, Director of National Intelligence Avril Haines, and Chairman of the Joint Chiefs of Staff CQ Brown all got on the line with Sullivan. US intelligence, they said, contradicted any prediction of further escalation or invasion by Hezbollah.

IDF intelligence indicated otherwise. It had even picked up signs of a possible Hezbollah paraglider invasion from Lebanon into the Galilee, as Hamas had done on October 7 into southern Israel. "If we're going to be attacked and invaded with gliders from the air," Netanyahu recounted to us, "what choice do we have? We have to fight." Israel would have to go big in response, the prime minister thought. The Biden administration, however, was not persuaded. The US military wasn't picking up the same signs, the officials said on the call. Certainly, the US officials added, whatever Israel was seeing didn't justify any major strategic escalation against Hezbollah.

Sullivan later dictated a message to a Dermer aide: "Jake to Ron: Your information is false. You're making decisions in the fog of war. Slow down."

General Erik Kurilla, the chief of US Central Command, told US envoy to the Middle East Brett McGurk, "My J-2 [US military intelligence directorate] says there are no paragliders.... There is no sign of this. It's a phantom."[5]

US intelligence was right. "I actually let the planes take off to have a full-scale attack on Hezbollah," Netanyahu told us. "And you know why it stopped? It stopped because it turns out the gliders were geese. We called back the planes." Israeli radar had mistaken geese for invaders. The entire war could have turned on such a misreading.

That would have been enough excitement for one day. Yet later in the afternoon, after the call with US officials, Gallant met with Dermer and Halevi. The defense minister had not given up. Gallant told Dermer, "We're ready to engage in a surprise attack. This will not leave the Israeli home front quiet"—meaning there would be a harsh Hezbollah counter-strike—"but it would be the best possible scenario." Hezbollah's attack capabilities would be weakened before the terror group had a chance to escalate in earnest. A vast majority of the IDF high command supported striking north.

When Netanyahu joined their meeting, he said without equivocation, "I am opposed. We would face massive destruction on the home front. Hezbollah just has too many rockets. Also, we need the full backing of the Americans for invading Gaza. The blow to the Israeli home front will be so horrible that it will cause a deep demoralization."

Left with this standoff, Gallant departed, disappointed. He hoped to try again later.

Not long after, Gallant tried to call Netanyahu. The prime minister's National Security Council chief, Tzachi Hanegbi, refused to put Gallant through. Netanyahu was evading again. It would not, Gallant explained later, "be politically good" for the prime minister to take the call, because openly rejecting Gallant's proposal would make him look weak. Gallant then sent his own chief of staff, Shachar Katz, to the prime minister's office. Hanegbi wouldn't let him in. Gallant himself left a meeting with David Barnea, the head of the Mossad, to walk over to Netanyahu's office, yet "even I was barely let in!" he recalled. Gallant was refused entry at first, even though he was defense minister and a war was on. Only after Gallant accused Netanyahu and his staff of playing childish games on matters of national security was he let in.

Netanyahu convened another war cabinet meeting. It started in the early evening and included all the key players: Gallant, Gantz, Eisenkot, Netanyahu, Dermer, and Hanegbi. Again, Gallant presented his argument for an attack right away, roughly summarizing to us later what he told the war cabinet at the time: "We would get a head-start in striking Hezbollah and eliminate Hezbollah's central assets. The strike would have a major impact on their functionality and would make it very hard for them to respond."[6]

He recounted that "there were those who thought we wouldn't be able to get up again from the Hamas invasion, that we were in a passive, fearful, and defensive posture," but he disagreed. "We could emerge from this to grab the element of surprise. We had legitimacy globally. We had our Iron Dome batteries and troops in position and on the border."

"The close [Israeli] border villages were already evacuated, so we could handle more attacks from Hezbollah without facing civilian casualties in those villages. Domestic Israeli support was strong," Gallant later told us, still utterly convinced of his position. He felt there would be no better time for the inevitable confrontation, for which Israel had prepared for a decade. Besides, Gallant worried that even if the IDF had significant achievements invading Gaza, "this would not be sufficient to restore full deterrence of Israel's enemies, especially with Hezbollah's forces remaining right on the Israeli border in the north."

In considering Israel's options in hindsight, General David Petraeus, the former head of US Central Command, chief of US forces in Iraq and Afghanistan, and CIA director, asked us an interesting question: "What was the real threat from Hezbollah? It was 10,000 missiles simultaneously—and that never materialized." Instead, he notes, Israel would successfully "contain the war to a relatively small area" in northern Israel. While politically painful, this would allow Israel to focus on Hamas. That was a must, Petraeus says, "given what it had done, and nobody knew what else it might do either."

Whatever the strength of Gallant's arguments, they did not carry the day. Netanyahu told the war cabinet that he had spoken to Biden and "a decision to significantly escalate the conflict with Hezbollah with a preemptive strike could radically alter Israel-US relations." Until that point, Gallant said, there had been "tremendous support" for a major strike from all levels of Israel's government outside the war cabinet—military, intelligence, diplomatic, economic, and public messaging. Gallant, Halevi, Barnea of the Mossad, Ronen Bar of the Shin Bet security agency, and IDF Military Intelligence Chief Aharon Haliva were all in favor. Incidentally, despite voting in favor in the end, at earlier points, Barnea had wavered on the issue, and then even turned against it, before ultimately supporting the attack. Although some top officials viewed him as waffling on what he believed in, Barnea had been clear that he was focused on maintaining US support.

Their advocacy was not enough. The prestige of those security experts had taken a hit on October 7. The war cabinet, led by Netanyahu, decided against attacking Hezbollah. This included the two other voting members, Netanyahu and Gantz, as well as the war cabinet's three observers, Dermer, Eisenkot, and Shas party leader Aryeh Deri.

Later, Dermer would tell Sullivan, "The prime minister and I were never supportive of this. It was being driven by the military, and this is a good outcome basically."

Netanyahu would reflect similarly. "I told Gallant, 'You can't do that,'" he recalls. "For two reasons: One, we cannot leave the south"—Hamas in Gaza. "We have to engage these people who committed the worst massacre against the Jewish people since the Holocaust. So, we're not going to leave them alone when God knows what will happen in Lebanon."

"Two," Netanyahu continued, "We shouldn't conduct an intensive two-front war. One intensive front at a time. Our decision, and what I said at the time, was: 'What we're going to do in the north is active defense,' which means we're not just defending ourselves; we're also pushing Hezbollah back. But the full force of the IDF, at that stage, goes to the south." That was where the war started. Netanyahu did not think he could or should put it on the back burner.

As the Biden team would tell it, it had helped save Israel from a catastrophic regional war based on poor Israeli radar detection—the geese—and Israeli bravado to prove how tough they were after the October 7 failure. Secretary of State Blinken said the Israelis were "30 minutes from launching a preemptive, or preventative in their minds, attack based on totally erroneous information."[7] The Biden administration would allege that the Israelis often put out partial intelligence findings alleging major conclusions, but when the intelligence was examined, it was often immaterial.

There was certainly some truth to these allegations about Israeli leaders and their intelligence establishment. But that is only half the picture. The other half is that US officials typically do not fully understand just how seriously Israel is threatened. Hamas's October 7 attack, Hezbollah's October 8 attack, the multiple attacks by Iran directly, and those by the Houthis from Yemen have made this clear. At each point, US officials urged Israel to scale down its reply and accommodate itself to an ever-more-dangerous status quo. If Israelis sometimes jump too easily at partial intelligence, it is because perfect intelligence has often arrived too late, and many Israelis have died waiting for it.

"Generations of Israelis will cry out in regret," Gallant warned, for having missed the opportunity to roll back Hezbollah's power and to secure Israel from the threat of the terrorist group's missile arsenal. This was not mere posturing. It was a very real sizing up of the immense work Israel had in front of it to restore deterrence against its enemies on what would grow to seven different fronts.

For the next ten or eleven months, while Israel worked strenuously to avoid a major confrontation with Hezbollah, Gallant's concern seemed vindicated. "What is happening now, just as I predicted," Gallant would reflect to us toward the end of that waiting period, "was exactly what I had hoped to stop"—an endless conflict with Hezbollah with no clear way out.

There would be a new way out in September 2024, but this would come only after nearly a year of military exchanges that would displace eighty thousand Israelis from their homes, divert critical troops and munitions, and draw Iran into a direct fight with Israel in ways no one could have imagined only months earlier. In hindsight, Gallant and the IDF high command's idea of an early strike on Lebanon was an opportunity to skip all that and wage a far different war than the one we saw from 2023 on. It could, however, have gone badly for Israel—bogged down in Lebanon, not for the first time, losing American support even before reckoning with Hamas, and perhaps leading to an early, direct confrontation with Iran. We cannot know what price Israel would have paid on the home front.

The later success Israel would have in its escalations with Hezbollah and Iran makes it hard to second-guess Netanyahu's strategy on those fronts. But those results can also be used to argue that Israel could have found the same or even greater success much earlier in the war. This would have denied Hezbollah the triumph, and spared Israelis the tragedy, of depopulating the north of Israel for thirteen months.

The October 7 attack was of such a magnitude that many thought Israel could not play it safe in response. It needed to think big, do something unexpected—reset the regional balance and secure Israel for a generation. In short, an opportunity had emerged from the crisis and come to look like a necessity. "We are going to change the Middle East," Netanyahu said in an official statement on October 9.

CHAPTER TWO

HAMAS WAS NOT DETERRED

Yahya Sinwar, also known as Israeli Prison Inmate No. 7333335, was a minor figure in Palestinian politics. Had Israel not released him, along with 1,026 others, as part of the 2011 prisoner exchange to free a kidnapped IDF soldier, Gilad Shalit, Sinwar might have spent the rest of his life forgotten in an Israeli prison.

Sinwar was born in the Khan Yunis refugee camp of Egyptian-occupied Gaza in 1962. His family had lost its home in the Ashkelon area during Israel's 1948 War of Independence. This is not an unusual Palestinian story. In the 1948 war, the Arabs of Palestine, soon joined by five surrounding Arab states, took up arms to crush the nascent Jewish state. They failed, and as their armies were repulsed, hundreds of thousands of Arabs were driven out. Many fled the fighting, as civilians often do in war when they can, but many others were expelled by the new IDF.[8]

This was an ugly war. Only a few years after the Holocaust, Arab leaders sounded the theme of extermination. "They thought they were going to win," historian Benny Morris, the leading scholar of the birth of the Palestinian refugee problem, told us at his home. Both sides fought dirty, and the Jews fought for their survival.

One result was a democratic State of Israel with a Jewish majority. Another was the *Nakba*, or catastrophe, as the Arab defeat and later the Palestinian displacement came to be known. Egypt occupied Gaza in the 1948 war and did not integrate the Arab refugees who came its way—as Israel had done with the hundreds of thousands of Jews driven from Arab lands around the same time. Instead, Egypt kept the refugees confined in what became the Gaza Strip. Refugee camps, such as the one in which Sinwar was born, became permanent.

The plan of the Arab bloc at the United Nations was not to resettle the displaced Palestinians and help them move on with their lives, as the UN tries to do for other refugees.[9] John Bolton, a former US national security advisor and ambassador to the UN, told us that Palestinian refugees in Gaza "were taken advantage of by radical Arab states in the 1950s and 1960s. They wanted them to be a wedge to drive Israel into the sea," he said. "Unlike any other refugee population since 1945, they were made into hereditary refugees." Egypt kept the Palestinians of Gaza trapped and stewing in their defeat as a reserve army of the displaced. Israeli troops conquered Gaza from Egypt during the 1967 Six-Day War, and Egypt made peace with Israel in a series of agreements in 1978–1979, but the Israeli-Palestinian conflict was left unresolved.

It was in this environment, in the early 1980s, that Sinwar received a degree in Arabic studies at the Islamic University of Gaza. Established in 1978 under Israeli rule, the university became a hotbed of anti-Israel and Islamist activism.[10] Sinwar involved himself with the Muslim Brotherhood, the major Islamist activist group, and was first arrested by Israel in 1982. Imprisonment allowed him months to get to know other Palestinian activists, including Salah Shehade, who would become a legendary Hamas bomb maker.

In 1987, Sinwar was a founding member of the Muslim Brotherhood's Gaza offshoot, Hamas. He went on to start Hamas's internal police, which performed counterintelligence operations to catch and kill Palestinians suspected of spying or otherwise "collaborating" with Israel. He gained a reputation for brutality against other Palestinians. This time also seems to have influenced Sinwar to think carefully about operational secrecy—how to keep information about upcoming attacks from leaking to the enemy—a key factor in the October 7 invasion's success.[11]

In 1989, Sinwar was sentenced to four life sentences for orchestrating the abduction and killing of two Israeli soldiers and four Palestinians he accused of collaborating with Israel, at least one of whom he confessed to killing with his bare hands.[12]

Hamas's goal, outlined in its covenant and oft repeated, is the total destruction of Israel and its replacement by Islamic rule on the way to founding a larger caliphate.[13] The war against Israel takes on special theological significance for Hamas as part of the jihad against the Jews that is supposed to culminate in their annihilation on Judgment Day. In this way, Hamas merges the powerful stream of Palestinian nationalism with wider Islamist and jihadist currents. Part of a movement with global ambitions, it nonetheless focuses on killing Israelis any way it can.

Dr. Yuval Bitton, a dentist in the Israeli prison system, saved Sinwar's life by diagnosing a brain tumor in time to stop it. During that time, Bitton spent hundreds of hours talking with Sinwar, including about the costs of Hamas's strategy. "I said to Sinwar, 'Tell me, is it worth 10,000 innocent people to die in order to free 100 [Palestinian] prisoners?'" the dentist recalled. According to Bitton, Sinwar replied, "Even 100,000 is worth it."[14]

Released in the 2011 Gilad Shalit hostage deal, Sinwar had spent twenty-two years in prison, during which Israeli authorities alleged that he somehow caught additional Israeli informants and ordered other prisoners to kill them and sever their body parts.

Sinwar returned to Hamas activity after his release and rose in the ranks. But when he took over Hamas's Gaza leadership in 2017, it was in the shadow of his predecessor Ismail Haniyeh, who had become Hamas's worldwide leader. Sinwar's first big move in 2018 was to organize a mix of protest marches and violent attacks on Israel's border fence with Gaza.

At the time and until October 7, Israeli intelligence viewed Sinwar as a relatively weak figure. It believed he wanted to avoid the continuing rounds of conflict with Israel that had been decimating the leadership of Islamic Jihad, another Iran-backed terrorist group in Gaza. Israeli intelligence assessed that Sinwar wanted to remain above it all as the relatively comfortable ruler of Gaza, rather than start large wars and endanger himself.

Sinwar had bigger plans. By 2019, he was ready in principle to start pursuing a mass invasion, IDF intelligence would later learn, though he may have been delayed by the coronavirus wave in early 2020. Hamas took COVID-19 seriously, keeping many of its forces compartmentalized to avoid infection. This made it difficult to plan or train for a large-scale operation.

Not long after Hamas's eleven-day war with Israel in May 2021, however, Sinwar and Hamas's military chief, Mohammed Deif, began to push harder to convert their lofty ambitions into concrete military plans and drills. As Ali Baraka, head of Hamas's National Relations Abroad in Beirut, would explain on October 8, 2023, Hamas fooled Israel. "We made them think that Hamas was busy with governing Gaza, and that it wanted to focus on the 2.5 million Palestinians," he told Lebanese TV.[15]

We don't know whether Sinwar decided more concretely on the mass invasion after Hamas's May 2021 conflict with Israel or only after watching Israel's judicial-overhaul debacle in 2023. Shin Bet Director Ronen Bar also accused Netanyahu of having a role in antagonizing Hamas by allowing unnecessary controversies to escalate over the Temple Mount and al-Aqsa Mosque in Jerusalem. The prime minister and other coalition officials countered that this was a mere fig leaf for Hamas's violence and that a small number of Jews praying at Judaism's holiest site is not a legitimate cause for offense. The terrorists had called their October 7 attack the "al-Aqsa Flood," a metaphor for a flood of invaders into Israel, though they did not make it anywhere near Jerusalem.

The 2021 war, however, had inspired Hamas to believe it really could destroy Israel. Hamas had succeeded at igniting violent riots among some Israeli Arabs as well as Palestinians in east Jerusalem and the West Bank. Hezbollah also stirred up some trouble during that conflict, firing missiles on Israel, raising the prospect of a two-front war on Israel while it faced disorder at home. This, Hamas realized, could make a potent combination.

Israel misread Hamas. The IDF high command and Netanyahu incorrectly concluded that the 2021 war had shown the terrorists how badly and quickly they could be harmed by the IDF's new style of artificial intelligence–based war, which used fancy algorithms to accumulate a large digital bank of targets for Israeli planes to strike. Hamas had made a number of small-scale attempts to invade southern Israel during the war, but the mix of IDF forces and advanced sensors on the border thwarted it easily. The system worked, and Israel's top decision-makers assessed that Hamas would learn its lesson.

Then, in August 2022 and May 2023, Islamic Jihad fought Israel alone from its base in Gaza. Hamas remained on the sidelines of those conflicts, losing stature both among its fighters and throughout Gaza, while Islamic Jihad's standing grew. As Israel saw it at the time, Hamas was focusing on its position within Gaza, not on provoking a conflict with Israel.

Convinced that they faced no imminent danger from external enemies, Israelis spent 2023 tearing themselves apart over an internal dispute: the judicial-reform plan. Opponents saw it as a right-wing attempt to topple the judicial branch and seize unchecked power to remake Israel—or a blunt mechanism to help Netanyahu beat lingering corruption charges. Supporters viewed it as a corrective measure after a decades-long "judicial revolution" that had seen the Supreme Court remove all the usual democratic constraints on its authority.

Nearly all Israelis agree that the domestic fight got out of hand, leading to a weaker IDF and a damaging perception among Israel's adversaries. If weakness is provocative, Gallant, Gantz, and the top commanders of the IDF and the Shin Bet have accused the Netanyahu government of provoking Hamas in precisely that way with the judicial overhaul. During the worst of the judicial-reform debate, more than ten thousand IDF reservists publicly announced that they would refuse a call up to serve until the policy was dropped. Israel's enemies may have believed them. When the Hamas attack did come, Israel was at its most polarized. Its government had already become unpopular and politically vulnerable, with a large, existing domestic protest movement organized and dead set against it. This was no way to enter the longest war in the country's history.

Whatever the final trigger, there is no doubt that October 7 was part of a patient, calculated, long-term plan. The only open question was when to launch the surprise attack.

By March 2022, Sinwar and a small group of top Hamas officials had developed tactical plans for their invasion, called Operation Walls of Jericho, and lined up support from a small group of leaders of Hezbollah and Iran's Quds Force. Sinwar even obtained what he thought were promises from Hassan Nasrallah to start a second front in Lebanon. This threatened to divide Israel's forces and bring in the larger axis of Iranian proxies. The Hamas plan was intercepted by Israeli intelligence, but it was ignored as the stuff of fantasy.

Sinwar's plan showed a cold disregard for his own Palestinian civilian population. He believed that, win or lose, Hamas would come out on top psychologically. Since Israelis were less willing than Palestinians to tolerate losses, their losses would hurt more. This was typical of Hamas thinking. Speaking on the Saudi al-Arabiya TV network on October 19, 2023, another top Hamas leader, Khaled Mashal, was asked about the suffering Hamas had brought on Gazan civilians by launching the war. "Nations are not easily liberated," he shrugged. "The Algerian people sacrificed six million martyrs" to expel the French in the 1950s and early 1960s.[16] The Palestinian national movement views itself similarly. Mistaking Israelis for European colonialists with some other home to return to, Hamas would gladly follow Algeria's example. In messages viewed by *The Wall Street Journal,* Sinwar told other Hamas officials in the middle of the war, "We have the Israelis right where we want them." By that point, more than thirty thousand Gazan civilians and fighters had already been killed in the war, according to Hamas.

* * *

The plan itself was closely guarded.

According to foreign sources, Sinwar, Deif, Mohammed Sinwar (Yahya's brother and deputy), Sinwar confidant Rouhi Mushtaha, and Deif confidant Ayman Nofal were physically together to plan the October 7 invasion.[17] A few others would be let in on the plan, but the list of those who knew the precise details did not even include Hamas's nominal leader, Haniyeh, and his deputy Saleh al-Arouri, who lived in Qatar and Lebanon, raising funds and conducting the group's global alliances. For reasons of information security, the list also did not include many of the five Hamas brigade commanders or any of Hamas's twenty-four battalion commanders. The brigade commanders who had been left out of the loop learned of the invasion only around three days before, and even then, they were not told the timing. Gradually, in the countdown to the invasion, brigade commanders started to inform their battalion commanders, though again the timing was left undisclosed.

In these final days, Ayman Siyam, the leader of Hamas's rocket units, was brought into the plan and received instructions to be ready to fire a vast number of rockets simultaneously, but yet again with the timing left to be determined. Only on October 6, the day before the invasion, did the top Hamas leaders decide that the best moment to strike would be early in the morning of the Jewish holiday of Simchat Torah.

Even though there is ample precedent for Arab attacks on Jewish holidays—most famously the 1973 Yom Kippur War—the IDF largely was set to take the day off. Israeli soldiers would be sleeping off a night of national celebration, and many of the army posts near Gaza were at only 40 percent strength. Complacent to the extreme, half the region's standing IDF force was off duty.[18] The number of border guards on the Gaza frontier was some six hundred, or around 0.1 percent of Israel's five hundred thousand soldiers, and there was no credible second line of defense if the front line were breached. Military intelligence had declared that adding troops to the border would be a waste of resources.

Hamas's high command finally looped in its top field commanders around midnight as October 6 gave way to October 7.

Then, in the hours before the attack, Deif almost called it off. He found it difficult to believe that Israel could be so unprepared and do so little to defend its border, and worried that the Jewish state might be setting a trap. After all, Israel had known about the general Hamas concept of overwhelming the border. It had even obtained Hamas's Operation Walls of Jericho plan in 2022, though it had dismissed it as unrealistic. That year Hamas also broadcast a TV series dramatizing such an attack to overrun Israeli military bases and nearby communities. Hamas had released more such videos in 2023.

Had Israel not noticed Hamas's daylong training in July 2023 for Operation Walls of Jericho? Or its twice-a-week battalion drills, with units of six hundred to eight hundred men, leading up to October 7?[19]

In fact, Israelis had noticed, but concerns that the drills were in preparation for something imminent were ignored at different points in the chain of command. No action was taken. A warning from an intelligence analyst in Israel's elite Unit 8200 (equivalent to America's NSA) was ignored. Israel's female border watchers had warned for months about signs of preparation for a large-scale Hamas assault, yet their mostly male higher-ups dismissed them as hysterical. Didn't their female subordinates know that Hamas was deterred? Didn't they understand the meaning of Hamas's decision to sit out Israel's wars with Islamic Jihad? Hamas had lulled Israel to sleep.

Yes, it was unbelievable that Israel could be so unprepared, so thoroughly fooled. Yet that's what Deif saw before him on the morning of October 7. Finally, he went forward. Around seventy top Hamas field commanders started to rally their forces in the late morning, many as late as 5:30 a.m. The delay, however, worked in Hamas's favor. All the meetings of Israeli military and intelligence leaders that were held to examine warning signs between 2 a.m. and 4 a.m. ironically were held too early, before the real Hamas troop movements, leading Israel to underestimate the danger.

Israeli officials could imagine little more than a pinprick from Hamas. But Sinwar's plan was to carry out an invasion so grandiose that it would rattle Israel to the bone, throwing into question its viability as a state. He sought to ensnare Israel in a grinding, multifront war that would plunge it into international isolation. At an October 2, 2023, meeting of the Hamas Politburo, the minutes of which were reviewed by *The Wall Street Journal*, Sinwar said the hope was to revive the global diplomatic importance of Hamas and the Palestinian national movement. He wanted to accomplish this, he said, just as "Saudi–Zionist normalization" threatened to "open the door for the majority of Arab and Islamic countries to follow the same path" of accepting Israel, at long last. An "extraordinary act" was needed to blow it up, Sinwar told his Hamas colleagues.[20]

* * *

Where was Israeli intelligence in all this? Missing in action.

Nor was this its first miss. IDF intelligence failed to notice or detect at least three prior aborted mass invasions by Hamas. The near invasions were in April 2022, October 2022, and April 2023, but Israel learned of them only during the current war by capturing Hamas documents and interrogating Hamas prisoners.

Before October 7, Israel was not looking for mass invasions and failed to see them. The IDF probes into its October 7 debacle showed that Israel's defense and political establishments for a decade or more believed that Hamas was completely deterred. IDF intelligence sources say that many of their analysts and collection officers had been trained to dig deep into tiny pixels of an intelligence picture, but had lost the capacity to track a long-term plan. One of the few Israelis who predicted this war was Yigal Carmon,[21] a retired IDF intelligence officer and the president of the Middle East Media Research Institute (MEMRI), which monitors Hamas's public communications. "They said it all. They said everything," he told us afterward. He had publicized Hamas's videos of its drills for an invasion of Israel.

But Hamas is always publishing threats, and most of the time it comes to naught. "If they publish it many times, then you can ignore it?" he asked us in response to that point. "I say just the opposite. If they publish it many times, it suggests they mean it and you cannot ignore it."

Israel would do the opposite of taking the threat seriously. By the time the IDF had intercepted a copy of Hamas's Walls of Jericho plan for invading Israel in March 2022, however, only "V," a lowly noncommissioned female intelligence officer in Unit 8200, seemed all that interested in raising the alarm. V had followed drills and chatter among various Hamas forces talking about killing all the villagers in certain southern Israeli communities. They spoke about much larger Hamas invasion forces than had been envisioned by Israel in even the worst-case scenarios.

V had started warning about a mass invasion in 2022. The IDF did not realize how close Hamas came to carrying it out around that time, so V's subsequent warnings were viewed by most of her colleagues and superiors as melodramatic. Sure, Hamas wrote up a plan, but it was a fantasy. Hamas could never pull it off. It wouldn't even try. V's superior officer in IDF Gaza Division Intelligence, Lieutenant Colonel "A," was so dismissive of her warnings and so insistent that a major Hamas invasion was a chimera not worth taking seriously, he never bothered to properly pass along V's warnings to the top echelons of IDF intelligence or the political decision-makers.

According to IDF intelligence, V never came close to giving the timing for such an invasion. While V continued to warn of disaster, the IDF probes found that V did not "jump up and down" about how imminent the threat was. Some emails were sent up the chain after a September 2023 meeting, and she and Lieutenant Colonel A both agreed to continue to discuss the issue in future forums—sometime after October 7.

To defend themselves from criticism later on, Unit 8200 and others in the IDF would point out that they did warn of potential danger in April 2023. When Hamas failed to attack at that time, however, this was then viewed internally as a false alarm and a waste of resources. Given additional information acquired during the war, IDF intelligence now looks back on the April 2023 incident differently. The invasion came deadly close to taking place then.

There's a good reason IDF intelligence was so reliant on assessments of intent rather than facts on the ground. In 2012, the Israeli government decided to end the IDF's collection of human intelligence in Gaza. This meant no IDF spies. The elite Unit 504, the army's own mini Mossad, was pushed out to handle only some signals intelligence in Gaza, presumably to pick up communications. Only the Shin Bet—Israel's equivalent of the FBI, except more powerful and facing fewer constitutional constraints—was left to spy in Gaza. There would be no duplication of efforts or agency turf war, but if the Shin Bet failed, Israel would be flying blind.

Later in the war, it would become possible to contrast Israel's stunning intelligence penetration of Hezbollah in Lebanon, the responsibility of the Mossad, with Israel's equally stunning ignorance in Gaza, the responsibility of the Shin Bet. Tough questions would be asked about the latter agency.

First, what happened to the Shin Bet's Gaza spy rings in 2023? Some intelligence sources claim the agency had lost most of its human spies in Gaza during Hamas counterintelligence crackdowns. For example, on November 11, 2018, a group of IDF special forces was intercepted by Hamas in the middle of a clandestine mission in Gaza. A senior IDF commander was killed and a wide crackdown on Israeli spies in the Strip followed. Hamas had been taught by Iran how to probe any penetrations of its territory or systems to quickly locate spies and loose ends.

Other intelligence sources have said that, leading into the war, the Shin Bet still had extensive sources in Gaza, and that at least one of them actively fooled his Israeli handlers into complacency. Others were not highly placed enough to know of the invasion. Either way, leading into October 7, Israel's defense establishment was mostly reliant on electronic spying tools. Even though Gaza is right next door, Israel had accepted that it would no longer have enough human intelligence to stay informed. Technology would fill the gap.

By 2023, however, Hamas had learned where it was penetrated electronically and deliberately left a misleading trail of information that suggested it was deterred from starting a war. This left Israel conceptually blind as well. Limited in its sources, Israeli intelligence failed in its most important task. It was unable to deliver a clear warning of war in time for policy makers to act.

Nobody woke up the prime minister or the defense minister until the attack had begun and there was no longer a chance to prevent it. "They woke me up at 6:29 in the morning," Netanyahu would tell us, still heated about the delay more than a year later. "6:29!" He would use this to attack the defense establishment, though even his own military secretary declined to rouse him after receiving a call from the Shin Bet at 6:13 a.m. No one even mentioned Hamas's Walls of Jericho plan to IDF chief Halevi on the night of October 6, the morning of October 7, or at any other useful time. Only weeks after the invasion did Halevi learn of the plan, even though IDF intelligence had held a copy since March 2022.

* * *

Even still, all could have been salvaged on the eve of Hamas's attack, when Israel's legendary Unit 8200 saw hundreds of Israeli SIM cards, used to connect cell phones to cellular networks in Israel, lit up in Gaza. At 9 p.m. on October 6, the IDF's Gaza Division intelligence officer and Southern Command chief Yaron Finkelman received notice. More SIM cards would be activated in rolling waves later in the night. This should have been a blinking-red warning of a potential storm, but Israeli intelligence didn't want to act rashly and jeopardize its sources. By "playing it safe," Israeli intelligence actually took an extraordinary risk. Only a hardened ideological preconception kept it from seeing that.

Between 9 p.m. and 11:30 p.m., there were extensive communications between the IDF's Gaza Division, Southern Command and the Shin Bet about this development. While it might seem obvious that Hamas would only need so many Israeli SIM cards if it expected to send a large contingent across the border, explanations were provided by intelligence officials to reassure commanders that this had happened before without leading to any real threat.

At 11:30 p.m., classified indications that we still cannot reveal increased confidence that the SIM cards were a sign of a Hamas military drill. Around midnight, Finkelman and IDF Southern Command intelligence chief Colonel "A" began a detailed dialogue about three scenarios to explain the SIM-card activity. They decided it could be either a military drill, some kind of undefined but not terribly serious attack move or, in the worst-case scenario, a localized attempt to penetrate Israel at between two and eight spots on the border, involving dozens of Hamas fighters at most. They scheduled a wider and deeper situation assessment for ten the next morning, October 7. It could wait.

There were calming factors to take into account as well in these hours. For instance, none of the Hamas invaders were mobilized. They would not do so until much later, closer to 4:30 a.m. and 5:30 a.m. Israeli intelligence in some ways was forming its impressions too early.

Between 2 a.m. and 3 a.m., IDF Chief Herzi Halevi's bureau chief woke him up and started to update him. Halevi left his bedroom and moved to his home study to be as alert as possible. He tried to organize his thoughts amid the drowsiness. "We cannot just convince ourselves that this is nothing," he wrote to himself in one haunting note. Halevi ordered additional Air Force drones into the sky and more intelligence collection. He also ordered his aide to update the Air Force, but there was no urgency to his orders, and the aide updated only the midlevel Air Force manager on rotation, not Air Force chief Tomer Bar.

Between 3 a.m. and 4 a.m., IDF Operations Command chief Oded Basiuk and his top deputy, Shlomi Binder, began a dialogue of their own with the Shin Bet, ordering some additional drones into the sky. They said this should be limited, however, so as not to "burn sources" and reveal intelligence methods.

From 3:10 a.m. to 3:30 a.m., IDF intelligence analysis chief Amit Saar and Unit 8200 chief Yossi Sariel were updated for the first time about the situation. Aharon Haliva, the overall IDF intelligence chief, was on vacation. None of these officials took any proactive measures.

The IDF chief ordered the head of Southern Command to give him an update, but Finkelman was in the middle of his own update with several IDF intelligence and Shin Bet officials. Halevi's update was delayed until 4 a.m., reinforcing the sense that nothing was imminent.

Halevi's bureau chief informed Basiuk of the Operations Command that the IDF chief and Finkelman would be speaking at 4 a.m., and Basiuk decided on his own to join the call. At 3:30 a.m., the Shin Bet issued a warning that Hamas might be seeking to conduct a small, localized penetration of the border, but that for the moment, Hamas forces still appeared to be in peacetime positions.

Around 4 a.m., Halevi held the virtual meeting with Southern Command chief Finkelman, Operations Command chief Basiuk, and some other IDF officials, including from the intelligence agencies. Crucially, Halevi did not demand that IDF intelligence chief Haliva be roused from his vacation, nor did Haliva's aides, who knew about the SIM cards, deem it necessary to wake Haliva again after having briefly spoken to him. The IDF chief also did not demand that the Air Force chief participate.

Further, Halevi did not see fit to wake up Gallant or Netanyahu. Both have since said that had they been woken up, they might have advised some additional defensive measures. It turns out that Shin Bet chief Ronen Bar did order his aide to notify Netanyahu's office at 5:15 a.m., but this was done only an hour later, at 6:13 a.m., sixteen minutes before Hamas initiated its invasion. During that time, Netanyahu's military secretary Avi Gil chose not to wake the prime minister, also believing—like everyone else—that there was no large, imminent threat.

Halevi's focus was still on not taking too many visible actions, endeavoring not to tip off Hamas to the IDF's penetration of its SIM cards. He ordered some minor changes: transferring one aircraft to the south, and drone intelligence collection regarding any suspicious movements in the Gaza area. Inexplicably, his subordinates delayed carrying out his orders, and once the invasion started, they were never executed.

At some point, the Shin Bet sent its elite, dozen-member "Tequila Team" to gather more specialized intelligence at the Gaza border and potentially to help with striking Hamas officials if it were to become necessary. Many of the team's members, grossly outnumbered, would be killed by Hamas invaders in one of the heaviest battle losses in Shin Bet history.

Between 4:15 a.m. and 5:40 a.m., Finkelman of Southern Command called back from holiday his brigade commanders with the rank of colonel. Based on a recommendation from Gaza Division chief Avi Rosenfeld, however, he did not call back battalion commanders, at the lieutenant-colonel rank, who led a few hundred soldiers each. The IDF would end up fighting without its key battlefield leaders.

* * *

When Hamas opened hostilities at 6:29 a.m. on October 7 with some three thousand seven hundred rockets and an invasion force of around five thousand six hundred men invading at 119 different spots to take over a couple of dozen villages, Israel's top officials went into shock. "It was the worst military-readiness failure in history," General Petraeus, the retired commander of US Central Command, told us. Classified video footage of the IDF high command "pit," which we viewed, shows not a single general was in the room and the midlevel officer in charge and his deputies were yelling at each other in chaotic fashion as individual reports of invasions flooded in. They had no overall defense plan.

A full hour into the invasion, at 7:30 a.m., the IDF high command knew about only 40 percent of the border penetrations. By 10 a.m., three and a half hours into the invasion, and with hundreds of Israelis already dead or kidnapped, the IDF high command still knew about only around 60 percent of border penetrations. The IDF's leaders did not really start to direct the country's defense until around 1 p.m. At this point, the vast majority of the hostages had already been taken, and most of the Israeli victims at places near the Gaza border like Be'eri, Kfar Aza, Nir Oz, and the Nova Music Festival had already been murdered.

Netanyahu, Gallant, and Halevi all set out to Israeli military headquarters in Tel Aviv, arriving somewhere in the eight o'clock hour. Gallant and Halevi spoke on the phone as both were heading in their cars toward Tel Aviv. Netanyahu received updates from his military secretary, who was in touch with the IDF's top brass. The prime minister's first orders were to seal Israel's northern and southern borders, to ward off a possible assault by Hezbollah in Lebanon and prevent the Hamas invaders from escaping back across the Gaza border. "It's clearly not another 'round'" of conflict, Netanyahu told colleagues, not the typical Gaza skirmish. "It's going to be a long war."

We reveal now for the first time that Netanyahu and Halevi did not speak until almost four hours into the war. Instead, they both were at military headquarters, a couple hundred meters from each other, for around two hours before speaking. We can disclose that they finally spoke at a meeting that began between 9:55 a.m. and 10:15 a.m., for which Netanyahu came to the IDF underground situation room. Halevi and Netanyahu both expressed that they were stunned at what Hamas had accomplished. Several Israeli security officials at headquarters appeared "white as ghosts." The two leaders also still felt very much in the dark about the full scale of the unfolding disaster, even debating whether a limited or full call up of the reserves would be appropriate, before the prime minister decided on the maximum.

Netanyahu had waited until his chief of staff, Tzachi Braverman, had arrived to military headquarters to assist with the Halevi meeting. Braverman was initially pinned down in his house with rocket siren alerts. But this is no excuse for the country's two most important national security figures not to speak for so long amid a crisis. Why did Netanyahu not want immediate updates from the army chief, so that he could best lead the way? Why would Halevi not reach out to the prime minister, if Netanyahu did not call, to make sure they were on the same page?

There is no good answer. It is clear that all of the country's top officials were not only stunned but racing to keep pace with the evolving picture, minute by minute, of Hamas's invasion. The collapse of the IDF's Gaza Division, with its headquarters besieged and its commander, Brigadier General Avi Rosenfeld, failing to convey the true extent of the assault, along with a general system overload from the sheer number of disparate Hamas invasions, led the army to underestimate the problem in these first hours. When Netanyahu and Halevi did finally meet, the prime minister did not come away with a substantially altered picture of events on the ground.

As a result of the confusion, the IDF high command often sent only small special-forces squads to trouble spots on October 7, when it should have deployed large infantry or armor units. Israel lost many of its best troops when, deployed to kibbutzim to face what commanders thought were a few infiltrators, they found themselves outnumbered by dozens or hundreds of Hamas fighters.

Midlevel officers on the Gaza front were sounding the alarm that a full-scale war was on already before 7 a.m. Higher-level commanders did not fully understand until hours later. Netanyahu issued orders in his meeting with Halevi for the Israeli Air Force to prevent movement across the Gaza border. The Air Force has said it had reached a parallel conclusion around the same time. Eventually, it did stop additional Hamas fighters from invading and helped eliminate a large number of the around fifteen hundred Hamas invaders whom the IDF killed in Israeli territory. But whether the Air Force moved too slowly, could not arrive fast enough, or did not know how to handle situations where civilian hostages were mixed in with Hamas invaders, the results were grim. Many of the 251 hostages the Air Force might have prevented from being kidnapped if it had acted differently were abducted to Gaza.

To his credit, Netanyahu did issue a video before 1 p.m. telling the Israeli public that the country was at war. But by then, Hamas had already accomplished most of its hostage taking and killing. Netanyahu, Gallant, and Halevi did not appear at a live press conference for an extended period. The only live presence speaking to the public and the media on October 7 was the IDF spokesman, Brigadier General Daniel Hagari.

The prime minister took a call from President Biden on October 7 and conveyed a message that would become a staple of his and Israel's early rhetoric: "Hamas is worse than ISIS." He also requested US assets be moved to the region to deter a Hezbollah attack. On October 8, Defense Secretary Austin ordered the USS Gerald R. Ford Carrier Strike Group to the Eastern Mediterranean.

One of us, Yonah, saw how wrong Israel had gotten the situation when he went to Be'eri, one of the Israeli border villages, on October 11. Four days after the invasion, fresh blood, contorted and burned houses and cars, and other signs of carnage were spread across the village. Hamas invaders remained nearby and rockets exploded directly overhead, leading him to hit the deck.

Between late 2023 and early 2025, after a far longer wait than most Israelis had expected, IDF chief Halevi, Southern Command chief

Finkelman and his deputy, and IDF intelligence chief Haliva and his deputy all resigned. Others were expected to follow after the worst Israeli military and intelligence failure in half a century.

* * *

Prime Minister Netanyahu never saw it coming. He thought Hamas was contained and deterred. Worse, for the sixteen years since Hamas took over Gaza, Israel's Shin Bet, military intelligence, and IDF chiefs all made the same mistake as the prime minister.

Netanyahu cannot help but feel that had the IDF made even basic preparations, or had the intelligence agencies been able to see what was right under their noses, the attack could have been thwarted. That may be true, but the buck must stop with the prime minister. On some level, he knows that, though he has avoided discussing it publicly and delayed an inquiry into his decisions. Netanyahu has used his parliamentary majority to vote down several attempts by the opposition to initiate a state inquiry, a customary Israeli practice with huge public support.

Initially, he argued that it was improper to hold such an inquiry at the most intense points of the war. By March 2024 and July 2024, however, the IDF itself started to set aside significant time and resources to probe its own failures. At this point, Netanyahu's rationale started to lose support even among many of his supporters, so it shifted. He now focused on the political ideology of the "deep state" and Supreme Court that would lead the probe, yet tended to disregard compromise proposals, digging in on his demand that political appointees be involved. Netanyahu has paid a significant price on this issue in opinion polls, but probably not as high as he would pay if he let a state inquiry proceed. He knows that would threaten to end his political career because he likely would be found as responsible for the failures of October 7 as the IDF and Shin Bet.

It helps Netanyahu that his chief opponents are also heavily implicated in the strategic conception that was discredited by Hamas's invasion and the war that followed. The past several IDF chiefs of staff emphasized the need for a "smaller, smarter army," relying on special forces, intelligence, and the Air Force. The era of big and dumb—with the tanks, artillery, and infantry needed to fight large ground wars on multiple fronts—was deemed over. Gantz and his political partner, Eisenkot, both favored this approach in their tenures as IDF chiefs, which would leave Israel at a disadvantage in this war. As Gantz told an interviewer in 2018, "I am saying, unambiguously, that I prioritized cyber and intelligence over infantry and armor.... Unlike the threat of ground invasion, the threat of cyber is realistic."[22]

Eisenkot, as IDF chief, celebrated the shift to a billion-dollar high-tech Gaza border wall along with Netanyahu. They said it closed the door on Hamas, which Israel would see coming miles away, and which would not be able to breach the border, above or below ground. Israel's prime minister, cabinet, military, intelligence agencies, and opposition all wore the same blinders.

* * *

Even so, why leave an armed jihadist group and proxy of Iran, sworn to Israel's destruction, in a position to get lucky? The original Israeli mistake in this case was to allow Hamas to rule a statelet on its border. Naturally, it came from a desire for peace and quiet.

Years of peace negotiations, from 1993 on, had failed to resolve the Israeli–Palestinian conflict. After the collapse of the Camp David II negotiations in 2000, the Palestinians launched a wave of violence with the Second Intifada (2000–2005), leading to a harsh Israeli crackdown lasting years. The experience of those years, arguably, should have taught Israelis that Hamas cannot be "contained."

In 2005, Ariel Sharon, then the right-wing prime minister of Israel, grew tired of the terror attacks on Israeli troops and civilians in Gaza and of the international opprobrium involved in maintaining security control. Each had worsened since Israel began withdrawing from Gaza City in 1994. Sharon decided that Israel would now pull out of the Strip entirely. More than eight thousand Israelis were forcibly evicted from Gaza by the IDF, and full control was handed to the Palestinians. They would have a chance to build something better of their own in Gaza.

The plan went awry, however, when Hamas won the subsequent 2006 Palestinian legislative election and carried out a coup in 2007, pushing its less extreme Fatah party Palestinian rivals out of Gaza by force. Fatah, which Israel had expected to police Hamas, found itself outvoted and outgunned. Suddenly, Israel was confronted with a much more radical enemy in control of a quasi-state. But the West pressed Israel not to return to war and control over Gaza. Perhaps the task of governing would lead Hamas to moderate. Rocket attacks on Israel were increasingly tolerated, especially when they "only" targeted the small, nearby Israeli border communities.

As crazy as it now sounds, Israelis got used to the jihadist fiefdom next door. Every so often, when the rocket fire got out of hand, or when the jihadists would tunnel into Israel to carry out a kidnapping, there would be a small war at a manageable diplomatic price to set Hamas back. Israel's governments—center-left Prime Minister Ehud Olmert (2007–2009), right-wing Prime Minister Benjamin Netanyahu (2009–2021, 2022–present) and centrist Prime Minister Naftali Bennett (2021–2022)—decided to isolate, contain, and deter Hamas, but not to oust it from power. After all, how much damage could Hamas really do from Gaza?

Netanyahu in time went even further. Hamas had started a war with Israel in 2014 after Fatah in the West Bank had cut Hamas off financially and the Gaza terror group had run out of money. To avoid letting Hamas get into such a dangerous financial situation again, Israel allowed Qatar to provide the terrorists millions of dollars on a regular basis following the war. In the wake of the October 7 attack, these payments would become a major anti-Israel talking point. They were used to suggest that Israelis, the victims of the massacre, really had only themselves to blame, not the Palestinians. Among the conspiratorial, they were cited as proof that Israel or Netanyahu specifically supported Hamas.

A little bit of context, however, is enough to provide a much more credible explanation. The move to allow Qatari funding to reach Hamas was a centrist consensus in Israel, advocated by both the security establishment and Netanyahu as a way to maintain stability and put off further rounds of pointless fighting. International support for the monetary transfers was also strong. Without them, it was argued, the humanitarian situation in Gaza would deteriorate—and Israel would be at fault. Though everyone knew much of the money would be diverted to Hamas's military purposes, it was nevertheless supposed to keep Gaza stable and grease the peace.

To his right-wing allies who protested that it was wrong and dangerous to allow such money to reach the terrorists of Hamas, Netanyahu found a savvy reply: The right-wingers were once again being shortsighted. He told them that there was a strategic advantage in the already existing division of the Palestinian national movement between Hamas-run Gaza and Fatah-run West Bank. When the Palestinians lacked a unified front, with whom could Israel be pressured to make concessions for a two-state solution that right-wingers opposed as suicidal?[23]

The Israeli left still supported talks for a two-state solution led by the Obama administration. But since negotiations stalled and overthrowing Hamas was too costly and out of the question, the center, Left, and Right in Israel all found ways to rationalize the status quo and even find virtue in a policy to prop it up. This view, however, came to depend on an inordinate faith in technology as a substitute for strategy and even basic preparedness. Israel's Iron Dome missile-defense system could shoot down most of the rockets that would have endangered Israeli citizens—so Hamas was allowed to keep shooting. Technology had provided Israeli policy makers flexibility to a fault. They didn't have to go to war because Israelis weren't dying. By this logic, Hamas was permitted to accumulate more and better rockets until it had amassed the arsenal that overwhelmed Israel on the morning of October 7 and provided excellent cover for an invasion.

Netanyahu and the IDF also believed that new technologies to counter Hamas's attack tunnels would be sufficient to prevent Gaza's rulers from posing any real danger. This is partly because they were focused on cross-border tunnels breaking into Israeli territory. They were far less focused on the tunnels within Gaza because no one believed it would be necessary to carry out a deep invasion to uproot Hamas, or that an Israeli governing coalition would ever approve it. This led the Israeli defense establishment to vastly underestimate the extent of the tunnels.

With carrots (Qatari cash and letting Hamas stay in power) and sticks (occasional airstrikes and small wars), the Israeli political and security establishments believed they had deterred Hamas. One important moment in the development of Israel's containment policy toward Hamas came in 2014. When Hamas escalated its rocket fire at Israel that year, there was an opportunity for a larger Israeli response. Instead, Prime Minister Netanyahu and then–IDF chief Gantz decided to limit the subsequent Gaza invasion rather than risk losing an estimated five hundred to one thousand soldiers in a full-scale invasion. In the end, Israel's action on the ground was superficial, taking a backseat to business-as-usual strikes from the air.

Much later in the October 7 war, as Netanyahu sought to fire Shin Bet Director Ronen Bar, the latter would accuse the prime minister of further responsibility for failures leading to the October 7 disaster. One reason, Bar said, was that Netanyahu had refused his repeated requests to assassinate Sinwar and his military chief, Mohammed Deif. According to the Shin Bet director, Netanyahu had warned him that such assassinations would threaten the peace, provoking an unnecessary war. Netanyahu never denied Bar's specific allegations. But when Netanyahu pressed Bar before October 7 to assassinate Hamas's deputy chief, Saleh al-Arouri, the prime minister said the Shin Bet chief balked—for similar reasons. Bar never denied Netanyahu's specific allegations either.

Why provoke Hamas when the Palestinian issue had been "parked"? The two-state solution was going nowhere, Netanyahu believed, because Israel lacked a Palestinian peace partner interested in it.

Palestinian leaders rejected offers to divvy up the land with Israel (and the Jewish Yishuv that predated it) in 1937, 1947, 2000, 2001, and 2008. The longer the Palestinians wait, the argument goes, the more of a pariah Israel will become, and the more the Palestinians will get in the end. That is part of what made the 2020 Abraham Accords between Israel and the United Arab Emirates, Bahrain, Morocco, and Sudan such an earthquake. It showed that time was no longer on the Palestinians' side. They could remain recalcitrant, but the Middle East was moving on. A deal with Saudi Arabia, a generational achievement that seemed to portend an end at last to Israel's regional isolation, was all teed up. Rather than make self-defeating concessions to Palestinians, Israel could contain them and bypass the old "Palestinian veto." It never occurred to Netanyahu that Hamas could strike Israel hard enough to upend the entire paradigm.

Yahya Sinwar would not be parked.

CHAPTER THREE

THE BLITZ OF NORTHERN GAZA

Hamas's invasion and massacre brought on a fury that the world had not seen from Israel in decades. From October 7 to October 27, Israel bombarded Gaza, especially northern Gaza, with harrowing air and artillery strikes, paving the way for its largest-ever ground invasion of the territory. Israel began attacking using a huge prewar target bank. It updated the target bank constantly, in real time, from drone and aircraft surveillance analyzed by artificial intelligence systems, though humans made the decisions. But few realize just how much debate it took to launch the invasion of Gaza.

While Netanyahu had directed Gaza wars in 2012, 2014, and 2021, and many smaller ones, too, he had never ordered an invasion of Gaza with all Israel's might. Even though some Israeli generals had previously pushed for larger invasions, never before had there been international legitimacy to topple Hamas. The US, both Democratic and Republican administrations, had cut short the previous Gaza wars, pressuring Israel into ceasefires in a matter of weeks or less. Even in Israel, there had been insufficient support for a more thorough operation, given the IDF casualties it was expected to entail. Besides, the assumption was that Hamas could always be weakened and contained, posing little threat beyond the small rockets it fired at Israeli border communities.

The October 7 attack had upended many of those assumptions—but not all. Netanyahu, despite his tough talk about "annihilating Hamas," dreaded that the IDF, which had failed on October 7, might fail again. It could get bogged down in Hamas's morass of tunnels, human shields, and booby traps. "There will be thousands of dead Israeli soldiers," Netanyahu warned Gallant in the early days after October 7, with a look of horror in his eyes that had not fully left since the attack. This was a very different Netanyahu from the one the public thinks it knows, and from the image he has cultivated.

The real Netanyahu may be a hawk, but going into the war he was also a conservative—cautious, even hesitant about the use of military force. He did not want Israel to blunder into a quagmire—though Israel did ultimately get stuck at war in Gaza for around two years.

As prime minister from 1996 to 1999, and then as finance minister from 2003 to 2005, Netanyahu led the free-market reforms credited with revolutionizing the Israeli economy. Despite that record, he lost elections in 1999 and 2006. It would only be as "Mr. Security" that Netanyahu would roar back to the prime minister's office in 2009—and stay on for twelve years to become the country's longest-serving prime minister. This was a remarkable run in the unforgiving world of Israeli politics. The 2020 Abraham Accords could have capped it off, and October 7 would have been on someone else's watch, if he had retired after being ousted in June 2021.

But instead of retiring, Netanyahu stayed in politics—contesting public corruption charges in his long and still-running trial, which was part of what had united a coalition against him—and eventually regained power in December 2022. The danger of the Iranian nuclear program still loomed, and he had been the lead player working to confront it for years.

Within Israel, Netanyahu has supporters who cannot imagine anyone else being prime minister and keeping the country safe, as well as opponents who believe he has deeply harmed democracy and endangered the country to stay in power. Either way, "formidable" is a descriptor that few would contest. He would now be put to the test with the toughest challenge of his long career.

If everything seemed to move at light speed on October 7, for the next twenty days, it felt as though the world had ground to a halt. Netanyahu wanted to slow down and think, but the political clock was ticking, and the war room knew it. The Israeli people were enraged and newly unified in demanding action.

Gallant, whose Lebanon offensive had been nixed, pivoted to push for the largest invasion of Gaza ever—and soon. In this, he received significant support from the IDF high command. Gantz was largely in favor, though as was typical, he wanted to be more circumspect about the timing and the details. Gallant liked to make quick, decisive moves. Gantz thought of himself as a more sophisticated thinker, seeking additional time to consider factors that Gallant might miss.

Netanyahu was mostly reacting to the ideas of his war-room partners at this stage. He was not driving the conversation but, on the contrary, seemed to be drawing out the process. It is not that he supported an alternative to a ground invasion. After October 7, however, he needed extra convincing the plan would succeed. The prime minister would not be rushed into invading Gaza before he was ready.

Gallant and Gantz mostly remained in their black dress shirts, no tie. Netanyahu sometimes would do the same, as if the war room had a strange and dark dress code, but at other times, he paired a suit with his favorite blue tie. They all were sleep-deprived, which surely contributed to the alternating moods. The war room was unusually subdued, humbled by the immense failures of October 7. Then, suddenly, at an errant word or suggestion, the leaders would lose patience with one another and raise their voices.

Rivalries simmered from the start. Netanyahu always worried that Gantz, who had been leading in Israeli opinion polls before October 7, would try to use wartime developments to oust him as prime minister. After October 7, Gantz suddenly had double Netanyahu's support from the Israeli public. He would keep that margin for at least five months and stay in the lead until August 2024. Netanyahu also was wary that Gallant would try to steal the spotlight, or else stab him in the back politically to great acclaim from the media—a repeat of the judicial-overhaul experience, as the prime minister saw it.

Gantz kept trying to figure out where Netanyahu stood on the war, concerned that he still could not read the prime minister who had fooled him into coalition deals in 2020 and then taken advantage. Gallant was incensed by Netanyahu's slow decision-making process for the first week or so, but afterward fell in line on the issue, especially once Biden administration pressure to rethink the invasion heated up.

A big push for the invasion came from IDF Chief of Staff Herzi Halevi, who was more confident in those early days, and who was convinced that Hamas had to be met with a massive Israeli ground attack. Already on October 8 and 9, even before the last of the Hamas death squads had been cleared from Israel, Halevi had several calls with Southern Command's General Yaron Finkelman about specific offensive plans. The massacre, Halevi felt strongly, must not go unanswered.

Israel felt it had international legitimacy for a major military response, but it did not know how deep that support went or how long it would last. Would this war follow the familiar script of past Gaza conflicts, in which media pressure weighs on a US president until he tells Israel to make a ceasefire?

Portions of the US campus left, especially under the media spotlight at Harvard and Columbia, had even cheered the October 7 attack. The day after the massacre, National Students for Justice in Palestine (SJP) celebrated "a historic win for the Palestinian resistance." Its instructions, sent on October 8 to its campus chapters across America, were to "normalize the resistance," noting, "there is no 'right' way for Palestinians to fight.... Resistance comes in all forms" and "all of it is legitimate."[24] SJP is the largest anti-Israel protest group in the US, and its actions would later be hailed in mainstream press coverage as "anti-war" and "pro-ceasefire."

Also on October 8, more than thirty Harvard student groups declared that Israel was "entirely responsible for all unfolding violence," absolving Hamas. Columbia's chapters of SJP and Jewish Voice for Peace declared themselves "in full solidarity with Palestinian Resistance" and celebrated the massacre as "an unprecedented historic moment for the Palestinians of Gaza." These student groups, operating under the new name of Columbia University Apartheid Divest, would lead the construction of a protest encampment in April 2024 that garnered international media attention, spurring the creation of similar encampments at more than one hundred US universities in the spring of 2024.[25] The story, already predictable, would be that President Biden was losing young voters.

When Halevi called Finkelman on October 8 to ask him to start working on the war plans, Finkelman replied that the work had already begun. Many in the IDF were itching to redeem themselves. Finkelman in particular, despite taking the failure of October 7 very hard, would come across during the war as one of the most confident commanders in the IDF. Halevi told his military colleagues that he had not assumed the best invasion plan would need to originate with him. It was typical of Halevi, who is unusually modest for a top general, to play down his role.

It was a problem, however, that there was no war plan on the shelf for a full invasion of Gaza, let alone an army built or trained to carry out a plan like that. Neither the IDF nor the government had been ready for the possibility, which had always seemed politically unlikely and too costly in soldiers' lives. Privately, Gallant and Halevi blamed Netanyahu's resistance over the years to major action in Gaza, while the prime minister blamed the defense establishment for not being prepared for all eventualities. Either way, the plans needed to be redrawn. These disputes would later break out in public.

According to Halevi, while Gallant was strongly in favor of invading Gaza at the very start, the defense minister had many serious strategic and tactical questions he wanted addressed. In particular, Gallant worried that Israeli tanks could be surrounded and captured, as on October 7. Halevi explained that it would be very different. He described to Gallant how invasion forces with tanks would have the clear and coordinated support of the Air Force and Israeli intelligence. "Bad things can happen. [S—] happens, but the bottom line is that Hamas cannot stop us. If they cannot land big punches, they cannot stop us," Halevi told Gallant.

Netanyahu would ask big-picture strategic questions to Halevi. The prime minister made it clear that he had never loved ground-war operations. Nor did several others. Halevi was asked by Israel's top decision-makers, "Why can't we just attack Gaza from the air?" He replied that it wouldn't be enough: "There are goals you cannot achieve without troops on the ground standing on the neck of the enemy."

Much of the war room was still afraid that there would be a repeat of IDF ground forces' failure during the 2006 Lebanon War. Halevi could feel the fear in the room. He told them, "I failed on October 7, but I am sure we can do this." Halevi referred to American tennis phenom Serena Williams and her difficult life story. "Like Serena Williams says," he told the war room, "the champion is not the one who wins many games, but the one who recovers from a failure and fights back to win."

During early meetings relating to an invasion, some described Netanyahu's legs and voice as shaky. Halevi has said that he saw the demoralized faces of many of the top IDF generals and the security cabinet officials and how hard it was on those below him and above him. Netanyahu, Gantz, and Eisenkot all appeared very worried. In difficult moments, Halevi himself would try to remember one of the families that was wiped out on October 7 or one of the hostages. This reminded him that he could not let his own personal struggle take him off course.

According to Gallant, Netanyahu was not the only top official with initial doubts about a deep invasion of Gaza. Eisenkot, the former IDF chief who had joined the unity government from the opposition, and Shas party leader Aryeh Deri, both war cabinet observers, were in a state of shock and fear.

While the debate raged over a large-scale ground invasion—as opposed to an air war like what Israel had carried out several times from 2021 to May 2023, or a more limited ground invasion like in 2014—Israel was not letting Hamas relax. It attacked from the air with great intensity. With little risk of Israeli casualties, and the war already begun by the other side, the prime minister sought aggressive action. When Halevi told him on October 9 that the Israeli Air Force had already struck fifteen hundred targets in Gaza in forty-eight hours, Netanyahu banged on the conference table. "Why not 5,000?" he demanded.

Halevi replied, "We don't have 5,000 known and approved targets to strike."

Netanyahu countered, "I don't care about approved targets. Bring down the houses. Bomb with everything we have."

Halevi was astounded by the prime minister's attitude about targeting in an urban battlefield. Halevi, Gallant, Gantz, Eisenkot, and others would later describe Netanyahu as having lost his sense of balance in those early days. We also spoke to Netanyahu on October 10. When asked about slowing down the war to avoid collateral harm to hostages or Palestinian civilians, who might be caught in the crossfire, he waved his arm, as if to suggest that he would not be deterred from bombing Hamas everywhere and anywhere it was hiding.

Israel had suffered its greatest single blow in fifty years, and its prime minister was not about to let Hamas escape by using its own people as human shields. The resulting devastation and some public statements by Israeli ministers in the heat of the moment, however, would later lend a superficial plausibility to allegations of indiscriminate Israeli bombing and even genocide. The impression would develop that Israel was merely venting its anger in pursuit of vengeance against Gazans rather than what it actually did: Conduct a highly targeted military campaign until civilians were evacuated.

"I had to be the adult in the room," Halevi has said. He felt Netanyahu was making decisions from the gut. The IDF chief found it childish, especially all the yelling. "If we carry out too many attacks in one day, then we just use up munitions," Halevi told military colleagues. He also worried about the potential damage to Israeli legitimacy and the consequences afterward, though for him, too, the leading concern was to dismantle Hamas as a national army.

Fatalities in Gaza were highest in that first month of bombing—more than eight thousand combatants and civilians, according to Hamas's

Gaza Health Ministry—and Israeli officials acknowledge that the pace of fatalities stayed elevated for the first three months before slowing. Israel would run low on munitions anyway in these early months, and eventually on diplomatic support, but it could have been worse.

* * *

Bombing from the air is one thing, but sending in an invasion force, which could take heavy casualties, was something else entirely. That debate among the war cabinet was not yet settled and would drag on for weeks that Israel did not have. Halevi recalled that Netanyahu's hesitancy had been reinforced by former generals like Itzhak Brik, who told Netanyahu the IDF was not ready. Halevi viewed Brik's conduct as disgraceful and misleading, including to the Israeli public, and was distressed that few had called him on it.

General Brik had been a lone voice in the wilderness before October 7. As a former Army ombudsman, he had warned in 2019 that the IDF was not prepared and that Hamas could attack. Even a few weeks before October 7, he spoke of "IDF disintegration" and declining competence and preparedness, with overreliance on air power and technology. When his concerns were tragically vindicated, he suddenly gained influence. But his inability to adjust to radically changing realities led his predictions after October 7—that the IDF would continue to fail in every theater—to miss the mark. Essentially, he had one prediction: that the IDF was unprepared and would fail. Yet the IDF would rout Hamas's best forces in northern Gaza in a matter of weeks. Had Netanyahu continued to heed Brik, the IDF may never have taken apart Hamas's twenty-four battalions.

Half the Hamas force was stationed in northern Gaza, with a small portion in central Gaza, and the rest in southern Gaza. Each battalion had distinct communications, intelligence, and logistics teams, as well as at least one thousand fighters, though some had significantly more. This was not merely a terrorist group; it was a national army.

Some pessimistic generals visited IDF brigades and told them, "You're making a big mistake in getting ready to invade Gaza." Halevi was furious when he heard about this. The IDF chief was accusing Brik and a few others of gravely misleading Netanyahu and undermining his own authority with subordinates. It was clear to Halevi that these dire predictions were both inaccurate and an obstacle to the action necessary to achieve Israel's two war aims in Gaza: Freeing the hostages and destroying Hamas as a military and governing force. From Netanyahu's point of view, however, serious military men were giving him vastly conflicting advice.

In fact, nobody in the war cabinet really knew what would happen once infantry troops were sent into Gaza. During meetings, the normally confident politicians and generals wore their anxieties on their sleeves. Would there be huge losses or would changes in IDF tactics keep Israeli casualties low? At one point, Netanyahu pulled Gantz aside and asked him point-blank, "Is the IDF capable of invading Gaza?" Gantz said it reflected the prime minister's fear after October 7. Netanyahu would later tell us, "Nobody had ever fought with such intense tunnel warfare in such a dense urban area."

In 2014, the last time the IDF had seriously considered a full invasion of Gaza, its estimates had ranged from five hundred to one thousand Israeli soldiers killed in a relatively short period of time. October 7, however, showed that the IDF had underestimated Hamas's strength, leading Netanyahu to wonder if these ghastly numbers were overly optimistic. As the war continued, Israel would also learn that it had greatly underestimated the size and scope of Hamas's tunnel system. It turned out to be around 450 miles long—snaking around the Gaza Strip, which itself is only twenty-five miles long. "Our intelligence was completely wrong about Hamas's capabilities, not only about its intent," a Netanyahu adviser told us.

Gallant and Gantz, regarded by the Israeli people as more dovish than Netanyahu, in fact renewed their push to get the prime minister to be more aggressive. They all but threatened to go public with his unwillingness to order the invasion. Netanyahu didn't appreciate the pressure.

The past conflicts of the three war-room rivals kept coming back to haunt them. Gantz had helped push Netanyahu out of power in mid-2021. Gallant had overshadowed Netanyahu with public speeches against their government's judicial overhaul in March 2023. This had led the prime minister to announce Gallant's firing before walking it back amid mass protests. Netanyahu was never sure if these two were trying to ensnare him in a political trap.

Likewise, Gantz had been stewing since 2020, when Netanyahu broke a promise to make him prime minister under their rotation agreement, whereby each man would take a turn in the top chair of their coalition government. Gantz was never sure whether Netanyahu's policy arguments represented what he truly believed was good for the country or what was best for him politically.

Gallant strove throughout the war to show his serious, no-nonsense focus on the battle, frequently showing up in enemy territory on every front, side-by-side with the soldiers and aircraft. This was a good look for Gallant, so much so that Netanyahu complained privately: "Is he ever photographed without war planes in the background?"

The defense minister started the war with substantial distrust of Netanyahu. This suspicion grew as the war progressed until Gallant lost faith in the prime minister, as Gantz had previously. Israeli right-wingers came to mock Gallant and Gantz by calling them the same name: "Gallantz." The two men, for their part, were always asking themselves a provocative question: Is Netanyahu really so worried about the Israeli body count or about the narrow vote count of his government?

* * *

It didn't help Gallant, Gantz, and Halevi's case for invasion that the Biden administration put up obstacle after obstacle to stop Israel or delay it. Though the US wasn't always at the war-room table, it could not be refused a seat.

After Hamas's October 7 attack, three US generals were sent to try to talk Gallant and Halevi out of a massive invasion of Gaza. "This is a very dangerous invasion plan," the US generals told Gallant. "You'll need longer to prepare. You'll pay a big price."

Gallant recalls their appeals to US experience. "We were in Fallujah and Mosul. We had to do carpet bombing. Are you going to carpet bomb Gaza?"

Gallant responded, "We won't do it for two reasons: We don't have to and also"—unlike the US—"we don't have the B-52s to do it anyway." More important, he added, "Why do we have this army if we don't use it" in a case like this? A large ground invasion seemed to him the clear choice.

When the US generals saw they were not getting anywhere, they pivoted and tried to freeze the invasion by getting the Israelis mired in the details of everything that could go wrong tactically. Gallant came to realize that they were trying to run out the political clock.

Multiple times amid this debate, US Secretary of Defense Lloyd Austin also tried to talk Gallant down. "Please don't forget who started this," Gallant told him. "Hamas and Hezbollah started against us, and then all the other regional adversaries [Iran's proxy militias in Yemen, Syria and Iraq] came against us. Doing nothing is not an option."

US Secretary of State Antony Blinken also tried to entangle Gallant in a debate about details. In diplomatic, economic, and public-relations terms, he kept asking Gallant, "What is the price of the invasion?" Israeli defense officials refused to be drawn into that debate, countering that the larger mission was too important to be dissected in this manner. Their thinking was guided by Israel's war aims, which said nothing about international opinion. All that seemed to matter in that regard was to keep the US president on board.

Netanyahu summarized the Biden administration's questions in one: How are you going to manage a full-scale operation? "That was a legitimate question," he told us. "The army said we had to have a ground invasion, and it was fraught with risk," he said. "All of Gaza, we knew, was full of defensive tunnels and booby traps. People could emerge from the tunnels and kill us. So nobody really knew."

Netanyahu wanted to give the IDF time to drill and prepare for the operational plan, including training soldiers on new tunnel-fighting techniques.[26] The prime minister's office believed it saved many Israeli lives that would have been lost had it rushed ground troops into Gaza.

Top US generals predicted disaster if Israeli ground troops were to enter Gaza. The US did not issue Israel an ultimatum, Netanyahu said, but advised against invasion. "That's what our experts say," they told him. The US military mavens thought a ground invasion was doomed; Israel would incur massive casualties, get bogged down, and struggle even to conquer Gaza City. "We thought otherwise," Netanyahu recalled, yet the warnings had to be taken seriously—another reason the prime minister was slow to decide.

On October 13, the IDF issued an evacuation order for northern Gaza. Israel demanded that 1.1 million Gazan civilians head south, painting a big target on the north of the territory. This helped clear the way for a ground invasion.

The US generals preferred an air war, special-forces raids, and the threat of a larger invasion to force Hamas to negotiate, but Netanyahu was not convinced those lesser options would work either. "We've already tried that four times," Netanyahu told them, and listed the prior Gaza wars that had left Hamas intact. "From the air, you can mow the lawn. You can't pull out the weeds," the prime minister told us. That, in common Israeli parlance, is the difference between damaging and dismantling Hamas.

All this talking took time—which seemed to be the Biden team's intent. Contrary to some of their expectations, the members of Israel's war room began to understand that US support for overthrowing Hamas was something less than ironclad.

In public, however, US support for Israel's mission was effusive. President Biden came to Israel and delivered a speech on October 18, 2023, that signaled no daylight between the US and Israel as well as moral clarity about the need to defeat Hamas. Even after relations between Biden and Netanyahu soured, the prime minister would emphasize to us the trip's importance as a signal to Israel's enemies, praising "Biden's decision to come to Israel and the backing he gave us at the beginning of the war."

It was one thing for Israel's war room to dismiss the Biden administration's advice verbally; it was quite another to make the final decision to invade Gaza expressly against the wishes of the US government. Ironically, given what would come later, Netanyahu gave US relations more importance at this stage than did Gallant or Gantz, both of whom argued that Israel had to make its own decisions, whatever the diplomatic consequences. The prime minister worried about losing US support so early.

At a critical juncture in the debate about what the Israeli military could accomplish in Gaza, Gallant put the matter starkly to Netanyahu: "Use it or shut it down," he said.

There was no point in devoting such immense resources to one of the world's best militaries, Gallant argued heatedly, his face now twisted into a snarl, if after the worst slaughter of civilians in its history, Israel was afraid to use it. Gallant also believed that the brutality of Hamas's invasion would ensure that Israel would retain US support indefinitely, even if Israel launched a deeper than "usual" invasion of Gaza.

Trying to pile on with Gallant, Halevi told Netanyahu and other cabinet members on the fence, "If we do not initiate a ground invasion, we will need to give up on the war aim of taking Hamas apart." This was the unvarnished truth, and Netanyahu knew it. He had said as much himself to the Biden administration. Halevi told his military colleagues that when he had made this clear to the prime minister, Netanyahu "understood he could not run away and hide behind his advisers."

Gallant and Halevi started to see a change in Netanyahu's body language when addressing the issue. If earlier in October he had expressed fear or put on a poker face without making commitments, he was now starting to engage much more concretely on the invasion.

Halevi had one last move to bring Netanyahu around. Fifteen years earlier, when Halevi was commander of the IDF paratroopers brigade, he had brought Prime Minister Ehud Olmert to speak to frontline commanders before the December 2008 invasion of Gaza. This had reassured Olmert and given him the confidence to move forward, Halevi felt. He decided to repeat the tactic with Netanyahu and brought him to meet a wide range of field commanders who believed in the mission and were ready to execute it. There is no substitute, the IDF chief thought, for speaking directly to the officers who will be risking their lives on the front lines. Halevi believes it helped Netanyahu draw the confidence he needed to move forward with the operation.

A senior Netanyahu adviser agreed. "He wanted to see that they were confident in the army's capability to do what needed to be done. And once he was convinced about that, he gave the go-ahead," the adviser recalled.

Despite US concerns, the Israeli war cabinet united. Israel could not limit its mission to deterring Hamas or "teaching it a lesson," as in the past. This time, the goal had to be to topple Hamas's rule in Gaza and dismantle its military capabilities. Ultimately, Israel's objectives dictated some kind of serious operation on the ground. Top Israeli officials were unclear at this point exactly how and when they would be able to negotiate, on terms they found acceptable, to retrieve the 251 hostages Hamas had kidnapped. But they were certain that without a broad ground invasion, Israel would not have sufficient leverage in those negotiations.

Gallant revealed to us that he had already decided by October 8 what the new general plan would be, and had assembled it with Halevi by October 15. This would take up the crucial first week. Gallant based his approach to the invasion of Gaza on a 2008 plan that he and Brigadier General Moshe "Chico" Tamir had proposed when he was still the IDF commander of the southern front. At the time, Prime Minister Olmert had refused it, Gallant said, and instructed him to develop a more limited invasion plan.

"Herzi [Halevi], who had led the paratroopers during the 2008–2009 conflict, also knew it," Gallant said. "We took the IDF's 2008 Gaza invasion plan and made personnel adjustments to fit the current army." The IDF, like all armies, adjusts its structure periodically, and the balance and makeup of many of the IDF Southern Command units had changed over fifteen years. The plan was not actionable until these adjustments were made.

Gallant saw Hamas as "very strong in the shell, weak inside." He believed that once Israel broke through the outer ring of Hamas fighters, the rest of its fighters would be vulnerable and could be cleaned out at Israel's leisure.[27]

On October 15, Gallant presented to Netanyahu and the war room his and Halevi's plans for invading Gaza. To maintain the element of surprise and minimize IDF casualties, Gallant and Halevi decided that Israel's forces would be constantly on the move, hunting for Hamas. Critically, they would not be trying to conquer or hold onto territory. The tactic was to penetrate and then tear apart the Hamas battalions' abilities to function in any organized manner, followed by a return to Israeli territory.

While Gallant was fending off the US generals who were still in uniform, he sought out the advice of the retired General Petraeus, the former commander of US forces in Iraq and Afghanistan, who supported the ground invasion. Petraeus lodged a complaint with Gallant, however, on strategy. "You'll kill a lot of bad guys" with the raid-and-leave approach, Petraeus granted, "but when you leave, the enemy can replenish the losses" and reestablish itself. The operational means, he argued, did not seem to fit the war room's stated aims of ending Hamas's rule and returning the hostages.

Hamas may no longer be an effective military organization after the fighting, "but certainly it could be a dangerous insurgent force," Petraeus said. He advised Israel to employ the strategy he had developed in Iraq: Clear an area of terrorists, hold it, and then build something better for the people. In other words, a comprehensive civil-military counterinsurgency campaign.

Gallant had an answer: "We don't have a counterinsurgency field manual. We've never done it before," he said. That was fair, Petraeus had to concede. Israel had no history of that sort of operation. Yet he said that Israeli soldiers were more than smart enough to figure it out. "This is not rocket science," he added. "Go one kilometer into the country, set up an east–west wall and three north–south walls, and you have four gated communities. Clear everything in those painstakingly. Block every tunnel entrance as well, so the enemy can't backfill behind you. Then you give biometric ID cards to all those who should be in that area"—and repeat. This advice would come to look prescient, but at the time, Gallant was not persuaded.

Another key tactical question was how the invasion would start. "The invasion was designed to run from the west side of Gaza," by the sea, "to the east side," Halevi explained to other commanders. "This was part of a plan to fool the enemy, which was set with strong defenses in the east," facing Israel territory. "We came from the opposite side and gained a huge advantage. But when I presented this to the cabinet, they were dismissive."

One cabinet minister asked Halevi straight up: "Why are you afraid of Hamas? Why are you playing games? Just go straight at them." The generals were not amused.

Halevi had an unusual idea that helped Netanyahu shift from supporting an invasion in theory to approving the concrete invasion plan placed in front of him. The plan promised interim points at which Netanyahu could halt the invasion or undertake a situation assessment before deciding to press forward. Halevi could see from Netanyahu's reaction that this gave him a greater sense of calm and control. This would be an invasion in stages.

For example, Halevi showed Netanyahu a map of cutoff points for Divisions 162 and 36. He told Netanyahu he would have the ability to make changes in real time. This was important to the prime minister, who is known for preserving his options whenever possible—even to the point of exhausting his colleagues. Gallant and Halevi told Netanyahu that if the invasion didn't go well initially, they could make a different decision. But if the invasion did go well, it could continue. It would not be a monolithic invasion or a package deal. Netanyahu would not need to go all the way. They explained to the prime minister that they had cut up the invasion into small pieces, thinking this would be easier for him to swallow. The flexibility made the risks of a massive invasion more tolerable.

Gallant said, "The IDF might stop at any point, with the cabinet needing to approve the crossing of each 'reporting line' goal." He added, "Bibi and Eisenkot did not want to invade. Normally, moving on from each reporting line goal is approved just by the IDF Southern Commander or, at most, the IDF chief. But their doubts led Netanyahu and Eisenkot to insist on approving each advance point," he said.

By this time, Gallant, Gantz, and Halevi had convinced Netanyahu to commit to an invasion. He still, however, wanted to delay it until after Biden's October 18 visit to Israel—a powerful display of wartime solidarity that the prime minister did not want to undermine. By October 21 and 22, the rest of the war room could see that Netanyahu was fully committed to an invasion. Now, they were down to picking a start date in the near future.

Later in the war, Halevi noted with frustration that some cabinet members who had been skeptical initially of any invasion of Gaza were criticizing the IDF for having failed to invade Gaza City, Khan Yunis, and Rafah all at once, instead of spreading them out over seven months. Where were they at the time? "The political echelon often just yelled; we planned," he said.

Why did the initial invasion focus only on northern Gaza rather than hitting Hamas from all sides?

Even in mid-2025, after stepping down as IDF chief, Halevi has defended the decision to separate the invasion into stages. "We did not have a sufficient volume of soldiers to invade all parts of Gaza at once. We needed to keep forces ready for threats from Hezbollah in the north. In retrospect, Hezbollah did not invade," he has granted, "but at the time, there was a high chance it might. In fact, maybe it would have if we had thrown all our forces into Gaza all at once in October 2023." Halevi also maintained that it was important to first invade Gaza City and the north of Gaza, where Hamas's two strongest battalions were located.

With the benefit of hindsight, it can be argued that Israel was too cautious. Top IDF officials told us that even weeks after October 7, the IDF always had more aircraft and more naval vessels based in the north, ready to fight Hezbollah, than it had in the south, ready to fight Hamas.

The threat of a Hezbollah invasion of northern Israel never left their minds in the early period.

Israel would not launch its full-scale ground invasion until October 27—after a twenty-day period of bombing and worsening headlines following Hamas's October 7 invasion. By the time Israel was ready to advance, much of the world's shock from the Hamas massacre had worn off. As one recently retired Israeli military official put it to us, "You can do during the first week of the war what you can't do later on, or is much harder to do later on." The elevated diplomatic costs of invading Khan Yunis in December 2023 and Rafah in May 2024 would attest to that.

Israeli leaders, however, were not only arguing among themselves during those crucial first weeks. They were also buying time for the IDF. Even after the invasion plan was made, a best practice is to drill soldiers in its operational elements before sending them to execute in a complex urban environment. Ideally, the planning and the drilling is done before the war, but nothing about the start of this war was ideal. "Take the time," Netanyahu said. "Take, whatever, another ten days to prepare. Then, go in," he added, despite the American advice. Where others saw politics at play in the delay, Netanyahu saw due diligence.

By October 25, Gallant and Halevi had held enough meetings and addressed enough of Netanyahu's and the Biden team's objections. Netanyahu determined the IDF was ready to execute the plan.

There's no doubt the delay for a ground invasion in October 2023 was strategically costly. It gave Hamas time to prepare. Though the terrorists had their tunnels ready before their invasion, other preparations could be made only in real time, once they had the hostages in hand and were able to observe Israel's bombing campaign as well as the type and location of IDF forces being assembled. This would make the subsequent IDF advance more difficult. The delay also wasted critical weeks after October 7, when Israel would not have faced as much Western opposition as it did later.

* * *

When the IDF finally got the order, on October 27, it went into Gaza in full force and started smashing Hamas's forces to pieces.

Israel advanced rapidly on the ground, faster and with far fewer soldiers lost than expected. "We had a political wind at our back. Everybody supported us at that time," Netanyahu recalled. "That was terrifying for Hamas and Sinwar," who had expected Israel to face the usual political constraints, Israel had learned. Much of the time, Hamas forces cut and ran. Wherever Hamas stood and fought, it was overwhelmed by Israel's better-trained troops, superior firepower, or fighter jets.

On November 14, 2023, IDF Division 162 Commander Itzik Cohen, the first general into northern Gaza, told us that his forces had already killed more than one thousand Hamas terrorists and reduced rocket fire from northern Gaza on Israel by around 80 percent.

Northern Gaza was the only battle of the war in which Hamas tried to stand toe to toe with the IDF, fighting it aboveground, one urban block at a time. Hamas believed, wrongly, that its enormous number of ambush positions in tunnels and high-rises would allow it to inflict so much pain that the IDF would have to withdraw. Instead, the IDF consistently sidestepped Hamas's main forces and ambush positions, eventually coming up behind them, achieving the element of surprise.

IDF forces first subdued the Atatra neighborhood of Beit Lahiya, north of Gaza City, then pressed south to Hamas's command center. From there, Israel attacked Gaza City's military quarter and its vast underground network, before heading west to a Hamas naval command center, the Shati neighborhood near the coast, and finally Shifa Hospital and its underground command center. In difficult urban terrain, this was an impressive maneuver.

Hamas also was not ready for the lethality of the Israeli Air Force, which used mass drone surveillance and AI to strike precisely at hundreds and then thousands of targets in a matter of days and weeks. This meant that no matter how well hidden they were, any Hamas fighters who opened fire became targets almost instantly.

At this stage of the war, most IDF ground forces maneuvered in highly armored Namer personnel carriers, which could withstand whatever Hamas could throw at them. One Namer driver told us that his vehicle had been hit up to seven times and managed to keep chugging along.

The Biden administration did not like that Israel entered Gaza City in such force, with the consequent harm to civilians, and that it took over Shifa Hospital. Yet that's where the terrorists were. "They weren't happy with that, but we did it," Netanyahu told us. "We told them what we were doing."

Together with the campus movement, human-rights groups played a key role in shaping progressive opinion. On October 7, many of these groups equivocated. "Civilians on Both Sides Paying the Price of Unprecedented Escalation Between Israel and Gaza" was Amnesty International's headline on the day of the massacre. Afterward, these groups would act as if the war began on October 8, representing the Israeli war effort in response as pure malevolence. "Damning Evidence of War Crimes as Israeli Attacks Wipe Out Entire Families in Gaza" read a typical October 20, 2023, Amnesty headline. Later on, it would accuse Israel of genocide.[28]

As Gallant would write many months later, "Early in the war, the IDF learned a simple rule: if you want to find a tunnel, look beneath a school. If you are searching for an enemy headquarters, start under a mosque. If you suspect an arms depot, check the basement of a hospital."[29] This was not only Hamas's military strategy to protect its assets; it was Hamas's political strategy to win the war. The longer it would take Israel to maneuver, and the more schools and hospitals it would destroy to pursue Hamas, the more US and international pressure would mount on Israel to stop short of its objectives. No one expected Israel to carry on the fight for two years—not even the Israeli war room. Certainly, Hamas did not foresee that Israel would use the time to smash the Iranian proxy axis itself, and then take the fight all the way to Iran and its nuclear facilities.

In one sign of the toll that the IDF's early operations took on Hamas in northern Gaza, twelve exhausted Hamas terrorists, cut off from food and water, surrendered together near Shifa Hospital in mid-November 2023. This would be followed by the mass surrender of a couple hundred Hamas fighters in Jabalia, another sector of northern Gaza.

One of the IDF's key early victories was capturing Hamas's underground military headquarters in Gaza City. Senior Israeli officials were surprised by the scope and sophistication of what they found, comparing it with Israel's underground "pit" at its military headquarters in Tel Aviv and the Pentagon's underground command center in Washington. Part of the Hamas tunnel network included a special shaft with an elevator that went to an almost unheard-of tunnel depth of one hundred feet below ground. Unlike other cramped tunnel elevators, this one was large enough to fit seven people.

The IDF found signs that Hamas's high command had hidden at the bottom of the elevator shaft. A top official speculated that this could have included Yahya Sinwar and his military chief, Mohammed Deif. One of the signs was Deif's wheelchair, which he used ever since a prior Israeli assassination attempt had wounded him.

The early victories flowed from the IDF's investment of tens of thousands of troops to invade northern Gaza, while surrounding all of Gaza with an even larger force. Gaza City's northern Shati neighborhood alone took four thousand five hundred heavily armed IDF forces. One negative development, however, was that several IDF sources said that they knew little about where Hamas was holding the hostages.

Another sign that there was more work for Israel to do, even in northern Gaza, was that IDF forces largely circumvented the Shejaya neighborhood. They would have to circle back there to deal with remaining Hamas forces. This move, as well as the tactic of marching through houses that were to be bulldozed, as opposed to on main thoroughfares, were key to avoiding Hamas booby traps and ambushes. The terrorist group had expected the IDF to operate as it did during past Gaza conflicts. There was an eight-kilometer area in which Hamas had hoped to bleed the IDF so profusely that it would give up before arriving at the center of Gaza City. Israel declined to play along.

The IDF also approached Hamas's tunnel system with a different objective in mind. Unlike in the past, when it had caused cave-ins at certain spots, believing that would neutralize the tunnel network, this time the IDF was seeking to destroy the network. By November 14, 2023, the IDF believed it had destroyed 30 percent of Hamas's tunnels in the area.

Those initial estimates proved wildly optimistic. Much of the IDF's Gaza war strategy in 2023–2024 centered on staying in motion and not trying to hold ground. This meant that in almost every neighborhood where it had "cleaned out" Hamas, it had missed significant aspects of the tunnel network. The IDF moved at such a rapid speed in Gaza City, raiding and then withdrawing, which allowed Hamas to regroup, that Netanyahu and the IDF would have to send forces back into the same area repeatedly over the next two years.

This first time, the findings were stunning. On November 22, Yonah was part of the first group of journalists to embed with IDF forces at Shifa Hospital deep in Gaza City, as well as at Hamas's underground command center connected to that hospital. Laid out before Yonah's eyes, next to one of the medical facilities within the sprawling Shifa complex, was a huge quantity of Hamas's guns and grenades, which the IDF had found hidden throughout the hospital. There were also RPGs, large and small advanced drones for delivering explosives, and a variety of sophisticated intelligence platforms. The vastness of the tunnels themselves, with a variety of rooms and blast doors, suggested this location was critical to Hamas, and gave a sense of how secure Hamas had felt operating under the hospital until the Israeli invasion.

As the invasion unfolded, Israel's war room worried that US government support for the war would not last. But Hamas did not know that yet. "They saw us moving, moving, moving, with American support," Netanyahu would reflect. "And there's no counter-vector yet. There's not yet the buildup of public pressure," he told us. Radicals on campus continued to make noise, and many media outlets had moved on from Hamas's October 7 atrocities to focus on the devastation in Gaza from Israel's counteroffensive, but neither had yet endangered the continuation of the war. The US was helping Israel to plan and scale down some of its attacks. It was not, however, exerting pressure to end the fighting.

Israel was rolling in a way that Hamas had not expected. Neither had the Biden administration. In a short period of time, and with far fewer casualties than anticipated, Israel had blitzed through Gaza City, Hamas's capital.

Sinwar was in shock and began to recalibrate his plans for a showdown in his hometown of Khan Yunis. Hamas might need time to regroup and break Israel's momentum. Hezbollah's Hassan Nasrallah was cursing himself for not having invaded along with Sinwar on October 7, to hit Israel when it was weakest. He was also cursing Sinwar for starting a larger war that could in time weaken Hezbollah and the entire Iranian proxy axis.

Nasrallah liked a meticulous plan with a clear goal, benchmarks, and an endpoint. He had no idea where Sinwar was leading him, after Hezbollah had joined the fray with some limited rocket fire on October 8, and he was not sure that Sinwar knew either.

Iranian Supreme Leader Ayatollah Ali Khamenei saw opportunities to permanently weaken the Jewish state by wearing it down on multiple fronts, but he also feared that he might lose one or more of his proxies to Israel's furious counterstrikes. Multidecade Iranian investments, core to the regime's ideology, were on the line.

As Israel advanced in northern Gaza behind massive firepower, Hezbollah was holding back and Iran was staying out of the fight, at least directly. Netanyahu, Gallant, and Gantz believed that all this, in combination with the perceived lack of daylight between Israel and the US, scrambled Hamas's planning. Israeli intelligence backed up the claim. Early military and political success created an opportunity for a hostage deal.

CHAPTER FOUR

MOSSAD GOES TO DOHA FOR A DEAL

The message had reached its destination. From Qatar it had traveled all the way to southern Gaza, descended into the tunnels of Khan Yunis, and snaked its way to the hiding place of Yahya Sinwar, the revered leader. A trusted courier passed on its contents. The news was good, and Sinwar made his decision. A new message would make the return trip, from the tunnels to the streets and all the way back to Qatar, where men in expensive suits claimed to lead Hamas and speak for it. They received the message and followed Sinwar's orders. There would be a ceasefire after all.

From November 23 to November 30, 2023, the fighting paused. Hamas would return around one hundred hostages in exchange for the release of more than three times as many Palestinian security prisoners from Israel. This deal—or ransom—was hammered out by Mossad Director David Barnea and Qatari Prime Minister Mohammed bin Abdulrahman bin Jassim al-Thani, two men who influenced the course of the war from the shadows.

Al-Thani served in the Qatari Foreign Ministry and in high-profile economic positions before being promoted by the emir, the country's ruler, to run Qatar's day-to-day operations as prime minister. He is a distant relative of the emir, not a direct descendant, but he has earned strong enough reviews from global leaders to become a force in regional politics.

Barnea took over the Mossad in June 2021. His key mission was to continue to thwart the progress of Iran's nuclear program, which the Mossad had done with repeated success since the 1990s. Only three weeks into his tenure, Iran's Karaj nuclear facility was destroyed. From April to June 2022, around a dozen Iranian nuclear scientists, drone developers, and terror managers from special units like Islamic Revolutionary Guard Corps (IRGC) Unit 840 were killed or otherwise taken out of action in mysterious circumstances. Barnea also inherited the Qatar file. This was the bizarre setup in which Israel allowed or facilitated the transfer of funds from Qatar to Hamas to keep the terrorists in Gaza "happy enough" that they would not start an unnecessary war over a lack of money, as had occurred in 2014.

Yossi Cohen, Barnea's predecessor, had organized the financial pipeline with Qatar, which the Mossad maintained. This meant Barnea already knew al-Thani extremely well even before October 7. The two had spent time together at Mossad headquarters as well as on al-Thani's intimate "glamping" desert trips, sitting in regal chairs and enjoying expensive and exotic foods. All of those visits, however, had been in the shadows, which Barnea preferred from decades of maneuvering.

Soon after October 7, Cohen visited Qatar to see if al-Thani could mediate hostage talks with Hamas since the Jewish state and the Gazan jihadists would not negotiate directly. Netanyahu tapped Barnea to lead Israel's team in the resulting talks. This time Barnea's flights and travels were advertised in the media by Netanyahu to show the Israeli public that he was working hard to return the hostages. Suddenly, everyone knew when Barnea was off to Paris, Cairo, or Qatar—and when he had returned without results.

The Mossad chief loathed this public attention. He also worried that too much of his personal attention had been redirected from his primary mission against Iran's nuclear program. But he agreed with Netanyahu that his personal ties with al-Thani could be the difference between life and death for Israeli hostages.

These negotiations were a difficult game of cat and mouse. Hamas's Sinwar believed he needed to hold the majority of the hostages as insurance for his and other top Hamas officials' survival and as a trump card to eventually force Israel to end the war. Israel sought to return all the hostages but found its military options limited. The war room was stuck dealing with the very terrorists whom it had pledged to pursue aggressively.

Three to four times a week from the outbreak of the war through November 2023, al-Thani met with Hamas leaders in Doha, the Qatari capital where the terrorist group had its political headquarters. He invested nearly all of his time trying to achieve a hostage and ceasefire deal, in no small part to try to save Hamas from being destroyed by a furious Israel. Negotiations would shield Hamas's "political" leaders from Israeli attack for a long time.

These Hamas leaders had little authority to make decisions of their own. Worse, Israel's negotiators at times suspected their Hamas counterparts had fallen out of touch with the real shot-callers in Gaza. Sinwar, from his hideouts, at first used electronic communications only sparingly. Soon, he dropped off the grid entirely, relying only on couriers.

The Israelis were immensely frustrated by Hamas's approach. The terrorists often took several days to issue every little response—ostensibly due to the courier process—only to speed up when Hamas needed it. Speaking only to mediators, who had their own interests in advancing or dragging out the talks at different points, also aroused suspicions. "We don't even know if the answers Qatar passes along are really from Hamas," one member of the Israeli negotiating team told us. When Hamas would go back on its word, was that the terrorists' doing, or had the mediators simply gotten ahead of themselves? Everything was opaque, and lives were on the line.

The first two hostages released by Hamas, in an isolated "goodwill gesture" to try to split the US from Israel, were Americans Judith Tai Raanan, fifty-nine, and her daughter Natalie, seventeen, from Illinois. Al-Thani said that Qatar was involved in every step of this release, nearly two weeks after their abduction, which Hamas used to show that it could hold up its end of a bargain. The release operation was very complicated and took twelve hours, al-Thani said.

Qatar's influence with Hamas, which it funded and whose suit-wearing leaders it still hosts, raises uncomfortable questions. Was it really an honest broker, or did it lean toward Hamas's side, trying to help it escape the war intact? On October 7, Qatar released the following statement: "The Ministry of Foreign Affairs holds Israel solely responsible for the ongoing escalation due to its ongoing violations of the rights of the Palestinian people, the latest of which was the repeated incursions into al-Aqsa Mosque under the protection of the Israeli police."[30] Its leverage over Hamas was three-pronged, Barnea thought: It hosts some of Hamas's top diaspora leadership; it hosts some of those leaders' families; and its banks, at points in time, have held up to 80 percent of the terror group's funds.

Barnea also knew he had strong credibility with al-Thani and the Qataris. This stemmed not from telling them what they wanted to hear, but the opposite, from his reputation for assassination operations and his loud criticism of allowing Qatar to send Hamas funds. Accordingly, when Barnea made the Qataris an offer, they knew it was real and concrete, and he was not just a diplomat trying to be smooth.

One challenge for Israel was to get the US to pressure Qatar to pressure Hamas, in turn. The major Air Force base of US Central Command is at al-Udeid in Qatar; without it, the Gulf monarchy could be in serious danger. On one hand, this gave the US leverage. On the other hand, the Pentagon greatly valued its relationship with Qatar and feared that threatening Qatar could damage US interests and forces in the region.

Barnea's first success was to seal the late November 2023 agreement with Hamas, which returned more than eighty Israeli hostages and twenty-four foreign hostages. It was a tightrope walk from start to finish. The Mossad director was no mere messenger but a critical operator in his own right, retaining discretion on a variety of issues in dispute. He often made recommendations or took positions that decisively influenced the course of the negotiations.

The critical point came in early November, when Barnea pushed for a temporary ceasefire to ransom fifty hostages. According to some top sources, Defense Minister Gallant, IDF chief Halevi, and Shin Bet Director Ronen Bar were all against such an offer initially. Later, they supported it and much later, they would champion the pursuit of hostage deals. Crucially, Netanyahu's close ally Ron Dermer was in favor of Barnea's initiative, as were Benny Gantz, Gadi Eisenkot, and Shas party leader Aryeh Deri in the war cabinet. Netanyahu himself did not take a hard stance, but he approved the initiative once Barnea was able to nail it down. It would be one of the last times Dermer would see eye to eye with Gantz and Eisenkot on the correct balance between progress in the war and returning the hostages.

Twice during the week when negotiations were playing out, Sinwar in Gaza tried to alter the terms of the deal. First, Sinwar tried to switch out some of the female hostages for male hostages. Perhaps he thought the women were more useful for tugging on Israeli heartstrings. Barnea responded with an unequivocal "no." Israel was ready, Barnea said, to proceed to the next stage of the invasion and destroy Sinwar's hometown army in Khan Yunis. Then, during that same week, Sinwar demanded that he be allowed to provide Israel with dead bodies instead of the agreed-upon living female hostages. It would have been a coup for Hamas. Again, Barnea shot it down, and the deal got back on track.

Officials who were present at these discussions during that period have differing accounts of what transpired. At least four cabinet ministers said that General Halevi had convinced them to vote in favor of the hostage deal despite the cost; evidently, he supported the deal himself. Officials with whom we spoke claimed that Halevi was pushing for a hostage deal but nonetheless believed that Barnea had made serious tactical errors in the negotiation. We were able to review Israeli documents that support the idea that this was Halevi's position in November 2023.

According to IDF officials to whom we spoke, Halevi argued during a senior-level discussion in mid-November 2023 that the negotiations were being mishandled and that the negotiating team was eroding the pressure the military had placed on Hamas. Halevi pointed to a reduction in the number of hostages to be freed—the Israeli negotiating team had started at one hundred and fallen to seventy-five and then fifty—and argued that Israel's position was being pushed backward in Doha even as the IDF had the upper hand on the battlefield. Was Israel folding in negotiations, offering to compromise at the first sign of resistance?

In additional meetings at the time, Halevi explained that Israel was losing momentum because of the manner in which the negotiations were handled. The IDF chief claimed that even the way Israel's position was phrased in the negotiation documents expressed weakness—"giving in without a fight"—which Hamas exploited.

In one of the discussions, Halevi argued that the length of the ceasefire and other terms were secondary. "Whether it's five days, seven days, this is *shtuyot*"—insignificant nonsense. "Another three tankers per day [of fuel for Hamas], versus five tankers? *Shtuyot.* Fifty more trucks of bread? This is unimportant. We need to maximize one thing: the number [of hostages], and about this, we need to be determined."

Officials with whom we spoke claimed that the Mossad chief's position in these negotiations was not approved by Israel's war cabinet, and that he had moved too quickly to agree to receive only fifty hostages. "You made a mistake," Netanyahu told Barnea. "Fix it."

The assumption of critics of Netanyahu from his right flank was that once the war's momentum was halted, it would be politically impossible for Israel to get it going again. A ceasefire could signal the end of the war, well short of Israel's objective of dismantling Hamas's military and governing capabilities. Netanyahu thought that Sinwar himself made the same mistake. "I think he thought it was just bravado on my part, and that once I stopped the war—even paused in the war—I wouldn't come back." As Netanyahu put it to his colleagues, "I know we're telling the truth, but I don't mind that he thinks I'm lying."

Even supporters of the deal, however, had to admit that Hamas was suddenly interested in a ceasefire for a reason: It thought it was to its advantage. Hamas needed to regroup its forces, protect its leaders, move hostages, and reset the political horizon. But at least Israel could begin bringing its people home.

* * *

On November 22, 2023, Israel and Hamas struck a deal. The agreement was a four-day ceasefire, extendible day by day after that, with the release of twelve or thirteen Israeli women and child hostages a day in exchange for three times as many Palestinian security prisoners—terrorists or suspected terrorists. Israel also agreed in November to allow more aid and fuel into Gaza, which Hamas used to sustain its underground operations.

The deal was initially for fifty hostages, but Netanyahu and President Biden, with pressure also from Halevi and other Israeli defense officials, agreed they could push Hamas to keep the deal going for some additional days to get the figure up to eighty hostages. They succeeded, bringing home the eighty Israelis and twenty-four foreign hostages as well. But by November 30, Hamas no longer saw the utility of giving up so many of its hostages at such a rapid rate.

Hamas stopped handing over the agreed-upon hostages on that final day, and Israel did not want to let that become a precedent.

No one in the security cabinet other than Eisenkot was ready to end the war having only eliminated Hamas's battalions in northern Gaza. The job was not finished. Netanyahu, Gallant, and Gantz were united in their determination to resume fighting, and the IDF waged some additional battles in northern Gaza. In Shejaya, IDF Division 36 killed an estimated 935 Hamas fighters, with forces eyeballing 735 of the bodies directly. In Jabalia, IDF Division 162 killed around a thousand Hamas fighters and arrested five hundred. On December 19, the IDF announced it had operational control over Jabalia, and on December 21, over Shejaya. That all but wrapped up the war for northern Gaza before Israeli troops would turn south.

The victory was only partial because the politics of the war had changed. As we have seen, many on the radical Left were ready to condemn Israel on October 7 and 8. On October 13, 2023, a professor of genocide studies had somehow already declared Israel's counterattack "a textbook case of genocide."[31] But it was on October 17 that biased coverage of Israel went out of control.

That day, Hamas said an Israeli air strike on Gaza City's al-Ahli Arab Hospital had killed at least five hundred Palestinians. That would be the headline in *The New York Times* and across the world. By the next day, however, it would turn out that the attack wasn't Israeli, it wasn't an air strike, it didn't hit the hospital, nowhere close to five hundred people were killed, and Hamas knew it. Israeli intelligence indicated that the culprit was a rocket launched by Islamic Jihad from a cemetery. It had fallen short, as the terrorists' rockets often did, and landed in the hospital's parking lot. President Biden affirmed that finding less than twenty-four hours after the incident, a key early moment of support for Israel.

But in the half-day period of uncertainty, the media leaped to echo the Hamas report. The BBC explained that the Israelis "said they are investigating, but it is hard to see what else this could be, really, given the size of the explosion, other than an Israeli air strike, or several air strikes." The world received the story essentially as Representative Rashida Tlaib, the Michigan Democrat, put it on social media: "Israel just bombed the Baptist Hospital killing 500 Palestinians (doctors, children, patients) just like that." The damage was done. The October 7 attack was only ten days old, but a new narrative was already forming.

By early November, the Hamas-run Gaza Health Ministry claimed that nine thousand Gazans had been killed in all. The IDF said that 30 to 50 percent were Hamas fighters. Hamas did not differentiate between civilians and terrorist combatants, but international media often left this out—along with the ministry's Hamas affiliation. At this time, Biden and Secretary of State Antony Blinken urged Israel to implement "humanitarian pauses" in the fighting. Tens of thousands of Americans protested for a ceasefire in Washington, DC, and across the country.

"As the [Gazan] casualties began to mount," Netanyahu recalled to us, "and the pictures began to mount, the pressure on the Biden administration and the president grew." Part of this, the prime minister pointed out, was because Hamas used violence to try to stop its own civilians from evacuating the battle zone. Better for Hamas to have Gazans caught in the crossfire, so it could use their suffering to spur an international outcry against Israel's war effort. To immense Israeli frustration, Hamas knew how to play the media. By immediately (and unrealistically) providing precise death counts, along with a stream of images of the aftermath of Israeli strikes, all context fell away. The picture provided was of wanton Israeli aggression.

It was working. When the north of Gaza fell into IDF hands, pressure on Israel from the Biden administration escalated to "shift to another phase" of the war. Only one thing about this new phase was clear: It would involve fewer troops, less firepower, and, the US president hoped, fewer Palestinian casualties and less pressure from his increasingly inflamed left flank. More than five hundred US government officials, including many Biden political appointees, sent a letter to the president protesting his support of the Israeli counteroffensive in Gaza. Several Western leaders, such as Canadian Prime Minister Justin Trudeau, agreed. "The world is witnessing this—the killing of women and children, of babies," he said. This was not merely the campus radicals anymore.

Netanyahu appreciated the difficult situation Biden was in, "I think you have to be fair to the Americans," he told us. "It's not easy to be president, let's face it, with these very radical fringes in his party. It wasn't easy to do what Mr. Biden did." From the "ultraprogressive wing" of the Democratic Party, Netanyahu continued, "the pressure was beginning to mount on the Democrats. And from them, it came back to us."

Toward the end of the ceasefire, Democratic Senator Chris Murphy of Connecticut, chairman of the Senate Foreign Relations subcommittee on the Middle East, made noises about newly conditioning US military aid to Israel on compliance with international law, a signal of disapproval. Vermont Senator Bernie Sanders demanded "an end to indiscriminate bombing."[32] By this point, Hamas's Gaza Health Ministry had reported around fifteen thousand dead, again with no distinction between combatants and civilians. The scale already greatly surpassed that of previous Gaza wars. The IDF was estimating around 40 percent of those killed were Hamas, while characterizing the rest as tragic but as mostly Hamas's human shields.

As the ceasefire ended, Secretary of State Antony Blinken said Israel had to take "more effective steps to protect the lives of civilians." The question was how. Netanyahu had grumbled more than once about the impossible conditions in which Israel was being made to fight. Usually in war, many civilians flee the fighting. Neighboring nations have a legal obligation to accept such refugees, saving civilian lives. When Israel fights, however, all that is turned on its head. Israeli orders that civilians should evacuate areas soon to be engulfed in fighting were condemned and even resisted by international rights and aid groups. Egypt reinforced and closed off its border with Gaza, locking refugees into the war zone, and threatened its peace with Israel. As a senior Israeli official wryly noted to us at the time, "It isn't over the killing of Palestinians that Egypt threatened to rip up the peace treaty, but over us asking them to save Palestinian lives."

Instead of leveraging the billions of dollars in US aid to Egypt or working to find a compromise—such as accepting only women and children, fenced off in an area of the empty, adjacent Sinai—the Biden administration backed Cairo's blockade of fleeing Gazans. On the other side, there was little trust that any movement of Palestinians out of Gaza would be temporary. Would Netanyahu's messianic coalition partners not seek to make it permanent and resettle Gaza themselves?

Either way, while keeping everyone trapped in the war zone hurt Palestinians, increased casualties, and lengthened the war, most of the world saw it as aiding the Palestinian national cause. More civilians caught in the gears of Israel's war machine meant a slower Israeli advance at greater political cost.

"As long as the international community blames Israel for Hamas's use of Palestinian human shields, Hamas will continue to employ this tool of terror," Netanyahu wrote in *The Wall Street Journal.* But the propaganda war against Israel was not primarily waged in print, where context can be restored. It was being waged with viral images and video clips on TikTok, Instagram, and X, formerly Twitter.

Where were the videos of Hamas terrorists? Since Israel limited journalists' access to Gaza, the only reporters giving the world a picture on the ground were Gazans under the thumb of Hamas. To show the other side of the war would be to risk deadly punishment by Hamas.

Israel's logic was that if biased international media outlets were given access to Gaza, they would make it worse or get caught in the crossfire. But some of Israel's most capable defenders, including Gil Hoffman of HonestReporting, believe this decision was a costly error. Given the importance of the public-relations war, you could call it a strategic error: Israel gave Hamas a near monopoly on reporting from Gaza.

One Biden administration refrain during the war was to permit more humanitarian aid to enter Gaza. Israel had briefly cut off the Strip after October 7, while Gaza used up supplies from peacetime, but Israel could not commit to a siege policy. Netanyahu and Dermer internalized this more quickly, while Gantz and Gallant saw a siege as an effective tool to squeeze Hamas and force it to cough up hostages at this time. Politically, this proved impossible. Early statements such as Gallant's on October 9—"I have ordered a complete siege on the Gaza Strip. There will be no electricity, no food, no fuel, everything is closed"—would play well domestically but cost Israel abroad.

This Israeli disagreement, running counter to what one might expect based on ideology, may have had more to do with the leaders' orientation to the West. Dermer had come from Florida and Netanyahu had spent significant time in the Boston area in his younger days. For true-blue Israelis Gantz and Gallant, by contrast, the consequences of such a blockade at this early point, following October 7, would simply be Hamas's responsibility. Israel agreed to reintroduce aid to Gaza before long, on October 18, 2023, under US pressure.

By the middle and end of the war, when the diplomatic implications had become clear, the war room would switch sides on the issue. Gantz and Gallant would press for more humanitarian aid, and Netanyahu and Dermer would come to advocate using it to pressure Hamas, but this was an evolution from the starting point.

The continued presence of civilians in the war zone complicated not only aid efforts, but also the fighting. For this next phase of the war, Blinken demanded "avoiding further significant displacement of civilians inside of Gaza." From northern Gaza, they had fled south to the central camps and especially to Khan Yunis, which was next up for the

Israeli advance. Would they be moved again and again? Civilians properly belonged in safe zones within the Gaza Strip, Blinken said, leaving Netanyahu to ask whether those zones would also have to be safe for Hamas.

Further, Blinken wanted Israel to do better at "avoiding damage to life-critical infrastructure like hospitals." To the inevitable Israeli protest that Hamas was fighting out of those hospitals, Blinken had a preemptive reply: "Intent matters, but so does the result."

Defense Minister Gallant said that Israel was ready to fight for many more months to defeat Hamas.

"I don't think you have the credit for that," Blinken shot back.

Jerusalem found the situation perverse. Hamas was being rewarded for abusing its own civilian population. Hamas was breaking all the rules of war, and Israel was paying the price for it.

The dire predictions of starvation did not materialize during this period of the war, but there was no doubt that the Palestinian population was suffering. Stuck in the crossfire between the IDF and Hamas, it would continue to pay an appalling price. Whether measured in deaths, wounded persons, loss of housing, loss of education, or the theft of an opportunity for a normal life, this was a humanitarian disaster.

For many observers, however, this became the entire story, as if Hamas had not started the war and was not holding onto a vast number of Israeli hostages and systematically using human shields. This narrative did not place merely contributory blame on Israel for mistakenly killing civilians while targeting Hamas, or for a strategy that led it to fight in the same neighborhoods over and over until they were leveled. It placed all the blame on Israel, or at least the primary blame. Accordingly, instead of demanding that Hamas release the hostages and surrender, global humanitarian sentiment was channeled into the demand that Israel give up on its war aims, leaving Hamas victorious.

Israel's position was becoming more difficult. Globally, the initial horror of October 7 had passed, and Netanyahu felt that the media, the West, and even the US had begun to turn on him.

As December wore on, the IDF started to release the reservist Division 252 from active duty. Fewer troops were required now that almost twelve of Hamas's twenty-four battalions had been defeated in northern Gaza, with several thousand fighters killed and several thousand more wounded. This meant there was no large, coordinated, armed Hamas force in northern Gaza anymore. Those who survived were broken down into tiny, disconnected local cells, many of which had fled south to Khan Yunis. Further, the IDF announced that some southern Gaza border communities in Israel could start to return to their homes. The continuing rocket fire by Hamas was down from hundreds a day at the start of the war to some seventy a day, and then to around fourteen, with Hamas mostly losing the capacity to fire into Tel Aviv or central Israel. The government had the statistics to convince itself that its strategy was working.

At this point in the war, the IDF's main attention was shifting from northern Gaza to Khan Yunis, Hamas's southern capital and Sinwar's hideout. The question now became how well Israel would fare under new political conditions in the dangerous tunnel maze of Sinwar's hometown turf.

CHAPTER FIVE

THE BATTLE FOR KHAN YUNIS

Why did it take Israel two months, until December 2023, to invade Hamas's southern capital of Khan Yunis? Halevi, the IDF chief, had started to plan the invasion much earlier, on October 12, and we have seen classified documents to prove it.

Still, there were concerns that delayed the Israeli advance. Neither Halevi nor any of the war cabinet wanted to invade Khan Yunis simultaneously with northern Gaza. All were concerned early on that Hezbollah might invade northern Israel in response to a large Israeli investment of troops in Gaza. The IDF now had to ration troops and ammunition, limiting its operations on any one front because it feared it lacked the ability to fight intensively on two fronts at the same time.

Even the IDF of old might have struggled to sustain such a prolonged fight on two fronts; the 1967 war lasted six days and the 1973 war lasted twenty. But this was not the IDF of old. Netanyahu had sponsored the Locker Commission (2014–2015) to reduce the IDF budget by more than $2.5 billion per year and the length of mandatory service for IDF soldiers by several months. Under pressure, successive IDF chiefs including Gantz (2011–2015) and Eisenkot (2015–2019) had shrunk Israel's conventional forces in favor of special operations units and high-tech platforms. Over the past few decades, about one hundred seventy thousand troops were dismissed from the reserves because IDF leadership felt they were no longer needed and could not justify the cost. The number of tanks fell to around a third of its 1980s peak, and the number of fighting field divisions was halved.[33] So much for multifront fighting. But after the IDF had performed beyond expectations in northern Gaza, the group of Gallant, Gantz, and Halevi was ready to roll the dice again and take on Khan Yunis in isolation. Still, this invasion was not automatic.

Netanyahu again took more convincing. He worried that Hamas's battle-hardened Khan Yunis battalions would do serious damage to the IDF. Further, Israel knew that there were hostages held in Khan Yunis, and their presence would force Israeli troops to tread cautiously.

Gantz, the supposed dove, along with Gallant and Halevi, once again pressed Netanyahu to green-light an invasion. They told the prime minister that there was no way to get additional Israeli hostages back from Sinwar without cornering the Hamas leader to a point where he would fear being caught. They also noted that so long as Khan Yunis was in the hands of Hamas, the terrorist group would retain the strength to operate as a national military organization.

Khan Yunis was less developed than Gaza City, which eased some of the IDF's concerns. In its agricultural areas, the IDF could be ambushed only from tunnels. In its urban areas, Israeli troops would confront antitank missiles guided by lookouts—usually unarmed, and in many cases children—though the smaller number of high-rises made the IDF's job easier.

On December 1, 2023, right after Sinwar stopped providing the agreed-upon hostages to Israel, causing November's seven-day ceasefire to break down, the IDF advanced on Khan Yunis. The logic of Israel's two war aims, toppling Hamas and freeing the hostages, had left Netanyahu little choice. The prime minister was right, however, to anticipate a bit of a slog. The IDF would spend longer than expected in Khan Yunis. "We were stuck there," Netanyahu told us, "because our forces discovered an underground tunnel network, which was bigger than anything we had seen.... It took them weeks to begin to clear it up."

Halevi agreed that the tunnels were very developed and took a long time to handle. "But we got very close to Sinwar and the hostages, and eventually destroyed the tunnels. This forced Mohammed Deif," Hamas's military chief, "to flee above ground to the house in al-Mawasi," where the IDF would later assassinate him, "and forced Yahya Sinwar to flee to Rafah," where the IDF would later kill him as well.

On December 21, 2023, Yonah was part of the first group of journalists to visit Khan Yunis midbattle with IDF forces. Colonel Omer Cohen, head of the IDF Commando Brigade, and some of his men described intense house-to-house and door-to-door fighting that their team had encountered at the heart of Khan Yunis. Considerable imagination was required to follow their account, as the houses they were describing had all been destroyed in the gunfights on the way to the home of Yahya Sinwar—which the Israeli Air Force had turned into a massive crater. The crater was so large that several journalists fell, and had to be caught and helped by IDF forces, as they tried to climb to its summit to look down at the scorched belongings of the Sinwar family.

Standing over the crater in the frigid December air, IDF Division 98 Commander Brigadier General Dan Goldfus, tall and imposing, taunted Sinwar and Hamas to stand and fight, and see what would happen to them. Goldfus said the military was cutting Sinwar's hometown forces to pieces. He explained that the IDF's artillery and Air Force had undertaken 1,300 attacks in the city alone and eliminated half its 150 tunnel shafts, sending Sinwar's men scurrying for new places to hide. By the third week of December, Goldfus said, Hamas had lost the capacity to stage counterattacks. This meant that as Israeli forces penetrated into new areas of Khan Yunis, there was at most sporadic resistance, but not much sustained and organized counterpunches of gunfire, drones, and RPGs. At that time, the emphasis was on forcing Hamas out of its tunnels, while watching for antitank missiles guided by unarmed lookouts.

Soon after, the IDF discovered Sinwar's underground lair, including twenty-four cages in which he had kept hostages. The mastermind of

October 7 had escaped only hours, or possibly minutes, before the IDF arrived.

By January 29, 2024, the IDF was close to defeating Hamas in Khan Yunis. Goldfus estimated that the group's ability to fight in the city as a collective force could be broken within weeks or less. Close to three of the four Khan Yunis battalions, originally commanding around 4,500 fighters, were beaten already. Of those 4,500, the IDF had killed 2,700 and wounded many others. As Goldfus explained, almost no fighting force could maintain a unified command after losing two-thirds of its men. The rate at which Hamas needed to replace fighters with different roles within the brigade was simply too fast for it to keep up.

On January 20 and February 7, Goldfus's forces found two massive tunnel complexes where Israeli hostages had been held in cages. Top Hamas officials, including Sinwar, had stayed there for months. The tunnels even included artificial turf. Evidence that the hostages had been there ranged from DNA to diapers for hostage children as well as their drawings. One of the tunnels was 830 meters long and 20 meters deep. "Twenty hostages were held there at different times in harsh conditions…that make it difficult to breathe," said Brigadier General Daniel Hagari, the IDF chief spokesman.

We learned from Goldfus that IDF troops had raided a tunnel located under the Bani Suheila cemetery in the heart of Khan Yunis, which turned out to be one of Hamas's largest headquarters. Inside, the IDF unearthed the office of the eastern battalion commander from Hamas's Khan Yunis Brigade. From here, he directed the October 7 attacks and most of Hamas's defense of Khan Yunis. IDF troops found operations rooms, a battalion war room, kitchens, electricity, and bedrooms of top Hamas officials. The tunnel under the cemetery was part of another elaborate underground labyrinth dug by Hamas over half a mile long, some sixty-five feet deep.

The Hamas tunnel system posed an immense challenge. "No military had faced anything like it in the past—not even Israeli ground forces," writes John Spencer, the chair of urban-warfare studies at West Point's Modern War Institute. "The IDF faced a Hamas military organization that had spent over fifteen years engineering the infrastructure of an entire region—to include over twenty major cities—for war."

According to Israeli intelligence estimates, Hamas invested at least hundreds of millions of dollars in these tunnels' construction. As Hamas Politburo member Mousa Abu Marzouk explained on Russian TV on October 27, 2023, the tunnels were for fighters only. As for the civilians? They are refugees, he said, so "it is the responsibility of the United Nations to protect them."[34] That's why Hamas built hundreds of miles of tunnels, but no bomb shelters. Hamas's strategy relied on Israel to use up its time fighting among the tunnels, and the civilian sites above which the tunnels were built, until the US and other states would force Israel to give up the fight.

* * *

Israel understood the Hamas strategy well, but how could it be thwarted? A change in the IDF's countertunnel strategy drove the Israeli advance in western Khan Yunis in mid-January 2024.

Netanyahu had worried that the tunnel warfare in Khan Yunis would lead to far more Israeli casualties than the IDF had suffered in the fight for northern Gaza. Initially, neither Goldfus nor other Israeli generals would allow full units to enter and maneuver through the tunnels. Those forces that did, Goldfus told us, had to slowly and clumsily feel their way around in the dark. When Goldfus and his forces went in—and he insisted on entering a large number of tunnels himself despite the risk—they usually did not yet know what to expect.

Goldfus believes that anyone who saw the Shifa Hospital tunnels in northern Gaza at the start of the war was, in some sense, misled. Yet in his telling, northern Gaza tunnels were different from Khan Yunis tunnels, which were different from Rafah tunnels, Jabalya tunnels, and Shejaya tunnels. Using the tactics from Shifa Hospital in another region could end up costing the IDF time and Israeli soldiers their lives. It was better to treat each region's tunnels as a unique project to study and overcome.

Goldfus said his forces needed to become accustomed to how the tunnels looked, to dig into them, record their sizes and put together photos and studies. Over time, this systematic approach built confidence, and Goldfus realized that even as Hamas's tunnels were different regionally, they were not entirely separate systems but one massive decentralized network. This was a conceptual leap.

Some top IDF officials thought Goldfus was crazy. But he was convinced that under the soldiers' feet was one unified network. In his telling, you could enter around Erez in northern Gaza and come out in a different region like Rafah or Egypt to the south. Hamas's movements would flow south to keep ahead of the IDF advance like water seeping and flowing down a mountain.

In January 2024, Goldfus and his forces had another breakthrough. They asked themselves: What level of risk should we take to explore the tunnels? What are the tunnels worth to the enemy? Surprisingly, Goldfus realized that Hamas had not come to fight underground. It used the tunnels merely to survive and rest. While Hamas used the tunnels constantly to move around outside Israeli surveillance, it did not seem to resist much when IDF forces entered any one branch. This meant the IDF could be much more aggressive underground.

Sending large forces down into tunnels at the same time as fighting raged above them was a radical move. But if Hamas was not standing and fighting, preferring always to flee to other parts of the network, then the IDF did not need to delay.

Yahalom, an Israeli special-forces unit, began entering the tunnels in larger numbers, including full platoons all at once, to combat Hamas terrorists with greater frequency and to cover larger distances. Asaf, a twenty-one-year-old Yahalom soldier who fought in the tunnels of Khan Yunis, told us that armed Hamas fighters were not even the main danger underground; it was the remote-controlled bombs they would leave in or around the tunnels, relying on cameras or child spotters to aid them with timing. Once Israel had developed techniques to thwart these, regular infantry units also went into the tunnels. By mid- to late January 2024, Israel had shifted fully to attacking above and below ground simultaneously. This allowed the IDF again to move with haste, rather than the slow crawl Hamas had intended for it.

Did all these breakthroughs help the IDF succeed at destroying Hamas's tunnel system? Goldfus said that the military would not get to all the tunnels. Rather, it would succeed in destroying a critical mass of tunnels closer to the border or those central to the Gaza network. Goldfus suggested that this was more realistic, pointing to the several dozen kilometers of Japanese tunnels from World War II in Okinawa. Many are still around. But the general is disapproving of people who lack the patience to be systematic about destroying tunnels. In Shejaya, his forces destroyed eight tunnels in only two weeks. In other areas, his forces were nowhere near that effective. It would take time.

Goldfus's work beating Hamas's tunnel network brought him closer to catching Sinwar. In January, IDF soldiers started to reach places where hostages had been held. In March, they penetrated to the heart of Khan Yunis and arrived at another underground compound where Sinwar had fled. Goldfus said they were so close to catching Sinwar that the coffee he and his team had left behind as the IDF was closing in was still hot. Goldfus wondered if the war would have ended, or gone very differently, if they had found him then. Despite the IDF's many achievements in northern Gaza and Khan Yunis, it lost the trails of Sinwar and Deif, as well as those of the Israeli hostages held in Khan Yunis. To encourage civilians to flee the city before the fighting, the IDF left them an open corridor south. The price was to allow many Hamas fighters to flee with the masses. It would take an entire additional year, until April 2025, for the IDF to find the strategic tunnel Sinwar was likely using to move between Khan Yunis and Rafah to command Hamas forces.

The new Khan Yunis victories also seemed to mean less than the victories in northern Gaza. The earlier successes restored Israeli confidence that the IDF could protect the country, beat Hamas, and coerce it to release hostages. But after the IDF showed it could win tactical battles, and months passed without another hostage deal, many Israelis, and much of the world, started to wonder whether the IDF could ever get the hostages back or track down Sinwar and Deif. Meanwhile, Hamas was reorganizing in areas of northern Gaza that the IDF had already cleared. Israel had built up the drama around Hamas's elite Khan Yunis battalion, along with the notion that once the IDF bested those forces, the terrorists would have to sue for another ceasefire, releasing their remaining hostages or giving up. It did not happen.

The reason was as diabolical as it was simple: Hamas did not need to win or even make it a close fight. It just needed to hide and hold onto the Israeli hostages long enough for Israel to lose focus and momentum or face more international pressure than it could bear. Hamas could weather tactical military defeats. The sense of futility made it all the more crushing when Israeli troops accidentally killed three escaped hostages they ran into on the battlefield in December 2023.

In late December, former Israeli national security advisor Meir Ben Shabbat explained that Hamas "feels confident enough" to insist on victory and reject ceasefire deals that offered anything short of it. In his view, "while the conditions under which our forces operate are more difficult than in the past, for Hamas fighters, things have improved." Under Biden administration pressure, Israel had been using less firepower to prepare its military advances while increasing the flow of fuel to the civilians in Gaza Strip, which Hamas would steal and use to stay underground.[35]

Israeli casualties were also rising. In a video that made the rounds in December, an Israeli infantry officer complained, "How can it be that an area isn't cleared from the air before allowing our soldiers to enter?" Israel did that earlier in the war, he said, but now "our firepower is being restrained because our leaders may have started prioritizing the enemy's lives over the lives of our soldiers."[36]

Israeli sacrifices were not always appreciated in Washington, however, where President Biden criticized Israel for "indiscriminate bombing." The White House subsequently walked back the claim, but it reflected the administration's growing frustration with the length of the war, its rising Gazan death toll, and the stream of images that exacerbated Biden's political problems on the left wing of the Democratic Party.

There were many reasons for demoralization. Even as the IDF won piecemeal battles in Khan Yunis, the longer it failed to rescue more hostages or eliminate Sinwar, the more Israelis started to wonder if those goals were even achievable at all or in a reasonable timeframe.

Brigadier General Goldfus told us he was sure that if his forces cornered Sinwar, the man was a coward who would surrender his hostages to get more lenient sentencing. But in two years of war, no major Hamas leaders would surrender.

* * *

As the conflict dragged on, the debates over humanitarian efforts to improve conditions for Gaza civilians took on a life of their own. Israel would eventually have to defend itself from allegations of genocide brought by South Africa at the International Court of Justice. The South African government had recently welcomed a Hamas delegation, but Pretoria's extreme anti-Israel bias did not preclude it from advancing the case at The Hague.

Top Israeli political and defense officials were still in denial at this point regarding how quickly and decisively world opinion would turn against Israel. It would come with greater intensity than at any time since the infamous 1975 "Zionism is racism" UN resolution, which was overturned in 1991. When Israeli legal officials or friendly pro-Israel media outlets warned Israel's war leaders of the stakes, they were mostly brushed off. Israel would have to fight on, this view went, and so long as President Biden stayed on board, would the media yelling and international denunciations really matter? In the case of Netanyahu and Foreign Minister Israel Katz, top European and Arab leaders were telling them behind the scenes to finish off Hamas and not to take their public condemnations too seriously.

Biden, Secretary of State Blinken, Defense Secretary Austin, National Security Advisor Jake Sullivan, and others had been pushing Israel on humanitarian issues from the moment the war started. It first bore fruit, as we have seen, on October 18, 2023. "Based on the understanding that there will be inspections and that the aid should go to civilians, not to

Hamas," Biden announced that day, "Israel agreed that humanitarian assistance can begin to move from Egypt to Gaza."

"Let me be clear," the president continued, "if Hamas diverts or steals the assistance, they will have demonstrated once again that they have no concern for the welfare of the Palestinian people and it will end. As a practical matter, it will stop the international community from being able to provide this aid." But when Hamas did steal, divert and tax aid shipments to sustain its power, Washington felt that it had no alternative but to push for the aid to keep flowing to avoid food security problems.

When the war started, the US had no ambassador to Israel in place. That changed on November 3, 2023, and Washington's lead player on the ground would be the new ambassador, Jack Lew. Not long after October 7, his confirmation was rushed through. Israel received only forty-eight hours' notice that the new US ambassador was on his way, and Lew was practically airdropped into meetings run by Blinken with Israeli leaders on November 3.

Lew had served in the Clinton and Obama administrations and was one of the highest-ranking Orthodox Jewish officials in US history. He had been deeply familiar for decades with Israel's leaders and culture. One of his first major accomplishments was a six-week campaign to get Israel to open the Kerem Shalom Crossing for humanitarian aid. Kerem Shalom is a southern Israeli kibbutz situated on the triple Gaza-Israel-Egypt border. This, along with other efforts, would significantly increase the quantity of aid reaching Gazans.

During those first series of meetings on November 3, Lew worked to build a strong new relationship with Defense Minister Gallant. The defense minister was highly conversant in both the practicalities and the policy issues of humanitarian aid. As a former head of IDF Southern Command, he could weave in and out of esoteric aspects of the relevant geography on both sides of the border for delivering aid. Eventually, Lew could too, which was reflective of the extraordinary interest the US would take in the matter. Right from that first meeting, Lew felt he had captured Gallant's attention.

As the ambassador saw it, it was in Israel's strategic interests to open the Kerem Shalom Crossing to aid, and it was the right thing to do. Lew told us, "I deal with this night and day, and I do mean night and day. There has been incredible progress, and there are large quantities of humanitarian aid going into Gaza, but there needs to be more." He reasoned that Israel needed additional political and diplomatic "space" to continue the war long enough to defeat Hamas. Without opening Kerem Shalom to help the people of Gaza, Lew thought that the war would "not wear well" with the US or the world. Warnings of mass famine—which UN agencies and NGOs repeatedly projected but which did not materialize in these early and intermediate months of the war, in part due to increasing aid—filled the international headlines.

This forced Israel into a no-win situation: Let Gazans go hungry and be deemed war criminals, even by allies, and lose support for the war, or facilitate all the aid Hamas would need to continue fighting and drag out the war—and take the blame when this, too, hurt civilians. Unable to settle for either option, Israel for most of the war seemed to get the worst of both. The food situation remained poor, increasing suffering and incurring opprobrium, while Hamas would steal or tax all it needed.

Around early December 2023, supporters of the Palestinians at the UN Security Council initiated an additional campaign to pass a resolution requiring Israel to end the war, even though it had not yet defeated Hamas militarily or retrieved all the hostages. Until that point, the US had summarily vetoed every call for a ceasefire that would hamstring Israel's campaign to finish off Hamas's battalions. But pressure was rising worldwide and within the Democratic Party regarding the increasing Palestinian death toll and food shortages.

Lew said to Gallant that he knew facilitating more aid to the enemy mid-war brought up a complex and sometimes toxic mix of politics and security issues for Israel. Nevertheless, when a vote was forced at the UN Security Council, Lew told Gallant point-blank: We'll veto the resolution, but you need to help us on the aid problem.

Gallant told Lew: "Let me get this done."

The US ambassador and Gallant began a detailed conversation on how to get the aid through to Gazan civilians, not Hamas. Lew, Austin, Blinken, and other top US officials thought that, unlike Netanyahu, who might promise to do something but then reverse course under fire from his right-wing coalition partners, Gallant's word was his bond. If he made a promise on serious issues of war and peace, they thought, he would push it through, come what may in the political arena.

There was one more twist. For a short but notable period of time, a group of Israelis started blocking the roads to Gaza to prevent humanitarian aid from entering. The grassroots group, called Tzav 9, argued that aid should enter only if Hamas returned Israeli hostages. After Israeli police had failed to secure the humanitarian aid from the protesters, US officials said the protests were unacceptable and could not be allowed to thwart aid delivery. Later on, in June 2024, the US would even impose sanctions on the domestic Israeli protest group.

There was a second talk between Gallant and US diplomat David Satterfield, who knew the geography better than any other US official. Satterfield convinced Gallant that Israel must finally use the IDF to hold off the protesters if the police could not or would not do it.

That did the trick. Kerem Shalom was open and the IDF cleared the protesters so that the aid could enter Gaza. On December 8, 2023, the US vetoed a UN Security Council resolution calling to end the war.

* * *

By early February 2024, Hamas was beaten in Khan Yunis. Civilians streamed south to Rafah, though eventually that would be the next war zone, because it was one of the few places left to go. Hamas's remaining forces in Khan Yunis's west were encircled. Netanyahu, facing condemnation abroad and what he saw as rising defeatism at home, was eager to point to Israeli accomplishments on the ground.

He could recite them quickly, one after the other: Nearly twenty thousand of Hamas's thirty thousand men—at least that was the number used then, though later the IDF admitted the total number of Hamas fighters was closer to forty thousand—were killed, incapacitated, or arrested. Seventeen of Hamas's twenty-four combat battalions were dismantled, no longer able to mount military maneuvers or fight in an organized fashion. Rocket fire against Israel was down more than 95 percent from the war's early days. From the November deal and a few IDF operations, Israel had freed 110 hostages, already more than some had predicted at the start of the war. The tunnels were much larger than expected, and soldiers reported finding munitions in nearly every home they searched, but Israel was persevering.

Some of the prime minister's aides viewed Israel's political achievements as even more impressive. The 2009 Gaza war was brought to an end after three weeks, the 2014 war after six weeks. This war had been sustained for more than 120 days, and still, the US and Europe were not insisting on a ceasefire.

General Goldfus's tunnel revolution—understanding how Hamas used tunnels and how Israel could maneuver quickly in them—paved the way for the IDF victory in Khan Yunis. With a variety of moves to satisfy the Biden administration's humanitarian demands, Israel managed to continue the battle for Hamas's southern capital from December 2023 to March 2024. With no sign, however, that the takeover of Khan Yunis would make Hamas budge, the Mossad's Barnea and Qatar's al-Thani were stuck restarting round after round of hostage negotiations. "We want it too bad," a senior Israeli official complained. Many in Israel also wondered if Qatar was putting any pressure on Hamas, and if the US was putting any pressure on Qatar. In January 2024, CNN broke the story that the US had agreed to extend its presence at Qatar's al-Udeid Air Base, crucial for Qatari security, prosperity and influence.

While the Gaza war faced increasing criticism at home and abroad, Hezbollah continued to fire away at the north of Israel. That region had been evacuated since the war's early days, displacing tens of thousands of Israeli civilians. Kiryat Shmona, Israel's northernmost city, was a ghost town when Elliot drove through in March 2024. It received thirty Hezbollah rockets that day. But Kibbutz Manara, in the Upper Galilee, was even worse.

"In peacetime, this is heaven," Orna Weinberg, a fifty-seven-year-old caregiver, explained from atop a mountain ridge overlooking the Hula valley. But the only conclusion from a brisk walk through her battered, dangerous, evacuated community was that Hezbollah has made the north of Israel into hell. Rockets from Lebanon and Syria were nothing new to northern Israel, "but the antitank missiles changed everything," Weinberg said. Her home was the second in Manara to be hit.

When were they going to return to their homes? When was Israel going to stop the tit-for-tat and make Hezbollah pay a real price for, in effect, shrinking the borders of Israel? The answer had always been: after Israel had tamed Hamas in Gaza. But that was taking much longer than expected. Israel still had not touched Rafah, Hamas's stronghold to the south, which was now home to the bulk of Gaza's population.

CHAPTER SIX

"WHERE CAN RAFAH CIVILIANS BE EVACUATED TO—THE MOON?"

By early 2024, Hamas appeared to be running out of room. Defeated in northern Gaza and then Khan Yunis, the terror group had only two regions left that had yet to face Israeli invasion. One was Gaza's central camps, where the IDF had not fought out of fear that it would endanger the many hostages it believed were held in that relatively small area. The other was Rafah, Gaza's southernmost city, and a much larger area where fighters had fled from Khan Yunis. Trapped by the Egyptian border, would this be their last stand?

Most Israeli officials believed that Hamas could not be allowed to maintain its Rafah stronghold, which provided access to smuggling routes in Egypt. But the rest of the world, including Washington, saw something else when they looked at Rafah: a potential bloodbath. More than one million civilians had found shelter there.

The fight over whether Israel should invade Rafah would dominate long months of the war, from February to early May 2024, and precipitate Israel's biggest confrontation of all with the Biden administration. Inside the war cabinet, the debate was no less fierce. At first, Gantz, Gallant, and Halevi were trying to convince Netanyahu to invade Rafah. The prime minister was not yet ready and used the US opposition to hold off his colleagues. Over time, however, these positions would nearly reverse. Netanyahu came to lead the push for a Rafah invasion. Gantz, Gallant, and Halevi did not oppose it, but they became ready to trade in the threat of invasion for a hostage deal that could end the war and potentially add Saudi Arabia to the Abraham Accords. This is the story of a pivotal shift in Israel's war room.

Netanyahu started to appear alone at news conferences, without Gallant and Gantz at his side. Likewise, Gallant and Gantz began to hold more news conferences of their own and leak more criticisms of Netanyahu's decisions. Something was breaking down. Inside the war room, the three rivals were regularly raising their voices at each other instead of trying to find common ground. Gallant was often the loudest, though Netanyahu could be forceful as well. On other occasions, the prime minister would greet unwanted advice with an icy silence. Gantz was more soft-spoken, yet regarding substantive policy, he and Netanyahu were at loggerheads more than ever. Sometimes, the arguments made in the war room were offered as much for the future transcript as they were to persuade other cabinet members or to influence events, reflecting how the three wanted to present themselves to history. Israel's war leaders became less interested in an exchange of views and more cognizant of how they might need to frame their eventual breakup.

The war cabinet was struggling with a number of questions. One was how to deal with US pressure to discuss strategy for managing Gaza after the war. Gantz, and eventually Gallant, were convinced that Israel had to engage the Biden administration on these issues, even if it meant agreeing to a place for the West Bank–based Palestinian Authority (PA) in Gaza. Netanyahu did not want to engage the US on "day-after" issues and did not even want to hear about the possibility of the PA gaining a new foothold. "There's no politics if Hamas puts a bullet in your head," he told us in March 2024. Israel would have to win the war first, before planning the day after.

Gallant and Gantz told Netanyahu he risked losing US support with this attitude, but the prime minister believed Biden would stick with Israel, and that the dilemma was too great for Jerusalem to give Washington a veto. He also wondered if he could secure better terms should a different US president, a certain Donald Trump, win in November.

The friction between the war room's principals on this question was trickling down to their aides and starting to destabilize some working relationships. But it was far from the only question. Another was how long the war would last. IDF projections had been pushed back time and again. The US and Europe, unlike with past Gaza wars, had so far resisted calling for an unconditional ceasefire. October 7 may simply have been too brutal. By now, however, everyone could see the cracks in Israeli domestic and international support.

To this, Netanyahu had an answer. First, the Biden administration had been slowing him down. The new rules and restrictions made the fight for Khan Yunis take longer than the blitz of Gaza City.

Second was John Spencer. The chief of urban-warfare studies at West Point's Modern War Institute became a favorite citation for the prime minister. Spencer, unaffiliated with Israel, pointed out that the 2016–2017 battle of Mosul to defeat ISIS had taken the US-led coalition nine months. "Mosul," Spencer wrote, "was one battle, in one city against 3 to 5k [3,000 to 5,000] militants with limited defenses. Israel is fighting multiple battles in seven cities against 30k [30,000] militants with military grade underground cities built under civilian areas." Israel had been clearing urban terrain and tunnels at a "historic pace," Spencer explained,[37] yet the tunnels were vast, and soldiers were finding Hamas munitions in most civilian homes. Israel needed more time.

But if there were some disagreements between Israel and the US about how aggressive Jerusalem had been in northern Gaza and Khan Yunis, the gaps over invading Rafah developed into a chasm. This was a major reason that little fighting—only minor clean-up operations—took place in Gaza from late January 2024 until May 2024. This was when Israel saw the largest antigovernment protests of the war to date. Abroad, the "Gaza Solidarity Encampment" at Columbia University was erected on April 17, 2024, in the middle of this period. By May 6, encampments, occupations, sit-ins, and walkouts had spread to 140 US university campuses. These were Israel's lost months, in which it paid the price globally of "continuing the war" even as there was little war continuing on the ground.

* * *

By February 2024, Gallant and Gantz had started to push loudly for an invasion of Rafah to root out its four Hamas battalions. Netanyahu said the same in public, but in the war room, he was stalling. He was not sure the IDF could handle the job or had sufficient munitions for a new offensive while remaining ready for any escalation with Hezbollah. He worried again that large IDF casualties would sink his government and the war effort. But he found a politically potent explanation for delay: President Biden would not let Israel advance.

The Biden administration was pressing Israel to wrap up the war with a hostage deal, even while Hamas controlled Rafah. The pressing need, Washington argued, was to end the suffering of Palestinian civilians—and, as Netanyahu and many Israelis saw it, to quiet the political protests from the American Left. In exchange, the president and his deputies offered that Israel could finally grasp the prize of normalizing diplomatic relations with Saudi Arabia. Then, virtually all remaining Arab countries would sign on to the Abraham Accords, Biden predicted, transforming the region.

As Secretary of State Blinken put it to Biden, "Right now the prime minister's legacy is October 7.... But if he could actually produce normalization with Saudi Arabia," all that would change. "It's the holy grail, or the golden ring. It's what Israel has wanted from day one, which is normal relations with its neighbors."[38]

The prevailing conception was that a Saudi deal, which would include a US military guarantee requiring Senate approval, could pass only with Biden in power. Otherwise, Biden's past—and the Democrats' present—hostility to Riyadh would sink it.

US Senator Lindsey Graham, the senior Republican from South Carolina, said to Biden, "I'm telling MBS [Saudi Crown Prince Mohammed bin Salman], if you recognize Israel, I'll get you forty-five votes for the defense agreement.... Democrats wouldn't vote for it if Trump introduced it," he explained, "because they hate Bibi and they hate Trump." That is, if Trump would win the November 2024 election. But Republicans could be persuaded to back a deal under Biden "if Israel encouraged us to. We can get 45 Republican votes," Graham told the president. "You have to get the rest from your caucus."[39]

"I can do that," Biden responded. "Do you think you can deliver?"

"I can deliver," Graham assured Biden.

Graham told the president they were "good to go," adding that Netanyahu had "lit up like a Christmas tree" about the possible US–Israel–Saudi deal.

After a meeting in early 2024 with bin Salman, Graham told Blinken and National Security Advisor Sullivan that the "only way you can do this is to get a ceasefire. And during that ceasefire, close this deal."[40] That was the trick: ending the Gaza war and closing the Saudi deal in one fell swoop.

We will never know if the US could have delivered on Saudi normalization at that juncture, or at what price, because Netanyahu, Gallant, and many other top IDF officials viewed ending the Gaza war while Rafah remained in Hamas's hands as unrealistic. "Four [Hamas] battalions were in Rafah and we couldn't leave them there," Netanyahu told us. "We also couldn't leave them with southern control. We either have to create a new southern barrier south of Khan Yunis," cutting off Hamas, "or we capture the Philadelphi route."

That's the key strip of land by Rafah on Gaza's southern border with Egypt. The border itself was sealed at this point, but there were massive tunnels underneath that facilitated the smuggling of weapons and other contraband. Though Netanyahu was not ready to invade Rafah yet, he wasn't giving it up as a future target either.

At a minimum, Israel's post–October 7 war aims required that Hamas would not rule territory on its border. Leaving Hamas in control of an entire city, with access to its resupply route via Egypt, was unacceptable to most Israelis. Minister Ron Dermer, who handled much of the back and forth with the Biden administration for Israel, told us, "Our existential nerve has been touched. There's no way we're not finishing this war."

The Biden administration, and especially Blinken, did not understand that. "Hamas is an idea. You can't destroy it," the US secretary of state told Israel's war cabinet in January 2024. This argument failed to persuade. "They say you can't destroy Nazism, the idea," Netanyahu reflected. "I say, sure, but there's no Nazi regime anymore." Netanyahu was confident that Hamas could be destroyed as an army and denied territory in Gaza that might allow it to flourish again, even if some elements of Hamas and their idea of a jihad against Israel would live on.

It didn't help that Hamas was encouraged by the public US pressure on Israel. Hamas reasoned that by holding out, it could extract a deal that ended the war while leaving it in charge of Gaza—a major victory. On February 14, 2024, Netanyahu told us Hamas's demands had become "stratospheric."

Biden told Netanyahu on a February 15 call: "We already said we were not going to support an operation [in Rafah] absent a plan to get the civilians out of harm's way…We don't see how you can do that. It doesn't add up…and it doesn't lead anywhere because you have a long-term problem on your hands."

In a meeting shortly after the call, Blinken told the prime minister that his Rafah and "day-after" plans would lead to either Hamas rule in Gaza, an Israeli occupation that few wanted, "or there will be nothing left, just anarchy."

"Well, you're right," Netanyahu answered. "We'll have our hands full for decades."[41]

The US objections gave Netanyahu cover to delay the Rafah invasion that he was not yet confident about initiating, but as always, he tried to keep his options open. If Hamas would not accept a hostage deal that fit his parameters, Netanyahu could invade Rafah later.

Biden believed the Palestinian Authority (PA) was the best candidate to run a postwar Gaza, with help from Egypt and the United Arab Emirates. Many in the Israeli defense establishment agreed, including Gallant and Halevi. Netanyahu wanted no role for the Ramallah-based PA.

Everything was stuck. The UAE, Egypt, and Saudi Arabia would not lift a finger unless the PA was involved to give their interventions a stamp—or even a fig leaf—of Palestinian approval. Since the Arab states could not be viewed as collaborators with Israel, they would need an invitation from the PA. "Its letterhead is its most valuable asset," a Netanyahu confidant told us. But the prime minister would not swallow the bitter pill even under heavy pressure from Israel's defense establishment.

Netanyahu would recount how John Kerry, as President Obama's secretary of state, used to tell him that the PA security forces could in time be trusted to hold back Hamas in the West Bank on its own. In those days, Kerry would offer the Afghan army as an example of how local forces could be trained successfully. This, Netanyahu knew, had become a sore spot for the Biden team. The Afghan army had gone on to crumble even before the US could evacuate its forces. The prime minister expected the PA would fare no better in Gaza.

Blinken spoke often of the need for a "revitalized" PA. What this would mean in practice was not entirely clear. PA President Mahmoud Abbas, then approaching the twentieth year of a supposedly four-year term, displayed no interest in reform. At most, he would shuffle the deck of close confidants in the posts beneath him. "Revitalized? To me, that means going to a day spa," one senior Israeli official told us in March 2024.

Blinken felt helpless. The prime minister usually modified policies only in response to threats from Biden himself, and even then, only in some instances. Blinken, who had spent considerable time in France during his youth, was viewed by Netanyahu's allies as a "European diplomat" in American guise. He could not influence Netanyahu to wrap up the war and make a push for Saudi normalization, and his attempts to pressure the prime minister by undermining him at home only backfired. While portions of the Israeli Left also wanted to end the war at this point, Netanyahu gained politically for being seen as resisting US pressure to stop short of Israel's goals. "Biden should be our campaign manager," a top aide told us. "If they really wanted to undermine the PM, they'd thank him every day for his help on aid." That would upset many right-wing and even centrist Israelis who found it painful to facilitate supplying Gaza and Hamas while hostages were still in captivity.

In March 2024, the US intelligence community published an assessment that Netanyahu's "viability as a leader" was "in jeopardy," anticipating large protests to bring down his government. Netanyahu was not amused. He felt it was not a professional assessment, but a Biden wish list. A senior Israeli official observed that there were "more US comments about protests in Israel than about protests in Iran."

The White House strategy seemed to those around Netanyahu to go big on sympathy for the Palestinians and hard "anti-Bibi" while trying to stay pro-Israel. This was not an easy line to toe when the issue was Rafah, the rare subject on which Netanyahu was backed by an indisputable majority of the Israeli people. This was driven home to us when interviewing the Israeli historian Benny Morris. He did not hesitate to call Netanyahu "incompetent" and "cowardly" and compared him to Hajj Amin al-Husseini (1895–1974), the disastrous Grand Mufti of Jerusalem. But when asked about Rafah, Morris replied: "In this, Netanyahu is right."

Gantz, then topping Israeli opinion polls, told US officials, "Finishing the war without demilitarizing Rafah is like sending in firefighters to put out 80% of a fire." The Biden team had chosen to fight Netanyahu on an issue where he had the high ground.

The dispute over Rafah turned out to be the breaking point in relations between Washington and Jerusalem, with Biden feeling betrayed by Netanyahu after he had protected Israel from international pressure. He did not understand that Netanyahu was posturing, using him as a reason not to invade Rafah for some months when debating Gallant and Gantz in the war room. In public, Netanyahu could signal to the Israeli people that he wanted to invade Rafah and was resisting US pressure vigorously, while in private he held off his colleagues who wanted to invade by saying that Biden would not let him. If Netanyahu could no longer market himself to voters as "Mr. Security," at least he could now say he was the only one strong enough to stand up to a US president when he believed Israel's core interests depended on it.

He had done so with Barack Obama over the 2015 Iran nuclear deal and even before that, with Bill Clinton over Israeli–Palestinian negotiations. Both times, it ended with the Americans swearing. (Clinton: "Who the [f—] does he think he is? Who's the [f—]ing superpower here?" Senior Obama official: "Chicken[s—].") Already on February 4, 2024, it was reported that Biden had called Netanyahu a "bad [f—]ing guy." The US president was deeply suspicious that Netanyahu would drag him into a wider Middle East war.[42]

Then, on February 12, EU foreign-policy chief Josep Borrell called for the US to rethink its military aid to Israel due to the high number of civilian casualties in Gaza. "Netanyahu doesn't listen to anyone," Borrell said at a press conference. Israel had promised to evacuate the civilian population of Rafah first. "Where? To the moon?" Borrell asked. "Where are they going to evacuate these people to?"

That same day, Karim Khan, the prosecutor leading the International Criminal Court (ICC), all but threatened to bring war crimes cases against senior Israeli officials if they went through with the invasion of Rafah. At that point, the Hamas-run Gaza Health Ministry pegged the number of Palestinians killed in the war at 28,340, without distinguishing civilians from combatants.[43] The IDF, meanwhile, said it had killed around ten thousand five hundred Hamas fighters. This figure was based overwhelmingly on soldiers eyeballing a Hamas fighter firing on the IDF, firing back at him, and then viewing his dead body up close. Some others were judged based on observing Hamas fighters entering a structure that was subsequently destroyed by an air-to-land missile.

Taken together, the Hamas and IDF figures seemed to imply nearly eighteen thousand civilian deaths. But the numbers could not be mashed together so easily. The 13 percent misfire rate recorded for Hamas rockets meant that several hundred Gazans, if not a couple thousand, could have been killed by Hamas's own rockets. The Hamas statistics could also be exaggerated. It never corrected its false claim that 471 Gazans were killed by Israel at al-Ahli Hospital in the war's first month, and it was not nearly true that 70 percent of deaths were of women and children, a widely cited claim from Gaza's Government Media Office.

After all these allowances, IDF sources would admit unofficially to a split of fatalities from its forces of around 40 percent combatants and 60 percent noncombatants. Even if the number of civilians killed at this point were "only" fifteen thousand, that would dwarf the approximately two thousand one hundred Palestinians killed during the 2014 Gaza conflict. In that light, the ICC's Khan expressed concern about Rafah and added, "those who do not comply with the law should not complain later."

All of the relevant top US officials—Blinken, Sullivan, and Defense Secretary Austin—renewed their push against a Rafah invasion. NBC News reported on February 11 that Biden had recently called Netanyahu an "a—hole" on at least three occasions. Netanyahu, ostensibly blocked, breathed a sigh of relief and temporarily "backed down," to the consternation of Gantz and Gallant.[44]

Austin frequently warned Gallant and Netanyahu that they were driving out of control at high speed into a dangerous intersection with no thought as to how to come out of the inevitable crash. Austin would invest well over one hundred phone calls in speaking with Gallant, but he still felt there were times when the Israelis simply decided they wanted to kill someone or blow something up, and damn the strategic consequences.

Netanyahu, though glad to buy time, increasingly came to feel that the Biden administration was crossing the line. Every day in February and early March 2024 seemed to bring a new US shot across Israel's bow. There were new strings attached to weapons transfers. A call from Blinken for a "timebound, irreversible path to a Palestinian state"—a major ask at the least promising juncture for a peace process. Most worrying was Biden's February 8 statement to reporters that, "the conduct of the response in the Gaza Strip has been over the top." Israel again was blindsided. Later in the month, Biden changed US policy to deem all Israeli settlements in the West Bank illegal, whereas many prior administrations had labeled them merely in dispute. Why now, amid a war? Netanyahu wondered.[45]

Jerusalem arrived at two answers. First, Biden was motivated by the February 27, 2024, Democratic presidential primary in Michigan, where a substantial population of Muslim and Arab Americans were threatening to vote "uncommitted" as a protest over the war. "At the start, Biden was working to help Israel," went the joke going around the halls of power. "Now, he's working for the two-state solution—Michigan and Nevada." Sarcasm aside, Biden knew he was in political trouble with the anti-Israel populations in Michigan. Second, the loud US opposition to an Israeli offensive in Rafah colored all the other moves. Many Israeli officials thought that whatever the Biden administration said about settlements or humanitarian concerns, these issues were mainly raised to pressure Israel on Rafah.

Then came Ramadan, from March 10 to April 9. The Muslim holy month was viewed as an opportunity by all sides. Israel had set a Ramadan deadline for Hamas to return the hostages or face an invasion of Rafah. This was largely a bluff; Israel preferred not to risk fighting over the holy month. US opposition to the invasion also undermined Israel's threat—and with it the Biden administration's own desire for a ceasefire.

Hamas chief Yahya Sinwar instructed his negotiators to refuse a deal in March 2024, according to the messages reviewed by *The Wall Street Journal.* Sinwar said Hamas had the upper hand, the Journal reported, "citing internal political divisions within Israel, cracks in Netanyahu's wartime coalition, and mounting US pressure to alleviate the suffering in Gaza."[46] All three were real—and to Hamas's advantage. Understanding the stakes, Netanyahu's plan was not to launch the Rafah offensive during the sensitive month of Ramadan. The IDF also needed time to plan the evacuation of Rafah's civilians and muster ammunition.

In the end, Hamas was unable to set off another intifada over Ramadan. "Hamas's plan," as Gallant put it, was to "take Ramadan, with an emphasis on the Temple Mount and Jerusalem, and turn it into the second phase of its plan that began on October 7." If the terrorists could set off violence at the al-Aqsa Mosque in Jerusalem, raising international outrage and opening a new front inside Israel, maybe it could force Israel to cut short its mission in Gaza. It did not work; Israel planned ahead and its extensive police preparation avoided major disruptions on the Temple Mount. But Israel did not advance in Gaza either. Its troops stalled, giving Hamas a de facto ceasefire—for free—while the terrorists held out for victory.

* * *

"What is 'victory'?" Ronen Manelis, a former chief spokesman of the IDF, asked us at a bar in Tel Aviv on March 12, 2024. For Netanyahu, "it's just a slogan," he said. Manelis, a confidant of war minister Gadi Eisenkot, bet us a beer that Israel would never invade Rafah.

Throughout the month of Ramadan, from early March to early April, Netanyahu was coming around to the idea that the IDF was ready for the job in Rafah. "Arm yourself to the teeth," he had instructed the military. Despite the slowdown in US weapons shipments, Israel had used the delay to amass enough ammunition that it was no longer a central reason to delay. "We are a step away from victory," Netanyahu told the Israeli cabinet during his statement to begin an April 7 meeting, one of many such predictions that did not age well.

The prime minister and his lieutenants were no longer waiting for a green light from the Biden administration. "I don't care if they give us a red light," one said. "We'll do it anyway." Netanyahu increasingly viewed Rafah as the crux of Israel's war effort. You couldn't oppose one and support the other. "There are those who tell us they support our right of self-defense so long as we don't exercise it," he told us in March 2024. "They support our right to defeat Hamas so long as we don't carry it out." By mid-April, the Netanyahu team had no illusions of reaching an agreement with the US over Rafah; he could try only to mitigate any fallout from the dispute.

In one meeting, Blinken told Halevi, Gallant, and Netanyahu that an Israeli invasion of Rafah would quickly kill thousands of civilians—perhaps twenty thousand, according to one estimate. "I have studied the maps," Vice President Kamala Harris explained in an interview with ABC News. "There's nowhere for those folks to go." Netanyahu would disagree. "Of course they have a place to go," he told the Israeli cabinet. "There's a safe zone on the beach," a few miles away, in the Mawasi area.

Blinken told Israel's war cabinet that it would take four to six months to evacuate most of Rafah's civilians. At other points, top Israeli security officials said that US counterparts had told them it would take four months, but never less than that. Halevi, the IDF chief, had matter-of-factly said it would take ten days. In the end, it took six.

Halevi said that Blinken later admitted to him that he had been right, and US estimates had been wrong. Gallant said that Sullivan admitted the same, though Sullivan told us the exchange was more nuanced. "I was lighting Dermer up regularly about civilian casualties and food access," he said. He believes it paid off. US officials would claim that their suggestions are what made the evacuation so successful. The Israelis had a different view of the matter from the start. The first artillery round, Netanyahu thought, would get civilians out of Rafah in a hurry.

It was not that there was "daylight" between the two leaders and governments over this issue, the prime minister felt. There was planetary distance. The way it looked from Jerusalem, when Biden started paying a domestic political price for his support for Israel, it began to wilt.

The pressure from the campuses and human-right groups, amplified through the American media, had come to dog the president. Protesters called him "Genocide Joe" for refusing to impose a ceasefire on Israel, and the attacks only escalated as Election Day 2024 drew closer. From Biden's perspective, he had supported Israel's war effort and shielded it from worldwide critics for half a year—with nothing to show for it but political headaches. Netanyahu was not giving him the concessions he needed to manage the fallout.

Netanyahu believed the Biden administration was already slowing the transfer of ammunition to Israel to discourage an invasion of Rafah. According to Gallant and other officials, if not for an IDF air strike on March 31 that disastrously and mistakenly killed seven aid workers from the World Central Kitchen (WCK), the Rafah invasion might have taken place a month earlier in April 2024. In the strike's aftermath, Biden, Blinken, and Austin excoriated Netanyahu, dashing all hopes of convincing Biden that Israel could manage a Rafah invasion without major civilian casualties. Sullivan told Dermer the air strike was unacceptable and demanded a thorough investigation. When we later asked if he accepted Israeli claims that the WCK attack was a negligent mistake rather than a war crime, Sullivan declined to say.

On April 1, top US and Israeli advisers held a two-and-a-half-hour meeting by secure video conference as Washington "encouraged" the Israelis "in constructive conversations" to avoid an all-out assault on Rafah.

Biden told the press on April 2 that he was "outraged and heartbroken" by the WCK strike and then went further. "This is not a stand-alone incident," the president said. "Israel has not done enough to protect civilians." Austin told Gallant in a phone call on April 3 that he was "outraged." Austin indicated to us the tragedy reinforced US concerns over a Rafah invasion.

On April 5, Biden threatened Netanyahu with serious consequences if Israel did not change the way it was waging its war in Gaza, the first time he had issued such an explicit threat. Biden also gave Netanyahu a nonnegotiable list of improvements Israel needed to make regarding humanitarian aid. He told Netanyahu that Israel must "immediately" open the Erez Crossing to aid by land and the port of Ashdod to aid by sea, and ramp up the aid already coming through the Kerem Shalom Crossing.

"You need a 'deconfliction cell' to make sure humanitarians are in the room with the IDF and your command units to make sure that something like World Central Kitchen can't happen again," Biden told Netanyahu. "If you don't do that and we don't see results, then you've lost me. I'm out."

"Joe, we're gonna do it," Netanyahu replied. The president had made his point.[47]

* * *

Back in Israel, the war-room debate had shifted. If in February 2024, it had been Gantz, Gallant, and Halevi trying to persuade Netanyahu to authorize a Rafah invasion, by April, it was closer to the opposite. The prime minister, as we have seen, had come around—but the others were no longer so sure that invading was Israel's best option.

Halevi saw a new opening for a hostage deal. He said, however, that Netanyahu disagreed. So, Halevi withdrew Israel's troops from Khan Yunis on April 7. Though he acknowledged this reduced pressure on Hamas, his view was that anytime a hostage deal was not in the offing, and pressure was not needed imminently, he had to pull out his troops to give them a break. This was especially true to let reservists see their children, work their jobs, or return to their studies—so that they would be more likely to volunteer to return the next time they were called up. Besides, Halevi said, leaving troops to sit in Khan Yunis was not a serious option. The Biden administration would have pulled all support for the war to block anything that smacked of an emerging Israeli occupation.

Halevi also worried there would be insufficient munitions for Israel to invade Rafah and carry out a major operation against Hezbollah simultaneously. Taking Rafah, he told Netanyahu and the cabinet, would mean delaying a resolution of the northern front. The tens of thousands of Israeli evacuees who were displaced for around half a year would remain so for the whole summer, which probably meant an additional year for them if the start of the school year passed.

Among the politicians, Gantz, and eventually also Gallant, had become more focused on returning the hostages, avoiding tension with the US, and seizing a Biden proposal to normalize relations with the Saudis. The price would be ending the war. Driven by a heartfelt sense of responsibility for the lives of the hostages, Gantz, following his political partner Eisenkot, had gradually come to the view that it was now safe to wind down the fighting. Israel had already achieved enough, even without clearing Hamas from Rafah, if it won normalization with the Saudis in exchange for its restraint. This was also the Biden administration's view, and it was shared by some IDF leaders. Netanyahu told us that Gallant eventually also came to make the same argument.

"We've delivered tremendous blows to Hamas," Gantz told the war cabinet. Israel had killed many of the group's commanders and thousands of its fighters, so "let's maximize our gains and minimize our losses" by cutting a deal to spring the remaining hostages. "We can always come back," Gantz argued, in a year or two after a ceasefire. In June, he would make this point on Israeli TV: "If there is a change in the fighting and our hostages are returned, and we do what needs to be done in the Gaza Strip in a year, or in two years, that's not an issue."

Netanyahu was not convinced. Who knew if Israel would have the diplomatic capital to restart the war so far down the road? Besides, "It's not enough to destroy Hamas if you don't control the southern closure," he told us. Otherwise, Hamas would rearm. "It'll be a great victory for Hamas, Hezbollah, and Iran," the prime minister countered to Gantz. "It's not going to happen."

In the prime minister's view, Gantz could not conceive of saying no to the US, Israel's great ally and patron, or of fighting a US president on Fox News, in *The Wall Street Journal,* or in Congress when it mattered most. For the former army chief, Netanyahu believed, the US was an unapproachable black box, which spits out a presidential policy and will not budge.

Gantz, however, had legitimate reasons for his view. He believed the risk of a broad break with the US was too high a cost to pay when Israel needed help and had so few friends to rely on, compared with whatever limited benefit might come from more fighting. For Gantz, maintaining bipartisan US support was a more important strategic issue than Rafah. He did not believe that invading Rafah would lead Hamas to admit defeat. To borrow the analogy Gantz had used earlier with the Biden administration, maybe the fire could not be extinguished entirely. The terrorists would fight on either way.

* * *

In Israel's war room, policy disagreements gave way to deeply personal spats. In one instance, Netanyahu ordered Tzachi Hanegbi, his national security advisor, to block Gallant's senior aides from attending a key war cabinet meeting in order to prevent leaks. When Gallant objected, Hanegbi responded, "Even I didn't keep my aides here," to which Gallant responded, "You forgot that you're also an aide." Known for his short fuse and unwillingness to be pushed around, Gallant yelled at Netanyahu and Hanegbi, "Stop disturbing me!" and stormed out of the meeting without giving the standard military update.[48]

The incident came shortly after Netanyahu had prohibited Gallant from meeting with Mossad chief David Barnea unless Netanyahu was present. Such one-on-one meetings were standard and often necessary to maintain operations, but the prime minister did not trust the two not to plot together to pursue their own initiatives to reach a deal with Hamas on freeing hostages.

As Israeli forces stood still and the hostages languished, Gantz and Gallant tried to maneuver the US—behind Netanyahu's back if necessary—toward supporting an invasion of Rafah that would be followed by and connected to a hostage deal that would end the war. The Biden administration would not like the invasion, but it might accept it if it could get the war over with right afterward, they reasoned. Netanyahu, by contrast, wanted to invade Rafah and then continue the war. He could pursue a hostage deal, yet he would agree only to a temporary pause in the fighting. The Israeli defense establishment assessed that the prime minister was willing to extend the war after Rafah even if this meant endangering the return of the hostages.

The gap between the members of the war cabinet widened over time. Gantz would tell Netanyahu that he was stuck in the Gaza mire and blind to the hostages' fate, to long-term strategy, and to the escalating Iranian threats. Gantz said Netanyahu "did not look the public in the eye and tell the truth. He won't bring the hostages home, he won't truly protect the south, he won't return the residents of the north to their homes, he won't prevent Iran from obtaining a nuclear weapon." Most of these predictions would not age well, but at the time, it landed hard on Netanyahu.

The approval that Gallant and, even more so, Gantz had won from the Biden administration did no favors for their relationships with Netanyahu. The perception among the prime minister and his top allies was that Biden wanted Israel's leader to be a *schmatte*, a rag, that would fold whenever he liked. Gantz, it seemed to them, was the candidate to replace Netanyahu. Gantz's views were of course more complicated, but he welcomed the American acclaim as a sign to the Israeli people that he was the real statesman, and that Netanyahu no longer was welcome in Washington's halls of power. If an Israeli election had been held during this stretch, Gantz was favored to win it.

Israel was not invading Rafah, yet it was not ending its war either. Hamas continued to reject all temporary ceasefire offers in return for the release of hostages. They had been stuck for months; something had to give.

A hint came in what Ophir Falk, Netanyahu's foreign-policy adviser, told CIA Director William Burns after each round of the hostage negotiations leading up to May: "I have a message for you from the PM," Falk would say. "'We're going to achieve our war objectives,'" which included the destruction of Hamas. From the experience of the war, the prime minister's office had reached a conclusion about its US counterpart: "This administration never supports anything we do until we do it."

The Israelis had taken their time. Will they or won't they? That was the question, repeated until most observers became cynical about Israel's tough talk on Rafah. For three months, Netanyahu had been debating with Gantz, Gallant, and Halevi about how to handle Rafah, while each of them also debated it with the Biden administration. For three months, nothing happened. Then, everything changed.

CHAPTER SEVEN

VINDICATION IN RAFAH

On May 6, 2024, just when it seemed as though Israel would never make a decision, the war cabinet gave the order. The IDF was invading Rafah, on Gaza's strategically critical border with Egypt, come hell or high water.

The early days of the attack went by in a fog of mystery typical of older wars, prior to the digital age. The Israeli military provided small anecdotes about the progress of its forces, but no full picture of how the invasion was going. Likewise, Hamas put out many notices about Gazan deaths, as usual conflating combatants with civilians, yet it did not give a picture of how much, if at all, it was succeeding at countering the IDF invasion. After all the hype, and the dire predictions of catastrophe, the story went strangely quiet.

It was also upstaged. News leaked on May 7 of a partial US arms embargo on Israel. That same day, Biden declared his commitment to securing Israel, pledging never to forget the October 7 attack during a speech for Holocaust Remembrance Day. On May 8, however, the Biden administration went public with its action. "We've paused one shipment of high-payload munitions," Defense Secretary Austin announced, linking the move to US fears about Rafah. Israeli troops were advancing, but had not yet entered the large population center. This gave the Biden administration one last chance to stop Israel from embarking on what it was certain would cause a humanitarian disaster before it was too late.

The administration would acknowledge only that it had embargoed one shipment of two-thousand-pound bombs, which it claimed were too destructive to be used in Rafah. Some experts disagreed with that judgment, noting that a professional force can limit the blast radius by fusing them to detonate below ground as well as adjusting the angle and velocity of their delivery.[49] When Israel did not execute this properly, however, the damage to civilians was often significant. Yet the weapons freeze was always much larger than the president or his deputies let on. While only one shipment was officially blocked, many of the rest were stalled and delayed. These included five-hundred-pound bombs; Joint Direct Attack Munitions (JDAMs), which convert unguided bombs into precision "smart" bombs; small-diameter bombs; tank shells; mortar rounds; bulldozers; and military vehicles.

All kinds of ammunition and spare parts were no longer arriving, which also had to do with the two hundred fifty thousand shells the US had positioned in Israel but transferred to Ukraine in 2022. Leading up to the Rafah invasion, Israel's main shortage was in aerial bombs. Netanyahu considered such bombs the central reason Israel was able to smash Hamas in Gaza so far without suffering large casualties. They were saving IDF soldiers from having to enter booby-trapped buildings. Without enough bombs, Israel would be faced with worsening options.

This was the Biden team's way of letting Israel know it meant business in trying to block an invasion of Rafah. The president even went on CNN in prime time on May 8 to make his point. "Civilians have been killed in Gaza as a consequence of those bombs and other ways in which they go after population centers," Biden said. "I made it clear that if they go into Rafah, I'm not supplying the weapons that have been used historically to deal with Rafah, to deal with the cities." He let the American people know that Rafah was his red line: "We're walking away from Israel's ability to wage war in those areas."

Israel's leaders were both incensed and concerned—their troops were already on the move. "The US withheld critical weapons," Netanyahu would later admit. "We briefed them about what we were doing, but they still withheld the weapons." Gallant spoke to Austin immediately, on May 8, and the US defense secretary said he would look for ways to end the freeze. In a conversation soon after with Austin and National Security Advisor Sullivan, Gallant expressed disbelief and said that the weapons freeze was illogical. Israeli defense officials knew that many US weapons were Israel's bread and butter.

At earlier points, Gallant had warned Netanyahu and Dermer the US could freeze weapons sales. According to Gallant, the two replied that it was nonsense—an empty threat or something that would soon blow over. Yet when it became open and undeniable, the costs of ignoring Gallant's warnings appeared stark. Senior Israeli defense officials knew how much the IDF relied on American platforms, munitions, and spare parts. If Biden said no to Rafah, the implication was, Israel might have to listen. It was not that Israel could never attack, Gallant thought, but it would have to shift its plans somewhat to reach a compromise with Washington. Otherwise, Gallant warned in May, US opposition would lead to a total weapons embargo, producing a severe ammunition shortage that would block Israel's offensive throughout Gaza and put it in grave danger of a Hezbollah escalation from Lebanon. Israel could not simply flout Biden's red line.

"That's a legitimate case," Netanyahu told us. "But if we don't go into Rafah, we can't exist as a sovereign state. We'd become a vassal state and we won't survive."

This was of course a significant exaggeration, but the prime minister knew the region was watching. If Israel allowed itself to be restrained from defeating Hamas, after what it had done on October 7, the country would pay dearly in weakened deterrence.

"We have to go in." Netanyahu told Secretary of State Antony Blinken. "We'll fight with our fingernails if we have to." A weapons embargo wouldn't stop Israel. "We had a little more than fingernails," the prime minister recounted to us, "but it made the point." Netanyahu would later complain that Gallant acted as a US "veto player" inside the Israeli cabinet, insisting that Israel had no choice other than to comply with the US ultimatum.

That ultimatum was laid out quite frankly by President Biden. "The Americans said to me," Netanyahu told us, "'If you go into Rafah, you're on your own, and we're not going to send you the critical arms,' which is tough to hear." Faced with that, the prime minister recognized that Gantz and Gallant had grounds to hesitate, even though he disagreed.

"I don't confront America with relish...but in this case, we had no choice," Netanyahu told us. *Ein breira*, a few Israeli prime ministers have said over the years, *no alternative*.

* * *

Amid a collapse in US–Israel relations, the likes of which had not been seen since President George H. W. Bush threatened to cut off assistance to Israel in the early 1990s, Israel had no room for error in Rafah. Biden had vehemently opposed the invasion plan, and he was prepared to act accordingly if it got ugly. No number was given for what would constitute "too many" civilian casualties; if it filled the US airwaves, that would be a sign. The partial weapons freeze could harden into a full embargo.

From the president's perspective, with thirty-five thousand Gazans killed by May 2024, according to the Hamas figures, the toll was simply too great. Even discounting for Hamas combatants and likely exaggerations, some pro-Israel estimates still had the number of civilians killed at twenty thousand or higher. The civilian-to-combatant ratio might theoretically be within the civilized military norm, but the absolute numbers were large, troubling, and beyond what Western militaries had seen in recent years. Biden would no longer give Israel a pass just because the civilians weren't killed deliberately. The president had reached his limit. Israel would have to be near perfect in Rafah—and it was, surpassing all expectations.

The debate over Rafah died down rapidly over the course of May as one striking fact undermined the Biden administration's case: The disaster predicted in Rafah failed to materialize. By May 20, two weeks in, top

IDF officials were just about ready to claim victory. They told us that the IDF had succeeded in evacuating around nine hundred fifty thousand Palestinian civilians in only two weeks. This was supposed to have been impossible. For months, the Biden administration loudly opposed any invasion of Rafah on grounds that Israel had "no credible plan" to evacuate the city's 1.3 million civilians—which they said would take four or more months—and that thousands would be killed.

Even as the evacuation began, Secretary Blinken repeated that mantra: "No credible plan." National Security Advisor Jake Sullivan did too: "We still believe it would be a mistake to launch a major military operation into the heart of Rafah," he said on May 13. Then, after the evacuation succeeded far faster than they had ever dreamed and with relatively low civilian casualties, the Biden team changed the subject.

Around a third of Rafah was already under IDF control by May 20, and around two-thirds of the city had been completely evacuated. Though Israeli troops initially met resistance from Hamas's four Rafah battalions, the IDF said it had largely taken them by surprise. Top military officials told us that the Hamas battalions had started to unravel, their soldiers fleeing or going into hiding, so that at some later date they might fight back using guerrilla warfare tactics. They had already accepted defeat in the main battle, and their battalions did not put up nearly as hard a fight as they had in Gaza City or Khan Yunis.

After advancing toward Rafah from the east, Israel declined at first to enter the city. Instead, it rapidly seized most of the Philadelphi Corridor along Gaza's border with Egypt, a thin strip just south of the city. This plan, Netanyahu explained to us, was part of how Gallant and Gantz came to support the final invasion. "They said, OK, we'll tell the Americans that we'll do a pincer movement.… From along the Philadelphi Corridor and from the side, so we don't go into the buildings," the heavily populated city center, until civilians have left.

Netanyahu told us he believed people would have moved away anyway once it was clear the fighting had begun in earnest. "The important decision was to go into Rafah despite the American ultimatum." Even as Israel flouted Biden's demands, however, there was utility in making adjustments and gestures toward his concerns. Israel needed the relationship to survive this stress test.

"Once the Americans understood that I'm going in anyway, they did indeed hold up the weapons, but they couldn't do very much about it," Netanyahu said. By the end of May, the Biden team was telling the media that Israel's invasion of Rafah was really a "targeted strike" and somehow had not crossed its red line. The partial arms embargo continued, yet the administration declined to escalate to a full break with Israel's war effort.

Israel's great gamble had paid off. If it hadn't, the Gaza war might not have continued for much longer. "All eyes on Rafah" went an online protest slogan, derived from the warning of a World Health Organization official, which went viral in May 2024. The world was watching, fully primed for a catastrophe that never arrived.

The IDF had destroyed some cross-border tunnels on the Philadelphi Corridor, and by controlling the Rafah Crossing, Israel knew Hamas could no longer drive trucks of supplies over the border. Egyptian officials were privately embarrassed by the smuggling, but did not show it. In fact, once Israel advanced, Egypt had moved in anger to close the Rafah Crossing to humanitarian aid. Contrary to fears and threats, however, Israel's relations with Egypt did not collapse. There were no violent border incidents between the sides and very few Palestinians had penetrated into Egypt, which had been Cairo's primary concern.

More broadly, Sinwar was on the move and starting to run out of places to hide, while Hezbollah in Lebanon was still being held back from helping Hamas. In the meantime, Israel was handing the Lebanese terrorist group a beating, gradually and cumulatively, that would leave it flat-footed at later critical points in the war. Nasrallah still had no idea how to extricate himself from a fight that he joined only reluctantly, but now could not call off. Ayatollah Khamenei in Iran still had not figured out an effective way to stop the slow-motion routing of his proxies.

Despite these Israeli successes, there were also clear shortcomings. As of May 20, the IDF had no updates on the status of the hostages held in Rafah. It seemed less sure than ever about where Sinwar was hiding.

Only a year later, in April 2025, the IDF finally found a large strategic tunnel between Rafah and Khan Yunis, which Sinwar had probably used to flee Khan Yunis to Rafah and then possibly to flee again during the Rafah invasion. Nevertheless, the IDF expressed pride that it had managed such complex challenges during the Rafah operation, defeating Hamas while still limiting civilian casualties and avoiding misfires that could hit nearby Egyptian troops. Israel had also seized and destroyed a large number of rockets and launchers in Rafah, the last place where the IDF said Hamas might still have a substantial arsenal.

A big open question, however, was the future of Hamas. Before the invasion, Netanyahu had described Rafah as Hamas's final stronghold and last stand. He had often implied that the terrorist group would collapse after the city had fallen, which could lead to an end to the war. That did not happen.

Top IDF officials told us that even after beating Hamas in Rafah, fighting a Hamas insurgency would require significant military resources at a minimum until October 2024, and possibly beyond. Even these estimates would prove wildly optimistic. Amir Avivi, an influential right-wing retired general who had pushed Netanyahu hard for a Rafah invasion, was more realistic about the aftermath: It would take several years to mop up Hamas and pacify the Gaza Strip, he had predicted to us, just like it had after Israel's 2002 operation in the West Bank to break the back of the Second Intifada.

This was not what the world or Israelis wanted to hear. There also seemed to be little new hope for returning more hostages to Israel—until a June weekend surprise.

* * *

It began in earnest on May 12, 2024, when Israeli intelligence identified the general location of four hostages in central Gaza's Nuseirat. Undercover spies, known as *mista'arvim*, were deployed. Disguised as local families, including modestly dressed women, they rented a nearby house and blended in by frequenting markets and interacting with residents, discretely gathering information.

Soon, they identified the precise locations. Hostages Almog Meir Jan, twenty-one, Andrey Kozlov, twenty-seven, and Shlomi Ziv, forty, were held in one building. Noa Argamani, twenty-five, was in another nearby. All had been kidnapped by Hamas from the Nova Festival on October 7.

At one point, the planned operation was only to rescue Argamani. At a later stage, it was decided to carry out a higher-risk, simultaneous operation in both locations. Otherwise, Hamas guards might kill the other three hostages upon hearing of a nearby attack.

The operation's chances of success were enhanced by the hostages' locations: They were held in civilian apartments, as opposed to tunnels. That some of those holding the hostages were not Hamas members but paid civilians, which was thought to help conceal the hostages' location, was a complication. Many of these civilians, especially the children, could not be targeted.

The operation was delayed several times to improve the intelligence, yet by May 31, Israeli intelligence was ready. On June 5, the operation was approved by the war cabinet, including Netanyahu, Gallant, and Gantz. Israel's defense chiefs were given the final call on timing. One key would be a diversion carried out by thousands of IDF soldiers in central Gaza for several days before the rescue. The idea was to desensitize the guards to nearby IDF operations, making them confident Israel had no idea hostages were present. This allowed Israeli special forces to set up a rescue operation from close by without raising alarms.

Around 11 a.m. on June 8, 2024, Halevi and Shin Bet Director Ronen Bar gave the go-ahead for a joint operation with the Yamam SWAT team. Israel would do it in broad daylight to achieve greater surprise, despite the risk of being seen.

Both buildings where hostages were held were three to four stories high. Four Israeli lookouts kept an eye on them, and twenty-eight commandos were involved in the raid. Thousands of soldiers were nearby in support. Most of the commandos entered the immediate area in a couple of trucks. Beds and belongings hung out from their vehicles, as if they were civilians displaced from Rafah. This got them close enough to spring into action.

The operation to free Argamani went smoothly: The commandos achieved complete surprise against her guards. After eight months in captivity, Argamani heard a knock on the door: "It's the IDF; we've come to rescue you." She was hustled out of the location in only six minutes.

The operation to free the other three hostages, around 650 feet away, led to a significant exchange of gunfire. The hostages were secured, but how to get them out? Dozens of Hamas terrorists used machine guns, grenades, and even RPGs against the Israelis. Arnon Zamora, the SWAT team's commander, was hit. He later died of his wounds.

Eventually, the commandos eliminated the guards while shielding the hostages and spiriting them to an escape vehicle. Then, the operation really went sideways. The escape vehicle was damaged and got stuck. It would not move. At this point, the hostages were exposed and the entire operation could have ended in disaster.

The Israeli Air Force and ground troops let loose a massive barrage of suppressing fire, causing a stampede at the crowded nearby market. The Israelis were going to shoot their way out. Hamas claimed that 276 Palestinians were killed and around seven hundred wounded. The IDF estimated that closer to ninety were killed, a majority of them Hamas forces. Leaving bodies strewn across the streets of Nuseirat, reinforcements and rescue helicopters succeeded in evacuating the commandos and hostages. Four more were now free.

The operation put new wind in the sails of the IDF and the Israeli public. But it also led Hamas to up its guard on other hostages, and Israel would not be able to replicate its success at any scale. This would be the high point of rescue missions. Israel would have no way to free its hostages other than to trade for them. For the IDF, it was back to the grind in Rafah and throughout the Gaza Strip.

That same month, June 2024, Yonah embedded with IDF troops in Rafah. Colonel Yair Zuckerman, the Nahal Brigade commander, revealed to Yonah the stunning theory that Hamas itself pressed for an earlier and quicker evacuation. In all prior battles, the terror group had tried desperately to prevent Palestinian civilians from following IDF evacuation orders. Hamas had always wanted to use its own civilian population as human shields from Israeli attacks. Either the shields would work and protect Hamas, or they would not work, and Israel would pay a political price for the casualties. But this time, Hamas wanted more time to set booby traps in the city center, Colonel Zuckerman thought.

Zuckerman said the IDF had started almost immediately to probe Hamas's tunnels in early May 2024, with a focus on eliminating weapons smuggling from Egypt. Despite ongoing progress, the following year, in March 2025, a new IDF assessment would admit that only 25 percent of tunnels in the whole of Gaza had been destroyed.

On September 12, 2024, Yonah visited Rafah a second time. He entered the largest cross-border smuggling tunnel of the Philadelphi Corridor, in an area that had previously held a mosque and a hangar bay, only around one hundred feet from the border fence with Egypt. This was very different from his June visit. Back then, Yonah had been driven by the exact same spot where this gigantic tunnel was hidden, but no one had any idea what was directly underneath them. By this time, 2,308 Hamas terrorists had been killed in Rafah and eight and a half miles of tunnels had been destroyed in the area. Gaza itself is only twenty-five miles long.

During the September visit, IDF Brigadier Generals Itzik Cohen and Daniel Hagari said that the main use of the Philadelphi Corridor tunnels was not to smuggle weapons, but to facilitate the firing of long-range rockets. Hamas placed the rockets next to the border with Egypt to deter Israel from striking them, lest it cause a diplomatic incident. The IDF had not invaded Rafah during any of the large conflicts since 2005, giving Hamas's Rafah rocket crews a sense of impunity.

IDF generals emphasized that the proportion of weapons smuggled underground was likely small. Rather, they said that three other means were likely responsible for the vast majority of Hamas's prewar build-up. First, Hamas could simply drive weapons through the aboveground Rafah Crossing. The crossing was manned by Egyptian officials who could either be bribed or outfoxed, if they were not already complicit.

Second, Hamas produced weapons domestically from at least fifty-five facilities in Rafah and northern Gaza. Third, the IDF believed that when the Muslim Brotherhood's Mohamed Morsi was president of Egypt in 2012–2013, he allowed unprecedented smuggling. Hamas itself is an offshoot of the Muslim Brotherhood.

Although these points were made in a technical military context, they also supported the Israeli defense establishment's argument against Netanyahu that the Philadelphi Corridor could be given up temporarily for a hostage deal, without endangering the gains of the war. It would take Hamas years to rebuild its cross-border tunnel network, the generals said, and Israel could always retake the corridor. "It will take us three hours to get back there," Tamir Hayman, a former head of Israeli military intelligence and the leader of Israel's top security think tank, told us. "OK, I'm exaggerating—four hours."

Netanyahu saw the issue differently. Securing Gaza's southern enclosure was a must, no matter how the arms were smuggled. "Otherwise, what's the point?" he asked us. "Even if you destroy Hamas, you leave, and somebody—some new Hamas or another terrorist group—will rearm itself through that southern route." It had taken twenty years since Israel's 2005 withdrawal, and several small wars, to muster the support to retake the Philadelphi Corridor in 2024. The defense establishment's assurances could be unrealistic given Israel's diplomatic situation, he thought. If Israel left now, it might not return. Netanyahu and his allies would portray Gantz and the generals as inviting defeat in so many words.

* * *

Israeli success in Rafah may have sufficed for the Biden administration, but Israel's hardline critics were as outraged as ever. On May 20, ICC Prosecutor Karim Khan hastily canceled a planned visit to Israel, in which he was supposed to hear Jerusalem's side of the story. Instead, he requested that the ICC's Pre-Trial Chamber issue arrest warrants for Netanyahu and Gallant alongside Hamas leaders Yahya Sinwar, Mohammed Deif, and Ismail Haniyeh.

Israel was taken by surprise. Its leaders learned about the request for arrest warrants right as Khan went on CNN to announce them, Secretary of State Antony Blinken said. Biden called the arrest warrants "outrageous" and stressed "there is no equivalence—none—between Israel and Hamas." The US was particularly perturbed about Khan's highly abnormal decision to use Christiane Amanpour's CNN show to announce the court's business.

Khan, a British lawyer, rose up the ranks as a Crown prosecutor before going international to work on human-rights cases in the former Yugoslavia, Rwanda, Sierra Leone, Kenya, Cameroon and Iraq. Ascending to lead the ICC, on the back of British and American support, was to be the crowning triumph of his career.

Most of Israel's legal establishment believed Netanyahu had not been taking the risk from the ICC seriously enough. For months before and after the announcement, however, it was never far from the top of his mind. And only a month prior, a leading international lawyer had advised Netanyahu's office that Khan was highly unlikely to seek arrest warrants for many months, despite his threats. After all, the ICC had yet to conduct a proper investigation while its staff was busy in Ukraine, investigating Russian war crimes.

Similarly, Blinken and British Foreign Minister David Cameron, plus a bipartisan group of US Senators who had met the ICC prosecutor, had reassured Netanyahu that Khan would take the necessary time. Israel thought it was cooperating toward providing evidence to Khan; indeed, ICC staff had a meeting planned with Israeli officials for May 20 to arrange the details for him to visit. But none of the promises about Khan waiting to hear both sides turned out to be true.

Netanyahu was not about to give up the Rafah invasion because of the ICC, whose jurisdiction Israel did not recognize. But would the cost of disregarding the court be to turn Israel into a true pariah?

Israel had declined to open any kind of state inquiry into the legality of the decisions made by Netanyahu, Gallant, and the war cabinet, though top Israeli lawyers had urged it to do so to buy time, if nothing else. Khan had once acknowledged that Israel has a "robust" judicial system. Indeed, the Israeli Supreme Court is renowned for its activism to balance out the still strange situation in which the country lacks a formal constitution. Had Khan bothered to visit Israel, he probably would have received more details about the around seventy criminal probes (this would later reach close to one hundred) Israel had already opened into the wartime conduct of individual soldiers. Some Israeli troops would be indicted and even convicted for instances in which they disobeyed orders or the rules of engagement, and acted violently against Palestinian civilians or terrorists who had already surrendered.

Khan's decision to pair indictments of Israel's leaders with indictments of Hamas's leaders seemed like precisely the false equivalence that Israelis found most offensive.[50] It appeared the ICC was erasing many of the critical moral distinctions established in the Nuremberg Trials. The Hamas leaders who ordered death squads to slaughter innocent Israelis on October 7 were to be lumped together with the leaders who responded by ordering bomber pilots to strike those terrorists in their Gaza hiding places.

Netanyahu would notice something else about the indictments: The ICC had named only two of the three members of Israel's war cabinet—himself and Gallant, but not Gantz. All three had approved Israel's war decisions, yet Gantz was at this point the world's best hope of unseating Netanyahu as prime minister.

Khan would also accuse Israel's leaders of using "starvation of civilians as a method of warfare." Seven months into the war, however, Israel had facilitated the entry of 28,255 aid trucks and 542,570 tons of aid. While Biden condemned the ICC, Netanyahu felt betrayed. Earlier in 2024, Israel had been given a very strong impression, including from Senate Democrats, that there would be a bipartisan bill imposing sanctions on the ICC if it moved against Israel. But after the indictments, the White House declared itself opposed to such sanctions.[51]

Responding to US and Israeli characterizations of Khan's handling of engagement with Israel, the ICC told us, "Despite significant efforts, the Office [of the Prosecutor] has not received any information that has demonstrated genuine action at the domestic level to address the crimes alleged or the individuals under investigation." This was the essence of the Khan's argument: Yes, Israel was investigating many individual soldiers for violating its own open fire rules or humane treatment of detainee rules, but it was not investigating Netanyahu and Gallant themselves.

It was by no means inevitable that Khan would pursue Israel's leaders. From 2009 until 2021, Israel had succeeded at preventing the ICC from opening a full war crimes probe against it, holding it at bay with a preliminary review of jurisdictional issues. That didn't change from June 2021 to October 2023, with Khan at the helm.

Then, in less than a month, everything changed. After October 2023, Khan issued statement after statement warning Israel about war crimes. He also tried to visit Gaza through the Rafah Crossing. Next, he visited Israel and the West Bank in an unofficial capacity to meet with Israeli victims of October 7 as well as the PA in Ramallah. Whether the Rafah operation sealed the deal, or whether it was the multiple political blows the US had delivered to Israel in early May, Khan finally decided to go after Israel. Israel would learn only later that Khan had been confronted by sexual assault allegations and that distracting from them might explain his abrupt switch. Until Elliot and a few others broke news of the details of the allegations in October 2024, Khan succeeded in sweeping them under the rug.

The arrest warrants were a disaster for Israel, a stain on its name. On the flip side, it actually could have been worse if the ICC had issued arrest warrants for Israeli soldiers as well. None of this diminished the deep fury of most Israelis at Khan and the ICC, which targeted Israel in a war that had started with Hamas's slaughter of close to one thousand two hundred Israelis.

* * *

Israel's war room united against the ICC's characterization of its actions, but it was otherwise bitterly divided. Especially after the IDF had already beaten most of Hamas in Rafah, Gantz was furious with Netanyahu for refusing Biden's offer to end the war, install the PA in Gaza to replace Hamas, and arrange a Saudi normalization deal. Netanyahu continued to oppose a permanent ceasefire and the introduction of the PA, both on grounds where he could legitimately debate policy and because they would spell the end of his power.

If Netanyahu were to install the PA in Gaza, his right-wing coalition partners would bring down the government, and Israelis would elect a new one, he believed, that would wrap up the war short of its objective. "I want victory over Hamas. The Left wants victory over me," the prime minister told us. To Gantz, these were Netanyahu's rationalizations for putting politics over country.

Gantz, and much of the Israeli defense establishment, had another reason to want to end the war in Gaza: to focus Israel's attention on Hezbollah. For more than half a year, the north of Israel had been turned into a no-man's land. "The country has been shrunk," Daniel Hagari, Israel's top military spokesman, told us in June 2024. Gantz, like many Israelis, saw an urgent need to stop Hezbollah's rocket fire on Israel's north, so that the tens of thousands of Israeli evacuees could return to their homes. "All eyes may have been on Rafah," Hagari said, referencing an anti-Israel protest slogan, "but we need our eyes on Hezbollah."

No one knew exactly what it would take to re-establish deterrence. Gantz was ready for a larger war to get it done. Hezbollah had already fired several thousand missiles and drones at Israel since October 7, but in small increments, typically targeting radar stations or the already evacuated homes of northern Israel. Though Israel responded with tit-for-tat air strikes, Hezbollah had managed to avoid incurring a major Israeli attack.

Pressure had been building on Gantz to do something, and not only about the northern front. Many opposition leaders and voters, to whom Gantz needed to appeal, worried he was being used by Netanyahu to legitimize the continuation of the war in Gaza. If he could not decisively influence the government to make the sacrifices necessary for a final hostage deal, many in the media asked, what was he still doing there? Better to work to precipitate its fall and then lead the opposition to the election victory to which it expected to cruise.

On May 18, Gantz set Netanyahu a deadline of June 8 to begin winding down the war in Gaza and turning his attention northward. "Lately, something has gone wrong," Gantz told the nation. "Essential leadership decisions to ensure victory were not made. A small minority has taken over the command bridge of the Israeli ship of state and is steering her toward the rocks." He meant the two parties to Netanyahu's right that formed part of his governing coalition. "Personal and political considerations have infiltrated the Holy of Holies of Israeli security," Gantz added, accusing Netanyahu of being blackmailed politically by National Security Minister Itamar Ben-Gvir and Finance Minister Bezalel Smotrich into continuing the Gaza war despite the recommendations of the defense establishment.

Gantz listed six objectives to which Netanyahu would have to agree if the prime minister wanted to keep him in the unity government. Many of them were starting to achieve consensus within the defense establishment, to which Gantz was strongly linked as a former IDF chief and defense minister. The six were:

i) Return the hostages;
ii) Demolish Hamas and demilitarize the Gaza Strip;
iii) Provide an "American-European-Arab-Palestinian" governing alternative in the Strip that "is not Hamas and not [PA President] Abbas";
iv) Return the residents of the north to their homes by September 1;
v) Promote normalization with Saudi Arabia as part of "a treaty with the free world and the Arab world against Iran";
vi) Adopt a framework for a program of national service for all Israelis, including Haredim, also called ultra-Orthodox Jews.

"If you choose to lead the nation to the abyss," Gantz said, "we will withdraw from the government, turn to the people and form a government that can bring about a real victory."

Many of Gantz's conditions mirrored Netanyahu's goals, yet on Gaza, the difference could no longer be bridged. Liberal voters and allies wanted Gantz to leave a government that had no intention of making the concessions needed at this point to bring all the hostages home. These voters faulted Gantz for propping the government up for so long, and he worried about the decline in his lead in the public opinion polls. This was Gantz's way of fighting back.

Netanyahu ignored the threat, and on June 9, 2024, Gantz and his party quit the coalition. He was out of the war room. This altered the war's course, giving Netanyahu a freer hand but also fewer excuses for not taking action to coalition members further right. No longer could he try to place the blame on Gantz for being less aggressive than his critics on the political right would tolerate.

Many had thought—wrongly, it turned out—that Gantz's exit would soon force Netanyahu into new elections. At the time, Gantz remained the prohibitive favorite to be the next prime minister. Over the course of 2025, however, his lead in the polls would continue to slip and eventually collapse, with other centrist and liberal parties grabbing many of his supporters. He had risen to answer Israel's call of duty in October 2023, but the association with Netanyahu would come to tar him for many opposition voters.

* * *

The war room was down to two main players. Gantz had not been the only one losing patience with Netanyahu; starting in mid-May 2024, Gallant began to take public what had been mostly private or leaked criticisms of Netanyahu over what was to follow the Rafah invasion. On May 15, Gallant said that the military had been pushing Netanyahu to decide on a plan for the "day after" the war in Gaza—any plan at all—to no avail. Eventually, he said, the defense establishment sent Netanyahu proposals of its own, yet the prime minister ignored them. That left military rule, which Gallant said would be paid for "in blood and victims" and "come at a heavy economic cost." Like Gantz, he accused Netanyahu of avoiding these critical decisions for political reasons, to avoid angering his further-right coalition partners who could topple the government.

Likewise, he accused Netanyahu of seeking to make permanent the exemption from IDF service for ultra-Orthodox Jews. All other Jewish men, and most Jewish women, were obligated to serve in some way, and amid the great sacrifices of the war effort, they had come to deeply resent the shirking of their Haredi coreligionists. Israel needed all the troops it could get. The prime minister doubtless agreed, but he was unwilling to take action that would prompt the Haredi political parties to bring down the government.

Netanyahu was politically vulnerable. While the Israeli public was increasingly demanding the return of all hostages in a deal with Hamas, he believed Israel needed "total victory" over Hamas. He also thought he needed an overwhelming victory to face the voters or redeem his legacy after October 7. To give himself the time to achieve those aims, Netanyahu had to keep the ultra-Orthodox parties on board. This was easier said than done when their continued support was conditioned on passing an extraordinarily unpopular draft-exemption law that was unlikely to pass legal muster. Few observers expected the government to survive another year, let alone to its natural expiry date in October 2026.

Eventually, Netanyahu gave a major speech detailing his reasons for refusing a hostage deal with Hamas until the terror group accepted Israeli control over the Philadelphi Corridor bordering Egypt and dropped its demand for a permanent ceasefire up front. He criticized the defense establishment for its contrary position on this issue, but most defense leaders could not respond as long as they were in uniform.

So the next day, it was Gantz and Eisenkot, both former IDF chiefs, former war cabinet ministers, and now top opposition figures again, who shot back. They tried to refocus the nation's attention on the larger threat of Iran, which was managing much of its proxies' effort against Israel in the multifront war. To make the contrast clear, Gantz and Eisenkot stood in front of a large map of the Islamic Republic and the entire Middle East. They brushed off Netanyahu's claim that withdrawing from the Philadelphi Corridor would be an existential threat to Israel, calling it a complex operational issue, not a strategic one. They accused Netanyahu of being stuck in the Gaza mud, missing the growing Iranian threats which for years had been at the heart of his own message.

They also accused Netanyahu of lying about fully pursuing a hostage deal and about being tough and hawkish. On the contrary, they said, the prime minister had worked cunningly to frustrate a hostage deal. The concern about not being able to return to the Philadelphi Corridor was merely Netanyahu showing his own personal fears of using force, they said, just as he had been afraid to invade Gaza in October 2023 and Khan Yunis afterward.

Netanyahu had said that there was no way to stop Hamas from re-arming without boots on the border, citing Hamas's massive smuggling during Israel's absence from Philadelphi from 2005 to 2024. Gantz and Eisenkot countered that the IDF now had technological solutions it had lacked in the past. Most important, they argued that Netanyahu's refusal to compromise to get a hostage and ceasefire deal was losing Jerusalem support globally in ways that were much more dangerous than a temporary withdrawal from the Gaza-Egypt border. After all, US support would be needed to handle the Iranian nuclear threat and to avoid global diplomatic isolation.

Overall, Gantz and Eisenkot tried to redeem the value of defense expertise in the cynical, post-October 7 eyes of the Israeli public. The titles of general and retired general should mean something, they seemed to be urging—and should not come with the label of naïveté that Netanyahu was assigning them.

* * *

With no end to the war, and no US trust left in Netanyahu, Gallant was left to negotiate the restoration of US military support for Israel. "The process to convince them was very hard," Gallant told us. He had been discussing the issue with the Biden administration for months. Top US officials had wanted to see how the Rafah operation actually panned out before committing.

Looking backward, Gallant told us his perception that, even before the Rafah invasion, he had nailed down the core elements of what would eventually emerge as the deal with the US. "The deal was that these bombs won't be used in Rafah, though we could still use other bombs which had already been delivered." Under the circumstances, this struck Gallant as a good compromise. "I presented the deal to Netanyahu and

Dermer. They were against it! They said it was problematic. I asked them, 'What's the problem?'" But Netanyahu was not to be persuaded. He vetoed the deal, Gallant said. "Gantz," who was still in the war cabinet at this point, "didn't know about it at all—or at least I didn't tell him," Gallant added. The fight over weapons therefore extended through the summer of 2024.

This was a perfect example of war-room dysfunction. Gallant had decided to cut a deal with the US without fully consulting Netanyahu, his boss and prime minister, on the terms. Netanyahu then vetoed the deal, even though it was probably in Israel's interest. Amid all this, Gallant could have turned to Gantz, who held significant power until the moment he quit and no doubt would have agreed with him. Instead, Gallant made sure to leave him out of the loop because the defense minister still detested Gantz from their rivalry a decade earlier over who would run the IDF. That feud was reinforced by how each of them handled the judicial-reform crisis of 2023, in which they both fought Netanyahu, but also took swipes at each other. Gallant seemingly would rather lose the battle with Netanyahu on this substantive issue than be seen by Gantz as needing his help. Once Gantz withdrew from the unity government, Gallant was left alone to try to moderate Netanyahu in dealing with Washington.

There would be no US-Israel military deal during the Rafah invasion. After that invasion had succeeded, Gallant sensed another chance to secure the US arms the IDF needed. He planned a visit to Washington for June 25–26, 2024. He had arguments ready, including reassurances about how Israel would use America's large Mark 84 bombs, but the results in Rafah did most of the talking. Biden's Middle East envoy Brett McGurk, perhaps the most pro-Israel official in the administration, told Gallant he would succeed at finalizing the deal on his visit to Washington. "Don't buy a plane ticket to fly back," he said. "You can go back on the boat bringing the weapons with you."

During a June 16 visit to Israel by US envoy Amos Hochstein, Gallant again understood that the deal was on track. On June 18, Israeli Minister Dermer and National Security Council chief Hanegbi flew to

Washington for high-level meetings. Afterward, they also told Gallant that the deal was proceeding apace.

"Then the video of Netanyahu attacking Biden came out," Gallant related to us, still with a look of disbelief. In an English-language video released by Netanyahu on June 18, 2024, the prime minister explained that Biden was holding up more than the one shipment of two-thousand-pound bombs.

"It's inconceivable that in the past few months, the administration has been withholding weapons and ammunitions to Israel—America's closest ally, fighting for its life, fighting against Iran and our other common enemies," Netanyahu said, just as Gallant was close to nailing down a deal to fix the situation.

Gallant was not the only one gobsmacked. "The White House called me and said, 'We wanted to give you the bombs, but now we can't give them to you,'" he recounted. The insult and the optics made it more difficult. Israel's defense minister started to argue, insisting that regardless of the politics, Israel needed the weapons.

Shared national interests would ultimately prevail. Gallant flew to Washington and met with McGurk, Hochstein, Blinken, and, finally, Austin. "With Austin I closed the whole deal—except for the Mark 84. This was the heaviest bomb. I wanted another day because Sullivan was preparing with Biden at Camp David" for the now-famous US presidential debate. This was the embarrassing failure that would lead Biden to drop out of the race after an agonizing month of criticism. Gallant spoke with Sullivan on July 26.

"What about the Mark 84?" Gallant asked.

Sullivan complained that Netanyahu had also sent two additional tweets attacking Biden on top of the video, Gallant said. It had come down to tweets.

"Listen," Gallant said, "you understand this. The bombs and the airplanes—this is defensive and not just offensive." There was no way but serious air power for Israel to reach Iran, Yemen, and deep into Lebanon or Syria to deter its enemies.

Finally, Sullivan relented. "What do you need?" he asked.

Gallant and the IDF high command asked for the bombs to be based in Israel. This was the crux of the deal: The US would base the bombs in Israel, but Israel could not use them without US permission. It allowed the Biden administration to keep possession of the heavy bombs, so it could say it was not handing them over to Israel, while also making them readily available to Israel should it truly need them. It was an elegant workaround. Sullivan signed off and "we got the weapons to Israel," said Gallant. If not for his personal relationships with Austin and Sullivan, their distrust of and anger at Netanyahu as well as their criticism of the number of Palestinian casualties might have left Israel lacking for critical weapons.

Weapons pauses and delays would reappear on and off through the rest of the Biden administration. This was partly due to real policy disputes between Israel and the US, but partly, according to Gallant and US officials, because Netanyahu continued to frustrate and undermine Biden diplomatically and politically. The prime minister disagreed with Biden on policy and felt he needed to press Israel's case. He also hoped to delay as many major policy decisions as possible to the next presidential term. Should Trump be elected, Netanyahu expected terms he would find more favorable.

The prime minister also frustrated Gallant. In October, Netanyahu would cancel his defense minister's already scheduled flight to Washington to prevent him from taking additional credit for improving US–Israel relations. That was supposed to be one of Netanyahu's calling cards. But after all their disputes, this White House no longer wanted to speak to him.

CHAPTER EIGHT

ISRAEL VS. IRAN—OUT OF THE SHADOWS

On April 14, 2024, Israel's two-front war with Hamas and Hezbollah suddenly exploded into a three-front war. Amid the fierce debate about whether to invade Rafah, Iran attacked Israel with some 170 drones, more than 110 ballistic missiles, and dozens of cruise missiles. One of the largest single drone and ballistic missile assaults in military history, this was an act of aggression that permanently altered the Middle East.

Unlike Hamas or Hezbollah, Iran does not share a border with Israel. Sitting more than one thousand miles away, Israel for years had no dispute with Iran at all. But since the 1979 Islamic Revolution, the ayatollahs who took power in Iran have been virulently hostile toward the US, which it calls the "Great Satan," and Israel, which it calls the "Little Satan."

Until this point, though, Tehran and Jerusalem had engaged in a shadow war, one that had been going on for forty-five years with little fundamental change. Both sides preferred to kill each other's operatives and destroy each other's assets through proxies or their own clandestine services. This preserved plausible deniability and avoided a direct confrontation that would have unpredictable consequences.

Why did this enduring pattern break down? One reason is that each party became too successful at its own mode of operation. The Islamic Republic achieved "too much" on October 7, 2023, via its junior proxy Hamas. But this Iranian "success" awakened the sleeping Israeli giant, shifting it from the limited retaliations of the past against Hamas to a far more aggressive strategy that sought to overthrow the terrorists running Gaza. Both Gaza City and Khan Yunis, Hamas's northern and southern capitals, were not merely subdued by the IDF. They were destroyed.

Hezbollah, Iran's most powerful proxy in its campaign to destroy the Jewish state, had fired rockets, missiles, and mortars at Israel since October 8, 2023. Hezbollah began to feel the change in the Jewish state's temperament that December, when Israel started to rout its forces in southern Lebanon. But in a way, this only increased the frustration among Israel's leaders that Iran had managed to inflict on Israel a two-front war without suffering any direct consequence. Everyone knew that Hamas and Hezbollah were armed, trained, and funded by Iran to menace Israel. Would the proxy strategy again be allowed to grant Iran immunity?

Not this time, Israel decided. In December 2023, the Israeli Air Force assassinated Sayyed Reza Mousavi, a senior Islamic Revolutionary Guard Corps commander, in an air strike near Damascus, according to foreign sources. In general, Israel started to increase its attacks on IRGC officials traveling to Syria, a key hub for the proxy war on Israel. On April 1, 2024, Israel took out Mohammed Reza Zahedi, the top commander in the IRGC's Quds Force for Lebanon and Syria, in an air strike on Damascus. Zahedi had also commanded the Quds Force's Unit 1800, which is responsible for smuggling ammunition and precision weapons into Lebanon. That went to the heart of Hezbollah's war effort.

Israel had kept silent on its responsibility for such occasional targeted assassinations of Iranians in Syria, and in the past, Iran's leader Ayatollah Khamenei had used that silence as an excuse not to take direct retaliatory action. This was how the game worked. But the killing of Zahedi, the manager of the Syrian and Lebanese proxy fronts for Iran, was a bridge too far. Khamenei needed revenge.

Iranian media reported that Zahedi had been meeting with leaders of Islamic Jihad, another Iranian terror proxy, at the time of the strike. According to later Israeli accounts—once the IDF eventually admitted to the strike—the Air Force had targeted a building adjacent to the Iranian embassy. But this was not the narrative presented to the world. The world heard that Israel had hit part of the Iranian embassy complex itself. Some reports at the time indicated that the building targeted had served as the residence for the Iranian ambassador to Damascus and was very close to Canada's embassy as well.

Herzi Halevi, the IDF chief, admitted that the IDF and the Mossad had misjudged the situation. "Netanyahu and the other senior cabinet members throughout the war told me they did not want to accidentally drag Iran into the war," he confided to other IDF officers.

Sources close to the Mossad sought to distance it from responsibility. "The [IDF] plan for the location of the assassination did not mention anything about the embassy of Iran. The Mossad saw that only afterward. The analytical assessment of potential scenarios could have been different if there had been information connecting it to the Iranian embassy," one source told us. "This was a fundamental error."

These intelligence sources focused not on whether the building was diplomatic in the formal sense, but on how the activities it hosted would cause the world to perceive it as diplomatic. Had the Mossad known this beforehand, it likely would have nixed the attack, in its telling.

Halevi was not having it. "After time had passed since the killing" of General Zahedi, he recounted to other military officers, "Dadi [Barnea, the Mossad director] said, 'I don't know if there were enough dapaot'"—contingencies listed in the prestrike IDF intelligence documents. Halevi responded to him, "You supported it, don't try to wriggle out'" of responsibility now.

We can reveal that the Israeli miscalculation was shared across the board and involved an inability to imagine an Iranian reaction larger than a counterattack against an Israeli embassy. On March 20, 2024, several senior and midlevel IDF and Mossad intelligence officials attended a planning meeting for the targeted strike, we can also disclose. Among the Mossad representatives were those with analytical responsibility for Iran as well as for Canada, suggesting that the Mossad understood the sensitivity of the target.

We can further disclose that there was a PowerPoint presentation at the meeting that showed the target location was close to the Iranian and the Canadian embassies, meaning it was enclosed with highly sensitive sites on both sides. At the time, the scenarios offered by the Mossad and the IDF for Iran's potential reactions to the strike were nearly identical.

Offering a rare explanation of the secretly discussed contingencies, Halevi said the prestrike dapaot by IDF Intelligence and the Mossad included a medium-to-high probability of a proportionate retaliation. The agencies thought Syria might fire some rockets or drones at Israel. These secret assessments from IDF intelligence and the Mossad also said there was a medium-to-low probability of Iran launching drones directly, which Israel could handle.

On March 21, Halevi gave his final approval. On March 22, Netanyahu gave his final approval at a meeting not only with Halevi and top IDF intelligence officials, but also including Barnea and the Mossad's top official for analysis. Again, the IDF and Mossad predictions regarding Iran's response were essentially the same.

But most decisively, on April 1, the same day as the strike, Barnea attended the first poststrike meeting of senior defense officials. He told the attendees that the whole world knew the airstrike took place close to the Iranian embassy, and that there was already evidence that Iran was trying to pretend this was its official consulate. The Mossad chief praised the Air Force and IDF intelligence for an impressive operation, adding that the latest dapaot estimate was that Iran's response would be more dangerous than some of the lowest prestrike estimates, but still not that high risk, perhaps attempting to attack an Israeli embassy someplace. Even attacking an Israeli embassy was not likely, Barnea said. That was probably the worst-case scenario, but Israel should look into it and be ready for changes.

All of this information makes it appear that the Mossad knew what IDF intelligence knew and had very similar views about the expected blowback from Iran both before the attack and in its first analysis after the attack. This would mean that the Mossad's narrative that it did not have the necessary information to properly advise on the issue would come only later.

Halevi clarified that the IDF gave the Mossad accurate information. "We didn't say 'embassy' because it wasn't the embassy. Nor was it a consulate. In the land records of Damascus itself, it was not listed as a diplomatic building," Halevi said.

Gallant concurred: The building had no flag. Afterward, Halevi said, the Iranians tried to put a flag there, but they knew the truth.

Even so, why did most of the world see it that way? The side of the building was adjacent to an Iranian diplomatic building. According to Halevi's version of events, because they were so close by, the Iranians sometimes used the second building, where Israel struck, to have more office space. Sometimes, the Iranian ambassador had even slept there. Israel's misunderstanding, sources indicated, was to believe it mattered that the Iranians had ceased sleeping in the building for some time. Tehran viewed it as every bit a diplomatic building nevertheless.

For three weeks, the IDF tried to clarify which floor and room Zahedi would be in, but it did not succeed. This meant the Air Force needed to use a larger munition. Pressed on why it was necessary to kill such a high-ranking Iranian official in the first place, Halevi explained to other officers that Iran was pushing the Syrians to fire more on Israel directly from Syrian territory, and that Israel wanted to stop that trend. In trying to deter attacks from Syria, then, Israel ended up escalating with Iran directly. But it did not know that at the time.

"After the fact, Iran immediately claimed it was an embassy and told this to the leader, Khamenei," misleading Iran's top decision-maker, Halevi has said. The IDF chief believes this changed everything. Ayatollah Khamenei does not often travel outside his palaces and command centers and relies on a small coterie of advisers to receive updates about the world. Had the ayatollah known that Israel had merely hit overflow rooms from the embassy, rather than the embassy itself, he might not have responded the same way.

If the ayatollah was misinformed, he wasn't alone. "Some of the top American officials really think it was the embassy and view Iran's claim as authentic," another senior IDF official told us.

Halevi, however, swears by his finding: "We know it was not a diplomatic building. If it was," he said, "I would not even have suggested the attack to the cabinet." To the IDF chief's regret, however, "fake news succeeded in Iran and in the US." Iran pressed the theme so hard that most top US officials, even in private, have told us they believe Israel struck an Iranian diplomatic compound.

The misinformation given to Khamenei led him to order the first-ever massive direct attack on Israel late on the night of April 13, 2024, and early in the morning of April 14. The decision stunned the Mossad and IDF Intelligence, which consider it their second-largest miss of the war, following only October 7, 2023. Indeed, IDF intelligence chief Aharon Haliva was shown the door later in April 2024 not because of the initial failure of October 7, which he had somehow weathered, but because he also underestimated Khamenei's response in mid-April. He would remain in office for a few more months, but his fate was sealed.

* * *

The US secretary of defense was furious. In Austin's view, Israel was obfuscating the significance of what it had done. He either did not accept Israel's story about the building or he thought Jerusalem was standing on a technicality that ignored what mattered: Diplomats used the building; therefore, Israel had broken the rules of the game. Austin told Gallant that the Iranians would now up the ante, and he was right. Khamenei would transform the Iranian–Israeli conflict.

Halevi's first call to the US on April 1, 2024, was to General Erik Kurilla, the chief of US Central Command. Kurilla saw the threat coming from Iran, for which Halevi gives him significant credit. Halevi warned the US general apologetically that his itinerary for the week was about to change. Contrary to preattack assessments, there was now intelligence that Iran was going to attack Israel very broadly, Halevi said. Israel and the US would need to activate all their regional relationships to defend against the threat.

On April 3, while Halevi was working with Kurilla, Gallant started to press Austin and Sullivan to form the multinational air-defense coalition that would help defend Israel. "To establish deterrence," Gallant said, US messaging also had to dovetail more with Israel's position. Iran needed to hear that Israel was not on its own—a message undermined substantially by Israel's mistaken attack a few days earlier on the World Central Kitchen aid convoy in Gaza and the ferocious US criticism that followed.

In the wake of the WCK strike, President Biden threatened to withdraw support for Israel's war effort unless it made certain substantial changes. Forty House Democrats, including Representative Nancy Pelosi, called on the president to cut off offensive weapons to Israel on April 5. By April 8, their ranks had swelled to fifty-six, including several Biden allies.

On April 9, New York Representative Gregory Meeks, the ranking Democrat on the Foreign Affairs Committee, accused Israel of "indiscriminate bombing" and threatened to block a weapons sale. That same day, Univision aired an interview in which the president seemed to call for a unilateral Israeli ceasefire, without mentioning the hostages.[52] The unintended signal to Iran, Netanyahu and others feared, was that the US was turning against Israel. That would be a green light for Iran to launch a larger attack.

The message got through to the Biden administration. "Our commitment to Israel's security against these threats from Iran and its proxies is ironclad," Biden announced on April 10. "Let me say it again: ironclad. We're going to do all we can to protect Israel's security." Secretary of State Blinken conveyed a similar message to Gallant, and General Kurilla traveled to Israel on April 11 to coordinate defenses.

Gallant would speak to Austin again on April 4, 9, 13, and 14 to prepare Israel's response should Iran strike hard. On April 9, Gallant also spoke to Blinken, and a separate message was sent directly to Biden just "to be clear." Halevi was constantly on the phone with top military officials on April 11 and 12 as the rushed alliance was formed leading up to Iran's April 14 attack.

Halevi and Gallant had made a clever argument to Austin and Kurilla. If the two Americans wanted to restrain Israel from a major counterattack on Iran, they would have to help give the Jewish state a nearly hermetic defense. If they did not, and if Israel took a pounding, the IDF would have to respond to Iran with greater force. That escalation was the last thing the Biden administration wanted. Washington wanted peace, but it would settle for quiet.

Hours before Iran's attack, Halevi and other military chiefs had already ordered hundreds of aircraft into the sky in preparation. When the ayatollah took his shot, Israel and an extraordinary group of American, European, and Arab allies helped block him from killing any Israelis. But this should not obscure the authentic terror that seized the Israeli nation when, around 1 a.m. on the morning of April 14, more than 110 ballistic missiles sped toward them from Iran, joining the hundreds of drones and dozens of cruise missiles already on their way.

It was unclear both in Israel and at the White House how the story would end. Austin sat with Biden, watching Iran's attack play out on the Situation Room screen. Initially, Austin told the president that the coalition defenses for Israel would hold. But this was when they detected a mere thirty ballistic missiles launched by Iran. When those numbers were multiplied, Austin was less reassuring.[53] October 7 had shown that Israel's "perfect" defense structure had gaping holes. What if Iran's attack would reveal another?

Interceptors raced to meet Iranian missiles, colliding and exploding in the night sky with precious little time to spare. It was an irresistible pyrotechnic show watched not only by Israelis, as the sky lit up above their heads, but by people all over the world on social media. As it turned out, Israel and its allies were able to shoot down 99 percent of Iran's rockets, missiles, and drones. This was an astounding success. A ferocious Iranian punch had been parried, leaving the regime humiliated—and vulnerable. All Iran managed to hit was a seven-year-old Bedouin

Arab–Israeli girl, Amina Hassouna, who was seriously injured by shrapnel from an interception in southern Israel.[54]

Gallant said Iran fired around three hundred aerial threats at Israel, Hezbollah another one hundred, and Yemeni and Iraqi militias fifty more. "There was an impact on the Israeli side of Mount Hermon in the north, four impacts at the Nevatim Air Force base in the south, and one ballistic missile landed near the Dead Sea," Gallant said, but "they did not hit anything important." Netanyahu and Gallant lauded the US military and intelligence cooperation, with the latter noting that General Kurilla personally may have been the US official most essential to Israel's defense.

The defensive coalition, Gallant said, "was built by the Americans to include England, France, Jordan, and other countries"—the latter being a code for the Saudis, according to foreign sources. A habit formed by years of caution and excessive sensitivity, Israelis still do not explicitly say the Saudis participated, even though Riyadh outed itself in the global media. Though Riyadh held out for additional concessions before there could be any official normalization of relations with Israel, according to foreign sources, it allowed the coalition to use its airspace to shoot down Iran's missiles and drones in the early morning.

* * *

After Iran's assault failed to kill even a single Israeli, President Biden immediately told Netanyahu that Israel should "take the win" and urged him not to attack Iran at all in response. US military officials told Halevi the same. Sullivan, the US national security advisor, told us that "the president was absolutely very direct to Bibi, very robust on this."

"I was not taking a sharper line than anybody else. This was really coming from the president," Sullivan added. Biden "insisted on calling Bibi that night [April 14] and laying it down hard. He told us, 'Don't back off of that.' None of us did," Sullivan said.

"It's not a win," Netanyahu told them in reply. "We were attacked. We have to respond." That Iran did not kill Israelis did not mean it hadn't tried to, crossing all kinds of lines.

The Biden team feared that any Israeli retaliation would draw the US deeper into the Middle East quagmire. For Biden, who in April 2024 was still very much in the presidential race, a wider regional war was seen as dangerous for international stability and for his electoral chances. The war had already split his Democratic Party base; for him, there was only downside.

De-escalation had been the Biden approach to Iran throughout his time in office. That was Plan A, noted Mark Dubowitz, the CEO of the Foundation for Defense of Democracies (FDD). It had failed as Iran rejected all overtures for a nuclear deal and pocketed a substantial increase in oil sales after Biden relaxed US sanctions enforcement. "But there is no Plan B from the administration," Dubowitz told us after the April 2024 attack. He said the Biden administration believed instead in what it called "CBMs," meaning confidence-building measures—the "off-ramps, incentives, deference approach to Iran."

After many phone calls back and forth, Gallant told Austin that Israel could not survive in the Middle East by standing down. The only question up for debate, he said, was how broad or narrow Israel's counter-attack would be. Austin, however, did not let up at this stage, continuing to oppose even a de minimis Israeli strike. Gallant told us this showed that Austin still lacked a deeper understanding of the Middle East. Whereas the Pentagon chief portrayed Iran's attack as a carefully calibrated counterpunch to Israel's crossing of the line at the Syrian embassy, Gallant considered it a major and reckless act of war.

It was also an attempt by Iran to lay down new rules to the game. "Henceforth," General Hossein Salami, the head of Iran's IRGC, said on April 12, "any assault by the Zionist regime on our people, property, or interests will trigger a reciprocal response originating from within the Islamic Republic of Iran."[55]

Biden, meanwhile, confided in Austin, Sullivan, and his other top aides that he knew Israel was going to act. He figured, however, that he could reduce the ferocity of Israel's counterstrike by arguing that it should not retaliate at all. This view explains Austin's subsequent attempts to pressure Israel into a symbolic response, one that would show off Israel's military advantages without killing Iranians. The US defense secretary understood that Israel had a national policy in many such situations of "having the last word." A symbolic response could do that while limiting Israel's risk of blowback, Austin explained to Gallant.

But coming as it all did after Israel's strikes on Zahedi and the WCK aid workers, Austin thought Israel was spiraling out of control. The defense secretary's priority was to avoid a regional war, but he had now counted multiple instances in which he believed Israel could have tamped down dangerous situations and instead chose to escalate them. Austin thought that whenever Israel saw a "tactical military window of opportunity," it seized it, thinking only later about the fallout.

Israel, however, was determined to break out of the "October 6 mindset." This was the way it used to push off responding to threats before Hamas's October 7 attack. To learn the lesson of October 7, 2023, many ordinary Israelis felt, Israel had to reject the Biden administration's advice after April 14, 2024.

Before Iran's attack, Gallant had conveyed the same message to Austin, Sullivan, and McGurk. "I was clear to them that if Israel is hit hard, we will respond harshly. We will weigh our reaction based on two issues: the intensity of the attack and the actual harm caused," he said.

Austin asked Gallant, "Why does intent have any relevance? Just look at the result."

Gallant responded with an analogy. "If a person drives through a red light at an intersection, they receive a punishment, a fine, or a judgment. An action was undertaken," he said. "If they also happen to crash, that is an aggravating factor," which makes the punishment harsher. "What business do they have with us anyway from 1,500 kilometers away?"

Gallant's compromise idea for a retaliation was to destroy Iran's Russian-made S-300 air-defense system in Isfahan, which protected its key Natanz and Isfahan nuclear sites. This would send Iran a serious message, exposing the vulnerability of its most sensitive assets without actually striking them. It would also send a message to Russia, both to avoid wasting its technology on Iran, where it could be embarrassed, and to be concerned that in any potential conflict with the West, beyond

Ukraine, it would be outmatched. Austin believed the attack on the S-300 was quite bold, as symbolic attacks went.

As the Israeli military saw it, Iran had made a strategic mistake. "It came out from behind its proxies," one official told us. This exposed the true nature of the war against Israel—it was waged by the Iranian axis, not by the Palestinians alone or by any individual proxy.

* * *

There were Israelis such as Barnea, the Mossad chief, who seemed to want broader action against Iran. Others, like IDF chief Halevi, wanted to retaliate in a restrained fashion. "Dadi [Barnea] can always repeat his mantra, 'We should destroy Iran,'" Halevi has said, but should the Iranians fire a massive number of ballistic missiles at Israel, responsibility for defense would fall to the IDF. Sources close to the Mossad told us that Barnea had hoped for a strong Israeli response, but always qualified this with the need to secure US support.

That is not how Halevi saw it. He needed to be the grown-up in the room, but also needed to be cunning and sophisticated. "King Saul pursued King David and got very close to him, but David turned the tables and caught Saul by surprise, even cutting off a corner of his cloak and handing it back to Saul as a clear message: I could have killed you, but I decided not to," the IDF chief offered by way of analogy. According to Halevi, this was the Israeli approach with Iran in April 2024: Hit something that will hurt, but without humiliating the Iranians, which might cause them to retaliate again even harder. By attacking the S-300, Israel made sure Iran understood that Israel can attack it anywhere, both Gallant and Halevi explained.

If one debate was the diplomatic clash between Gallant and Austin, and another was the operational clash between Halevi and Barnea, the third was a strategic debate inside Israel's war room. Here, everyone wanted to respond to Iran, but there was still a dispute over how far to go. Gallant argued that if Jerusalem attacked too lightly, it risked encouraging Iran to try again with another wave of drones and ballistic missiles. Gantz warned that if Israel attacked too aggressively, it risked inviting greater retaliation from Iran and Hezbollah, which could do immense damage to Israel if it attacked in full force along with its Iranian master.

Netanyahu initially took Gantz's position, but over a few days, he became convinced of Gallant's point of view. Gallant told the war cabinet that this could not be a normal "response to a response" that would be lost in the long line of moves and countermoves, as if nothing fundamental had changed. Iran had fired over 110 ballistic missiles at Israel out of around 2,500 in its arsenal. Unless Israel wanted this to become a new normal, it needed Iran to feel a "biting response." He emphasized that Tehran had carried out not "just another terror attack," but "an act of war."

Gallant and Netanyahu outvoted Gantz two to one. The stronger of the "symbolic" attacks would go forward. Despite initial Biden administration opposition, Gallant eventually got a green light from Washington to retaliate against Iran.

The attack came on April 19, when Israel fired long-range missiles from outside Iranian airspace. Iran's loss was significant; the S-300 was the most advanced antiaircraft system the Islamic Republic possessed, having spent years pressing Russia to sell it. "We also could have hit Iranian aerial threats," such as aircraft and drones, Gallant added, but "we carried out a precise strike on the radar unit of the S-300 in the heart of Iran at Isfahan, next to the airport. They still don't know how it happened, but they saw the hits." Halevi said that the Iranians were very cautious after Israel struck the S-300 on April 19. "Even on July 30, almost four months later, when the Mossad killed [Hamas Politburo chief Ismail] Haniyeh in a key IRGC facility in the heart of Tehran, they waited and did not retaliate."

While the attack damaged Iran's prized radar system that protected its largest uranium-enrichment site at Natanz and its key sites for weaponizing enriched uranium at Isfahan, it did not directly touch Iran's nuclear program or fundamentally alter the Middle East's balance of power. Though Israel demonstrated that it possessed aerial overmatch—both offensive and defensive superiority—both sides soon returned to their proxy wars. The quiet wouldn't last for long.

CHAPTER NINE

FROM BEIRUT TO TEHRAN TO GAZA

Almost as quickly as it had been diverted, the focus of Israel's war would return to Hamas. One of Israel's primary wartime missions was to hunt down and kill the leaders who had masterminded the brutal October 7 attack. This took time, but one after another, across the Middle East, top terrorists would meet their end at Israel's hands.

Hamas deputy chief Saleh al-Arouri was the first to go. The targeted strike on al-Arouri, a prelude of sorts to the even bigger fish who would follow, came out of the blue on January 2, 2024. He was visiting Beirut to meet with Hezbollah leader Hassan Nasrallah. The Mossad, IDF intelligence, and the Israeli Air Force carefully tracked al-Arouri's travels from his home base in Turkey.

Al-Arouri thought he was too senior to be targeted, especially while visiting Hezbollah's capital city. Israeli Hellfire missiles showed otherwise, eliminating al-Arouri along with six other Hamas comrades. No civilians are believed to have been killed in the attack. After October 7, Mossad chief David Barnea had vowed publicly to hunt down every last person involved in the mass slaughter of Israelis—just as the Mossad had done with the Palestinian terrorists who planned the 1972 Munich massacre of Israeli Olympic athletes. No Hamas leader was safe.

* * *

The next to die would be Mohammed Deif, Hamas's legendary military commander who seemed to have nine lives. He had already survived more than half a dozen Israeli assassination attempts, most recently in 2021. On one occasion, an Israeli missile struck the room he was in but only managed to wound him. He had happened to be in a tiny part of the room that was shielded just enough by surrounding objects and nearby cracking walls to allow him to survive.

Deif had been military chief several years before Yahya Sinwar took overall command of Hamas in Gaza. At minimum, Deif was the terrorist group's number-two man. Seemingly invincible, he was the ultimate symbol of Hamas resilience.

Born as Mohammad Masri in 1965 in the Khan Yunis refugee camp, Deif gained his nom de guerre after joining Hamas during the First Intifada, or Palestinian uprising, of 1987–1991. Israel arrested him in 1989 for Hamas involvement and Deif spent about sixteen months in jail.[56] Promoted up the ranks of Hamas over the course of thirty years, Deif had developed the group's network of tunnels and its bomb-making expertise. Jerusalem held him responsible for the murders of dozens of Israelis in suicide bombings. For years, he topped Israel's most-wanted list.

Israel believed that Deif had lost an eye and that one of his legs was seriously injured in prior assassination attempts. During the war, IDF intelligence would find videos of Deif to confirm this, though his legs were not as injured as they had thought. While Deif escaped time and again, the people around him were not so fortunate. His wife, seven-month-old son, and three-year-old daughter had been killed in an Israeli air strike in 2014. Deif, the strike's target, had put them in the line of fire.[57]

If Yahya Sinwar was the mastermind of October 7, and the one with the idea to provoke a multifront war against Israel, Deif was the one responsible for the plan's practical and military success.

Deif was fifty-eight years old on October 7, but the near mythic hero had rarely spoken to the public. When Hamas's TV channel gave a preview on October 7 that Deif would be speaking soon, Palestinians knew it would be no ordinary day. As Hamas fired thousands of rockets at

Israel, it broadcast an audio recording in which Deif dubbed the Hamas invasion the "al-Aqsa Flood." He framed the attack as retaliation for Israeli police raids at Jerusalem's al-Aqsa Mosque, though those raids had been temporary and practical, aimed at bringing rioting at the mosque under control. "Today," Deif told the nation, "the rage of al-Aqsa, the rage of our people and nation, is exploding. Our mujahideen," or holy warriors, "today is your day to make this criminal understand that his time is over."

In the months after the massacre, Israel could not follow Deif's movements as he continued to direct military operations from the vast tunnels and backstreets of Gaza. After Israel took over Rafah following the May 2024 invasion, however, Deif's network of available tunnels shrunk. By early July 2024, Israeli intelligence was finally able to track him down.

Israel was also tracking one of Deif's top deputies, Rafa'a Salameh, the chief of Hamas's Khan Yunis Brigade, who was hiding in the Mawasi humanitarian zone along the coast. Deif was slippery, however, and it took weeks until Israeli intelligence could determine that he was due to visit Salameh, including a short time above ground. While Salameh was regularly at al-Mawasi, using the displaced civilians as cover, Deif came rarely and briefly. Some Israeli officials thought he had come out of the tunnels this time only as a medical necessity; life underground was rough given his many health issues.

IDF intelligence and the Shin Bet had only hours to act on highly precise intelligence tracking Deif's location when he showed up in the humanitarian zone. He would be in an open area surrounded by trees, buildings, and low sheds, with tunnels close by but not in the immediate vicinity. Israeli Air Force chief Tomer Bar revealed to us that he kept five pairs of aircraft and drones on rotation to hover or pass by the residence where Deif was expected to visit Salameh. This way, the moment the war cabinet approved an operation, the Air Force would be ready to open fire.

On July 13, in broad daylight, the Air Force fired eight to ten missiles, some of which weighed two thousand pounds, at the location of

Deif and Salameh's meeting. Hours later, the IDF announced it had attempted to kill the two, and soon after, it confirmed Salameh's death. The outcome with Deif was unclear because the attack had been carried out from long range, the line of sight was obscured, and there were dozens of other casualties in the mix. The IDF estimated that most of those killed were Hamas terrorists, but it didn't deny the possibility that a significant number could have been civilians. Later, some IDF officials said that as many as seventy civilians may have been killed. The IDF high command, IDF legal division, and Israeli security cabinet deemed Deif important enough to justify that. It was thought that his killing could save many times that number of lives in the future.[58]

Such calculations, however, are no consolation to the families of those regular Gazans who lost their lives. They can blame Israel, which fired the missiles and so many others like them, or blame their Hamas leaders, who started the war and held the meeting in the humanitarian zone. But for the civilians, there is precious little justice to be found. They would pay so much of the war's terrible price.

The IDF knew Deif was in the room with Salameh when the bombs struck, but it would not be until nearly three weeks later, on August 1, 2024, that IDF intelligence confirmed Deif's death. Hamas would not own up to Deif's death until months later, on January 30, 2025.

Yossi Kuperwasser, the former chief of analysis for IDF intelligence, told us that Deif's killing could have an even greater strategic effect than the killings of archterrorists like Hezbollah military commander Imad Mughniyeh (2008) or Iranian Quds Force commander Qassem Soleimani (2020). Every terrorist gets replaced eventually, but in the case of Deif, Kuperwasser said, Hamas was already in danger of being permanently reduced to a fledgling existence. By July 2024, Hamas had lost the vast majority of its battalion commanders, three of its five brigade commanders, and most of its top rocket and drone commanders. Deif's two closest deputies were dead, and none of his successors were viewed by Israeli intelligence as anywhere near as formidable and creative an adversary. Deif was needed more than ever to train and shape a new generation of commanders.

Former IDF intelligence chief Tamir Hayman, the head of Israel's Institute for National Security Studies, had for months urged a deal with Hamas to free hostages, even at the price of freezing the war indefinitely. But he told us stridently that killing Deif, the man who made the October 7 invasion a success, was a strategic imperative separate and above all other considerations.

* * *

Israel hunted its next target in the Hamas leadership more than a thousand miles away from Gaza. Ismail Haniyeh had crafted the strategy for Hamas's takeover of Gaza and led it in the Strip from 2007 to 2017. At that time, he handed off his position to Sinwar and took the much more comfortable role of Hamas Politburo chairman. Haniyeh's was a long terror career, in which it was always someone else's turn to put on the suicide vest. Living outside Gaza, mostly in Qatari and Turkish hotels, Haniyeh became responsible for Hamas's foreign relations as well as its fundraising and long-term direction. This more political role, as opposed to the active military roles of Sinwar and Deif, was thought to provide him protection. He strutted about in suits and acted the statesman, meeting with foreign officials and publishing statements.

None of that could save him. Death arrived for Haniyeh early on the morning of July 31, 2024, during his visit to Tehran to celebrate the inauguration of Iran's new president, Masoud Pezeshkian. Haniyeh stayed in one of Iran's most secure Islamic Revolutionary Guard Corps facilities for visiting dignitaries, a location he had frequented many times. It was the guesthouse in a large compound called Neshat, located in a high-end neighborhood in northern Tehran. If Israel could reach him here, in the safest spot in the capital of its greatest enemy, nowhere was safe.

Unfortunately for Haniyeh, the Mossad had infiltrated the top ranks of the IRGC and, according to foreign reports, knew that its safe house was his favorite place to stay. This provided Israel's assassins a clear target for which to plan. In June 2024, agents had concealed a small, highly customized bomb in the room where Haniyeh would stay. The bomb was waiting for him when he arrived in July.

Mossad chief David Barnea is fascinated with cutting-edge technological solutions, such as the remote-controlled machine gun that reportedly was used in the 2020 assassination of Iranian nuclear chief Mohsen Fakhrizadeh. Israel used some similar remote-controlled technology with Haniyeh. The bomb was set to go off the night Haniyeh showed up, and it was developed to kill only him, not harming a single additional person in the nearby rooms. This is contrary to the rumors initially circulated that the attack had occurred by drone strike. The IRGC or its allies had hoped this narrative could shift some responsibility for the failure onto other Iranian military bodies, with which it competes domestically for resources and prestige.

While Iran immediately blamed the Mossad for the assassination, Israeli leaders initially kept silent. Israel wanted to avoid or limit escalation with Iran, and to make it clear that Haniyeh was targeted in Tehran only because he was a Hamas leader tainted by the October 7 attack, not because Israel was trying to challenge Iran on its soil. It would be six months, when Israeli officials were trying to intimidate the Houthis of Yemen to stop their attacks on the Jewish state, until Jerusalem finally took responsibility for having killed Haniyeh. In admitting what everybody already knew, Israel sought to make clear to the Houthis that even their highest officials would not have immunity if they continued to fire on Israel.

International press coverage of the attack on Haniyeh, which demonstrated Israel's breathtaking intelligence mastery in Tehran, was strangely fixated on the idea that Haniyeh had been a "moderate," and therefore his killing made a hostage deal less likely.[59] But multiple Israeli defense sources, including those usually critical of Netanyahu, agreed with him in this case that Haniyeh's removal could make a hostage deal more likely. The politburo chief had become more hardline in negotiations over time, they said, holding out for unrealistic terms.

US National Security Advisor Jake Sullivan and Defense Secretary Lloyd Austin, however, thought that Israel's killing of Haniyeh wrecked trust between Israeli and Hamas negotiators anew, making it much harder to reach a new hostage deal. Sullivan was heavily critical of Netanyahu, whom he believed to have thwarted a hostage deal to keep his right-wing coalition partners on board.

But Sullivan told us the primary blame for the lack of a deal in this period did not fall on the prime minister.

"Hamas was not really available to do a deal until the end of 2024," Sullivan said. "Then, when they were ready to do it," they kept sending mixed signals. "Neither Bibi nor Hamas were really that motivated to do it. But Hamas never came out and said, 'Let's go, here we go,' leaving Bibi to say no. That point never arrived. What's missing in this whole debate" about Netanyahu and his political interests, Sullivan told us, "is just how intransigent Hamas" was. He noted that Netanyahu had been ready to cut a deal for the hostages in May 2024, but Hamas had refused.

"August was more complicated. We had a window in August, and potentially could have landed it. But the killing of [dual US–Israeli citizen] Hersh [Goldberg-Polin] and the other hostages," by Hamas, "and the killing of Haniyeh—that period kind of crystalized the challenges," Sullivan said. Real opportunities were disrupted by actions on both sides. "Hamas was finally negotiating" for real, an exasperated Sullivan told us, "but they still never produced an actual list of hostages or prisoners to be released." Israeli officials were split on this question of whether Hamas was even open to a hostage deal in the summer of 2024. The uncertainty was maddening, but this was what negotiating with terrorists was like.

* * *

The story of the Haniyeh assassination, in the early hours of July 31, 2024, cannot be told without also telling the story of Hezbollah military chief Fuad Shukr, who was assassinated just hours earlier on the evening of July 30. This one-two punch changed the course of the war.

Hezbollah had joined the war on Israel on October 8, 2023, with rockets, missiles, and mortars. These were steady, low-level attacks that added up. In April 2024, the IDF counted some three thousand one hundred rockets that had crossed the Lebanese border into Israel over the preceding six months. These attacks intensified in May and June, and July 4 saw Hezbollah fire two hundred rockets and twenty drones after an Israeli targeted strike killed senior commander Mohammad Naameh Nasser. Slowly but surely, the war was heating up.

The Shukr killing, a precision air strike on an apartment building in the Haret Hreik neighborhood of Beirut, came in response to a Hezbollah missile attack on Israel three days earlier, which had killed twelve Druze Arab children. The missile had hit a soccer pitch near a playground in the town of Majdal Shams on the Israeli Golan Heights. Israelis were stunned, demanding action in defense of the Druze, a minority with strong communities in northern Israel and across the border in southern Lebanon and Syria.

Shukr was not only the commander responsible for the attack on Majdal Shams, but also Nasrallah's right-hand man and the primary architect of Hezbollah's military strategy. Those twelve Druze children would be his last victims. Shukr's death removed one of Hezbollah's most capable military figures, who had the ear of top officials in Iran's IRGC. It also sent a stark message to Hezbollah: If you kill Israelis—of any kind—the IDF will no longer shy away from killing your top leaders deep inside your capital.

Born in 1961 or 1962, Shukr spent his adult life rising through Hezbollah's ranks. Like many other Hezbollah military leaders, he was a founding member of its precursor, the Islamic Jihad Organization. By the time the IDF completed its withdrawal from southern Lebanon in 2000, Shukr was leading Hezbollah's ground forces. Israel regarded him as one of the group's most dangerous tactical minds.[60]

Shukr remained in command of Hezbollah forces in southern Lebanon for years afterward, including when the group kidnapped IDF soldiers in the summer of 2006. This is what sparked the Second Lebanon War. Shukr is also credited with expanding Hezbollah's rocket arsenal from a meager fifteen thousand around 2006 to one hundred fifty thousand by October 2023, making it the most feared nonstate actor in the region. Further, he played a significant role in commanding Hezbollah's forces in Syria, aiding the Assad regime's campaign of slaughter to stay in power. Finally, according to the IDF, Shukr was Hezbollah's point man for smuggling Iranian parts through Syria into Lebanon to construct guided missiles.[61]

On July 30, 2024, at around 7 p.m., Shukr received a telephone call telling him to ascend from his second-floor office to his seventh-floor residence, where the shadowy terror chief would be easier to strike. The call came via a channel the Hezbollah leader would trust, likely from a party that had hacked into Hezbollah's communications network, a Lebanese official said. Shukr did as he was told—upon which seven Israeli bombs pummeled his apartment and the three floors below. Shukr was killed, along with his wife, two other women, and two children. According to the Lebanese Health Ministry, more than seventy people were wounded.[62]

Shukr and Hezbollah likely never intended to kill those twelve Druze children specifically. The group prefers to kill Jews. But in firing thousands of rockets, missiles, and mortars on Israeli towns, Hezbollah was poking the bear. This time, the bear responded with breathtaking accuracy. Fuad Shukr learned the hard way.

* * *

One question is whether Israel planned to assassinate both Haniyeh and Shukr within the same twenty-four hours. And what led Israel's decision-makers to take out Shukr first and Haniyeh second? "Assassinating Haniyeh in Tehran could lead to an Iranian reaction. We didn't know for sure," Defense Minister Gallant told us. "All the intelligence analysis was being very conservative," especially after Israeli intelligence had underestimated how strongly Iran would react to the killing of a senior IRGC commander in April 2024. "But we thought this was a once-in-a-lifetime opportunity. If we didn't do it, we would not have another chance," Gallant said.

"We approved the assassination of Haniyeh on July 27, three days before that Saturday and before Hezbollah struck Majdal Shams. We only assassinated Mohsen," Gallant explained, using Shukr's nom de guerre, "because of the Hezbollah attack."

The initial plan was to kill Haniyeh for his leadership role in Hamas and negative effect on hostage negotiations. The strike on Shukr was a late addition after Hezbollah had killed the twelve Druze children in Israel.

"On Sunday at 7 a.m., I arrived at Majdal Shams and could still see the blood on the soccer field," Gallant recounted to us. "The rocket fell closest to the bomb-shelter area, which the boys who had been playing soccer were all running toward." They didn't make it in time.

"At 10 a.m., I flew back to military headquarters in Tel Aviv. I told Herzi" Halevi, the IDF chief, "'We are going to kill Mohsen.' This is the man who gave the order to fire on Majdal Shams," Gallant said to us.

Netanyahu and the war cabinet approved the assassination that same day. The only question was when. All acknowledged that a window had opened to take out Nasrallah's military commander. On Sunday and Monday, July 28–29, the cabinet and defense establishment debated what would happen if Israel killed Shukr first, before Haniyeh. Would Haniyeh change his schedule? Or if Haniyeh was hit first, would Shukr go into a bunker?

The decision was made to strike Shukr first. Whereas the Lebanese theater was already active, a sudden strike in Tehran would send shock-waves to Iran's proxies.

On Tuesday night, Israel struck Shukr in Beirut, with an anxious Gallant watching in the war room in Tel Aviv. "At 10 p.m., we did a situational assessment and asked to be updated the second that Haniyeh might change his travel schedule," Gallant told us. "But he didn't change anything," so his assassination went forward. Both targets went down, but if Gallant thought he could breathe a sigh of relief, he was mistaken.

At around 3 a.m. in Israel, Gallant received a call from the US secretary of defense. Austin was furious.

"What are you doing?" Austin demanded. "You're going to lead yourselves into a war with Iran!"

"What do you mean, 'what are we doing?'" Gallant responded. "We kill our enemies—whoever wants to kill us." Shukr, he explained, had ordered the attack on Majdal Shams. Haniyeh was responsible for October

7. "Both of them have the blood of Israelis and Americans on their hands," he told Austin.

Shukr had helped forge the plot to launch suicide truck bombings against foreign peacekeepers in October 1983, killing 241 US servicemen at the Marine Corps barracks in Beirut. The State Department still had a $5 million bounty on his head.[63] This constrained the Biden administration's ability to protest. Jerusalem had settled an account that Washington should have settled itself long ago.

Israel wasn't finished with the leaders of Hamas and Hezbollah, not even close. But that story would unfold only after a series of attacks that stunned the world. It all started with a beep.

CHAPTER TEN

EXPLODING BEEPERS

At 3:30 p.m. on September 17, 2024, pagers began to beep and buzz in Beirut and all over Lebanon, alerting Hezbollah operatives to a message from their commanders. But the message was not from Hassan Nasrallah or anyone else in the terrorist organization. Within less than ten seconds, the pagers would explode, sending Hezbollah, Lebanon, Iran, and even the White House into a panic.

Before anyone knew what was happening, the blasts had Hezbollah terrorists flying off their motorcycles or collapsing onto the floors of supermarkets, writhing in pain as a bizarre smoke belched upward from their pockets, belts, or fingers. From the sounds of the blasts and the fright that followed, it became clear that a massive sabotage operation was under way.

The beeper bombing killed or wounded some three thousand five hundred Hezbollah operatives. Between two and four children were killed, and there were some other civilians hurt, but what stood out to most observers was the attack's accuracy. "This was the most impressive supply-chain operation in modern intelligence history, and maybe forever," General David Petraeus, a former CIA director, told us. For an operation of its size, harming so many Hezbollah operatives and so few others, the targeting was unprecedented. "Usually," Prime Minister Netanyahu noted to us, "the guys who get beepers were important—command-and-control positions. That's why they need the beepers."

As Hezbollah tried to find its bearings and switch its method of communication the next day, a similar wave of exploding walkie-talkies, cell phones, and other devices wounded another five hundred or so terrorist operatives. What was going on? This was an astonishing reversal for Hezbollah, which only a day before had viewed itself as enjoying a substantial measure of impunity by virtue of the size of its rocket arsenal. It thought it had Israel deterred.

Back at Mossad headquarters in Tel Aviv, ten minutes before the pagers were due to go off, everyone was on edge. In the spy agency's state-of-the-art situation room, plasma screens waited for satellite video feeds to stream real-time updates from on the ground. If the pager operation failed, it could cause a collapse in confidence in the Mossad. So much money, so many years, and such great expectations had been poured into the project. If something went wrong, would Israel's vaunted intelligence service plunge the country into its most costly war since the fight for independence?

Even a few minutes after the beepers started to explode, the Mossad didn't yet know how successful the operation was going to be. There was no remote-tracking method to follow what was happening. Mossad Director David Barnea, a famously cool operator, was feeling the heat.

It was only as media reports started to arrive of beeper attacks not only in Beirut, but deep into Lebanon, in the Hezbollah stronghold of the Bekaa Valley, that the Mossad operatives allowed themselves to exhale. The project seemed to be succeeding; Hezbollah had been dealt a thunderous blow. "We had a surprise prepared," Netanyahu told us with a grin. "They didn't know what hit them."

* * *

The Biden administration was about as shocked as Hezbollah. "It was morning in Washington, and we received a request for an urgent phone call" on September 17, recalled Dan Shapiro, the deputy assistant secretary of defense for the Middle East, and a former US ambassador to Israel under President Obama. "Minister Gallant informed Secretary Austin that Israel had a 'special capability,' which he was about to exercise in Lebanon. He was vague about what it did or how it would work, but he wanted Austin to have advance knowledge," Shapiro said.

As a senior Israeli official close to Netanyahu told us on September 17, the day of the beeper bombing, "The US objective from the start was to de-escalate. Our objective is to win the war." Even up until the last minute, Shapiro added, Gallant felt compelled to withhold all the details.

"When the call concluded, we were still pretty confused about what he was describing," Shapiro told us. "But within less than thirty minutes, we started to see reports on CNN and other television networks about explosions happening in Lebanon," Shapiro explained.[64] They would learn what Israel's "special capability" was, like everyone else, by watching the news.

"It was unusual. And in some ways, you could say it was impressive," Shapiro reflected. The Biden team had reacted with genuine alarm at the escalatory potential of Israel's action, but it was colored by admiration. "They were impressed by the creativity, the ingenuity, the secrecy, and the careful targeting of Hezbollah members, ensuring that civilians weren't affected," Shapiro said.[65] How could you not be?

This is the story of how Hezbollah in Lebanon went from the "forgotten front" to one of Israel's greatest intelligence and military successes, and for some months the main focus of Israel's war effort.

For most of the war's first year, Hezbollah was a distraction. It loomed as a major threat, tied down Israeli troops and munitions, and forced tens of thousands of northern Israelis from their homes, yet for Israel it was a distinctly secondary concern. The priority was to take apart Hamas's battalions in Gaza. Israel would practice "active defense" against Hezbollah, but it sought to avoid a larger war. "One massive front at a time" was Netanyahu's watchword.

Avoiding a larger Lebanon war was not only a matter of priority. Netanyahu, no matter how tough he sounded in public, in private was chilled by the prospect of how many Israelis might die from an all-out war with Hezbollah. The IDF expected Hezbollah to fire six thousand to eight thousand rockets a day on Israel for the first several days of a full war. By comparison, the most rockets Israel successfully handled in one day during this war was three hundred.

The responsibility was Netanyahu's, but he was not alone in his concerns. "Towers will topple in Tel Aviv" was the universal expectation. In June 2024, Tamir Hayman, the former head of IDF intelligence now leading Israel's top security think tank, told us the fight in the north would simply have to wait. "War with Hezbollah? Not now," he said. "A couple of years from now. We don't have the resources, international legitimacy, or approval of the US to do Lebanon now." Even more-hawkish former generals believed Israel would never be the same after the damage it would sustain in such a war.

Everyone knew a larger war with Hezbollah was inevitable—how else would Israel ever become safe again? The question was not if but when, and the answer from Israel's political and military leaders was always "not yet." There was truth, a Netanyahu confidant pointed out, in Nasrallah's claim that it was cheaper for Israel to evacuate its northern citizens than to rebuild the skyscrapers of Tel Aviv.

For months, Israel and Hezbollah remained in a holding pattern. Both sides could point to accomplishments: Israel was winning the tit-for-tat war, steadily pushing Hezbollah back from the border. But Hezbollah's rocket attacks had depopulated the north of Israel.

"Nasrallah is losing every day at the tactical level. But he is very stubborn in his strategic assessment," Gallant told us. In effect, Hezbollah's leader had shrunk Israeli territory, and also prevented Israel from deploying the full force of its military in Gaza. While maintaining steady rocket fire on evacuated Israeli towns, he stayed within bounds that in turn allowed Israel to abstain from major retaliation. "He knows us too well," we were told by Oded Stein, the head of the Israeli premilitary academy of the Upper Galilee. "He knows exactly where the line is for us."

Gadi Eisenkot, the former IDF chief of staff and war cabinet observer, was firm in his belief that Nasrallah didn't want war. But, Netanyahu feared, Nasrallah thought Israel didn't want war even more strongly than he didn't. Gallant agreed: "Nasrallah is not afraid of a war." The grand leader of Hezbollah, he said, "is a very religious person. Eventually he could say, 'This is what Allah wants, so we'll do it.'" Hezbollah didn't want war, "but it might get it anyway," Netanyahu told us in June 2024, "the way it is playing this."

Benny Gantz had long pleaded with Netanyahu, to no avail, to use more military force against Hezbollah. The prime minister's failure to do so was one reason Gantz quit the government in June 2024. For months after, he would call on Netanyahu to transfer forces to the north and be willing to risk full-on war. "Nasrallah and Iran don't want it," he asserted with confidence. Gantz assessed that when Hezbollah's leader gave the order to shoot on October 8, 2023, to support Hamas, he had no idea that the Gaza war would go on for so many months. But Nasrallah had tied himself to Yahya Sinwar and Hamas, and now he was stuck with them for as long as it would take.

* * *

On August 25, 2024, three weeks before the pagers operations, Hezbollah escalated the fight and changed the way Netanyahu viewed the northern front. Hezbollah had planned to launch several hundred, and maybe up to one thousand, rockets that day, including on Israeli intelligence headquarters north of Tel Aviv. Yet the IDF did not only stymie Hezbollah; it cleaned house. With clear intelligence dominance, it blew up the vast majority of the rockets and drones Hezbollah intended to use as well as others—thousands of them—before they could even be launched.

How exactly the IDF pulled this off is highly classified, but at different points in the war, the IDF has allowed us to publicize details regarding: long-range, land-based radar detection systems; long-range, air-based surveillance systems; massive drone surveillance; cyber and other spying; and covert operations behind enemy lines. In some cases, this intelligence allowed the IDF to strike Hezbollah rocket crews before they ever fired. Nasrallah and Ayatollah Khamenei of Iran were left to hail as a great victory Hezbollah's firing of 210 rockets, hitting an Israeli chicken coop and not much else.[66] Suddenly, Netanyahu was euphoric and ready to press Israel's advantage.

The prime minister asked: What if instead of losing five thousand to ten thousand Israelis from tens of thousands of rockets over several weeks in an all-out war, he could pre-emptively destroy enough Hezbollah rockets and launchers to shrink Israel casualties by orders of magnitude? What if he could ensure that the terrorists would not be able to mount an effective strike in retaliation? This was the thought that changed the northern front.

After the successful pre-emption, Netanyahu was ready to strike north. There were a number of factors that had weighed in favor of caution before but now favored taking risks. For example, negotiations for a comprehensive ceasefire with Hamas had fallen apart. Nasrallah was also furious at Israel for killing his top military chief, Fuad Shukr, on July 30, and had become even less likely to agree to a bilateral ceasefire. Plus, if the IDF was going to take any major actions against Hezbollah, it wanted to do so before winter would set in and obscure Lebanon's mountainous landscape. That would cost Israel some of its air-power advantage.

"We should do it in October," Netanyahu proposed, winning backing from the Mossad's Barnea. "One of the reasons," the prime minister later recounted to us, "was that October is one month before November." Who knows what happens after a US election? But during the election campaign, Israel's chances of securing US support would be greater, he thought. Whether it would also have cost Biden politically, he did not say.

For a time after the May 2024 invasion of Rafah, however, Gallant and many leaders in the IDF had come to change their minds about the wisdom of escalation in Lebanon. Gallant, who had urged a massive strike in the first days of the war, now argued that Israel had reached a "strategic junction": It could make a deal with Hamas and save the hostages' lives, which could also lead to a ceasefire with Hezbollah, or it could continue fighting Hamas, risk the hostages' lives, and fall into a destructive escalation with Hezbollah.

"What's the point?" argued Gallant. "We don't need another war. It will end in an agreement, not so different from the agreement we can get now." So why go through the fighting? he asked. Better to skip the war with Hezbollah.

The hawk had become the dove, at least for the moment. Israelis were tired, Gallant saw, and the longer the hostages stayed in Gaza, the greater the chance they would die in captivity. Escalation would threaten to bring Iran into the war in an even bigger way while the Gaza front was far from closed. The West Bank, which Gallant like many Israelis calls Judea and Samaria, could also erupt. In fear of precisely this scenario, the IDF would have to divert troops in late August 2024 for a major operation against the simmering Hamas and Islamic Jihad cells of the West Bank, focusing on the neighborhoods of Jenin and Tulkarm still referred to as refugee camps.

Besides, what would a war against Hezbollah accomplish? Unlike with Hamas in Gaza, there could be no hope of destroying Hezbollah. It was too large, and Lebanon too big a country, with a porous border to Syria. Instead, Israel could aim to push the terrorists back from the Israeli border—the same goal being pursued by US diplomacy. Biden envoy and close aide Amos Hochstein had made a half dozen trips to the region between October 2023 and August 2024 to try to cajole Israel, Lebanon and Hezbollah into a deal.[67]

Unless Israel wished to continue an attritional fight indefinitely, it would have to extricate itself from any war with a deal. Along with Gallant, many senior IDF officials told us that it made more sense to take that deal instead of a war, rather than after it. And the only way to get a deal with Hezbollah, Nasrallah had made clear, was to first stop the fighting with Hamas. This had already been tested during the Gaza ceasefire in November 2023, when Hezbollah's rockets went quiet, only to resume once the ceasefire ended.

Netanyahu rejected the premise that a prewar deal with Hezbollah would be the same as a postwar deal. "It makes a hell of a difference," he told Gallant, "whether we make the ceasefire after we cut Hezbollah down to size or after we leave it intact." If Hezbollah still held a sword of Damocles over Israel's head, no terms on paper would secure Israel. Ultimately, there would have to be a fight. Israelis "aren't going to come back to the north if we don't change the equation and if they don't have a sense of security—which means actual security," he told us.

As we have seen, while pressure mounted in the months after the Rafah invasion in May to come to an agreement with Hamas, Netanyahu refused the key concessions the Gazan terror group demanded, calling them a "nonstarter." The war in Gaza would again come to drift in these months, yielding neither a new hostage deal nor major advances against Hamas. "This is the worst and most wanton government in the country's history," said opposition leader Yair Lapid, a liberal former TV anchor. "As far as they're concerned, there could be war here forever." Demonstrations of tens of thousands of Israelis demanded an agreement to bring the hostages home rather than fight on indefinitely.

"A step away from a victory that will never come, we're surrounded by enemies. The whole world is against us," a former Israeli official said at a June 1, 2024, protest.[68]

That same day, Netanyahu reiterated that "Israel's conditions for ending the war have not changed." They would have to be met "before a permanent ceasefire is put in place."

Netanyahu's right-wing coalition partners had threatened to bolt, and the prime minister may not have been able to cut a deal that Hamas would accept and that would keep his government from falling. Gantz offered support for such a deal with votes from outside the governing coalition, but this would have been only temporary.

There is a broader debate about how legitimate it was for Netanyahu to take the threat of losing power into account. All politicians do, but what can be said objectively is that no one stays in power in the fractious Israeli Knesset as long as Netanyahu has without a razor-sharp focus on politics. There is no question that Israel's options were limited by its prime minister's political constraints—in part because he genuinely felt his government's survival was essential for the country, and that no other leader would continue the war or take it to Tehran. Many Israelis, meanwhile, thought the fall of his government was essential for the country, as any other leader would free the hostages.

By not making the concessions necessary for a deal at that time, Netanyahu preserved the option for a decisive war to push back Hezbollah. Had the northern front been quieted, it would have been difficult to open it anew, and in such a large way, and easy to kick the can further down the road. Then again, Netanyahu also knew he could not make major concessions on the Gaza front unless he was willing to face an election he was likely to lose.

Hezbollah, meanwhile, began in September to expand the range of its rocket fire deeper into Israel to the cities of Safed and Nahariya, not merely the evacuated towns it had targeted before. Gallant's "strategic junction" analysis wasn't wrong: The logic of the war really was pushing Hezbollah and Israel closer to the brink of escalation.

Maybe that wasn't the worst thing for Israel, given the circumstances. Hezbollah had already fired eight thousand five hundred rockets over eleven months; US diplomacy had failed to stop them.

* * *

The real story of the beepers and walkie-talkies began almost two decades earlier. The earliest foundations were laid by Yossi Cohen for then–Mossad chief Meir Dagan from 2002 to 2006. Dagan led the Mossad for an unusually long nine years from 2002 to 2011. Already a legend in Israel, he would receive credit for a years-long campaign of assassinations of Iranian nuclear scientists, Israel's 2007 attack on Syria's nuclear reactor, and the 2009–2010 STUXNET cyberattack on Iran's nuclear program, among other exploits.

Cohen himself would go on to lead the Mossad from 2016 to 2021. He would be credited with seizing Iran's nuclear archives, destroying three Iranian nuclear facilities, and planning the targeted killing of Iran's nuclear chief and many others. Perhaps most important, he helped nail down the Abraham Accords. But at this time, he was the agency's project manager for operations to thwart Iran's nuclear program.

According to Mossad sources, Israel launched a new, systematic tampering campaign against Iran in 2002. Then, through a variety of fronts and straw men, Mossad sold the Iranians a substantial amount of tampered equipment in 2003 and 2004 with dramatic results. Without revealing what, Israeli intelligence sources told us the Mossad "added something" to each device or piece of equipment.

Sabotage is as old as war itself, but those prior operations took place in peacetime. The first Israeli operation to serve as proof of concept for large-scale technology tampering in wartime was against Hezbollah during the Second Lebanon War in 2006. Little has been revealed about such attacks during Cohen's reign as Iran project manager, or about the connection between those earlier Iran operations and the ones in this war, against Iran as well as Hezbollah.

Devising the spy agency's next move, Cohen always asked himself, "How do I tamper with your organization and disrupt it? How do I enter your secret defense program and your secret supply lines for purchasing nuclear-related equipment?" As of 2006, Hezbollah was sold a variety of sabotaged products. Some transmitted data, such as GPS locations. Some listened. Some, like the beepers, exploded.

By 2014, the Mossad and IDF intelligence wanted to expand into new areas of surveillance and sabotage, targeting Hezbollah's walkie-talkies. Tamir Pardo was the Mossad chief at the time, and Herzi Halevi was head of IDF intelligence. They worked on a plan that would allow Israeli intelligence to use the walkie-talkies as a surveillance tool as well as a "judgment day" weapon to be pulled out if the sides ever fell into a general war.

"The walkie-talkie was a weapon, just like a bullet or a missile or a mortar," Michael, a fictitious name for a former Mossad agent, said in an interview with CBS's *60 Minutes*.[69] Inside the walkie-talkie was a battery, made in Israel at a Mossad facility, which included an explosive device, he revealed. These walkie-talkies were designed to be placed in the chest pocket of a Hezbollah fighter's tactical vest. We were told that Hezbollah bought more than fifteen thousand of them. "They got a good price," Michael said, with no small dose of irony. But, he added, the price could not be too low because that could cause Hezbollah to get suspicious.

To conceal the source of the walkie-talkies and infiltrate Hezbollah's supply chain, Mossad agents established shell companies. "We create a pretend world," Michael said. "We are a global production company: We write the screenplay, we're the directors, we're the producers, we're the main actors," he added, "and the world is our stage."[70]

One limitation of the walkie-talkies, which Israel would detonate the day after the pagers, was that Hezbollah fighters were expected to carry them only during war or military exercises. This meant that on most days, they were sitting idle in military barracks. For the Mossad, this was not good enough. It wanted to plant devices on Hezbollah operatives that they would have in their possession at all times.

Cell phones? No. Nasrallah had been telling his operatives that Israel was using cell phone networks to track them, and that they needed to go low-tech to avoid detection. "You ask me where is the agent," Nasrallah told the Hezbollah faithful. "I tell you that the phone in your hands is the agent," he said. "Bury it. Put it in an iron box and lock it."[71]

Nasrallah preferred pagers because they could receive messages without giving away a user's location. They were safe, Nasrallah thought. This created just the lethal opening the Mossad had been looking for.

Already by 2018, the Mossad was thinking about the pager option. But the Mossad's technologists hit various snags. At the time, a Mossad division head said the plan was not technically viable. Aspects of the program were even closed down, at least officially. If that had been the end of the story, Israel might never have taken a sledgehammer to Hezbollah, and the entire Middle East war might have produced a different result.

Certain Mossad agents, however, were fixated on tampering with the beepers, no matter the obstacles. Within the spy agency, agents sometimes work clandestinely, on their own time, to keep ideas alive that have been officially shut down. The patriotic hope is to revive the idea for when the time is right. These Mossad agents, who will never be named, helped turn the tide of the war for Israel. Eventually, they solved a particularly difficult "physics problem," and the program was placed back on an official Mossad track.

The Mossad was the originator of the beepers plan, but it did not act alone. Once the Mossad presented the concept, Israel's military intelligence and operations arms began a push to transform it into an actionable plan, coordinated with the larger military. The IDF also established mechanisms to study and compare scenarios for when the pagers would be most effective. The goal was to achieve the maximum strategic advantage over Hezbollah.

By 2022, the Mossad had started to build up the intelligence and operations infrastructure for the plan to move forward, and by 2023, it had begun to solidify. A former Mossad agent referring to himself by the cover name of Gabriel told *60 Minutes* that the agency had learned Hezbollah was buying pagers from Gold Apollo, a Taiwanese company. He described the Gold Apollo pagers as sleek, shiny, and, most critically, able to fit into pockets. But the Mossad needed a larger variant of the pager to fit the explosives inside.[72]

The Mossad used dummies to conduct tests. Held inside a padded glove, the pagers were detonated next to the dummies' faces. This helped calibrate the precise quantity of powdered explosives required to harm a Hezbollah fighter while avoiding an innocent bystander next to him. The Mossad even tested the beepers' special ringtone, aiming for a sound that would seem urgent enough to compel Hezbollah fighters to take it out of their pockets, no matter what they were doing.

A former Mossad chief told us that these beepers lacked any intelligence capabilities. They could not even track and transmit their locations. Their entire focus was to explode, functioning as hidden miniature bombs. Inside lay only three grams of PETN, a concealed explosive compound.

According to Gabriel, the day he showed the pager to Barnea, the Mossad chief, "he was furious. He was telling us, 'There is no chance that anyone will buy such a big device. It's not comfortable in their pocket. It's heavy.'" Barnea sent Gabriel back to the drawing board, but Gabriel said he eventually convinced the Mossad chief to adopt the beeper.[73]

Later, it would be hyped in advertisements on YouTube as robust, dustproof, and waterproof, with a long battery life. "It became the best product in the beeper area in the world," Gabriel boasted. The spy agency's marketing was so convincing that many other clients besides

Hezbollah sought to purchase it. "Obviously we didn't send it to anyone," Gabriel said. "We just quote them with [an] expensive price."[74]

The Mossad set up shell companies, including one in Hungary, to fool Gold Apollo into working with it. According to the contractual arrangements, the front manufactured the pagers and had a licensing partnership with Gold Apollo. This made it look fully legitimate to Hezbollah. After the attack, pictures were publicized that showed the beepers with Gold Apollo's logo.

Gold Apollo's Taiwanese founder, Hsu Ching-kuang, denies that his firm manufactured the pagers. "The product was not ours. Our brand name was only on it. We are a responsible company. This is very shameful," he said. Instead, he accused BAC Consulting, a Budapest-based company, of responsibility for designing and producing the explosive beepers. The companies had been working together for around three years.[75]

After the news broke of its role in the beepers attack, BAC's website went dark. Records from Consultancy.org obtained by the BBC show that the company was founded in 2022. Its leaders were said to have "more than a decade of consulting experience" and a five-member team. The company had presented itself as active in the publishing, media, and oil-and-gas sectors. Cristiana Barsony-Arcidiacono, the CEO of BAC Consulting, told NBC News that her company worked with Gold Apollo, but denied any further involvement: "We don't make the pagers. We're just the intermediary. I think you're wrong in your trail." A spokesman for Hungarian Prime Minister Viktor Orbán said the exploding pagers were never in Hungary.[76]

BBC Verify has accessed BAC's records, which reveal that it has a single shareholder and is registered to a building in Budapest. A company brochure, published on LinkedIn, listed eight organizations BAC claims to have worked with, including the European Commission and the UK Department for International Development.[77]

The UK Foreign Office said it was still investigating, but an initial review indicated that its department had no involvement with BAC, despite the firm's claim. Barsony-Arcidiacono was the only listed employee on the BAC website.[78] While she did the phone interview with NBC, neither the BBC nor any other media outlet has managed to reach her since. The Mossad knew how to set up straw companies like no one else.

To preserve its cover, BAC also took on real commercial clients, but the purpose was always to be positioned to infiltrate Hezbollah's supply chain. "When they are buying from us, they have zero clue that they are buying from the Mossad. We make like the 'Truman Show'—everything is controlled by us behind the scene," Gabriel said. "In their experience, everything is normal."[79] To lend the scheme even more credibility, the Mossad hired Gold Apollo's saleswoman, with whom Hezbollah regularly worked, though she was as clueless as they were that she was helping a spy agency. The Mossad also created two other shell companies to conceal the identities of the intelligence officers developing the pagers.

Gabriel said the Gold Apollo saleswoman offered Hezbollah the first batch of beepers free of charge, as a perk, to keep the customer hooked. By September 17, 2024, five thousand bombs had been planted in Hezbollah terrorists' pockets. Israel's coup was to get the men of Hezbollah to place them there themselves.

* * *

After Hezbollah joined Hamas in attacking Israel on October 8, 2023, a brigade-size unit of IDF officers was established to gather the intelligence and operational details required to set the beeper operation in motion. Many of these officials worked at a clandestine IDF intelligence collection base in the north of Israel.

But when to trigger the explosions? The initial storyline leaked by Israeli security cabinet members and the IDF was that the beepers were activated on September 17, 2024, because Hezbollah was close to discovering the sabotage. "There were those who had misgivings about using it at all," Netanyahu later told us. "But since it was time-sensitive, I pushed it through." In this telling, it was either use it or lose it, and the operation had to be moved up some from the prime minister's desired October start date.

"'Let's not rush,'" he says he was told. "'Let's not open the war because of toys.'" After all, "'you don't decide strategy based on the means.'" To this, Netanyahu replied, "It's a strategic means. You're never going to have something as awesome as that to create the beginning of a shock-and-awe operation."

The prime minister says he rejected Gallant's argument that Israel should inform the Biden administration of its intentions beforehand. "I said, 'If we tell the Americans, we blow it. It could leak, and that's the end of it." This was not true in every instance, but when it came to a major move like this with the potential to blow another front or two of the war wide open, the prime minister had a good case. Even after eleven months of Hezbollah rockets, the Biden team urged Israel not to do anything that could escalate the fight. On September 24, after the pagers attack and its follow-ons, the president held to the same line. "Full-scale war is not in anyone's interest," Biden said.

Halevi, the IDF chief, told us that Israel's military high command had never opposed using the pagers. Rather, it said the government first had to shift its focus from Gaza to Lebanon and declare the northern front its main priority. In other words, the IDF wanted the government to make the political, military, and conceptual shift regarding its war effort, not merely roll out the beepers attack as a stand-alone gimmick.

It is doubtful that the pagers operation went forward on September 17 purely because it was at risk of being exposed. The story of an unscheduled rush to activate the devices resonated with the Israeli and Lebanese publics, which had been taken by surprise when, after 11 months of Hezbollah fire with limited Israeli retaliation, Israel suddenly went big. But intelligence sources told us that Israel had picked the timing carefully and not solely because of a discovery by Hezbollah.

Netanyahu had already decided to initiate a major strike on Hezbollah as of September 12, five days before the beepers were activated. Both Netanyahu and Gallant had made public statements about elevating the push to return Israel's northern residents to their homes to the list of the primary objectives of the war. The last of Hamas's twenty-four battalions, in Rafah, had been declared defeated a few weeks earlier, in a statement from Gallant. For weeks and days leading up to the beeper explosions, Israel had been shifting its force posture—both ground and air forces—toward the northern border.

None of this means that Hezbollah never got close to exposing the beeper or walkie-talkie plots. Israeli intelligence sources have indicated that Hezbollah got close not only in September 2024, but also at earlier times. Probably the most accurate version of the story is that some existing concerns about the program being exposed were renewed in mid-September—but not necessarily at the level of imminent crisis—and that this may have led to a decision to initiate the explosions and attacks a week or two earlier than they would have happened anyway. This is very different from the picture some have painted of one of the biggest decisions of the war, the move to stage a major attack on Hezbollah, coming almost accidentally, to protect an intelligence asset.

* * *

As devastating as the pagers were to Hezbollah in September 2024, and as effective a campaign as they would subsequently prepare, could they have been outdone by the walkie-talkie bombs on October 11, 2023, when Gallant had wanted to strike north? It does not pay to second-guess success, but the counterfactual that Gallant and others have presented, as discussed in Chapter One, is tempting. Israel might have saved itself more than a year of war in the north.

In a maximum-success scenario, Israel's use of the walkie-talkies in the first days of the war could have killed as many as fifteen thousand Hezbollah fighters in one fell swoop, Gallant told us and Halevi told a small group of reporters. There were far more booby-trapped walkie-talkies than pagers in circulation. If Israel made the right moves to get the maximum number of Hezbollah troops to mount their walkie-talkies, the impact would have dwarfed the around three thousand five hundred mostly Hezbollah terrorists who were ultimately wounded by the beepers and walkie-talkies on September 17 and 18. It would also have had the potential, Gallant and Halevi argued, to quickly end the war in the north and pressure Hamas into a better hostage deal for Israel.

In February 2025, the Mossad's Barnea rejected some elements of Gallant's story at a conference in Tel Aviv. Barnea argued the attack would not have been as effective if the pagers and walkie-talkies had been activated in October 2023. There were "ten times as many beepers" in Hezbollah's hands" when they were blown up in September 2024, he said, "and two times as many walkie-talkies were detonated." He also gave substantial credit to Netanyahu for moving ahead with the operation "in the face of the majority opinion in the room."[80]

Questioned about whether the US might have supported an Israeli attack on Hezbollah on October 11, 2023, if it had known about Israel's secret pager and walkie-talkie assets, Biden's national security advisor was skeptical. "I don't see any solid evidence to see that they would have had a better outcome. I can't disprove it either," Sullivan told us. "We didn't know about the pagers. I have my doubts about effectiveness," he said, if Israel had tried to use them "out of the blue during the complete psychological disarray of the Israeli body politic" in the days after October 7.

"They were still organizing themselves militarily," Sullivan noted. "Could it have been quick and decisive? That's for historians to debate. But the fact that they were seeing things that were not there"—such as the geese that almost spurred an all-out Israeli attack on Hezbollah—"is relevant to understanding their mindset just after October 7."

A year later, when Israel was far more organized and clear-eyed, it found success. Netanyahu, Gallant, IDF intelligence, and the Mossad were credited with paving the way for the Israeli air and land forces to crush Hezbollah over September and October, leading to a November ceasefire enforced far more favorably to Jerusalem than had been anticipated earlier in the war.

In our judgment, if the walkie-talkies had been activated on October 11, 2023, they probably would not have had anywhere near the maximum effect, as estimated by Israeli intelligence under optimal circumstances. All the same, if the IDF had taken certain maneuvers to prod Hezbollah into donning its battle vests along with the walkie-talkies, it is likely that exploding them early on in the war would have had an even greater impact than the beepers did in September 2024. That would depend, however, on Israel's tricking Hezbollah into that major mobilization.

Mossad sources told us that the walkie-talkies had been shifted internally from Plan A to Plan B three years earlier, losing the top spot to the pagers. Not for nothing were the pagers considered the more effective sabotage option.

* * *

When the Mossad finally pushed the button to explode the pagers at 3:30 p.m. on September 17, 2024, and then hit Hezbollah the very next day with the exploding walkie-talkies, the stage was set for Israel to smash the Lebanese terror group. While it was only later that Israel formally took credit for those attacks, it left no doubt as to who was responsible for the waves of strikes that followed from September 19 until November 27, destroying tens of thousands of Hezbollah rockets. At the operation's apex, on September 23, the Israeli Air Force bombed a jaw-dropping one thousand three hundred targets in one day.

In many ways, this follow-on campaign secured the triumph of the Mossad's sabotage, which could be remembered very differently today if it had prompted a deluge of Hezbollah rockets that devastated Haifa and dealt serious damage to Tel Aviv. Instead, none of that happened. Israel prevented the terrorists from firing the large, coordinated salvos that could overwhelm Israeli air defenses. "This was the big issue," Netanyahu told us—how to follow up the theatrics of the beepers and walkie-talkies to protect Israel and win the war.

The prime minister said he was not fully satisfied with the three follow-up options suggested by the IDF. He worked with the generals to develop a fourth option to take out Hezbollah's main missile stockpiles.

"Some of them were out in the open, which was an easy shot," he said, "but Nasrallah was relying on the missiles and rockets that he put in private homes because he knew of our concern over civilian casualties." There, protected by human shields, the terrorist leader thought his second-strike capability would be safe. Besides, the rockets were widely dispersed. Surely, Israel could not hit enough of them to save itself from mass damage. "I said to the Army, 'I want you to take them out,'" Netanyahu told us. He praises the IDF for coming up with "an improved plan, which was actually brilliant, because among other things they took over Lebanese television" to help evacuate civilians from their homes. Then, Israel could target the missiles in their hiding spots.

The plan succeeded. "In six hours, we wiped out most of the ballistic-missile stockpiles Hezbollah had amassed," Netanyahu exulted. This changed the course of the war. The fear that Hezbollah's response would kill "untold numbers in Tel Aviv, and that the towers would collapse, and so on," would not be realized, he said. "We took out the main thing they built, a good chunk of it."

Israel also ramped up its targeted strikes on Hezbollah leaders, including Ibrahim Aqil, the commander of Hezbollah's elite Radwan Forces, who was believed to have taken over for Fuad Shukr as military chief, and sixteen of his top subcommanders. Day after day, in one strike after another, Hezbollah leaders fell. Israel seemed to know their precise locations and refused to let up. It helped that the beeper and walkie-talkie attacks had maneuvered Hezbollah into moving many of its commanders closer together, given that the organization could barely communicate remotely anymore. In short order, Israel churned through Hezbollah's communications, missile arsenal, and chain of command. It left the organization dazed, confused, and battered. Hezbollah had been humiliated.

Less well-known is that the beeper attacks were not limited to Hezbollah. The attack struck more than one hundred of Iran's top IRGC operatives across the Middle East, who were using the same network of beepers. The Mossad's message to the Iranians was clear: If you arm terror proxies to hunt Israelis, don't be shocked when you are hunted too.

* * *

Two days after the wave of beeper explosions, Hezbollah chief Hassan Nasrallah, known for his fiery rhetoric, gave a subdued speech. He looked defeated.

The attack had "destroyed the fighting spirit of Hezbollah," a Mossad source told us, and not merely for the moment. "Thousands of Hezbollah operatives have been and will continue to walk around with no fingers or eyes—no eyes like Zedekiah, the last King of Israel" in the Hebrew Bible, who was blinded by the conquering King Nebuchadnezzar of Babylonia. They would serve as a standing reminder, more frightening than any bomb from a plane, of what happens to those who wage war on Israel by means of terrorism.

This one held the pager in his left hand. That one brought it close to his eyes. The medium was the message—and Israel was only getting started.

CHAPTER ELEVEN

ASSASSINATING NASRALLAH, INVADING LEBANON

At 6:20 p.m. on September 27, 2024, ten days after the beeper bombing, dozens of F-15I aircraft from the IDF's 69th Squadron pummeled Hezbollah's underground headquarters in the heart of Beirut. When the smoke cleared from some eighty-five bombs, Hassan Nasrallah was dead and the Iranian proxy axis was shattered.

Nasrallah was killed alongside around twenty Hezbollah military commanders, including Ali Karaki, the commander of the southern front, who had been designated Hezbollah's new military chief after Israel had killed his predecessor. How did Israel pull it off?

The story begins with a decade of meticulous intelligence collected by the IDF and the Mossad, including from Iranians working with Hezbollah. It ends with a variety of last-minute deceptions, such as Prime Minister Netanyahu's business-as-usual flight to the United Nations in New York to ensure that Nasrallah would not get suspicious. It also involved the GBU-31 bunker-buster bombs, likely supplied by the US, needed to drive down deep enough under the large residential building in Beirut that hid Hezbollah's headquarters.

This round of war-room drama was not limited to the standard situation rooms in Jerusalem and Tel Aviv. Instead, key talks took place while Netanyahu was on the plane to the US, and even at his hotel in New York. This gave the disagreements a different energy, depriving Netanyahu, Defense Minister Gallant, and IDF chief Halevi of the ability to point and yell in one another's faces. But mere physical distance could not eliminate the tensions built up by a year of fighting over the most important decisions of their lives. Netanyahu continued to bang on the table, even while speaking over the phone, and Israeli defense officials did not hesitate to push back when they felt that solid military strategy demanded it.

Eliminating Nasrallah had been an Israeli defense establishment priority for more than a decade. Halevi, Gallant and many intelligence officials had spent endless hours planning and collecting intelligence to keep a potential operation updated. During the crucial week leading to the Nasrallah killing, there were disagreements about who was first to be ready to approve the operation and who hesitated. Gallant and Halevi said they led the way. Netanyahu said he did.

On the question of how aggressive to be in butting heads with the Biden administration, however, the war room's long process of switching roles was complete. Netanyahu was now firmly the most willing to undertake risky military moves even if Washington would oppose them. Gallant and Halevi were now far more concerned about shoring up American support, in this case to ensure air-defense help against the likely massive Iranian ballistic-missile retaliation.

In the end, all the Israeli decision-makers approved the targeted strike on Nasrallah. Though each side of the war room would later suggest that the other had been reluctant to attack, this was an instance of the war room coming together to achieve a major objective.

* * *

That Israel killed Nasrallah is a fact. But exactly what the differences were in the Israeli war room over how to assassinate him remains hotly debated.

Halevi and Gallant's narrative starts with IDF successes against Hezbollah: First, the September 20, 2024 targeted strike on Hezbollah's new military chief of staff, Ibrahim Aqil, and the top brass of his elite Radwan invasion force. Second, dropping one thousand three hundred bombs on Hezbollah on September 23, the largest bombing of Lebanon of the war. Halevi said that Netanyahu opposed the Aqil assassination until he and Gallant had pushed it through, and that only afterward did the war cabinet seriously start to consider killing Nasrallah.

Netanyahu asked Halevi, "Why not tomorrow morning, now that we have seen our capabilities?"

Halevi responded, "We are up to a 70% chance of success. But a 30% chance of missing is very bad." He wanted to improve the intelligence and planning. "If it looks like Nasrallah will move, we have operational readiness and can attack fast," Halevi told the prime minister. Having previously invested huge resources to be prepared for such an operation, the IDF would be ready.

When the war room discussed the possibility, Netanyahu did not reveal his hand. Dermer, however, advocated waiting to strike until his boss's return from the US. Halevi said the entire defense establishment was in favor of a strike. Gallant said he was also strongly in favor and has called it a bald-faced lie that he had opposed eliminating Nasrallah.

In Halevi and Gallant's telling, it was Netanyahu who opposed such a strike in a key meeting on Wednesday, September 25, two days before the ultimate attack, preferring to get a deal with Hezbollah at the last moment. Only after facing right-wing political pressure, while he was on the plane to New York on Thursday, September 26, did the prime minister say for the first time, "I think the right move is to kill Nasrallah."

Halevi has granted that it was a "very brave move" for Netanyahu to order the assassination of Nasrallah while he was outside Israel, yet he insists that he and the IDF were also in favor. "It is a lie when anyone says the IDF did not want to do it. The IDF led the way on this."

The debate from there was merely about "exactly when and how to do it and whether to coordinate with the Americans," as Halevi would put it. He and Gallant argued in favor of informing Washington, and

Netanyahu argued against it. Nasrallah had also killed lots of Americans, and Halevi thought the IDF would get some extra intelligence and operational help from the US to be more precise. He added that the IDF did ultimately let the US know some things a few days before. Halevi had a special relationship with General Erik Kurilla, the chief of US Central Command, which went far beyond the political contacts between the two countries. Halevi was confident then—and remains so today—that Kurilla would have supported a strike on Nasrallah and should have been given a chance to convince Biden, or at least to explain to Biden after the fact that Israel had given him advance notice. The IDF chief believes Netanyahu missed this possibility in his fixation on personal fights with the US president.

Most important, Gallant, Halevi and the IDF brass did not want to risk upsetting the Biden administration by blindsiding it with the Nasrallah strike, which could cost Israel US air defenses should Iran retaliate. Without US help, the impact on Israel—civilians, military and essential infrastructure—could be disastrous. Better to keep Biden in the loop, even to do something he opposed, such as with Rafah.

Halevi did not think the prime minister's stance against telling the US in advance was patently wrong. Further, "The prime minister asked me a good question: Given that I was in favor of updating the US," if Netanyahu forbade him from giving that update, "would I then turn to oppose an attack? I said no," Halevi has explained. He added that "we would still need to speak to the Americans and explain afterward. But it was not a deal breaker." Despite disagreements over the course of the debates, the war room would unite on this point: Hezbollah's terrorist kingpin had to go.

* * *

Netanyahu has generally been averse to crediting his war-room partners for major successes. His narrative goes like this: The prime minister supported the September 20 strike on Hezbollah's Aqil, which he had the cabinet approve on September 12 while adding a new war aim: the return of northern Israelis to their homes. After approving the subsequent attack on Hezbollah's missile arsenal, Netanyahu had heard that the opportunity to strike Nasrallah was slipping away. On September 22, he secured the eager support of Mossad chief David Barnea to seize the chance while Israel still had it.

In this telling, however, Gallant and Halevi wanted more time. The IDF chief had a six-day attack plan to devastate Hezbollah and worried that the killing of Nasrallah would disrupt it. He wanted to achieve as much as possible before targeting Nasrallah, after which Biden might force Israel to halt. Gallant also pointed out that "Nasrallah gives us the best intelligence"—Israel had become adept at following him—during a meeting in which the defense minister still had not gotten to yes on killing Nasrallah.

Netanyahu replied that after he had rejected Gallant's push to attack Hezbollah at the start of the war, "I said we'd come back. Now," he asked Gallant, "you're saying we can't?"

Gallant has often countered that Netanyahu twists snippets of conversations out of context to his political benefit.

On September 24, raw intelligence provided by Gallant and Halevi via the famed Unit 8200 of Israeli military intelligence convinced Netanyahu that Nasrallah had to go. "He was literally taking over the command of military actions," Netanyahu later told us. "He had replaced Soleimani," the Iranian general who had commanded Iran's proxy empire until his death in a January 2020 US strike. "It's not only that Iran was using [Nasrallah]. He was using Iran." On September 24, Netanyahu said, "We can't let him go. We have to take him out. He's the axis of the axis."

For Israel, Nasrallah had become the most dangerous man in the region. "I was enormously impressed with his leadership. He had been the leader of his battle for thirty-two years. He built Hezbollah from nothing into a great force, even though he lost two of his senior commanders," the prime minister reflected, in rare praise for the skill of an enemy. "We had to take him out."

In the meeting on Wednesday, September 25, detailed operational plans were presented for the first time. Halevi and Gallant were now more positive about the idea. "In general, I'm in favor of doing this," Halevi said, "but I have two conditions—and they're difficult conditions": Coordinate in advance with the US and be prepared to absorb a retaliatory strike from Iran. "If you're not willing to get an attack from Iran, you shouldn't do it," he said. Gallant said, "I'm not against taking him out, in principle. But we're talking about escalating, and escalating is not right at this moment."

Halevi was right about Iran's massive retaliation, which would come only days later. Whether or not to tell Biden, however, became a sticking point. Defense Secretary Lloyd Austin had insisted that he be informed in advance of "any significant move" in Lebanon. "I said, 'absolutely not,'" Netanyahu told us. "The [IDF] chief of staff said, 'You can, it's possible,'" and advised telling parts of the US team of Israel's plan to attack Nasrallah. "I struck it out completely," Netanyahu added. "You could tell them when the planes are more or less in the air, that's fine, but not before, because it would leak and Nasrallah would escape. The chickens would flee the coop."

In the meeting, the prime minister's words were: "There's no option of calling them." Should US officials beyond General Kurilla find out, "It'll be 'don't' on steroids," Netanyahu predicted, referencing Biden's one-word warning of choice to Iran and Russia. Netanyahu said certain US officials would "jump out of their skin" if they found out and go directly to Biden to nix it. They would have been aghast at an Israeli decision to blow open the war like that.

Netanyahu acknowledges that Gallant supported the strike in the end. But in the prime minister's view, insisting on informing the Biden administration beforehand was a backdoor way to try to prevent the operation from ever taking place—the same way that Gallant had accused Netanyahu of calling Biden to avoid striking Hezbollah in 2023. Halevi, in this telling, genuinely wanted to attack but thought he could secure US approval through military channels. He also thought that foregoing it could cause Biden to refuse to defend Israel from a deadly Iranian missile response.

The prime minister disagreed. As Dermer put it during the debate, the Biden team "will be with us on the defense; they won't be on the offense." They were confident that Biden would help defend Israel against Iranian retaliation, given the president's overriding desire to prevent escalation. The only way to do that would be to stop Iran from scoring the kind of big hits on Israel that would force Jerusalem to escalate in kind.

Netanyahu approved one last try in negotiations as a decoy to provide Nasrallah false reassurance of his own security. But the war room was not yet ready to go ahead with the strike. Even Dermer, Netanyahu's right-hand man and typically steady support for aggressive military moves, was getting wobbly on it at this point. On the key decision, the prime minister told his top colleagues, "I'm flying to the UN—I'll get back to you."

The prime minister caught a few hours of sleep on the plane. In this time, French President Emmanuel Macron called repeatedly to push a ceasefire in Lebanon. Netanyahu's aides refused to wake him for the call.

When he awoke, instead of calling France back, Netanyahu convened a phone meeting with the Israeli war council to say that he'd decided in favor of the strike. On Thursday, September 26, after an unrelenting four-hour conference call from New York's Regency Hotel, the prime minister got his cabinet to approve the attack—without coordinating with Washington.

* * *

The timing, however, was not yet final until Halevi and Gallant called Netanyahu's military secretary, Roman Gofman, on the morning of Friday, September 27. They had what Gofman—who is expected to become the next chief of the Mossad—called a "golden nugget" of intelligence: Nasrallah was talking about moving locations. If Israel were going to strike, the time was now. "We are very close to carrying this out. There is talk about Nasrallah moving," Halevi told the prime minister. Netanyahu banged on the table, exclaiming, "do it today!"

Around 9:30 a.m., Halevi had a special closed meeting with select Hebrew media military correspondents, including Yonah. After an hour and a half or so, in a very unusual fashion, Halevi left the meeting for around twenty minutes. Later, Halevi related that two discussions had taken place at that time. First, Halevi and Gallant spoke, with the defense minister coming to Halevi's office. Halevi told Gallant they wanted to strike Nasrallah that day, and Gallant approved.

Second, the two then called Netanyahu together. Halevi has said that he presented the assassination plan since he had initiated the call. Halevi gave the prime minister a fifteen- to twenty-minute presentation of the latest tactical status of the operation, including how it had been improved since they last spoke. The three key decision-makers of Israel's new war room also discussed their next steps in the war and what might be Hezbollah's response.

Halevi recommended that the assassination take place around seven hours later, at 6 p.m. Netanyahu wanted the attack carried out at 6:30 p.m. He was concerned that if it were any earlier, he would still be standing on the UN podium, giving a speech. With the Jewish Sabbath starting at that later time, however, Halevi wanted the attack to occur early enough that observant Jews in Israel would hear about it and know to be on guard for Hezbollah missiles in response.

In general, Halevi has credited Netanyahu regarding the timing of Nasrallah's assassination: "Carrying it out around his speech on Friday was a good trick" to get Hezbollah to lower its guard. "We would do it right after his speech but before Shabbat began at 6:30 p.m." Gallant said that Halevi quoted Tomer Bar as saying the attack had to occur during daylight because of the heavy tonnage of the bombs. Missing the target in the dark even slightly could have been disastrous for civilians. Halevi explained to Netanyahu that waiting was risky because if the fighter jets did not all launch and drop their bombs at the same time—if there was even a small delay in between their attacks—the probability of success for killing Nasrallah could drop dramatically. In the end, "it was decided to carry out the attack at 6:20 p.m., as the last rays of daylight were still out."

Yonah was less than 100 feet away while IDF chief Halevi and Gallant held the call with the prime minister and made the decision to strike that night. Later, in the early evening, Halevi sat with Tomer Bar and was updated on the attack scenarios. "It cannot get any better than this," he told Bar. Taking more time to plan and gather more intelligence was no longer worth it. "Let's do it," Halevi told the Air Force chief.

"As I gave the UN speech," Netanyahu told us, "I knew that the planes would be leaving very soon. As I came out of the speech a short time later, basically it's done."

* * *

There are some discrepancies about when final changes were made to the operational plan to assassinate Nasrallah. Gallant, who says he was entirely in favor of killing Nasrallah, told us that the last changes were made on Sunday or Monday, around five days before the attack. "I met with [Air Force chief] Tomer Bar on Sunday night, September 22, after approving Operation Northern Arrows for the destruction of Hezbollah's missile arsenal," he said. "I asked Tomer, 'how many tons of bombs are you dropping?' He responded, '40 tons,' which had a 90% chance of success. I said to double it to 80 tons and to take another round of sorties against Nasrallah's bunker, which would raise the likely success rate to 99%."

In Halevi's view, the idea that the operation was finalized by Gallant on Sunday was "a complete lie." He recalls presenting the assassination plan to the prime minister on Tuesday. Then, it was agreed to try to make it more precise to increase the probability of success, so the operation was delayed for a short period. Between Tuesday and Thursday, there were two processes connected to the operation that changed the plan, making it more precise and leading to a higher probability of success.

The IDF chief also was not sure where Gallant was getting the idea that he ordered the munitions to be doubled. There was already enough explosive power. Halevi approved eighty tons and did not know anything about an earlier forty-ton munitions point: "Tomer also doesn't remember this." Sometimes people just get confused, Halevi has pointed out, which does not mean anyone is lying. Air Force chief Bar showed Halevi two scenarios for the assassination, one in which they added a bit of additional munitions to slightly increase the probability of success, but nothing dramatic.

Gallant told us that his meeting about increasing the munitions from forty tons to eighty tons took place with one of Bar's top deputies, Brigadier General Omer Tishler, not with the Air Force chief himself. It was important to the defense minister to make it clear how large his stamp had been on the assassination.

By Friday, September 27, the day of the operation, Halevi and the IDF had achieved a 95 percent probability of success. They improved the intelligence and changed the operation, Halevi has said, focusing more precisely on the target area. This dramatically reduced the potential collateral harm to civilians and the international criticism that would accompany it. Waiting, however, could come at a cost. "On Friday morning, we learned that Nasrallah was thinking about moving to another place," Halevi recounted with some of the military officials involved. Halevi and Tomer Bar agreed that they should not keep delaying as the plans had been substantially improved. Halevi has said it was his initiative to update Gallant and then Netanyahu because of the unpredictable situation with Nasrallah.

The IDF chief shortened the readiness-to-attack status to a few hours. "Not everyone thought he would go out" and change his hiding spot, Halevi has said. "Some thought Nasrallah would wait there longer before moving, so initially Ron Dermer and the National Security Council chief suggested we wait until Sunday night." Halevi rejected this idea: "I said to the prime minister, 'It will be very hard to maintain immediate Air Force combat readiness for the strike for that long. We want to do this today.'"

Netanyahu began his talk at the UN in an arresting fashion. "Mr. President, ladies and gentlemen, I didn't intend to come here this year. My country is at war, fighting for its life," he said. "Hezbollah is the quintessential terror organization in the world today," he added, detailing its attacks on Americans and more recent missile assault on the north of Israel. "Israel has been tolerating this intolerable situation for nearly a year. Well, I've come here today to say enough is enough"—a late addition to the speech. His audience could not have known how immediately he meant it.

* * *

Israel's F-15I aircraft, known as Hammers, descended on Nasrallah's headquarters in the Dahiya suburb of Beirut, dropping heavy bunker-buster bombs to land precisely where there were tunnel openings that allowed them to dig deep underground. They were aided by targeting systems that Mossad operatives had earlier planted inside the building above Nasrallah's bunker.[81] Brigadier General Amichai Levine, the newly appointed commander of Israel's Hatzerim Airbase, told us that a large number of aircraft dropped additional bombs, one after another every few seconds, to ensure Nasrallah would not survive.

General Levine also added that it was his birthday, and that he considered taking out Nasrallah to be an unusually good present.

Netanyahu described the blow to Hezbollah of taking out Nasrallah as not quite fatal, but "near fatal." He asked us, "Remember what Nasrallah said about Israel? That we're 'weaker than a spider's web'?" Those were the Hezbollah's chief's words, adapting a phrase from the Koran, during the terror group's victory celebrations following Israel's withdrawal from southern Lebanon in 2000.[82] "We would collapse, this was their assumption," Netanyahu continued. He let that hang in the air for a second before rendering judgment: "Wrong."

Netanyahu also went further in claiming the success: "None of this would've happened had I succumbed to the pressure from abroad and from senior staff to end the war. I mean, they were OK in the initial phase of the war. When we went into the ground invasion of Gaza, they were fine. But the minute we started having international pressures on us, many of them caved." He continued, "Imagine that we had agreed to stop the war before Rafah—not finishing Sinwar, not finishing Deif, not going into Lebanon, not doing the pagers, not doing the rockets, not eliminating Nasrallah and all his top commanders. Where would we be? It would be a tremendous victory for Iran."

Gallant and Halevi have accused Netanyahu of inflating his role and deflating that of everyone else on all these points. Though the battle over credit would continue, all the members of Israel's new war room had notched a major victory in removing Nasrallah.

* * *

After Israel's September 17, 2024, beeper attack on Hezbollah and September 27 assassination of Nasrallah, the Iranian axis was reeling. Sinwar in Gaza, himself on the run, could not do much to respond. Hamas had to endure the piece-by-piece demolition of its ally to the north. Khamenei in Iran, by contrast, still had the means to show his fury, which would not be far off.

The Biden administration was alarmed, but also in awe of what Israel had pulled off with the pagers. The US reaction to the killing of Nasrallah, however, was much more negative, bordering on terror at the consequences.

By this point, Gallant and Austin had been working together for around twenty-one months and had spoken well over one hundred times, sometimes several times in a day or a week. The worst phone call they ever had, Gallant said, came when Israel assassinated Nasrallah. Some media accounts have said that this was the only time Austin—famous for keeping his cool even when delivering a firm rebuke—yelled at Gallant. "What did you say?" was Austin's stunned reply when Gallant informed him that Israel's planes were in the air, already on their way to take out Nasrallah.

Netanyahu took this as a vindication of sorts. When the cabinet had debated whether to inform the US before the start of the operation, Gallant had suggested the Biden team might offer to help Israel with targeting. Halevi had thought so too. The prime minister did not buy it. He told Gallant that if they asked for the Biden administration's permission, "140% they won't approve."

A senior Pentagon official told us there was no actual yelling on the call, but that Austin was firm and direct with Gallant over the Israeli decision to kill Nasrallah. Israel had taken a major strategic decision that could reshuffle the entire Middle East. It could explode into the regional war with Iran that the Biden administration had worked so hard to avoid. A phone call in advance might have been nice.

After calming down, Austin questioned Gallant, pressing him on if he really believed Israeli citizens would get back to their homes via this strategy. Even after Nasrallah was dead, Austin contended to Gallant, the Hezbollah threat would continue to loom over the north of Israel.

Later, trying to soften the blow, Austin made it clear that he viewed Nasrallah as an archterrorist with blood on his hands. However, he added that it seemed harder than ever, post-Nasrallah, to manage the escalation in a way that would get Hezbollah to stop firing on northern Israel. Austin urged Gallant to alter Israel's trajectory, saying the point at which no ceasefire plan would be possible was fast approaching. He added that Israel's enemies were around before October 7 and would remain afterward; Israel would have to leave room for diplomacy and find a way to coexist with those enemies.

In some ways, Austin was correct. There was no ceasefire for nearly two months after Israel killed Nasrallah. Yet he was also wrong. Israel's use of force would achieve what restraint and US diplomacy had not: compelling Hezbollah to stop firing on Israel and disconnecting its fight from Hamas's in Gaza. That blow, felt by the entire Iranian proxy axis, is what would allow northern Israelis to return to their homes in 2025.

* * *

After the killing of Nasrallah, its revered leader, Hezbollah fired only ninety rockets over the next twenty-four hours and a couple of hundred more in the following days. This was one measure of Israel's achievement. Out of an arsenal that still contained some one hundred thousand rockets, Hezbollah could not muster salvos anywhere near as large as it needed to fluster Israel.

Senior IDF sources told us they were surprised at how ineffective Hezbollah was at responding to the onslaught against it, in particular after Nasrallah was assassinated. But Israel was aggressively undermining

Hezbollah's capability to retaliate, far more than the terrorists ever would have expected.

When the IDF started to pummel Hezbollah, Israel believed it could achieve some element of surprise and degrade the terror group's second-strike capability. Still, the Home Front Command slapped restrictions on the entire north of Israel. The IDF put Haifa, Israel's third-largest city, on lockdown, with the expectation that it could get hit very hard. Instead, not a single person in Haifa was killed by Hezbollah during this part of the war, and the city was barely touched until the Israeli ground invasion of Lebanon.

Small Israeli cities like Safed, Acre, Nahariya, and Kiryat Shmona and villages further north that had already been under short-range rocket fire for extended periods remained under fire. While tragic, this constituted nowhere near the strategic threat the IDF had expected Hezbollah to pose. The military had worried about Hezbollah killing thousands of Israelis, while hitting Tel Aviv and critical infrastructure. A third of the country would lock down, but air defenses parried Hezbollah's attacks and Israel's central population centers weren't seriously menaced. Hezbollah had been infiltrated, overpowered, and sent into disarray, and everyone could see it.

Netanyahu, Gallant, and Halevi—Gantz was no longer in the war cabinet—believed the death of Nasrallah could do three things: First, it could bring Hezbollah to a ceasefire that would make the northern border sufficiently secure to allow Israel's evacuated residents to return. Second, it could bring the newly isolated Hamas to the negotiating table and free Israeli hostages. Third, it could deter Iran from further adventurism and any more direct confrontations with Israel.

When these gains did not materialize immediately following two weeks of hugely effective Israeli targeted strikes, Netanyahu and Gallant, with support from Gantz in the opposition, ordered the first serious Israeli invasion of Lebanon since 1982. (There had been a smaller, much criticized invasion in 2006.) Israel's security cabinet, led by Netanyahu, Gallant, and Halevi, met to discuss the matter at 7:30 p.m. on September 30, 2024, and was given several choices for what kind of invasion to launch. The idea was to focus on Hezbollah's stronghold in southern Lebanon, closest to the Israeli border. The decision, however, was far from automatic. There were quite a few ghosts from the past still lingering in the war room.

The 2006 IDF invasion of southern Lebanon was viewed as a disaster. Following a Hezbollah infiltration into Israel that killed eight soldiers and kidnapped two, the sluggish Israeli response led to the early ousting of then–IDF chief Dan Halutz. The first Air Force officer ever to become Israel's military chief, General Halutz had de-emphasized ground-forces training. The disappointing offensive was also one of the reasons Prime Minister Ehud Olmert was forced to resign early in his term.

During the 2006 invasion, Israel's reserve units were exposed as untrained and undisciplined. Their gear was defective, and many Israeli soldiers were killed in ambushes when Hezbollah tracked their amateurish use of civilian cell phones in the field. At the war's end, Hezbollah was still standing and gained a new luster from facing down the IDF. Iran restored Hezbollah's military losses and before long, the organization grew stronger than ever before. This experience fed fears of any new invasion, even nearly twenty years on.

Halevi and other IDF officials, however, told the war cabinet that this was a different military than the one Israel had fielded in 2006. Not only had the IDF revamped its training for reservists, but some of these reservists had now spent nearly a year fighting intense battles with Hamas in Gaza. Others had spent a year sparring with Hezbollah in Lebanon, even if not in a large-scale invasion.

After the devastation of Hezbollah during two weeks of targeted air strikes, Israel's leaders were ready to finish the job in southern Lebanon. A key focus of the invasion was to remove infrastructure that Hezbollah's elite Radwan Force had set up to invade Israel and threaten its northern towns. The Israeli plan called for a narrow incursion limited to southern Lebanon, yet many in the IDF feared mission creep—that developments could drag it into a wider invasion. If Hezbollah were to cause more deaths or damage to Israeli soldiers or civilians than expected, this would become even more likely. Then, Israel would be stuck in the mire, which is the automatic association that Lebanon conjures in the Israeli mind.

The war cabinet approved the invasion plan and was mindful not to overreach. "With success, the appetite for more grows," Netanyahu's foreign-policy adviser Ophir Falk told us, "but our goals in the north are limited." Israel had maintained reasonable US backing, despite the Biden team's misgivings about escalation, and the war room wanted to keep it that way. Israel had already amassed huge achievements against Hezbollah at a lower cost than anyone had predicted; it did not want that to change either.

The clock ticked much faster toward an IDF ground invasion as signs of Hezbollah's weakness grew. President Biden and a raft of US officials issued warnings, but at 8:39 p.m. on September 30, 2024, the IDF took last-minute measures to prepare an invasion, declaring closed military zones at Metula, Misgav Am, and Kfar Giladi in the north of Israel. Shortly after, the Lebanese Armed Forces started to withdraw from several positions in southern Lebanon where it expected the IDF to invade. The Lebanese army had been a bystander to the war waged from its own territory by Hezbollah. Now it was a bystander to the war waged against Hezbollah by Israel.

IDF officials canceled some planned interviews with us to attend emergency meetings during the final few days. All hands were needed for the invasion. Even on the afternoon of September 30, however, sources told us that a decision was still not final about the shape and size of the ground invasion. In the final days and hours, a sudden Hezbollah missile success against Israel, a readiness to negotiate, or a sudden increase in pressure from the US could have delayed an invasion.

Israel was sensitive not to be seen as an occupier in Lebanon and to frame its coming invasion only in terms of enforcing UN Security Council Resolution 1701. That resolution had brought an end to the 2006 Lebanon war, and had expressly obligated Hezbollah to keep its military forces north of the Litani River—away from the border with Israel. Hezbollah had flagrantly violated the terms, reentrenching itself in the Shia Muslim villages south of the Litani, with the UN peacekeepers' and Lebanese government's acquiescence.

Just prior to the invasion, the IDF destroyed a significant amount of Hezbollah's long- and medium-range missiles and rockets, which could have threatened Haifa, central Israel, and the Tel Aviv corridor. Israel also took out Eid Hassan, the commander of Hezbollah's medium-range rocket array, to weaken the terrorists' ability to mount a coordinated response.

Key IDF officials confirmed on September 30 that a clear majority of Hezbollah's capabilities had been neutralized. This was a sea change from September 27, when many top IDF officials were warning that such statements were hubris. The extended vacuum of a Hezbollah response to Nasrallah's assassination had shifted the Israeli defense establishment's view of how deeply the terrorist group was reeling. Several days after Nasrallah's death, it still was not clear who was running Hezbollah.

By the time the ground invasion formally began, overnight between September 30 and October 1, the world was already resigned to it. It barely seemed to make the papers. What in the past would have been an earth-shattering risk for Israel, and a major global story inviting all kinds of condemnations, had now been priced in. After all, the IDF official pointed out, "We took out Nasrallah, and the world is still with us. This is a total failure for Hezbollah." The domination continued on October 4 when Israel assassinated Nasrallah's likely successor, Hashem Safieddine. He lasted not even a week in the top chair.

Unlike with Gazans, few tears were shed for the small number of primarily Hezbollah-associated civilians caught in the crossfire. Lacking the Palestinians' substantial territorial grievances, Lebanon could not easily be portrayed as the victim of the war started from its territory by Hezbollah. Israel had put up with Hezbollah's rocket fire for eleven months, providing ample time for diplomacy. After those US-led efforts failed, Israel put on an awe-inspiring show, picking apart the terrorist group with two weeks of precise strikes.

President Biden criticized the invasion, but his comments were viewed by Israel as almost pro forma, unaccompanied as they were by any threat. This was not Rafah all over again, nor was there any presentation of an imminent diplomatic solution that Hezbollah would accept. In their stubbornness to keep shooting, the terrorists had made Israel's invasion inevitable.

* * *

As Israeli troops advanced, the IDF published pictures and videos of the thousands of weapons, many of them high-end, which it had found in village after village, house after house, in southern Lebanon. These weapons were planted by Hezbollah's Radwan Forces to be ready at a moment's notice to invade and conquer Israel's Galilee region. This had been a public plan of Hezbollah's since long before Hamas started to consider a full-scale invasion of Israel.

What Hezbollah had amassed near the border took Israel's leaders' breath away. "The subterranean network turned out to be enormous—much bigger than we thought," Netanyahu told us. This was going to be Hezbollah's main thrust for an invasion of the Galilee, he stressed. They could reach Haifa, easily, and beyond.

Prior to October 7, 2023, Hezbollah's elite Radwan Forces had around six thousand men, divided into six brigades and sixteen battalions, available to quickly invade Israel. Over the course of the subsequent war, this was reduced to several hundred due to steady Israeli airstrikes. After Israel's ground invasion, the figure fell to the dozens, and eventually there were practically zero Radwan fighters positioned close enough to get anywhere near Israel's border.

On October 8, 2024, a year after the Hamas massacre that started the war, Yonah embedded with IDF forces to visit what had been the Hezbollah stronghold of Blida in southern Lebanon. There, he saw what could have produced another massacre, perhaps even larger than Hamas's. The IDF's supremacy in southern Lebanon during the ground invasion masked how dangerous a threat the Radwan Forces had presented before the war. The comparison between the flimsy Israel-Lebanon border fence, which Yonah passed through, and the cache of arms that

Radwan possessed, suggested a grisly scenario of what would have happened if Hezbollah had invaded a year earlier at the same time as Hamas.

When the IDF announced in early October that its Alexandroni Brigade had found around eight hundred military vests, along with numerous grenades, mines, guns, and other weapons in villages in southern Lebanon, we no longer needed to take its word for it. Yonah got to see Hezbollah's weapons in their "natural environment," where they had been newly found, camouflaged in Lebanese villages. In one house alone, he saw dozens of vests, dozens of grenades, high-caliber guns, and a variety of other weapons. In other homes, he saw boxes full of long-range Kornet antitank missiles, which had made entire Israeli towns uninhabitable for months.

* * *

Israeli troops advanced all the way to the Litani River and the Wadi Saluki area of southern Lebanon. Over the course of the invasion, the IDF would seize 85,170 Hezbollah military items from more than thirty villages. Among these items were 2,250 large rockets and 6,840 antitank missiles and smaller rockets, of which 340 were the more-advanced Kornet missiles. There were also sixty antiaircraft missiles and twenty vehicles, often capable of firing a dozen or several dozen rockets at a time. Next, the IDF seized nine thousand improvised explosives, 5,560 guns, and around sixty thousand eight hundred electronic items, equipment, and documents.

The IDF said that it had killed 3,851 Hezbollah terrorists and wounded around nine thousand more from October 8, 2023, until the end of the invasion on November 27, 2024. The vast majority of the dead, around 3,017, were killed after mid-September 2024, when the IDF started its massive bombing campaign and then invaded on September 30. Naim Qassem, Hezbollah's new leader, would offer Hezbollah's first official casualty figures only in August 2025. He said Israel had killed five thousand Hezbollah fighters and wounded thirteen thousand more during the war. Israel would lose some eighty soldiers and forty-seven civilians on the northern front.

While Gallant has said that the IDF eliminated 80 percent of Hezbollah's large-scale firepower, and others have confirmed this, the IDF officially said that 75 percent of Hezbollah's short-range rockets and 70 percent of its strategic weapons were destroyed. One category of around forty thousand Hezbollah mortars had also been reduced to six thousand or eight thousand. Another category of long-range rockets was reduced from one thousand to around one hundred. In total, Hezbollah was estimated to be down to tens of thousands of mostly weaker and short-range rockets. By the end of the war, its capacity to fire large numbers of rockets at a distance had been substantially reduced.

Within a few weeks, it was clear the invasion had mostly succeeded. Israel's task from here was to pressure Hezbollah to agree to a "separate" ceasefire, one on Israel's terms. This would allow the IDF to continue attacking Hamas in Gaza and hold onto portions of southern Lebanon until Israel was satisfied that Hezbollah would not blend back into the civilian population of the Shia villages.

Despite these achievements and talk of an imminent ceasefire, Hezbollah fired 250 rockets at Israel on November 24, 2024 and more than thirty rockets and some drones into the north of Israel on November 25, wounding at least one Israeli in Nahariya.

Finally, on November 26, the mix of Israeli military action and US pressure from the still-in-office Biden administration and incoming Trump administration brought Hezbollah to sign a ceasefire mostly on Israeli terms.

Crucial to Israel's confidence in the deal was a secret side letter it received from the Americans. This letter, secured by Minister Ron Dermer, was signed by President Biden and approved by President-Elect Trump—a golden combination. It assured Israel that the US interpretation of the ceasefire terms allowed Israel to strike Hezbollah essentially as needed, when the terrorists inevitably violated the deal by reconstituting or resupplying their forces.

Around December 12, 2024, the IDF started to withdraw from portions of southern Lebanon as part of its ceasefire commitments. From the start, however, Israel dropped hints that the full withdrawal it had agreed to would depend on Hezbollah's compliance with its own obligations to withdraw from southern Lebanon and disarm.

Israel's achievements in Lebanon were breathtaking. Hezbollah's rocket and invasion threats were set back by many years. Former US National Security Advisor John Bolton told us Hezbollah had been reduced "to a shadow of itself," though he suggested keeping it on the run and further reducing its capacity to fire missiles at Israel. The group had suffered a huge degradation as a military force and even as a political player in Lebanon, though it still possessed rockets and strong support among the country's Shia population.

The bigger picture, with Iran and its "axis of resistance," had never looked better for Israel. Taking Hezbollah out of the fight meant that Israel could shift its forces and focus back to Hamas, whose hope that the northern front would pressure Israel into ending the war had been dashed. Now, Israel could also bear down on Iran. "Hezbollah meant everything to Iran because that was its protection," Netanyahu told us. "It was built for that purpose, first of all, to protect Iran by targeting Israel."

Already in December 2024, Netanyahu recognized the damage to Hezbollah as a "catastrophe" for Iran. With Hezbollah's defeat, Iran had lost what many Israeli security officials termed the regime's "insurance policy" against an Israeli strike. Were Israel ever to attack Iran's nuclear program, the expectation had been that Hezbollah would rain down one hundred fifty thousand rockets on the Jewish state. No longer. The terror group's knockdown and forced abandonment of Hamas, which was left alone under Israeli fire, also called into question the strength and cohesion of the entire Iranian "ring of fire." It was about time Iran's proxies understood that Israel was done being passive in the face of enemies who wanted to kill its people and wipe it off the map.

CHAPTER TWELVE

TEHRAN VS. JERUSALEM—ROUND TWO

At 7:31 p.m. on October 1, 2024, Iran fired more than 180 ballistic missiles at Israel. The barrage nearly hit Mossad headquarters and destroyed significant parts of two Israeli Air Force bases, Tel Nof in the center and Nevatim in the south, home to many of Israel's prized F-35 aircraft. Shrapnel fell in around one thousand different spots in Hod Hasharon, a medium-size city near Tel Aviv. Iran had launched some 50 percent more ballistic missiles than last time, in April 2024, and while Israel again managed to parry most of them, this time was a much closer call.

Israel's defenses had been penetrated. "They were very happy with it, even though it failed to kill Israelis," Prime Minister Netanyahu told us. "It was much more successful than their first attack." The barrage saw the IDF "hack" simultaneously into every cell phone in Israel to warn with a loud sign of an impending Iranian salvo, spreading fear and panic throughout the Jewish state. The government had never done this before. The purpose was to send all ten million Israelis into safe rooms and bomb shelters, not for the standard ten minutes after Hamas or

Hezbollah rocket attacks, but for around an hour—and perhaps longer—in the face of an unprecedented and unpredictable threat.

Clearly, Ayatollah Khamenei had not been deterred. Many Israelis, including top political and defense officials, openly wondered if this proved that Israel's April 2024 retaliation against Iran, taking out an S-300 air-defense system, had been too light.

Defense Secretary Austin in Washington did not think so, and he let Israelis know it. Austin cited all that Israel had done in September 2024 to dismember Hezbollah, including the killing of Hassan Nasrallah, on top of Israel's assassination of Hamas's Ismail Haniyeh in Tehran. These were blockbuster events that had provoked Iran's supreme leader anew. Israel had to find the balance, Austin believed, between striking back at Iranian proxies and avoiding escalation with Tehran.

IDF chief Halevi believed that Israel's April strike on the S-300 air-defense system guarding Isfahan had closed the chapter. "Only after we killed Nasrallah did it become too much for them," he told us. "No one said that the April attack would protect Israel from retaliation for all possible future actions."

There was another view. We can reveal that in the Mossad, director David Barnea believed that Nasrallah's death alone had not pushed Iran into another major attack on Israel. He pointed instead to the killing of Abbas Nilforoushan.

Nilforoushan was and is essentially unknown outside intelligence circles. Until Israel killed him in the same September 27, 2024, attack in which it eliminated Nasrallah, he was an Iranian brigadier general and deputy of operations for the Islamic Revolutionary Guard Corps. His military career went back forty-five years and included a variety of top posts. According to Barnea, in the same way that the killing of another Iranian, Mohammad Zahedi, had set off Ayatollah Khamenei in April 2024, Israel's killing of little-known Nilforoushan had triggered him this time. Proxies were one thing, Iranians another.

Everything was moving quickly. The Iranians had attacked Israel the night of October 1, not even 24 hours after the beginning of the Israeli ground invasion of Lebanon. When the barrage was over, an IDF official playfully texted top generals, "Do you remember when we invaded Lebanon this morning?"

"Iran made a big mistake tonight," Netanyahu said on October 1, 2024, after the Iranian attack, "and it will pay for it. The regime in Iran doesn't understand our determination to defend ourselves and retaliate against our enemies." He cited the Hamas and Hezbollah leaders whom Israel had killed since October 7, 2023, adding, "and there are probably those in Tehran who don't understand this. They will understand."

The question was whether President Biden understood. Before the attack, Austin had warned Iran of "severe consequences," a pledge reiterated by National Security Advisor Sullivan afterward. But what did they mean by that? Asked the next day, October 2, if Washington would support an Israeli strike on Iran's nuclear facilities, Biden said, "The answer is no." He also brought out the leaders of the G7 democracies to help restrain Netanyahu. "We will be discussing with the Israelis what they are going to do. All seven of us agree that they have a right to respond but they should respond in proportion," he told reporters. A message not to hit Iran's oil export facilities was also transmitted.

But the US presidential election was only a month away, and Donald Trump, the Republican nominee, felt much less of a need to hold back Israel from striking the Iranian nuclear program. "Isn't that what you're supposed to hit?" he replied publicly. "It's the biggest risk we have, nuclear weapons." He also told Netanyahu privately, "Do what you have to do."

Israelis were split on how to respond. The retaliation needed to be much harsher than it was in April, former National Security Council chief Yaakov Amidror, a confidant of Netanyahu, told us late in the evening on October 1, only hours after Iran's attack. "They didn't leave us a choice. They are acting now as if they can do whatever they want," he said. But "what to do exactly is very complex," he said. "Do we want to do something while we are in Lebanon?" he asked. "There is no rush. They won't disappear," and "the weaker Hezbollah is, the weaker Iran is."

Late on October 1, the IDF said that Iran's attack that night, much of it focused on Israeli air bases as in April, had not harmed the effectiveness of the Air Force on offense or defense. In addition, the IDF said there had been no "significant hits." But how did it define "significant"? The IDF said that no one was wounded or killed directly by ballistic missiles, and that only a small number were wounded by shrapnel. One Palestinian was killed by shrapnel in Jericho. The IDF also said that it had shot down a very high number of the ballistic missiles, along with substantial assistance in identification and interceptions from the US and other allies. But given the greater number of Iranian hits this time, there was less public bragging than in April about the help of those allies.

Iran's attack on Israel embarrassed both sides. It embarrassed Iran because it failed to kill Israelis or hit any aircraft. The F-35s and all their pilots had been widely dispersed before the attack, thanks to warnings from US satellite intelligence, which keeps track of the movements of Iran's TEL vehicles for positioning and firing its ballistic missiles. It was embarrassing for Israel because even the combined might of the Iron Dome and Arrow defense systems, along with US and other allies' help, was insufficient to block Tehran from bloodying Israel's nose.

This meant that Israel was going to strike back harder. A number of top officials insisted Israel finally had the legitimacy to hit Iran's nuclear program. On October 6, Gallant continued to threaten a major response and also claimed that the IDF's southern Nevatim base, which he had visited, was fully operational. Satellite imagery from foreign reports would indicate thirty impacts from Iranian rockets on the base, including on at least one runway.

Gallant was expected to fly to Washington. While Israel had retaliated against Iran after five days in April 2024, it seemed that Jerusalem would take weeks or longer to decide how to reply in October. Meanwhile, Iran grounded all flights throughout the country for several days, hoping it would be easier to track Israeli aircraft or missiles in empty skies.

Even if Israel's October response was going to be tougher than the one in April, Austin believed it still needed to be carefully calibrated and linked to efforts to steer the region in the direction of coexistence. It was not that the Pentagon chief thought some kind of warm peace would break out anytime soon. But he believed that Israel needed to find ways to live in the region without resorting to military action so often. Part of this was due to a concern that Iran would lash back at Israel with nightmarish consequences, which the country had been lucky to avoid with Hezbollah.

"The Iranians had a growing confidence," Netanyahu told us. "We had to respond, obviously, and much more forcefully." For at least a few days after Iran's attack there was an expectation that, despite US opposition, Iran's second massive barrage of the year might finally compel Israel to "go big" and take out Iran's nuclear program.

Then, a surprising development cut against public Israeli threats. As we reported on October 8, 2024, Netanyahu and Gallant—Gantz was long out of the picture—became opposed to striking the ayatollah's nuclear program. Confronted with the report, sources indirectly confirmed to us its thrust, which predicted that Israel's retaliation against Iran for its massive October 1 strike on the Jewish state would fall more in the medium range of attack scenarios.

This was partly due to loud opposition from Biden, Austin, and Blinken. In this atmosphere, Netanyahu and Gallant now opposed striking nuclear sites and moved toward the idea of attacking military and intelligence installations, especially those that had been involved in Iran's two attacks on Israel, and which could threaten the Jewish state going forward.

Despite the sense that this could be a once-in-a-lifetime chance to attack Iran's nuclear facilities, top Israeli sources indicated to us that such a strike wouldn't be consistent with the goals of the war. These were to defeat Hamas and free the hostages, and later to return Israel's northern residents to their homes. But another goal was not to be dragged into a regional war, especially with Iran. That could significantly impair Jerusalem's ability to finish off Hamas and beat back Hezbollah, not to mention disrupting relations with Washington.

Some senior Israeli officials did not view Iran's attack as a sign of readiness to get into a broader war, but as an attempt to rebalance its own deterrence with Israel. Still, it was stunning to hear top officials who were megahawks on Iran find reasons to pass up this golden opportunity.

Had some bizarre alternate universe taken hold? Iran had attacked Israel directly for a second time in six months, this time with more than 180 ballistic missiles that did considerable damage to Israeli Air Force bases and other sensitive sites. What else could Israel be waiting for before deciding to strike Iran's nuclear program? When would it have a better justification to its allies?

Before this war, the prevailing theory among Western analysts was that the Iranian regime was a risk-averse, rational actor that would not directly attack Israel with conventional weapons and certainly would not do so with nuclear ones. After two extraordinary direct attacks, Netanyahu could contend that Khamenei had turned a corner and was now capable of anything.

A major risk of hitting Iran's nuclear program had always been related to its proxies, Hezbollah and Hamas. It was said that if the IDF ever attacked the nuclear sites of Fordow or Natanz, Khamenei would order both proxies to rain hellfire down on Israel. By October 2024, however, Hamas had been bludgeoned and no longer posed a rocket threat, and Hezbollah had lost the capability to devastate Israel.

Another decades-long objection to striking Iran's nuclear program was that it could lead the Islamic Republic to fire large numbers of ballistic missiles at Israel, potentially killing thousands. But it had already fired the missiles. Besides, those dire predictions came at a time of uncertainty about the performance of Israel's untested Arrow missile-defense system. Now, Israel had proven that its defenses could largely stand up to Iran's ballistic missiles, even in major salvos.

The case had never been stronger to attack Iran's most valuable and dangerous asset.

To be fair, many Western officials and analysts had said that Israel could not successfully attack Iran's nuclear program on its own. Unlike Washington, Jerusalem lacked the mega bunker-buster bombs to destroy Iran's underground facilities, especially the uranium-enrichment site at Fordow.

There was no guarantee that the US would join an Israeli attack. There were some former senior US officials like John Bolton who told us that "the US should cooperate with Israel and join the effort, as the most effective way to eliminate the [nuclear] program." He added, "there will be no permanent peace and security in the Middle East until the regime in Tehran is overthrown. It is very vulnerable now, more vulnerable than any time since the 1979 revolution." But both US political parties had soured considerably on Middle East interventions. Direct US action alongside Israel seemed unlikely, no matter who was president.

This, however, should not have been a counsel of helplessness. We had published that multiple smaller bombs could be dropped repeatedly in the same area to cause an underground cave-in, not so dissimilar conceptually from how Israel killed Nasrallah deep underground with eighty-five bombs. Fordow was a good deal deeper, but such a cave-in could slow and damage Iran's nuclear progress.

If Israel would not strike now, it seemed as though it never would. Failing to do so would defy decades of statements by Israeli leaders. Netanyahu and Gallant had both pronounced the removal of the Iranian nuclear threat hovering around Jerusalem's neck as one of the greatest purposes of their lives in public service. The decision to shelve that now, when the ayatollah had given Israel the perfect justification, seemed to mark a dramatic shift toward emphasizing Gaza and Lebanon as bigger security issues than Iran, jettisoning a generation of Israeli security thinking.

* * *

Then came another blowout, one of the last between Netanyahu and Gallant. The defense minister had already announced his trip to Washington to sort out joint positions on Iran when Netanyahu ordered him to cancel his visit. The prime minister's and Gallant's staffs both leaked that Gallant could not fly to the US until such time as Biden would call Netanyahu. Deputy Pentagon Press Secretary Sabrina Singh acknowledged the reports of Netanyahu's order, but offered no explanation for the bizarre situation, saying she refused to engage in "Israeli politics."

Top Israeli sources told us that Netanyahu had canceled the flight to prevent Gallant from getting credit for solidifying a joint strategy on Iran. If true, this would be a nakedly political maneuver, given that Gallant and Netanyahu had similar views of how to respond to Iran's October attack. It was unclear if or when Gallant's visit could be rescheduled. In fact, he never would make the visit because Netanyahu fired him the next month.

Austin had also been slated to travel to Israel in September, but his trip was canceled due to escalating tensions between Israel and Lebanon.

Biden did not speak to Netanyahu in the aftermath of major Israeli attacks in Lebanon, including the assassination of Nasrallah, even though the US took to the skies along with four other armies—from the UK, France, Israel and Jordan—to defend Israel against Iran's ballistic missiles. When the first anniversary of the October 7 attack arrived, Biden called Israel's largely ceremonial president, Isaac Herzog, underscoring the absence of a Biden–Netanyahu call.

The US president would help defend Israel, but he did not want to boost its prime minister. Biden was furious with Netanyahu for refusing to end the war in Gaza, for surprising Washington with the Nasrallah assassination, and for a variety of aggressive actions that he believed had provoked the crisis with Iran that the US had worked so hard to avoid.

On October 9, 2024, Gallant said the IDF's counterstrike on Iran would put the original attack to shame. "The Iranian attack was aggressive, but inaccurate," he said. "In contrast, our attack will be deadly, pinpoint accurate, and most importantly, surprising. They will not know what happened or how it happened. They will just see the results."

On October 13, the US announced it had deployed a Terminal High-Altitude Area Defense (THAAD) battery and its one hundred–member crew to the region. President Biden said he was sending the system "to defend Israel" against a potential third missile attack from Iran, to follow any Israeli retaliation.

Iran did not take kindly to that. "The US has been delivering record amounts of arms to Israel. It is now also putting the lives of its troops at risk by deploying them to operate US missile systems in Israel," Iran's Foreign Minister Abbas Araghchi warned.[83]

Gallant spoke twice with Austin during this period, and Biden finally held a conversation about Iran with Netanyahu. Biden pressed his Israeli counterpart not to attack critical Iranian infrastructure or nuclear sites, and Netanyahu said he agreed. Israel would ultimately attack one nuclear component in Iran, but it largely complied with the Biden administration's request.

Netanyahu had an important reason to listen to Biden: Israel's potential shortage of interceptor missiles. Boaz Levy, CEO of Israel Aerospace Industries, the state-owned manufacturer of Israel's Arrow interceptors, told us he was operating triple shifts to keep the production lines active. It was no secret, Levy emphasized, that Israel needed to replenish its stocks of ballistic-missile interceptors.

The US THAAD system saved Israel from using up as many of those critical Arrow interceptors. Estimates for the cost of each Arrow interceptor range from $2 million to $3 million, depending on the missile. This means that between Iran's April and October attacks, Israel easily could have used between $600 million and $900 million in Arrow interceptors to defend itself. The real number was likely higher since the IDF has admitted to firing more than one interceptor at the same target sometimes. Israel also had been using these interceptors to shoot down the missiles fired at it regularly by the Houthis in Yemen and occasionally to shoot down missiles from Hezbollah. Defense sources acknowledged that there were instances in which Israel might decide not to shoot down even a ballistic missile due to the cost. It needed all the Arrows it could get.

In contrast to the Arrow, Iron Dome interceptors had a much lower cost of around $50,000 a pop. Israel was prepared to mass-produce and use more of them against the immense number of smaller and weaker rockets Iran's proxies have fired. Still, given the twenty-three thousand rockets shot at Israel by October 2024, the IDF also had to be more conservative in its use of the Iron Dome.

Despite some reports on and around October 15, neither Mossad chief Barnea nor other top officials such as Netanyahu, Gallant, or

Halevi were ever seriously considering giving Iran a pass. Some US officials hoped, however, that sudden pressure by Iran on Hezbollah and Hamas to cut a deal, including returning all the hostages, could make it harder for Israel to rock the boat. But perhaps a comprehensive ceasefire would have a glimmer of a chance only after Israel struck Iran. Once the proxies saw Israel strike their main sponsor, they might be more pragmatic, Jerusalem calculated. That hope was quickly dispelled. Hamas was hoping for a regional war between Israel and Iran, on the chance that it could pressure Israel into agreeing to a ceasefire on the terror group's terms.

In any case, Israel decided to wait to attack Iran until after the US had put the THAAD system in place. Given the time this took, there was even a point when some Israeli officials weighed waiting until after November 5, 2024, America's Election Day, under pressure from the Biden team. But after some days of discussion, the Israelis, and especially Netanyahu, decided they preferred to have the attack play out before the election. Waiting any further risked missing their chance altogether.

* * *

Back in April 2024, Gallant and Halevi had been the most outspoken in the war room about striking back aggressively against Iran. Over time, Netanyahu joined them in favor of striking Iran's S-300 air-defense system protecting its Isfahan nuclear facility. Even Gantz supported this strike eventually. After Iran's October 2024 attack, however, the positions in the war room had shifted.

Gallant and Halevi still wanted to be relatively aggressive, but they were much more closely aligned with the US. Netanyahu, by contrast, had become more aggressive across the board, and also more ready to defy the Biden administration. The US election was only a month off and Trump was favored or even in the polls. "The first time we responded with a powerful signal, but it was a signal," Netanyahu told us. This time would have to be more forceful.

Still, the prime minister wanted the US and its allies to help Israel defend itself from any retaliatory Iranian attacks. Netanyahu also felt it important to express gratitude to America for its help in parrying Iran's attack on October 1. Securing US authorization to fly over certain Middle Eastern states on the way to striking Iran would also help. Barnea continued to support a somewhat aggressive approach to Iran, while always emphasizing the need for US buy-in as a restraining factor.

That's where the war room landed: The US should not be disregarded, but Israel would have to hit Iran hard enough—and intelligently enough—to deter further attacks. This was the logic behind Israel's decision to strike the four remaining S-300 air-defense systems in Tehran, as well as more than a dozen other air-defense and ballistic-missile-production targets, and one nuclear-related target at Parchin. Tough, but not too tough.

In the early hours of October 26, 2024, only ten days before the US election, around one hundred Israeli aircraft and drones, including the F-35 stealth fighters, struck in about three waves at some twenty Iranian military sites spread across the country. There were reports of widespread internet outages in Iran as the attacks continued until 5:45 a.m., just as the sun began rising over Tehran. Several of the strikes targeted military bases across southern and southwestern Tehran, according to Iranian media.

The US was notified by Israel ahead of its strikes, but it was not involved in the operation. In a typical pattern, Iran's foreign ministry at first denied the attacks, then slammed Israel for them. According to Israeli intelligence, whose sources and methods are classified, the effect of Israel's retaliation was to reduce Iran's ballistic-missile production capacity—at least temporarily—from fourteen new missiles a week to one a week, and to leave Iran's nuclear program undefended and more exposed than ever to a potential attack.

"Iran was battered," Netanyahu told us. "They were dumbfounded when we took out their critical air defenses." Gallant made it clear that defanging all of Iran's best radar systems was one of his proudest moments, an issue he had worked on for years.

A few weeks later, on November 18, 2024, the prime minister would issue a directive to the IDF and the Mossad to prepare to remove the

Iranian nuclear threat by April 2025. At this point, few knew how seriously Netanyahu meant it, but the strike on Iran's air defenses had done enough to make attacking the nuclear program—considered for at least twenty years an existential danger to Israel—a much more realistic possibility. The door had been opened.

The hit on Iran's ballistic-missile production, the prime minister told us, "means they now have to calculate how much ammo they have, because it'll take them several years to resuscitate it—assuming we don't hit it again." This assessment would prove unduly optimistic, but Israel's strike did convince Iran not to retaliate against Israel or escalate further.

The IDF had also targeted some drone production facilities and air defenses for critical military bases, especially around Tehran, to let the ayatollah know that his military would be defenseless should Israel ever be given reason to attack Iran again. That would be more or less how it played out eight months later in June 2025. But for now, Israelis could only marvel at the possibilities that had opened up—and the opportunities that had been missed.

It would leak that David Barnea, the Mossad director, had wanted in October 2024 to attack Iran on a larger scale, including its nuclear program. Both in April and in October, he was ready to be highly aggressive against Iran—but not without US support. Other top Israeli officials found this position frustrating. Why emphasize a readiness to attack Iran's nuclear program if your key condition for doing so, US approval, would never be met?

"Again, Dadi [Barnea] can talk about destroying Tehran," Halevi has said. "But how many munitions will it take? How much of the nuclear program will we strike? There are not enough munitions to do it all." He added, "No one suggested striking Iran's nuclear program in October, and that includes the prime minister."

Halevi was proud of what Israel had accomplished in its strikes. "Iran was totally naked" without its air defenses, he said. "We took out all of their industrial production of solid propellants for their surface-to-surface ballistic missiles on the border of Iran and Iraq," and "we showed how precise we can be by striking Parchin," where "there was a depot with remains from a machine used during the Amad project in 2003." Amad had been Iran's first nuclear-weapons development program. "The machine we struck at Parchin, we hit only one part of the hangar where the machine was, and did not try to blow up the nuclear site in a larger way," Halevi said, highlighting the finesse amid the heavy bombing.

In May 2025, Halevi said, "They are still freaked out, even now, trying to figure out how we struck them." By the following month, the Iranians would have more to worry about, but for now Israel's strategy with Iran, Halevi said, was "playing with the pot without letting it explode."

Israel's response to Iran could have unfolded at any moment after October 1. In fact, there was an earlier point before the strike date of October 26 when Netanyahu had wanted to get it done the very next day, Halevi said. Israel had many reasons to delay, as we have seen. One of them, however, was entirely unexpected, and for once it was not another complication but a success.

CHAPTER THIRTEEN

THE DEATH OF SINWAR

Gaza still rankled. How could it be, Israelis wondered, that after IDF military victories in Gaza City, Khan Yunis, and even Rafah, Hamas's rule of Gaza persisted? Gallant had declared victory over Hamas's Rafah brigade, but what did that mean if Hamas was still fighting, still diverting and taxing humanitarian aid, and controlling Gaza's population? Worst of all, how could it be that Yahya Sinwar still lived?

The IDF devoted every resource to finding Hamas's leader in Gaza, but it had come up empty, day after day. It was a standing insult, and a taunt, that one full year after Sinwar had masterminded the October 7 attack, Israel appeared no closer to tracking him down. The longer it went on, the more demoralizing it became. While Sinwar lived to tell the tale, what Israeli victory could there possibly be? It felt as though the IDF could blow up every inch of Gaza and still not find him.

In February 2024, an Arab media report suggested Sinwar had fled to Egypt along with Israeli hostages.[84] IDF and Mossad sources told us this was not true, and that Sinwar still had tight control over hostage negotiations from Gaza. They turned out to be right, but at the time, the media report seemed plausible. After all, if Israeli intelligence really knew where Sinwar was, wouldn't he be in IDF custody already? Perhaps he had escaped and was laughing at the Israelis from afar. The mere prospect was infuriating.

What if, unbeknownst to Israel, its bombs had killed Sinwar earlier in the war, and he was buried underground or beneath the rubble? Gallant had openly speculated about this and even suggested it was true. Was Israel chasing a mirage? Or was the archterrorist surrounded by so many hostages that Israel, as intelligence sources sometimes implied, could never get near without risking the hostages' lives?

The IDF's assumption for many months in 2024, backed by some intelligence findings along the way, had been that Sinwar was hiding in Rafah. It made sense: Until May, Israeli troops hadn't fought there, so it would have been relatively safe. It was by the Egyptian border, which offered a potential escape route. Given that Sinwar had previously been in Khan Yunis, his hometown, it would have been easy for him to flee further south to Rafah by tunnel or among the mass of civilians who did likewise.

That was the IDF's theory, and it stuck to it. It turned out to be true, but after Israel invaded Rafah in May and failed to turn up Sinwar in June, July, August, or September, the trail appeared to the public to have gone cold. The most wanted man in Gaza seemed again to have evaded Israel—if he was even there at all.

Those summer months when Sinwar was nowhere to be found featured some of the roughest war-room and public debates about whether a deal to end the war should be struck with Hamas before it would be too late to save the hostages. In July 2024, the IDF assessed that the war would end with hostages still missing like Ron Arad,[85] a soldier who was captured in Lebanon in 1986 and was never found. How many would die in prolonged captivity? We will never know for sure what might have been for those hostages who ultimately returned home in body bags.

It turned out, however, that Israel had Sinwar on the run. He never stayed in one location for long and avoided all electronic communications technologies, relying instead on messengers. But as the IDF advanced, the Hamas chief was running out of places to hide.

Military sources have leaked that an August operation in Rafah likely came close to killing Sinwar. Then, on August 31, 2024, six hostages—Hersh Goldberg-Polin, Eden Yerushalmi, Carmel Gat, Almog Sarusi, Alexander Lobanov, and Ori Danino—were discovered slain by Hamas in a Rafah tunnel. The IDF believes Sinwar had stayed in the same tunnel complex as them, a few hundred meters away. At times, they were likely his human shields. Soldiers found DNA from Sinwar that suggested he had been there soon before their deaths, likely between August 21 and August 27.[86]

The hostages' corpses also suggested that they had been badly malnourished. Their captors may have considered them too weak to be transported away when IDF soldiers came near and Sinwar himself fled. That an IDF advance near where hostages were hidden had led Hamas to murder those hostages rocked Israel and set off a political crisis for Netanyahu, who had argued that military pressure would save hostages, just as it had in November 2023.

Though the IDF and the Mossad did not know it, for the next two months, Sinwar was likely without hostage cover. Gaza's border with Egypt was also now blocked by Israel. If Sinwar had wanted to escape for good—against the view of Israeli intelligence that he was dead set on staying in Gaza to maintain control—he had missed his chance.

* * *

Then, on October 16, 2024, it happened. Unlike so many other terrorist leaders whose deaths are detailed in this book, Sinwar was not felled by any operation, immaculately planned by Israeli intelligence. Neither ingenious sabotage nor overwhelming air power took him down. Instead, it was the steady military pressure that limited Sinwar's options and forced him to take risks until he met an Israeli foot patrol, in the right place at the right time. Separated from his guards, he died alone. Sinwar's luck had finally run out.

In a badly needed vindication for Israel's war room, the big catch was in Rafah, the city everyone had warned Israeli leaders not to invade. Sinwar had been moving from home to home, on the run likely since fleeing the tunnel holding the six hostages in late August 2024. The IDF had been searching the area for tunnels and destroying buildings near where Sinwar would be discovered.[87] The pressure was on.

The fateful sequence began at 10 a.m. on October 16, 2024. Soldiers from Israel's Bislamach Brigade—a training battalion for squad commanders, called into the fighting during wartime—noticed several suspicious figures entering and exiting a damaged structure in a rubble-filled area. They fired on it and had a drone watch the area to detect movement. Sure enough, at 3 p.m., three armed men left the building, moving from house to house. Two of the men were checking the area in front of a third, Sinwar. The trainee soldiers fired again, wounding some of the three men, whose identities they did not know. Two fled into one structure and the third, Sinwar, fled into another. Now on his own, Sinwar climbed to the building's second floor.[88]

If Sinwar thought he could hide, he was wrong. A tank from Battalion 195, the armored training battalion known as Adam, fired on the building. Not taking chances, the soldiers then directed a reconnaissance drone through the window, taking footage that would become famous around the world. With wreckage strewn all about, a hunched Sinwar sat very still in a cushioned chair. He was badly hurt and gripping a chunk of wood. Stiffly, he swung his arm back and up to throw the wood at the Israeli drone. He was unable to twist his body to face his electronic pursuer, so the throw was weak.

It was one last gesture of resistance, futile but loaded with symbolism. As the drone retreated, the Israeli squad commanders in training began to fire once more. The building collapsed and took Yahya Sinwar's life with it.

The young soldiers had no idea whom they had killed. To them, this was just another rank-and-file Hamas fighter. Evidently in no rush, Israel took until the following day to confirm that the dead body was Sinwar's. Arriving the next morning to sift through the rubble, it was a different group of soldiers who wondered about the visual resemblance. The IDF said Sinwar was found with a bulletproof vest, grenades, and forty thousand Israeli shekels, valued at around $10,700.

"We unleashed a lot of gunfire and a lot of artillery," a soldier involved in the attack on Sinwar told Israeli media. "When we heard he was killed, we joked around, saying, 'How crazy would it be if it was us?'" Israel checked Sinwar's dental records and fingerprints with those from his time in Israeli prison. It was a match. This was the moment Israelis had been waiting for—they got him.

"I stand before you today to tell you that Yahya Sinwar has been eliminated," Prime Minister Netanyahu announced that night, October 17, 2024. "This is the beginning of the day after Hamas," he promised. "It's now clear to all, in Israel and the world, why we insisted not to stop the war—why we insisted, in the face of all the pressures, yes to go into Rafah, the fortified stronghold of Hamas, where Sinwar and many of the mass-murderers were hiding."

IDF chief Halevi emphasized not the chance encounter with Sinwar but the unified IDF effort that had ensnared the terror leader. The military operations to hunt down Hamas throughout Gaza, and in Rafah in particular, had paid off.

Benny Gantz, now from the opposition benches, applauded the troops' success. "It sends a very clear message to our enemies: Israel will not rest until those who harm us pay for their crimes," he said. "The IDF will have to continue operating in Gaza for years, but this moment must be seized and leveraged to bring the hostages home and topple the Hamas regime."

Defense Minister Gallant stressed the terror chief's cowardice. "Sinwar concluded his life defeated, chased, fleeing, and not as the commander, but as someone who only worried about himself," he said. But upon the IDF's release of the drone footage of Sinwar's last moments, many in the Arab world would take that feeble toss of wood as a demonstration of character, of true defiance. They would see a martyr.

How had Sinwar remained on the loose for so long? Top Israeli defense officials told us in April 2025 that a large strategic tunnel between Khan Yunis and Rafah, which they uncovered only then, had probably been one of his main ways to avoid detection while maintaining control of Hamas's southern forces. Israel had previously destroyed many tunnels during this war, but evidently not enough of them. Sinwar became more vulnerable only when he was likely cut off from much of that tunnel network, and had to come above ground.

To millions of Israelis, Sinwar's death signaled that at last there had been real retribution for the October 7 massacre. Its mastermind had paid the price, and the most basic of Israel's war aims had been achieved. As Netanyahu suggested, there was sudden optimism that the end of Hamas rule could be near. What would the group be, on the run without its fanatically committed leader?

On the theory that Sinwar had been obstinate where other Hamas leaders might be flexible, many thought this was the chance for a hostage deal. The Biden administration quickly picked up the opportunity, but it was not to be. Hamas had lost its most effective and now-legendary leader, but its fundamental strategy had been set: Outlast Israel, bleed it with hit-and-run attacks, and trust that international pressure over humanitarian suffering would eventually exhaust it. Hostages could be exchanged to head off extreme danger, but as many of them should be preserved for as long as possible.

Sinwar would be replaced by his own brother, Mohammed. In Hamas, there would be more continuity than rupture.

Biden administration officials even told us that the killing of Sinwar delayed a potential deal. Hamas, they said, could not be seen as caving in to Israel or even negotiating with it in the immediate period after Israel had killed its leader.

In some quarters, Sinwar would be mourned. Mahmoud Abbas, the president of the Palestinian Authority in the West Bank, offered condolences on Sinwar's "martyrdom," calling him a "great national leader." Turkish President Recep Tayyip Erdoğan also saluted Sinwar—while receiving Iran's foreign minister and Hamas's top terrorists in suits for meetings.[89] One other party may also have been hit hard by Sinwar's death: The Hague.

* * *

In May 2024, while seeking arrest warrants for Netanyahu and Gallant, the ICC's Khan also targeted three Hamas leaders. But when all three were killed, the prosecutor was stripped of even a fig leaf of moral equivalency. He would only be prosecuting Israelis. After applying for arrest warrants, he had faced little meaningful pushback from countries around the world. But on October 17, the day after Sinwar's death, Khan's world would begin to crumble.

An anonymous X account calling itself "ICC Leaks" and Britain's *Daily Mail* tabloid broke the story of sexual assault allegations against Khan by a female employee, including a cover-up. The alleged victim, an ICC lawyer, said she did not want to undermine Khan's case against Israel. Khan denied any misconduct. A whistleblower report, which Elliot obtained in October 2024, recounts the female lawyer's examples of Khan's alleged nonconsensual behavior: Locking her into his office and sexually touching her, visits to her hotel room in the middle of the night, demanding to be let in; claiming to have a headache and lying on her hotel bed, touching her sexually. The whistleblower says he was sent out of the country by Khan and threatened by Khan's wife.

Two and a half weeks after learning of the allegations, Khan announced his decision against Israel. Looking back, the timing appeared to head off any probe into the sexual allegations against him. The ICC kept quiet about the brewing scandal for more than five months. Khan suggested it could be a nefarious plot against the court. But the story gained steam following investigations by *The Wall Street Journal* and Associated Press and demands by the ICC staff union.[90]

* * *

Just as Khan's scandal broke, the US election campaign entered its final stages. Israel and Gaza were not major issues of the US presidential contest, which were focused on Joe Biden's, Kamala Harris's, and Donald Trump's competence for office and domestic-policy agendas. But for much of the Democratic Party's activist base, Israel and Gaza were highly salient. President Biden had been heckled repeatedly by left-wing and Muslim activists as "Genocide Joe" for his support for Israel and failure to end the Gaza war.

Dealing with the same hecklers after she took over the Democratic Party ticket, Vice President Harris typically brushed them off as helping Trump. Asked after the election if Israel was committing genocide, she said that was for a court to decide and added, "When you look at the number of children that have been killed…the refusal to give aid and support, we should all step back and ask this question and be honest about it." Postelection, Harris would suggest that the issue on which she had disagreed most with Biden was Gaza. She had wanted him to be harder on Israel.[91] It's little wonder, then, that preelection polls found Israelis overwhelmingly preferred Trump to Harris—by a four-to-one margin, according to Israel's leading TV news station.[92] American Jews went in the opposite direction, broadly supporting the Democratic Party, as they have in the past. Most US Jews backed Biden and then Harris over Trump on questions of social and economic policy as well as concerns about democracy.

Israelis, however, looked to their own region. In his first term, President Trump had moved the US embassy from Tel Aviv to Jerusalem, treating it at last as Israel's capital, and recognized Israeli sovereignty over the Golan Heights. He had built a "maximum pressure" sanctions campaign against Iran and negotiated the Abraham Accords to normalize relations between Israel and Arab states. Netanyahu retained some reservations about Trump's unpredictability. He had few doubts about what a Biden or Harris administration would look like regarding Iran or Gaza, however, and that was the problem.

Beyond the 2024 election, there were reasons to be concerned about the growing US partisan split on Israel. Many Israeli critics of Netanyahu slammed him for the increasing identification of support for Israel with the Republican Party and Trump. But in the here and now, the choice seemed clear to the Israeli public.

The prime minister had been taken by surprise by Biden's collapse in the June 2024 presidential debate, having expected him to survive for the ninety minutes and then see it declared a victory by the media. But even before, Netanyahu had been closely attuned to Biden's fading chances, and had bet big on a Trump win. Already in March 2024, an official in the prime minister's office had fantasized to us about a Trump golf course in Gaza.

Amit Segal, among Israel's most plugged-in political columnists, told us that same month that the Netanyahu government was "counting down the days" of the Biden administration. Rather than wrap up the Gaza war on Biden's terms, and be pressured to withdraw fully, dismantle buffer zones, hand over control to the Palestinian Authority, and lay groundwork for the creation of a Palestinian state, Netanyahu saw an opportunity to end the war on more favorable terms under a Trump administration.

Israel's prime minister also looked toward Iran, where his most important goals lay for Israel's security. Biden, and subsequently Harris, would be highly unlikely to countenance an Israeli strike on Iran's nuclear program, let alone assist. Netanyahu and Minister Ron Dermer thought that Trump, thoroughly unconventional and committed to a tougher stand against Iran, might well give Israel the green light. It is no coincidence that on November 18, 2024, only a few weeks after the US election, Netanyahu would issue a directive to the IDF and Mossad to prepare to remove the Iranian nuclear threat by April 2025.

If Biden had won, Israel likely would soon be under more pressure to shut down its multifront fight. With Trump, nothing was assured, but there was a chance to finally remove the Iranian nuclear threat. It was a strategic risk Netanyahu was willing to take. It would pay off for Israel, though Netanyahu's identification with Trump doubtless has contributed to weakening Democratic Party support for the Jewish state.

When Harris ascended to the top of the Democratic ticket in early August 2024, the matter became even clearer. She did not have the instinctive pro-Israel convictions of old-style Democrats, many thought. If Biden had often been "the most pro-Israel person in his own government," as one Israeli military official put it to us, Harris could be expected to swim more with her party's current.

On November 4, 2024, a day before the US election, while Israel remained on guard for an Iranian retaliation, a senior Israeli official put it to us bluntly: "If Kamala wins, Iran might shoot at us again. If Trump wins, it would be suicidal of them to do so." Such comments should trouble those concerned to keep US support for Israel bipartisan, but this is how many Netanyahu supporters saw it.

* * *

On Election Day in the US, Netanyahu fired Gallant. Though long rumored, the timing came as a shock. Indeed, it was almost unfair. The day's other news, of Trump's election, was simply too course altering for Israelis to muster the kind of protest wave in defense of Gallant that might have been expected. People did take to the streets, but not for long, and not in the way they did when Netanyahu had tried to fire Gallant in March 2023 after he had opposed the government's judicial overhaul.

Netanyahu had also tried to fire Gallant a second time in late September 2024, hoping to replace him with Gideon Sa'ar. A onetime Likud minister and Netanyahu challenger, Sa'ar was ready to rejoin the government from the opposition. Instead, Netanyahu decided to trigger the pagers in Lebanon, and wanted Gallant's steady hand for a bit longer. Then Iran's October 1, 2024, strike on Israel intervened and delayed the firing further.

With so many active fronts, it seemed inadvisable to fire a defense minister such as Gallant with serious military chops. Besides, while Netanyahu wanted Sa'ar to buttress his coalition, he was not enamored with the idea of installing another independent actor as defense minister. The prime minister wanted a trusted lieutenant pushing the military where he wanted it to go.

When Netanyahu finally fired Gallant, it was too busy and demoralizing a day for the Biden administration to object effectively to the loss of its preferred interlocutor, the one it trusted. "The surprising decision to fire Defense Minister Gallant is concerning, especially in the middle of two wars," a US official told reporters.[93] But that was about it. The Biden team viewed it as Netanyahu placing politics over talent in the cabinet, but Netanyahu, and no one else, was the prime minister of Israel. Politically, he would get away with it.

Netanyahu would explain that he had lost trust in Gallant, and that Gallant had lost trust in him. This was true enough, but it had been the case even before the war. The prime minister also knew that Gallant had frequently briefed reporters against his policies, but again, this was nothing new. More important, Netanyahu would complain of real policy differences, arguing that he was entitled to a defense minister who shared his priorities.

Fundamentally, Netanyahu said that Gallant had become Washington's man. He knew the US had tried to play him through Gallant, using the Israeli defense establishment as its forward position. "First, he wanted US approval before Rafah," Netanyahu told us, adding that Gallant had at times questioned the military necessity of taking the city. "Second, Gallant said we have to brief the Americans before the beeper operation" against Hezbollah. "Third, Nasrallah. He said the Americans must be informed."

Gallant responded that Netanyahu himself had wanted to check with the US before attacking Hezbollah in October 2023, and that he had never voted against any of the attacks against Rafah or Hezbollah. The two of them could continue the debate endlessly. Gallant, along with most Israelis, would interpret the firing differently—as a consolidation of power and the triumph of politics over security. In a speech after his dismissal, Gallant told the country it stemmed primarily from "my firm stance that everyone of conscription age must serve in the IDF and defend the State of Israel." This, the issue of conscripting Haredi Jews, had been the big story leading up to the firing. Gallant's principled, and popular, stance threatened the survival of the government, which relied on ultra-orthodox Jewish parties dead set against any military service.

While more than one thousand Israeli soldiers were killed during the October 7 war and more than sixteen thousand wounded, Israel's Haredi community largely sat it out. The arrangement had become untenable—socially, morally, and even militarily. Israel needed the troops, and its Jewish majority was outraged by the lack of solidarity from these fellow Jews.

Later, in June 2025, Gallant's narrative was strengthened when Netanyahu was recorded telling an important Haredi rabbi, "We had enormous obstacles that we removed. You know, when the defense minister is against you and the [IDF] chief of staff is against you, you cannot move. Now we can move."[94] The prime minister did not really think that the ultra-Orthodox should be wholly exempt from service, but he was unwilling to lose his government in wartime over the longstanding issue. Gallant would also argue that Netanyahu had blown potential chances at earlier hostage deals and cite his own advocacy for a state commission of inquiry on the failures of October 7 to explain his firing.

After Netanyahu dismissed Gallant in November 2024, Sa'ar would join the government not as defense minister, as originally planned, but as Israel's foreign minister. Admirers in the opposition called Sa'ar a flip-flopper and a traitor. The new minister, in turn, decried the "sanctimony on their lips and obsession with ousting Netanyahu in their hearts, as if we hadn't gone through the hardest year in our history." Sa'ar's small faction added four more seats to the government majority, bringing it to eight—sixty-eight seats out of 120 in the Knesset. This provided Netanyahu a cushion and denied his hard-right coalition partner Itamar Ben-Gvir the ability to bring down the government on his own. Ben-Gvir's faction contributed six seats to the coalition, five of which he could control reliably.

Gallant remained a persistent critic of Netanyahu's policies from within the Likud fold, but he had been alienated from his party, caricatured by Netanyahu supporters as someone who had folded to the Biden administration and held back the prime minister. Gallant's independent political appeal was limited by his role of defense minister on October 7, but he had gained new respect from centrist voters by taking on Netanyahu and the other, even less-popular coalition leaders on matters of principle.

The previous foreign minister, Netanyahu loyalist Israel Katz, would slide into the defense role. Katz had served as a platoon leader in the paratroopers, but no higher. An experienced government minister, he nonetheless lacked Gallant's stature. Katz's elevation signaled the shrinking of the war room. For better or worse, it would now be almost entirely Netanyahu's show.

CHAPTER FOURTEEN

WALTZ WITH BASHAR

After Israel's September 2024 offensive, Hezbollah had lost its fastball, curveball, and slider. It was without most of its top leadership, including its mastermind and charismatic leader; its rocket arsenal; and its ability to invade Israel on the ground. Eager to escape further punishment, Hezbollah went back on its word and agreed to a ceasefire with Israel on November 27, 2024, abandoning Hamas to fight on its own.

Planning could now begin for Israeli civilians, displaced for endless months, to return to their homes in the north of Israel. Their land would no longer be a de facto buffer zone, which had shrunk the usable State of Israel. Instead, that buffer zone would shift north, into southern Lebanon, where Israel would build five outposts to hold as an insurance policy against Hezbollah's return.

Perhaps if Lebanon were a real state, Prime Minister Netanyahu thought, Israel could make real peace. But—intractably divided and unable to rein in Hezbollah—it isn't, so he prepared accordingly. Part of the ceasefire's logic was that Israel needed time to rearm and refresh its troops. If Hezbollah flagrantly violated the terms of the ceasefire, Netanyahu expected Israel to be ready for a full-scale offensive after the deal's preliminary sixty-day quiet period. If not, he expected a steady stream of smaller Hezbollah violations, which would lead the IDF to strike back repeatedly and maintain those security outposts indefinitely.

The ceasefire, then, was largely a polite fiction. Force would still rule, but both sides had reasons to accept the fiction and limit the fighting for the moment.

With an estimated 70 percent of Hezbollah's best missiles destroyed, the balance of power had shifted. Israel could and did attack Hezbollah anytime it violated the ceasefire by trying to return arms and fighters to southern Lebanon, and anytime it tried to reestablish weapons depots and factories anywhere in Lebanon, including in Beirut. The ceasefire's enforcement was about power, not paper, and no one could question where the real power resided.

The weight of the north had been lifted from Israel's shoulders, and benefits redounded in every sphere. The most positive of all would come in Syria.

* * *

When the Assad regime in Syria fell in early December 2024, the Israelis were as surprised as anyone. Netanyahu had received zero early warning from Israeli intelligence. He found out along with the rest of us, as rebel forces led by Ahmed al-Sharaa captured Aleppo, then Hama, then Daraa and then the Syrian capital of Damascus.

In lightning-fast speed, more than thirteen years of civil war would resolve itself in less than two weeks of fighting—right after the ceasefire in Lebanon. And it never could have happened without Israel.

There's a short story and a long story. The short story is that Israel hit Hezbollah so hard that it and its Iranian masters were prevented from coming to the Assad regime's rescue, as they had done in 2012.[95] Turkey gave the Syrian rebels the green light to advance once Israel's fight with Hezbollah had paused. No one wanted to be seen as aligned with Israel, though the rebels' actions surely helped Jerusalem in the broader fight against Tehran.

Bashar al-Assad, the dictator of Syria ever since his father died in 2000, had plenty of armaments. He needed troops—shock troops, specifically—willing to put up a fight and drown the rebels in a sea of atrocities.[96] This time, in disarray after the Israeli campaign, Hezbollah was in no position to bail out the Syrian regime.

Iran itself tried to pick up the slack, unwilling to surrender its Syrian pawn so easily. Iran sent an airborne division on its way to Syria shortly before the Assad regime's fall in early December 2024, only for Israel to force the plane to turn around. For the Iranians, it was either that or be shot out of the sky. At the same time, Russia—Syria's other backer—had its hands full in Ukraine. Moscow had also grown fed up with Syria's ruler, whose uncompromising stance required more and more foreign intervention to sustain.[97] As a result, when the rebels began their final march, Assad was left to fend for himself.

The Syrian army crumbled and Assad fled to Moscow. Did the dream of the Iranian "resistance axis" die with Assad's regime? Suddenly, people began to ask the question.

Hafez al-Assad, Bashar's father, had ruled Syria since 1971 and invaded Israel in a surprise attack with Egypt to start the 1973 Yom Kippur War. Though an armistice was reached the following year, Syria never formally concluded hostilities, let alone made peace. A loyal Soviet client over the decades, Assadist Syria faced new challenges after the fall of the USSR in 1991. Another blow arrived in 1994, when the heir apparent, Bashar's brother, Bassel al-Assad, died in a car accident.[98]

This thrust Bashar into a role for which he had never been thought of before. At the time, Bashar was living a quiet life in London, training to work as an ophthalmologist. Unlike his father and brother, he had no military background.[99] The prospect of a weak ruler frightened many regime loyalists but delighted other Syrians, and many in the West, who saw hope for reform. Surely, Westerners reasoned, the London ophthalmologist would refuse to play by the brutal 1982 "Hama Rules" that governed his father's conduct in leveling much of his own Syrian city, with maximum disregard for civilian life, to put down dissent.[100]

The optimists were wrong. First, Bashar turned to North Korea for help to produce nuclear weapons. Israel's intelligence agencies almost missed this but eventually would eliminate the resulting Syrian nuclear reactor in a secret 2007 air strike.[101] Second, Bashar turned to aggressive repression of dissent in response to the pro-democracy protests of the Arab Spring in 2011. He had learned how to use force to crack down on opposition at least as harshly as his father had done. Next, as the country descended into civil war in 2011 and 2012, he would prove he had the sternness and brutality to save his throne.

To keep power, Bashar massacred his own people and flattened his own cities. When his army was not enough, he came to rely on Hezbollah, Iran, and Russia. Though he ruled a state, Assad in many ways became another Iranian proxy, propped up by and accountable to Iran and Hezbollah next door. Over the years of the civil war, Syria became the central supply and transit hub of the entire Iranian proxy network.

Islamic Revolutionary Guard Corps generals orchestrated the regional anti-Israel strategy from Syrian territory. They used it to transport weapons to Hezbollah in Lebanon, Hamas and Islamic Jihad in the West Bank, and various groups in Jordan. Syria's geographical position made it the critical link in the network.

Israel was well aware of this long before October 7, and in 2013, it began to strike Iran-linked targets in Syria. The idea was to take out long-range Iranian weapons before they could be transferred to Hezbollah, and to do so without sparking a larger war. Thousands of targeted air strikes would follow during the years of the Syrian Civil War, and Hezbollah and other Iran-backed groups would occasionally fire missiles at Israel from Syrian territory.

This was part of what Israelis called "the war between the wars." The occasional strikes became an accepted part of the regional dynamic. Israel did not want to provoke anything larger, the Assad regime had its hands full with internal enemies, and the Iranians were content to let the Jewish state bleed and expend resources fighting their proxies.

Though the Israeli strikes continued, they were never able to shut down the Iranian smuggling network. Hezbollah would become "the most heavily armed terrorist group in the world," as Yitzhak Gershon, a major general in the Israeli reserves, told us while he served on the northern front. The war between the wars had taken a large chunk out of Hezbollah's armament efforts, but not nearly enough. Likewise, Israel had failed to convince the Syrian regime to cease giving over its territory for Hezbollah and Iran's use. Israel was active, but one-off air strikes simply were not sufficient.

When Yahya Sinwar launched Hamas's October 7 attack, he looked to Hezbollah for help. While Hezbollah joined the war the next day, October 8, Syria stayed out. Direct fighting wasn't its job. Its role was to let itself be used as a command post and a land bridge, transferring weapons to the entire Iranian proxy network.

"We warned Assad not to let Iran supply Hezbollah with weapons through Syria," Netanyahu told us. "He played dumb. And I said, 'If you let stuff go through, we'll take care of you.' Well, it turns out we didn't have to. Somebody else did."

That somebody would be President Recep Tayyip Erdoğan of Turkey. Ankara had been committed to the overthrow of the Assad regime since 2011, seeing an opportunity to install an ideologically aligned Sunni Islamist regime to its south. At first, Turkey supported the Free Syrian Army, providing weapons and training. Then, it assembled a new rebel coalition that it would use as a proxy, along with regular Turkish troops, to occupy parts of northern Syria in 2016.[102]

The Turkish-backed rebel coalition became the Syrian National Army in 2017, and it would ally itself with Hayat Tahrir al-Sham (HTS), the Islamist rebel group of Ahmed al-Sharaa, who had been an al-Qaeda commander under the nom de guerre of Abu Mohammed al-Jolani. When Sharaa's HTS fighters took the major Syrian city of Aleppo on the path to victory in December 2024, some of them hung Turkish flags over its walls.[103]

Sharaa, born to a Syrian Sunni family originally from the Golan Heights, grew up in Damascus. He joined al-Qaeda after the 9/11 attacks but not long before the US invasion of Iraq in 2003. He fought US troops in Iraq until his arrest in 2006. For five long years, he was jailed—but also kept safe—by US forces. After his release, he was tasked by al-Qaeda in Iraq's Abu Bakr al-Baghdadi, later the leader of ISIS, to expand al-Qaeda's influence in Syria. Then, in 2012, Sharaa founded the Nusra Front, the Syrian affiliate of al-Qaeda. Its goal in fighting Assad was not to establish democracy, as it was for some of the rebels, but to impose strict Sharia law.[104]

In 2016, the Nusra Front announced a break from al-Qaeda, with whom the Nusra Front said it no longer had "external ties." Sharaa's idea was to focus solely on Syria, as opposed to al-Qaeda's global war with the West. But many were suspicious that this was merely an attempt at image management. Sharaa began to show his face and drop the outfit of turban and robes in favor of shirt and pants. In 2017, the Nusra Front merged with other Syrian Islamist and jihadist groups to form HTS, which presented itself as "an independent entity that follows no organization or party, al-Qaeda or others." Al-Qaeda condemned the merger, but for years the US government maintained that HTS kept a link with al-Qaeda. In HTS's designation as a foreign terrorist organization, the US government called Sharaa's group a "vehicle to advance [al-Qaeda's] position in the Syrian uprising."[105]

The debate about Sharaa's ideology still rages, but General Petraeus gives him his due as a military man. "In Syria, you had a well-trained and experienced leader who had actually spent years investing in building a military force, even including the equivalent of infantry officer basic course and advanced courses. They invested, with help from Turkey and Qatar, and others, and built a force that was really quite capable at the same time that Bashar Assad's force was collapsing around him."

Turkey, which had sustained the rebels through hard times, is believed to have given at least tacit approval for the final offensive that delivered the coup de grâce.[106] The success of that operation, however, is partly Israel's. "We had already cut off the supply" of Hezbollah fighters, Netanyahu told us. "That's why the Syrians were caught." Many analysts agree.

In late 2023 and through 2024, Israel had intensified its bombing campaign in Syria. What had been one-off strikes to trip up the Iranian transport network became heavy and sometimes daring attacks to shut down that network. This meant bombing Iranian weapons depots in

Syria territory, Iranian operations at Syria's international airports and in its largest cities, and senior IRGC officers operating out of Syria.

On December 25, 2023, an air strike outside Damascus killed Iranian Brigadier General Sayyed Razi Mousavi, the IRGC's senior adviser responsible for coordinating the military alliance between Iran and Syria, with Tehran accusing Israel. The message was that no Iranian would be safe in Syria. It was reiterated the next month, on January 20, 2024, when an Israeli strike on a house near Damascus killed five IRGC members, including the intelligence chief for Syria and his deputy. Iran's senior command in Syria was being wiped out.[107]

On February 1, 2024, Reuters reported that the Revolutionary Guard was pulling out most of its remaining senior officers from Syria along with many midlevel officers as well. It was simply too dangerous, and Israel's assassinations risked forcing Iran into a direct response it might have preferred to avoid at that juncture. Reuters's sources said "the Guards would manage Syrian operations remotely, with help from ally Hezbollah."[108] Some lower-level Iranians would remain in Syria, and Israel would continue to target them. As the Iranians were steadily pushed out, Syria became ever more dependent on Iran's other proxy, Hezbollah.

Iran did have one other wild card in Syria: its long-range precision-missile factory underground at Maysaf, in northwest Syria. The Islamic Republic had started building it in late 2017, with Israeli intelligence watching the whole way. Perhaps the best example of Israel's new aggressiveness in Syria was its spectacular September 8, 2024, covert operation, carried out by Shaldag special forces against that factory.

Several Israeli attempts to destroy the factory from the air had failed over the years, but in August 2024, the newly confident IDF began planning a radical new concept. It would attempt a combined ground and air operation at a size and scale that it had never done before so deep in Syrian territory. A series of prior operations to degrade Syria's air defenses cleared the way to the facility, 125 miles into Syria.

Then, more than 120 Israeli soldiers, backed by a large number of supporting aircraft, briskly dropped in on the facility's guards. The

Israelis took them by surprise and then fended off Syrian reinforcements during the precisely timed two-and-a-half-hour operation.

The IDF broke into the facility and placed charges meticulously at preplanned locations to blow it up from the inside. Soldiers involved told us it was the most significant operation in which they had ever participated.

The result was to close the door on a dangerous plot by Iran and Hezbollah to manufacture between one hundred and three hundred long-range missiles a year near the border with Israel. If successful, it could have obviated the need to smuggle missiles from faraway Iran, shifting the balance of power. But in hindsight, the success of Israel's operation, which proceeded almost without a hitch, may have been a hint of the Syrian army's growing weakness and Assad's vulnerability.

* * *

As the Assad regime collapsed, it didn't take Israel long to recover from the shock. The fall of an Iranian pawn—the linchpin of its proxy network—was already a victory, but Netanyahu saw in it an even greater opportunity. "I took a leaf from Churchill" in World War II, he told us. Churchill "had bombed the French Navy in Oran," on the coast of French Algeria, "because he thought that it would fall into Nazi hands" after the fall of France in 1940.

"Do you know about this?" the prime minister interrupted his story to ask. When Elliot told him that he did, and supplied the name "Mers-el-Kébir," the Algerian port that Churchill struck, Netanyahu let out a sigh of relief, audible over the phone, and lightened up. A son of a prominent history professor, the prime minister lives for this sort of thing. He often feels frustrated when people with whom he must work are ignorant of the historical parallels he sees all around him. How can they understand him, a man of history, if they don't speak his language or recognize the standard by which he tries to govern?

The day the Assad regime fell to Sharaa's rebels, on December 8, 2024, the IDF sprang into action. In quick strikes that went unopposed, Israel destroyed the major assets of the Syrian military: Chemical weapons, air-defense batteries, combat aircraft, helicopters, drones, the naval fleet, weapons stockpiles, production facilities, and even tanks.

Since Syrian air defenses were no longer operating, the Israeli Air Force could act freely. In forty-eight hours, Israel carried out 480 strikes, wiping out an estimated 70 percent of Syria's strategic capabilities. A Syrian rebel commander told the Syria Direct news outlet that it would take decades to rebuild the Syrian army.[109]

Netanyahu continued with his Churchill example. "I think he killed 1,300 French sailors, which is very tough. In our case, I don't know if we killed anyone, but we certainly smashed the weaponry of the Syrian army," the prime minister said. "We don't want all the stuff the Syrians amassed falling into the hands of the jihadists," who might use it in future attacks against Israel. "So, we knocked it out."

Taken from the pages of history, the operation put to bed the Syrian threat that had dogged Israel ever since its founding. The significance of the regional shift "goes back to the rise of the Assad regime 57 years ago," Netanyahu told us. "It's a huge change and it will affect everything." To start, it laid the groundwork for a very different balance of power and relationship with the new Syrian regime. In time, this would even open the door to peace negotiations, but nobody was certain of that in December 2024. Sharaa, after all, had been an al-Qaeda commander. He still had a US bounty on his head.

"Nobody knows what to make of the rebels," a senior Israeli official told us in the new regime's first month. "Anyone who says they do is lying." One question the prime minister's office had was why Assad's army didn't seem to fight back at all during the final rebel offensive. Speculations ran wild, and no one was ready to talk positively about Sharaa's government. "Distrust and verify" was Netanyahu's watchword, even as he gladly pocketed the win against Iran.

It was also a return to form for Israel. "Power isn't merely guns, missiles, tanks, and aircraft," Netanyahu told us. "It's the will to fight and seize the initiative."

In Syria, Israel seized the initiative not only from the air, but also on the ground. From the day the Assad regime fell, December 8, 2024,

Israeli troops advanced to take strategic positions on the Syrian side of the border. Assad's troops had abandoned their posts, and Israeli officials worried about jihadists taking their place.

They also saw opportunity—the high ground of the Syrian Mount Hermon was open. What if Israel never again had to worry, as it did for decades, about Syrian artillery taking up those positions? What if Israel could later trade back that land for peace? This was the action of an Israel unafraid, an Israel that knew it had a now-or-never chance to secure all its fronts and transform the Middle East.

Yonah embedded with the IDF in early December 2024 for the first Israeli media visit to Syria since the 1974 armistice following the Yom Kippur War. At a Syrian army base in Tel Kudne, the IDF had captured abandoned tanks and weaponry. No Syrian soldiers were in view for several miles. Meanwhile, Israelis were at work digging deep trenches to stymie potential invaders.

Yonah would visit Syria again in March 2025, ascending by helicopter 9,232 feet above sea level to the Syrian peak of Mount Hermon. With a view of dozens of miles in all directions—some days even to Damascus, not to mention the Iranian smuggling routes—the strategic value was obvious. Israeli alpine commandos and snowmobile drivers had by then settled into a comfort zone in the new territory.

The IDF began briefing reporters that the Iranian axis of Tehran, Damascus, and Beirut was gone. Israelis were not the only ones to notice; President Biden even started taking credit, never mind his constant push to de-escalate and contain the fighting. "Our approach has shifted the balance of power in the Middle East," he said in December 2024. "Neither Russia nor Iran nor Hezbollah could defend this abhorrent regime in Syria. This is a direct result of the blows that Ukraine and Israel have delivered upon their own self-defense with unflagging support of the US." To Netanyahu's pleasure and bemusement, Biden was coming to view the success of Israel's regional war as part of his legacy.

Netanyahu saw Israeli activity in Syria first as a way to prevent a resupply of Hezbollah. He also saw opportunities for peace, but most of all, the prime minister viewed it in terms of the larger fight with Iran.

Assad's fall "degrades the main problem," he said. "We always said 99% of our problems came from one place, Iran. And now its proxies—boom, boom, boom."

Many Israeli goals in Syria would be announced or intimated. Jonathan Schanzer, the executive director of the Washington-based Foundation for Defense of Democracies, told us that "Israeli action in Syria is all about containing Turkey's Neo-Ottoman expansion." The protection of the Druze minority, present in Syria as well as Israel, where the Druze are beloved for their eager participation in the IDF, was also a big one. Israel instructed the new Syrian army not to venture south of Damascus, creating a massive buffer zone, to shield Syria's Druze-majority Sweida province.

Both motivations were certainly in play, along with the pragmatic need to defend the Israeli border against a great many unknowns. Israel would urge both the US and Russia to keep their troops in Syria, in the interest of stability and security. But it all comes back to Iran, whose pipeline to rearm Hezbollah was disrupted and whose remaining forces were swept out of the country. For Tehran, it was an unambiguous defeat. The tide had turned. The war that Yahya Sinwar had set in motion had by now backfired worse for the Iranian axis than he ever could have imagined.

CHAPTER FIFTEEN
THE WAR THAT DIDN'T END

Israel was on a roll. The September to November 2024 victory in Lebanon had yielded December's unexpected gains in Syria, which gave way in January 2025 to a long-awaited hostage deal and ceasefire with Hamas in Gaza. For the outgoing Biden administration and the incoming Trump administration, it was a rare bipartisan achievement.

The Biden team brokered the agreement and deserved substantial credit. It took painstaking work to hash out the deal's key tenets and complicated implementation scheme among the parties and mediators. It also took resolve to stick to those terms as Hamas, now led by Yahya Sinwar's brother, Mohammed, bargained for more. This Sinwar was viewed as just as stubborn as Yahya and determined to present the war as a victory. But Israeli intelligence also thought that the defeat of Hezbollah and the fear of President-Elect Trump made him more likely to cut a deal.

"I laid out the precise contours of this plan on May 31, 2024," President Biden said. That was true. But there was a reason it didn't happen then, when Hamas rejected it, as opposed to January 2025, when Hamas was staring down the barrel of a Trump administration. For a year, the Biden team had pushed this rock up the hill only to see it roll back down each time.

Donald Trump had issued a threat to Hamas during the presidential campaign. "I tell you this," he said at the Republican National Convention. "We want our hostages back, and they better be back before I assume office or you will be paying a very big price." In Jerusalem, Israel's leaders were struck by the thought that this was more forceful than anything they had heard from Biden on the issue in nearly two years.

Trump kept it up after his election victory, threatening "all hell to pay" if Hamas failed to free the hostages by the day of his inauguration, January 20, 2025. Prime Minister Netanyahu was overjoyed. For months before the election, he and his advisers had sensed a chance for Trump to "pull a Reagan in 1980," when the incoming US president was able to orchestrate the release of fifty-two US hostages from Iran on his Inauguration Day. No one wants to spend four years on the bad side of a new US president. Now, "time is no longer on Hamas's side," a senior Israeli official told us. "There is again no daylight between us and Washington."

The threats—and the prospect of political relief for the Israeli war effort in Gaza—ushered in a hostage deal on January 15, 2025, only days before Trump's return to the White House. The deal freed thirty-three Israeli hostages held in Gaza, plus five Israeli guest workers from Thailand who were released separately. Included were the corpses of Kfir and Ariel Bibas, the redheaded Israeli brothers kidnapped at the ages of nine months and four years old. News of their loss was a crushing blow to Israelis, especially as Hamas made a macabre show of parading their coffins and celebrating their deaths. Israeli forensics would determine that the boys had been brutally murdered. Hamas's ugly hostage-release ceremonies also antagonized the new US president.

The freedom of the hostages still alive came as an enormous relief to the Israeli public, which seemed to have been holding its breath since October 7, 2023. But it also came at a cost. Israel released nearly two thousand Palestinian prisoners, including more than one hundred serving life sentences for involvement in murders of Israelis. Some of these were sure to return to the fight and cost Israeli lives in the future. Israel also withdrew from most of Gaza, including the Netzarim corridor that bisects the Strip into north and south, and retreated to the buffer zones it had created on the Gazan side of the border.

For one Israeli party, the price was too high. On January 19, 2025, Netanyahu's hard-right coalition partner Itamar Ben-Gvir quit the government, along with his Otzma Yehudit party. This was Israeli politics in miniature: While Netanyahu was fighting off a large political attack on his left flank, which pushed for a final hostage deal to end the war, he also had to worry about his right flank, where politicians like Ben-Gvir wanted a military occupation of Gaza and the return of Israeli settlers to the area. Since the other right-wing coalition partner, Bezalel Smotrich, stayed in the government, Ben-Gvir could not force an election by himself—nor did he really want to. Ben-Gvir would return to the coalition on March 19, 2025, after he was satisfied that the temporary ceasefire had failed to become permanent and that Netanyahu would fight on in Gaza. But the episode illustrates how shaky the political ground was on which Netanyahu was trying to stand.

Just as notable as the price that Israel paid for the ceasefire, however, was the price that it did not pay. Israel did not have to leave the Philadelphi Corridor separating Gaza from its Egyptian supply route or agree to end the war at the outset of a deal. Instead, negotiations over an end to the war would start in earnest only toward the end of the six-week ceasefire, the first phase of the hostage deal.

Despite high hopes for the release of all the hostages and a lasting end to the war, very few in Israel gave a second or third phase a high probability of occurring. Israel had secured side letters from both Biden and Trump assuring it that unless Hamas agreed to negotiate in good faith toward its own disarmament and exile (which it was not considering), Israel could resume the fight in March 2025.

This constituted a victory for Netanyahu. "No one expected Israel to get 33 hostages out without giving up on Philadelphi and a permanent end to the war," his foreign-policy adviser, Ophir Falk, told us. It had been widely predicted that Netanyahu's decision to oppose those terms would doom the hostages. Israeli opposition officials would say that the hostages could have been returned several months earlier, with more of them still alive, and with Israel's standing in the world less damaged. But in the end, Hamas did in fact budge on Netanyahu's two major demands.

Big news came during the ceasefire on February 4, 2025, when, alongside a rather stunned Netanyahu, Trump said that Gaza's population should leave the Strip during the long rebuilding process to come. The US, he added, should take it over and make it into the "Riviera of the Middle East." Calling Gaza a "demolition site," Trump expressed a desire to "resettle people permanently in nice homes and where they can be happy and not be shot, not be killed."

On one hand, this seemed finally to offer the people of Gaza their right to flee the war. On the other hand, a total removal of the population seemed unlikely without the use of force, which Israel opposed as illegal and wrong. The Trump administration would clarify that it also opposed forced relocation, but most of the world was aghast at the plan and ran out of adjectives to express dismay.

Israel accepted the Trump plan; no need to be more circumspect than the president. But few countries would take in Gazans, and none in significant numbers, so the plan stalled for months. Its larger significance may have been to shift the conversation. If only to ward off Trump's idea, Egypt, the UAE, and the Arab League finally released their own postwar Gaza plan with some more concrete commitments and price tags.

The Palestinians were now on the political defensive. Netanyahu had long resisted putting forth a plan of his own for the "day after" in Gaza, to the consternation of the Biden administration, the Israeli defense establishment, and most of the West. Now, however, it seemed more likely to proceed on Israeli terms.

The ceasefire's "first phase" wound down in March 2025, and Netanyahu removed his IDF, Shin Bet, and Mossad hostage negotiators. In their place, he picked Minister Ron Dermer, whom he knew he could count on to resist demands for a final end to the war other than on his terms. Hamas, in turn, was not ready for an unconditional surrender.

Both sides dashed the hopes of most Israelis that the deal would continue to bring home the rest of the hostages.

Yet as the ceasefire ended, the war didn't restart. For two and a half weeks in March, Hamas did not release more hostages, and Israel did not resume hostilities. Instead, the two sides bartered over numbers: Hamas would agree to release five hostages in exchange for another long ceasefire, while Netanyahu demanded a minimum of ten hostages. Eventually, the prime minister convinced US envoy to the Middle East Steve Witkoff to take the same position, but neither of them could convince Hamas. Again, the Israeli Left and center were devastated that the ceasefire was not extended to return some number of hostages, even if Hamas would agree only to give up five when Netanyahu was demanding ten.

Witkoff was named US envoy to the Middle East, but in practice, the billionaire executive was the all-purpose top diplomat of the Trump administration. Jetting from one conflict zone to another, he had a straightforward task: Make deals. He had learned the art in the real-estate business, where he became a friend and trusted adviser of the president, and also gained extensive business ties to the Gulf monarchy of Qatar. A hyperconfident American Jew—earlier in his career, he kept a copy of the book *Tough Jews* on his desk—Witkoff had no diplomatic experience and limited knowledge of Middle East politics. Yet the president's envoy had common sense, such as the need to set deadlines to avoid interminable negotiations. Having lost a son of his own to a drug overdose, he also spoke with genuine personal emotion about the plight of the hostage families and the need to save their loved ones.

Netanyahu stalled on the battlefield, eager to show the Israeli public he was trying with Witkoff for a deal. He also used the dead time to replace IDF Chief of Staff Herzi Halevi, who had brought Hezbollah to its knees and beaten Hamas militarily. He was forced out by Netanyahu, who sought stronger action in Gaza going forward whereas Halevi supported ending the war to return more hostages. Halevi also felt the need, in the end, to take personal responsibility for a portion of Israel's failure on October 7, 2023. Halevi believed Netanyahu was equally responsible, but the prime minister had the power to push Halevi out, and only a future election could force out Netanyahu.

Major General Eyal Zamir, Halevi's replacement, was a former military secretary to Netanyahu. Outside the military, Zamir was widely viewed as a more aggressive general, though inside the army, Halevi was also viewed as aggressive. Either way, Netanyahu tasked Zamir with leading a new Gaza offensive.

The first preparatory step for Israel, announced with the end of the ceasefire on March 2, 2025, concerned humanitarian aid. "In light of Hamas's refusal to accept the Witkoff outline," Netanyahu said, "we have decided to prevent any entry of goods and supplies into Gaza." Aid had flooded into the Strip during the six weeks of the ceasefire, and as a result, the Israelis estimated Gaza was stocked for at least two to three more months.

It was part of a plan to squeeze Hamas, which stole and taxed aid to pay its fighters, distribute patronage, and keep control of the people of Gaza. In theory, perhaps the Trump–Witkoff plan could have worked. But mixed with politics and nightmarishly complicated logistics, the plan would crater. The idea had been pushed by Netanyahu's right-wing coalition partners, and Gallant or Gantz were no longer in the war room to push back against it. Before long, it would turn out to be one of Netanyahu's greatest wartime errors, undermining his other policies going forward.

* * *

On May 10, 2025, *The Wall Street Journal* reported that the accusations against ICC Prosecutor Karim Khan were far more serious than had previously been known. Khan was accused by a subordinate ICC lawyer of forcing sexual intercourse upon her multiple times and then of pressuring her to disavow the allegations. While he had earlier implied it might all be an Israeli plot, it turned out the accuser was a Malaysian Muslim who strongly backed his case against Israel's leaders.

Finally, Khan took leave from his job. His deputies would stand by the arrest warrants for Netanyahu and Gallant, which the ICC's lower trial court had granted in November, but critics now had additional ammunition to question their legitimacy. The WSJ's headline said it all: "ICC Set Plan to Charge Netanyahu Just After Prosecutor Was Accused of Sexual Assault."

Also in May, General Zamir's long-awaited offensive began. The goal was to capture 75 percent of Gaza—essentially all of it except the difficult urban terrain of Gaza City and the hostage-laden central camps. This time, Israel would not raid and then leave the areas in which it fought, but stay and hold the territory. It was an implicit acknowledgment that the tactics of the previous eighteen months, approved by Netanyahu, Gallant, and Halevi, had failed to break Hamas's guerrilla war or political dominance in Gaza.

Israel's raid-and-leave tactic had come under heavy criticism internally for allowing Hamas to regroup in areas where the IDF had already fought and won, sometimes at heavy cost. Having to fight for the second or third time for the same neighborhood seemed to epitomize the problem with Israeli strategy in Gaza. Could Hamas ever be defeated in this way? As the war dragged on, right-wingers would blame the failure to hold onto territory. Pragmatic defense officials like Gallant and Halevi, along with Israelis on the political center left, would blame Netanyahu's refusal to hand the keys to Gaza over to new management, such as the Palestinian Authority or Egypt and the UAE, or a hybrid of the three. The raid-and-leave strategy would be left with few defenders.

Timed with the May 2025 offensive, and two months after Israel's aid squeeze had begun, the IDF resumed the flow of aid to Gaza—but with a twist. The brand-new, privately run Gaza Humanitarian Foundation (GHF) built and began operating four large distribution sites for Gazans to get aid directly. Previously, Israel had relied on the UN and other international groups to send out aid trucks, which Hamas or local gangs would often loot. Gazans had typically found themselves buying food aid from merchants, with Hamas taking a cut, rather than receiving it for free as intended. The GHF aimed to change all that.

The UN's Integrated Food Security Phase Classification (IPC) had been warning of famine in Gaza since December 2023, each time to a gusher of media headlines. In March 2024, the IPC projected famine "anytime between now and May 2024." No one was called to account when the famine failed to materialize. When the IPC warned on May 12, 2025 of an "imminent risk of famine," the Israeli public was not buying it. Netanyahu was now heeding the long-standing right-wing argument that the UN aid system was at least indirectly propping up Hamas.

Backed by Israel and the US, the GHF immediately generated controversy. The UN and other aid groups refused to work with it. They viewed the new competition as an arm of the Israeli military and objected to the danger its methods posed to Palestinians.

As large masses of Gazans traveled past IDF lines to reach the GHF distribution sites, there were several incidents in which the IDF admitted to mishandling crowd control. Dozens of civilians were killed before Israel got the problem under control, but it was too late for the new aid mechanism's reputation. The still-opaque casualty numbers were likely a fraction of what Hamas and many media outlets claimed, but top IDF officials acknowledged that too many civilians had died and Israeli troops needed to do better. It did not help that IDF forces had not been outfitted with nonlethal crowd-control measures, such as water cannons and tear gas. These were not police but soldiers in a war zone; bullets were all they had when crowds came too close.

It also did not help that Hamas worked to instigate stampedes to bring about the anti-Israel international headlines it desired. In two months, the BBC ran 33 separate headlines promoting claims that Israeli forces killed civilians seeking food at GHF aid sites.[110] Aryeh Lightstone, who worked on the Abraham Accords in the first Trump administration and fought for the GHF harder than anyone else in the second, argued that the new aid mechanism "caused Hamas more fear than anything else has in the past two years." He saw cutting out the UN as essential to ridding Gaza of Hamas in the long run.

In only a few months, by the end of September 2025, the GHF had distributed over 175 million meals to Palestinians in southern Gaza. If only Netanyahu had not waited to launch the new aid program until after Gaza's food stocks had been running low, its successes might have received greater notice. The Biden administration had been pressing for "day after" planning to replace Hamas politically on a variety of fronts since early 2024, and Gallant and other Israeli defense officials said they had pushed for programs similar to the GHF much earlier in 2024. An earlier start would also have given the GHF time to raise funds and scale up operations, including to northern Gaza where the hunger was the worst.

Instead, Israel's decisions generated a race: Would the new aid system first bring Hamas to its knees, or would it provoke a humanitarian crisis that would elicit more international pressure than Israel could bear?

CHAPTER SIXTEEN

RISING LION, MIDNIGHT HAMMER—THE TWELVE-DAY IRAN WAR

Israel's attack on the Iranian nuclear program was anything but inevitable. Iran could have crossed the nuclear threshold. Or there could have been a new and perhaps inadequate nuclear deal that might have pushed off the threat for a brief time. Until the very last moments, both alternatives had seemed more likely than what was to become Israel's most daring action of the war.

The Biden administration had long sought a nuclear deal with Iran, but negotiations never advanced enough to nail down anything final. President Trump got the talks he wanted by making clear that the only other option was force. "Something's going to happen one way or the other," he said, and military action would be "a terrible thing—for them." Iran long insisted it would never negotiate with Trump and spent the Biden years talking about killing him. But faced with a credible military threat, Iran relented.

The US and Iran began negotiating in earnest in April 2025. At the outset, Trump set a two-month deadline for the talks to ensure he could not be "tapped along" indefinitely. US envoy Steve Witkoff was sent to face off with the highly experienced and specialized Iranian negotiating team. You could fill textbooks with what the US envoy did not know about Iran's nuclear program, but Witkoff had a clear idea of what a negotiation should look like.

There were points at which they appeared to be closing in on a relatively weak, preliminary nuclear deal, sending shivers through Israel's political and defense establishments. Yet the US was unable either to swallow or dislodge Iran's demand that it be able to continue to enrich uranium at home. The only reason for Iran to insist on this, and to reject sensible alternatives even at the risk of inviting a massive attack, was to keep open a short path to a nuclear bomb—and everyone knew it.

With negotiations deadlocked on June 12, the last day of Trump's two-month deadline for a deal, the UN's International Atomic Energy Agency (IAEA) formally found Iran in violation of a wide variety of nuclear obligations. One of the IAEA reports included a devastating table of Iran's efforts to sanitize illicit nuclear sites. Over and over, once an illegal, undisclosed site had been exposed or the IAEA had made a request to inspect it, Iran would move containers, destroy the buildings, and sometimes even scrape the ground. When asked, Tehran provided false explanations that the IAEA said weren't technically credible. On at least one occasion, the Iranians acquired in advance the questions to be asked at inspections from what the IAEA called "highly confidential documents."[111]

Israel attacked the next day, June 13, 2025, stunning the world. Iran had run out of time. But there was nothing inexorable or obvious about that Israeli decision or the process that led to it. In fact, Iran's entire security doctrine was developed with the idea of making such a strike too costly for any adversary to undertake.

It took Israel a long time to prepare its attack plans for the twelve days that shook the world in June 2025. In early 2023, long before the war, the IDF had already started to shift its structure, personnel, and resources significantly toward readiness for a large attack on Iran. At that stage, however, the plan was still focused on Iran's nuclear program alone. By the summer of 2023, a top Israeli Air Force official presented us with a classified scenario for attacking Iran that contained a much wider range of targets.

Beginning in October 2023, the IDF shifted its thinking about Iran. Previously categorized as a "third-circle," faraway threat because of its thousand-mile distance from Israel, Iran had now become a "first-circle" threat, considered effectively to be on Israel's border. Tehran's missile capabilities meant it could reach Israel in as little as ten minutes, and its proxies could strike even faster. Israel's thinking had started to change with intelligence showing that Iran was pressing its proxies to open simultaneous fronts against Israel in 2023, and Halevi at the time ordered new military moves to be ready. No one foresaw the massive invasion of October 7, but the more-aggressive Iranian tactics prompted a change in Israeli thinking. The change crystalized when Iran attacked Israel directly with massive force in April 2024.

We can now reveal that in meetings in late April and early May among Netanyahu, the Mossad, and top IDF officials, a major event took place. For years, Netanyahu had given the Mossad the lead on thwarting the Iranian nuclear threat. There was also a potential plan for the Mossad to undertake an unprecedented wider operation to simultaneously destroy most of Iran's nuclear program. While Iran had accused the Mossad of sabotaging individual facilities one at a time in the past, this would have been a much larger undertaking. But in the late April and early May meetings, Mossad Director Barnea finally informed Netanyahu that this plan was too large, unrealistic, and unachievable.

At this point, Halevi and Gallant moved forward with their plans to prepare for a potential aerial attack on Iran, plans which Netanyahu had placed on the back burner until then, based on his hope that the Mossad could pull off a large-scale attack against Iran's nuclear program.

On June 4, 2024, Netanyahu told his ministers that it was their government's responsibility to prevent a nuclear Iran. "The threat needs to be removed on this watch," he said, according to a senior official in the room. The wars against proxies had other aims, and they were more than enough to occupy Israel's attention, but the prime minister deemed this task overriding. "We can't leave it for the next generation," he said in another closed meeting, "because there may not be a next generation."

Halevi and much of the IDF high command are convinced that even this was not actually the point when Netanyahu truly shifted to become ready to attack Iran. Rather, from his razor-sharp focus on Gaza at the time and refusal to turn his attention to Hezbollah, they viewed his statement as an interim point. Netanyahu was feeling the Iranian threat more intensely because of the April attack, but he was still unconvinced that it was time to attack and worth the risk of unleashing a massive Iranian and Hezbollah counterstrike. They also said Netanyahu was not yet fully convinced because it was not until months later in 2024 that the prime minister set a potential attack date.

In October 2024, the IDF started working not only on the retaliatory operation it carried out at the time against twenty Iranian radar and ballistic missile–production targets, but also on a much broader operation against Iran for the future. The idea was to smash its most precious assets, nuclear and otherwise, that could threaten Israel in a serious way. The IDF intelligence and Air Force units had previously developed initial ideas for hundreds of targets to strike in the event of a war. But these prior plans were divorced from the reality of the active Israel–Iran confrontation in October, and all its moving pieces.

On November 11, 2024, only days after replacing Gallant as defense minister, Israel Katz met with the IDF high command to be briefed on Iran operations. Katz was a veteran government minister, but on matters of policy, he was in place to serve as a trusted lieutenant of Netanyahu. For this reason, analysts and observers tended to belittle him. He would not advance ideas of his own, they said, and unlike Gallant, he would support the prime minister to the hilt in any disagreement with the

Israeli defense establishment. But at least on Iran, there were not too many disagreements.

On November 18, 2024, a few weeks after Israel's retaliation against Iran for its second missile barrage, Netanyahu had Katz issue a directive to the IDF and Mossad to prepare to remove the Iranian nuclear threat by April 2025. A senior Israeli official tells us the defense establishment still did not believe the prime minister was genuinely ready at this stage. Defense officials say they were surprised Netanyahu was finally taking their plans more seriously, but they were also more than prepared to invest additional concrete resources into a potential attack.

The Israeli government had high hopes. Strategic Affairs Minister Ron Dermer, a native Floridian, had met with President-Elect Trump at his Mar-a-Lago club a week earlier in November 2024. Dermer came away buoyant, assessing that Trump was likely to support an Israeli strike on Iran's nuclear program or even join in himself.

But for several months, all the way until Trump decided to support Israel's attack on Iran as it was playing out, the president was blocking such an attack. In early April 2025, Trump decided he preferred to give negotiations a try, as many of his less-interventionist advisers had suggested. This US decision followed "months of internal debate," *The New York Times* reported, with CENTCOM's General Erik Kurilla the most supportive of a strike. Kurilla lost the debate, and the next month, in May, Trump demoted Mike Waltz, his hawkish national security advisor. Secretary of State Marco Rubio, strongly pro-Israel and tough on Iran, seemed to be playing it safe and not asserting himself on the key policy decisions. Israel's leaders were left to wonder if they had misjudged the Trump administration and missed their chance to act against Iran.

An influential faction of the administration led by Vice President JD Vance opposed a resort to military force. Director of National Intelligence Tulsi Gabbard, who in years past had attacked Trump as a warmonger for his first-term Iran policies, warned of setting off a catastrophic larger war. Outside advisers, such as podcast hosts Tucker Carlson and Steve Bannon, made sure the president knew they also opposed a military conflict with Iran. Witkoff, who had Trump's ear, urged trying negotiations first. He believed in his ability to get a deal.

The first round of nuclear talks between the US and Iran began on April 12, 2025, the first of the sixty days Trump had allotted for negotiations. Many top Israeli officials were worried that Iran would use this time to fleece the unstudied US president and his rookie envoy, Witkoff, who seemed willing to make concessions. But the clock that Trump had set for Iran was ticking.

The IDF high command also discussed the possibility of preparing to attack Iran much later, in October 2025. That was when the "snapback" mechanism, a provision in President Obama's 2015 nuclear deal to restore United Nations sanctions on Iran, would expire. At that point, Western leverage would diminish. No one was even talking about staging an Israeli attack in June 2025.

* * *

At the end of November 2024, the IDF intelligence and Air Force units held a ten-hour conference. Their task was to arrive at a formula for striking as quickly as possible at Iran's military sites and power centers. The idea was to weaken any Iranian second strike against the Jewish state after an Israeli attack on Iran's nuclear program. IDF intelligence designated an office for some 120 soldiers and officers to work on the issue, dividing them into teams focused on different categories of targeting.

On December 25, 2024, top IDF officials started to make their plans for assassinating around thirteen Iranian nuclear scientists more concrete. Each of those scientists was marked red, orange, or green. Red meant there was not yet a plan to kill the scientist. Orange meant there were aspects of a plan, but more was needed. Green meant that a plan was ready to go.

Top Israeli defense officials discussed trying to get the US to attack not merely Fordow, but also the deep-underground portions of Iran's Isfahan nuclear facility. The hope was that the US could at least cause heavy damage, which turned out to be true.

From comments by top Israeli defense officials, it seems that if the US had stayed out of the fight, the IDF either would not have attacked the Fordow nuclear facility—Iran's key uranium-enrichment site buried beneath a mountain south of Tehran—or it would have had much lower expectations for how much damage could be caused.

If the enrichment site at Natanz was the workhorse of the Iranian nuclear program, Fordow was its warhorse, built to be invulnerable to conventional air strikes. Iran had steadily increased the site's capacities, such that, using Fordow alone, the regime could produce enough weapons-grade uranium for nine nuclear weapons within a month, according to the Institute for Science and International Security.[112] Even if Israel destroyed everything else, leaving Fordow, its centrifuges for enriching uranium, and its nuclear material intact would be extremely dangerous.

In January 2025, IDF intelligence's Iran experts and its analysis division both produced written warnings that Tehran's nuclear program was moving forward in newly dangerous ways, especially regarding its weaponization activities. These included advances in developing uranium metal and work on neutron reactions. Iran was even working on the cone-shaped hemispheres that wrap around the outside of a nuclear warhead.

Yet that same January, even as Iran was raising the stakes, many leading IDF intelligence officials thought their planning for a strike had reached a dead end. They seriously considered informing Netanyahu and the Israeli cabinet that a quick knockout war against Iran was beyond their capabilities.

Then, beginning in late February 2025, IDF intelligence had an epiphany. There was no one locus of Iranian power that Israel could quickly destroy. The intelligence officers shifted gears to focus on the many facets of Iranian power. This was much harder intelligence work, requiring many more elements of targeting. But once IDF intelligence accepted the scope of the challenge, it found that there was a more feasible path forward.

On February 16, Halevi flew to Washington for the only visit of his term to the US, meeting with all of the top Pentagon and CENTCOM commanders. Although Trump was still against an Israeli strike on Iran and against the US participating in any strike at this point, we learned that Halevi ironed out critical details of joint planning between the countries if Trump might later endorse a joint strike. Looking back, Halevi's meetings in Washington were another turning point toward being ready to strike Iran for real.

* * *

The plan to attack Iran received a boost when Eyal Zamir replaced Halevi as IDF chief of staff on March 5, 2025. Halevi had ordered attacks on Iran twice in the prior year, but Netanyahu felt that Zamir saw more eye to eye with him in general, leaving him at greater ease about giving the final strike order.

As smart as any other IDF chief, Zamir's unusual résumé and risk tolerance put him on the more aggressive end of the spectrum. He is also the first tank commander to lead the army in more than forty years. Colleagues called him a "soldier's soldier," a title earned during four decades that took him from the small development city of Eilat to the IDF general staff's fourteenth-floor command room in Tel Aviv. But not every soldier's soldier gets to spend a few years working elbow to elbow with Netanyahu as his personal military secretary. This experience did not hurt in convincing the prime minister to finally give the order to strike Iran when Zamir told him, "We're ready to do it in the best possible way."

By March 27, 2025, Katz was already discussing the ways to attack Tehran's command-and-control capabilities with Israeli defense officials. The plan, which now went far beyond striking Iran's nuclear facilities, had progressed in its potential to constrain the Iranian ability to strike back. By April, most of the plans were ready, and IDF intelligence now projected that sometime in May or June 2025 would be the right moment to strike.

Israel could not wait much longer than that. IDF intelligence assessed that Iran had made a quick and surprising recovery in ballistic-missile production after being hit by Israel in October 2024. This made war more dangerous for Israel with each passing month. "Within weeks," a senior Israeli official told us in June 2025, "Iran would be able to make 300 missiles a month." Israel had intelligence showing that Iran could double its production of such missiles by the end of 2025. Before long, Iran could amass enough missiles to exhaust Israel's best interceptors and score major hits on the Israeli home front in the event of a war.

There were also very worrying advances in Iran's nuclear-weapons development. As discussed above, these went beyond the usual enrichment activities. Between a potential stockpile of twenty thousand ballistic missiles and a potential nuclear weapon, "either one would kill us," Netanyahu said.

With all these negative trends, Katz ordered the IDF to move to a P+14 level of readiness as of April 17, 2025. This meant that if the order were given, the IDF had to be ready to attack Iran within fourteen days, or by May 1. This was no longer some distant future scenario. It was becoming very real, very fast.

Yet even at this late stage, there was still significant doubt about US involvement. Would Trump "always chicken out," as his domestic opponents had begun to allege? For now, Washington was assisting with some intelligence and logistics for a theoretical operation, but nothing imminent.

Critically, Israel's plan to kill top Iranian officials all at once—codenamed Operation Narnia—still had not been integrated into the larger plan's opening strike. Instead, it was classified as a potential response should Iran's retaliation for an Israeli attack on the nuclear program achieve particularly deadly results in Israel.

At this time, Israel enhanced its focus on destroying Iran's uranium metal conversion facility at Isfahan, critical for weaponizing highly enriched uranium to place it on a nuclear warhead. "If you can't metallicize, you have nothing," US Middle East envoy Steve Witkoff would later tell us.

On April 27, 2025, Zamir asked CENTCOM's General Kurilla if the US was now willing to join an Israeli attack. Kurilla told him the Trump administration still had not given the green light. The online isolationists who claimed the Make America Great Again mantle had been pushing hard against any US or Israeli strike on Iran. Tucker Carlson, the former Fox News host, said any such confrontation would "almost certainly result in thousands of American deaths." MAGA luminaries Steve Bannon and Donald Trump Jr. made similar noises. Carlson even claimed, "An attack on Iran could very easily become a world war. We'd lose."[113]

The conventional wisdom, in the US and Israel, was that Trump would not stand for a new war. As nuclear negotiations dragged on, a former senior Israeli official who had worked with Netanyahu for years told us something was not right with the prime minister. "He seems to have convinced himself that everything will come together perfectly," the former official said. "The Bibi I knew was always the most skeptical in the room."

But the prime minister himself, while worried about Trump's advisers and MAGA allies, retained some faith in Trump's commitment over the years to preventing an Iranian nuclear weapon. "There's no way Trump wants an Obama-style deal," Ophir Falk, Netanyahu's foreign-policy adviser, argued to us. At the time, most observers predicted Trump would do exactly that, while proclaiming it the deal of the century. Minister Dermer and Mossad Director Barnea took the lead for Israel in trying to convince the president and his team of the need for decisive action instead.

The Trump administration's position in Iran negotiations seemed to stabilize and harden in May 2025. Interviewed on NBC's *Meet the Press* on May 4, Trump was asked, "Is the goal of these talks limiting Iran's nuclear program or total dismantlement?"

"Total dismantlement," he replied.

"That's all you'll accept?"

"That's all I'd accept."

This and many subsequent comments helped resolve the confusion after Witkoff had stated in April that the Iranians "do not need to enrich past 3.67%," which seemed to concede that Iran could be allowed to enrich up to that point.[114] That 3.67 percent was the standard under President Obama's 2015 Iran deal.[115] To Netanyahu, it would be tantamount to leaving an Iranian sword of Damocles looming over Israelis' heads.

"End enrichment capability—EEC," Falk tried to drill into us. "If they have centrifuges, they can make bombs. If they don't, they can't. It's that simple."

Republicans rallied against concessions to Iran. A letter asking Trump to stand by his demand "that the regime must *permanently give up any capacity for enrichment*" was signed by fifty-two GOP Senators—that was all of them, save only the Kentucky libertarian Rand Paul—and 177 House Republicans.[116] Witkoff had clarified his remarks as well. "An enrichment program can never exist in the state of Iran ever again. That's our red line," he said in May."[117]

When *Time* magazine asked Trump if he worried that Netanyahu would drag him into a war with Iran, he said no. The question, however, echoed a long-standing worry of the Left that had found new support from the rising anti-interventionist wing of the American right. These Republicans saw former presidential candidate Pat Buchanan as a prophet and Israel as a malign and warmongering influence on US foreign policy. They were loud, but Trump had been consistent for more than a decade that Iran not be allowed a nuclear weapon. "You asked if he'd drag me in, like I'd go in unwillingly," the president clarified to his interviewer. "If we don't make a deal, I'll be leading the pack."[118]

But as May wore on, it became increasingly clear that Iran had not gotten the message. "We are witnessing completely unreasonable and illogical positions from the Americans," said Foreign Minister Araghchi of Iran. "Enrichment is absolutely nonnegotiable." Ayatollah Khamenei said the US "should try not to talk nonsense" and called it a "big mistake" for Trump to demand an end to Iran's enrichment of uranium.[119]

Trump still wanted to give diplomacy every chance to succeed. Asked on May 28 if he had warned Israel against actions that could disrupt talks with Iran, the president replied, "Well, I'd like to be honest: Yes, I did." Trump said he told Netanyahu that it was not "appropriate right now" to attack the Iranians. "Right now, I think they want to make a deal."[120]

On May 31, a senior US official told us that Israel needed to resign itself to a US–Iran deal, and to begin thinking about what Israel would want to ask Trump for in return for not kicking up a fuss. That same month, IDF intelligence chief Shlomi Binder wrote his own highest-level warning that Iran might only be a few months away from developing a nuclear weapon. Soon, Binder added, there might not be enough time to stop it.

At this point, Israel was deep in conversation with the US about an attack. But with no US commitment, the IDF could only hope that Washington would weigh in midbattle.

One trick Israel and the US did pull off in coordination during the month of May was to flood the media with stories about a potential attack until Iran started to disregard them, as in "The Boy Who Cried Wolf." As a senior Israeli official put it to us, "The deception was that there was no deception." It was all in the open, and it worked to give Israel the element of surprise and the upper hand. For the US, it preserved options.

On May 20, Netanyahu joined Katz to move the IDF to P+7, meaning the Air Force needed to be ready to attack Iran on a mere week's notice. We were later shown a copy of the order. By May 27, top IDF intelligence and Air Force officials had given resounding assurances that they were ready to initiate the grand operation against Tehran not merely in theory, but in practice. Then on May 29, Netanyahu, Katz, and the Israeli cabinet approved Operation Tornado, the part of the plan geared toward striking strategic sites in Tehran that represented the regime's rule.

But even at this late stage, nothing was certain. At the end of May 2025, Witkoff made the Iranians a US offer, handing them what he called a term sheet, or a framework for an agreement to be hashed out later. Many Israeli political and defense officials viewed the offer as a disaster. It would allow Iran to keep enriching uranium for a lengthy period during which a "regional consortium" would build a nuclear facility outside Iran, with the regime's involvement. This easily could buy the regime enough time to break out to a nuclear weapon.

Yet when Witkoff presented this plan to the Iranians, they were stunned. Its ultimate principle of no domestic enrichment went too far for them. Ayatollah Khamenei rejected it out of hand. "Uranium enrichment is the key to our nuclear program," he said in a televised speech. "The rude and arrogant leaders of America repeatedly demand that we should not have a nuclear program. Who are you to decide whether Iran should have enrichment?"[121] He was not alone in thinking the US would compromise further.

"Trump preferred a deal. I won't argue with that," a senior Israeli official told us. "Only Israel was enforcing that 60-day deadline of his." Though most had forgotten it, the deadline was set to expire on June 12. Trump wanted to try to get a deal right down to the last moments. But in the final two weeks, he began to more seriously consider a new line of argument from Israel, advanced principally by Dermer. This argument recognized that Trump wanted a deal, and held that an Israeli strike might be the way to get it. Only after an attack on Iran would the regime come to terms. Nothing else was working.

By June 4, Netanyahu moved the war with Iran to P+3. Finally, on June 9, Netanyahu set the war's starting point for June 12–13. The final date was selected in part because Israeli intelligence had assessed that on a Friday morning like June 13, Iranian targets would be at their most vulnerable and could be hit simultaneously. Israel would be enforcing a deadline which the US president set.

On deadline day, June 12, Iran responded aggressively to the IAEA resolution against it. The regime announced that it would begin operating a secret nuclear enrichment site and upgrade its centrifuges at its underground Fordow site. The secret enrichment facility, never previously disclosed to UN inspectors, was yet another breach of Iran's nuclear nonproliferation obligations. It was likely in the mountains by the Natanz facility. This was brazen.

Netanyahu had waited a long time to attack. "For decades, I argued that a nuclear Iran would pose a mortal threat to Israel. For years, I authorized clandestine operations that set them back but didn't stop them," he told us. He had even come close to attacking in 2011, though then–IDF chief Benny Gantz and Mossad chief Tamir Pardo opposed the move enough that the prime minister decided to back down. More than anyone else, Netanyahu had identified the existential threat that Iran's nuclear program posed to Israel, and the great danger it would pose to the West as well. Stopping Iran's theocratic, antisemitic, and revolutionary regime from obtaining the weapons to obliterate Israel had been his obsession at least since the 1990s.

In a famous 2012 UN speech, Netanyahu drew a red line on a cartoonlike bomb, insisting that Iran be prevented from advancing its enrichment of uranium. "The relevant question is not when Iran will get the bomb," he said. "The relevant question is at what stage can we no longer stop Iran from getting the bomb."

As Netanyahu saw it, the first wave of Israeli leaders was tasked with securing the Jewish state's survival against the surrounding Arab states that sought to destroy it. They succeeded, only to find that the task of destroying Israel had been passed to Iran. To thwart the ayatollahs and their nuclear program would be the historical task of Israel's next wave of leaders, born like him after the Jewish state's founding.

This centrality of the Iranian threat had not always been accepted in Israel. But over time, as Iran's nuclear program and forever war on Israel advanced, Netanyahu won the domestic Israeli argument. "Through five stints as prime minister, I was 'Iran, Iran, Iran,'" he told us. At great cost to Israel's relations with the US Democratic Party, he fought Obama over the president's 2015 Iran deal, and "went to the two houses of Congress to try to keep the flame alive."

For around twenty-five years, covert Mossad operations had delayed the nuclear program, but Tehran soldiered on. Certainly by 2025, many thought it was too late to stop Iran—and that Benjamin Netanyahu would never do it. He would only talk.

* * *

In the final security cabinet meeting only hours before the attack started, IDF chief Zamir warned that while Israel would see significant military achievements in the operation's first week, it would meet diminishing returns after 10–14 days. At this point, Iran would start to make a comeback and land more missiles on Israel.

The entire cabinet rose when Zamir left the room. Several of the religious ministers gave him blessings, and he headed back to the Air Force Headquarters "pit." One final ruse was to brief reporters that Netanyahu was going on a short family vacation in advance of his son's wedding, which was planned for a few days later.

On June 12, around 11:00 p.m., Israeli aircraft took off from a number of locations, but all with the common target of Iran.

We can disclose that the operation was nearly aborted. There were last-second dilemmas as various top Iranian targets left their houses and moved to other locations, such as bases or offices. Israel even lost track of IRGC Aerospace Commander Amir Ali Hajizadeh for some period of time. But eventually, Israel found him again in a command center with a host of other officials. When Israeli intelligence was able to adjust in real time and convey the new target locations to its aircraft, Zamir decided to re-approve the operation.

On June 13, 2025, at around 2:50 a.m., he gave the order: "Take action, attack approved. Good luck." Israel's Operation Rising Lion kicked off with some two hundred Israeli aircraft dropping 330 precision munitions on more than one hundred high-value targets, including nuclear sites at Natanz, Fordow, and Isfahan, IRGC command bunkers in Tehran, and missile factories at Yazd and Mashhad, in Iran's far northeast.

Over the course of twelve days, the Israel Air Force struck nine hundred targets in addition to the highest-value sites. It dropped four thousand six hundred bombs, killing at least thirty top Iranian military and intelligence officials, at least eleven nuclear scientists, and destroying more than half of Iran's four hundred ballistic-missile launchers, according to senior IDF officials.

By day three, Israeli jets had achieved full operational freedom in Tehran's airspace. "They can do anything they want, just about," General Petraeus, the former US CENTCOM commander, told us. Israel's power, and Iran's weakness and vulnerability, was astonishing. In part, Israel was able to use Iran's size against it. The vast country—Iran is twice the size of Texas—had to defend a huge surface area. Israel, by contrast, could channel Iran's ballistic-missile response into a bottleneck, as the salvos all took a narrow trajectory to hit the smaller Jewish state, the size of New Jersey.

Iranian state media confirmed that Israel's opening shot had killed IRGC Commander Hossein Salami and Armed Forces Chief of Staff Mohammad Bagheri, Iran's top two military commanders. Soon after, the IDF confirmed the killing of IRGC Air Force Commander Amir Ali Hajizadeh, considered Iran's most creative and dangerous military mind, along with the leaders of the IRGC's drone force, aerial command, and others as they met in an underground command center. In the span of a day, much of the top echelon of the Iranian army and IRGC had been extinguished.

Israel would wipe out nine Iranian nuclear scientists on day one, almost all at the same time, while sleeping in their beds. The targeted strikes were called Operation Narnia, reflecting the improbable nature, like something out of a fantasy. Two of the nine were working on nuclear weapons specifically, the IDF added, and all were pivotal figures in Iran's nuclear program, with many decades of accumulated experience.

Netanyahu announced to the world, "Israel will never allow those who call for our annihilation to develop the means to achieve that goal."

IDF chief Zamir added, "We cannot wait for another time to act. We have no choice"—the four most resonant words in the Israeli military vocabulary.

Israel would go on to score other hits in Iran, including eliminating the IRGC intelligence chief, Mohammad Kazemi, and his deputy on June 15. Israel would also strike a large number of nuclear sites. In addition to the Natanz enrichment site and several facilities at Isfahan, the IDF would land blows on Iran's old and new nuclear headquarters, the Karaj centrifuge manufacturing site, the Kalaya electric centrifuge site, the centrifuge manufacturing building at the Tehran Research Reactor, the Arak heavy-water reactor and weaponization sites, the Lavisan-2 campus, the Sanjarian testing facility, and more. There were also many strikes on air defenses, ballistic missiles, and missile launchers.

In the latter days of the war, Israel also attacked some IRGC and Basij paramilitary headquarters and bases. The idea was that targeting the Iranian regime's institutions of domestic repression could threaten the regime and weaken its will to continue the war. At the end of the war, Iran's Ministry of Health reported 610 deaths and more than four thousand five hundred injuries.[122] The nongovernmental organization Human Rights Activists in Iran gave a much higher death toll, at 1,190.[123]

Iran answered by targeting Israel with about 550 ballistic missiles and more than one thousand explosive drones during the war's twelve days. IDF figures showed that its multilayer air defenses—Arrow, David's Sling, Iron Dome, and US-deployed THAAD batteries—intercepted 80 percent to 90 percent of missiles and 99.9 percent of the drones. Six missiles slipped through to hit five IDF bases, and around thirty more got through overall, killing twenty-eight Israelis and wounding around three thousand. These hits left some awful scenes in Tel Aviv, as well as in the Israeli cities of Beersheba and Bat Yam. One strike hit the cancer-research facility at the Weizmann Institute in Rehovot.

For twelve days, millions of Israelis packed into shelters for long periods, experiencing much graver levels of fear and exhaustion than they had from Hamas, Hezbollah, or Houthi missile attacks. More than two thousand three hundred Israeli residences were heavily damaged and more than thirteen thousand roofs were destroyed. Prewar changes in the deployment of Israeli forces, however, meant there would be very little damage to the IDF when the war finally came. It paid to be prepared.

Israel is a country of ten million people, whereas Iran has ninety-two million. Yet Israel dominated Iran, free to take its pick of targets from the regime's most valuable assets—nuclear, military, and internal repression mechanisms. Iran caused Israel much less damage in its counterattack.

Incredibly, Israel did not lose any manned aircraft in all its strikes. As a senior US official told us, after the Twelve-Day War, "The really smart people in the world are saying, 'I don't have to be afraid of the Iranian Mafia anymore.'"

* * *

In addition to the two hundred jets flying round-the-clock sorties, hundreds of Mossad agents and special-forces soldiers were operating secretly inside Iran, along with untold numbers of spies and compromised Iranian officials. They had smuggled weapons and munitions across the border into Iran in preparation, and were ready when the day came. Swarms of Mossad drones, stunningly launched and operated from covert warehouses inside Iran, delivered their explosive payloads with pinpoint precision. Clusters of Iranian air defenses, rockets, shells, and ballistic missiles were blown up across the length and breadth of the country. Numerous car bombs went off, wreaking havoc. The Iranians didn't know what hit them.

The Mossad and IDF intelligence also made use of some of their former agents' expertise. An Israeli telecoms executive working in Europe had been asked to design a device that appeared to be a low-tech mobile phone, but which transmitted encrypted data disguised as social media traffic, according to foreign sources. The same sources noted that a techie working at an Israeli health startup had helped craft an algorithm that he had worked on during his military service to enable a dedicated internet server to sift through satellite images of fuel trucks. This rapidly identified which trucks carried missile propellant rather than oil.[124]

Many of the covert and crazy technological parts of the operation were the brainchild of David Barnea. This was the same Mossad director who had masterminded the exploding beeper attacks that so debilitated Hezbollah in September 2024. Within the Mossad, he was known as "a gadget-loving killing machine." We can reveal that Barnea also sent dozens of Mossad women to penetrate Iran and that they were on the ground performing operations, not merely surveillance, during Israel's attacks. The Mossad almost never reveals the gender of its agents, so as not to tip off adversaries. This reveal showed the importance of the operation and that Barnea wanted to give credit to the agency's female spies. Barnea and the Mossad's success at eliminating top Iranian officials created paranoia in the regime. Iran would detain an astounding twenty-one thousand suspects during the Twelve-Day War, its state media would report.

Shortly after the war, Iran's minister of information and communications technology announced that the country had been the target of more than twenty thousand cyberattacks during hostilities. Predatory Sparrow, a hacker group linked to the Israeli government, took credit for erasing the data and rendering inoperable the systems of Bank Sepah, the key financial institution of the IRGC and Iranian military. The attacks set off the collapse of Iran's currency, the rial.[125]

According to Iran International, a London-based news outlet that often breaks stories about Iran, malware implanted into Tehran's city security cameras located Ali Shadmani, the new commander of Iran's joint military headquarters, in the Zafaraniyeh neighborhood, where he was then killed by a drone strike. Shadmani's predecessor, Gholam Ali Rashid, had also been killed four days earlier, in Israel's opening strikes. The Mossad reportedly tracked Shadmani by digitally obtaining a DNA sample and then used artificial intelligence–based facial recognition and genetic profiling to locate him. Mossad sources said that not all of these details were 100 percent accurate, but that in some cases, the Mossad's operations had been even more audacious.[126]

Unusually, the Mossad admitted that it had used a mix of spies on the ground, remote-controlled weapons placed on standard motor vehicles, and remote-controlled drones. With tens of millions of Iranians who detest the regime—Persian, Azeri, Kurdish, or otherwise—there is a nearly endless supply of Iranians for the Mossad to recruit. And the regime knows it. This means that even if Tehran would manage a successful crackdown, and study how Israel penetrated it so completely, it would be nearly impossible to plug all the holes and to stop the Mossad.

The spy agency also had been involved in secret aspects of the April 2024 and October 2024 attacks by Israel, and in a daring operation to whisk Iran's nuclear archives out from Tehran in 2018. The Islamic Republic previously accused the Mossad of destroying two separate nuclear sites at Natanz in July 2020 and April 2021, as well as at Karaj in June 2021, and of killing its nuclear chief Mohsen Fakhrizadeh in November 2020. In some ways, the havoc that the Mossad brought down on Iran in June 2025 was simply a culmination of attacks it had been carrying out for years, almost at will.

An unofficial codename given to Israel's long-term policy of crippling Iran's military machine, disabling its air defenses, and hampering its nuclear program—the job of the Mossad—was "Death by a Thousand Cuts." But suddenly, after years of drips and drabs of covert operations, all the cuts were bleeding at once.

* * *

When Israel first launched its attacks on Iran on June 13, 2025, the Trump administration was wary. It hadn't given Israel a red light—a major diplomatic achievement for Jerusalem—but Secretary of State Marco Rubio released a statement saying Israel had taken "unilateral action" and warning Iran not to retaliate against the US. "We are not involved in strikes against Iran and our top priority is protecting American forces in the region," Rubio said.

But as the war played out, Trump made clear that Israel's success was drawing him closer to acting. Iran was exposed as far weaker than the world had thought. Its missile salvos were becoming smaller. The Israelis estimated that Iran now lacked the capabilities even to try to take on the US in the Persian Gulf in the event of an American strike. Its system of command and control had been disrupted, and all its assets were now vulnerable.

Around three days into the operation, Kurilla called Zamir. "How many drones have you lost?" the US general asked.

Zamir responded concisely: "None." The American general was stunned.

As Zamir summed up the achievement to those close to him, "We did assassinations in Tehran exactly like in Gaza and Lebanon." Now, Zamir wanted to convince his US counterparts to help finish the job. "They didn't understand how we were achieving so much," the IDF chief said. "But eventually doubt turned to curiosity, which turned to 'let's join the party.'"

The benefits of destroying the Iranian nuclear program were clear, and Israel had already taken most of the risk. Dermer made the effective argument to the White House that its intervention would no longer be a matter of starting a war—with all the uncertainty that entailed—but of ending it.

"This campaign can take five days or 50," a senior Israeli official told us. "The choice is Trump's." The isolationists were losing the argument in America as their dire predictions had failed to materialize. Iran had not responded to Israel by striking the US or sparking a "world war," involving Russia and China. Where were the "thousands of American deaths at bases throughout the Middle East" that Tucker Carlson had predicted? Where was the "$30 gasoline" that "could collapse our economy"? Iran looked more like a paper tiger.

Up until Trump saw Israel's military success against Iran's nuclear program in the first forty-eight hours of its operation, he did not commit. After that, he wanted in. It would also help that 80 percent of Iran's antiaircraft missiles in the relevant areas had been destroyed by Israel.

Early in the day on June 18, Trump announced he would give Iran two weeks to agree to nuclear and other terms before he decided whether to strike Fordow, Iran's deep-underground nuclear site that Israel had yet to touch. Was this Tehran's chance to save its nuclear program for another day? It seemed like it. But later that evening, Trump secretly told Netanyahu that he had already decided to attack.

Trump would come through for Israel on Iran. Netanyahu's biggest bet of all had paid off.

On June 20, a Trump administration official showed us a map of Israel's strikes on Iran. The more recent ones were heavily concentrated, seemingly clearing a flight path to the Fordow nuclear facility, he said. These Israeli strikes on Iranian air defenses paved the way for a US strike.

That same day came a crucial meeting, the contents of which have not been fully reported until now. Zamir went to the Israeli "pit" command center to talk with Netanyahu, Dermer, a few top IDF officials and Defense Minister Katz. They were all on a call with Vice President

JD Vance and General Caine. Netanyahu made some initial comments and then turned it over to Zamir to convince Vance.

Zamir's presentation built up to a key point: "We are already flying over Fordow freely," he told the vice president. "There is a straight-line aerial lane open."

Vance asked a few more questions, and then said "thank you." He had heard all he needed. Given the flight time of America's bombers, they were likely ordered into the air not long after this call.

When Vance later came to Israel on October 24, 2025, he asked to meet Zamir and said he remembered what the IDF chief had told him on that phone call. This was the first time a US vice president had ever come to an IDF chief's office to thank him personally.

* * *

On June 22, 2025, right around midnight, the hammer fell. In a strike that shook the Middle East and instantly altered the worldwide balance of power, the US Air Force attacked Iran's nuclear sites at Fordow, Natanz, and Isfahan. "Iran's key nuclear enrichment facilities have been completely and totally obliterated," Trump announced to the world.

This was an exaggeration. But politics and sensationalism should not obscure Trump's achievement. The nuclear facilities were so heavily damaged that they will take Iran some years to repair. Indeed, Iran might have to abandon them and try to rebuild somewhere else. This was a major success for the US and Israel.

The strikes set back Iran's nuclear program by two years, top Israeli and US officials told us, and that figure assumes Iran is allowed to rebuild unimpeded. Both Netanyahu and Trump repeatedly pledged further strikes if Iran were to attempt to reconstitute its program.

A top US official told us, "The original plan was to drop two to three MOPs," short for Massive Ordnance Penetrators, the mega bunker busters, "on Fordow. But we decided to go big and dropped 12." As veteran nuclear inspector David Albright of the Institute for Science and International Security assessed in a June 24 report, the Israeli and US attacks "effectively destroyed Iran's centrifuge enrichment program."

He added that "the IAEA also assessed that 'extensive damage' was done to the tunnel entrances" at Isfahan.[127] This was essential, as many Israeli officials believed Iran's stockpiles of enriched uranium—the key asset that was not hit directly—were stored in those deep-underground tunnels. They would now be trapped. Later, we learned that the Mossad knew exactly where the uranium lay and was prepared to act should Iran take any actions with the uranium which Israel might view as dangerous.

Trump congratulated Netanyahu, with whom he had worked "as a team, like perhaps no team has ever worked before." Netanyahu, in turn, praised Trump: "History will record that President Trump acted to deny the world's most dangerous regime the world's most dangerous weapons," he said. The US had "done what no other country on Earth could do," a reference to the mega bunker busters that smashed Fordow and Natanz.

The US president added that the Iranian regime's choice was now "peace, or tragedy for Iran far greater than we have witnessed over the last eight days." He also made it clear that the US had no further plans to intervene against Iran in this war.

Despite some suggestive statements by Israeli politicians, top IDF officials said that regime change in Iran was never a priority. Rather, they said that top internal regime power centers were not even hit until near the end of the war, when it was decided to increase pressure on the regime to agree to a ceasefire.

General Dan Caine, chairman of the US Joint Chiefs of Staff, explained on June 22 that America had not used bombers stationed in Guam, as many had expected. Instead, the aircraft took off all the way from Whiteman Air Force Base in Missouri. But the majority of those planes split off toward Guam as a decoy. Only seven B-2 bombers, all with stealth capabilities, continued to proceed east from the US toward Iran under virtual radio silence. Their mission would last thirty-seven hours, nonstop, with multiple aerial refuelings. The US had put on an air-force master class.

Escort fighter aircraft coming from another direction linked up with the B-2 bombers before they entered Iranian airspace. The mission would involve more than 125 planes in all. Around 1:45 a.m. in Iran, the B-2s dropped two MOPs on Fordow, targeting the site's two ventilation shafts with remarkable precision. This allowed the bombs to glide down into the depths of the facility before exploding. Iran had covered the shafts shortly before the attack with concrete caps, but it was not enough. Later, another twelve MOPs were dropped on Natanz and Fordow. More than two dozen Tomahawk missiles were fired at the Isfahan complex from a US submarine in the Gulf of Oman.

The concrete caps at Fordow, Caine explained, had been accounted for. "The cap was forcibly removed by the first weapon and the main shaft was uncovered. Weapons two, three, four, five were tasked to enter the main shaft, move down into the complex at greater than 1000 feet per second and explode in the mission space," he said. "There were six on each side. Weapon no. 6 was designed as a flex weapon to allow us to cover if one of the preceding jets or one of the preceding weapons did not work." Caine said the US used seventy-five precision-guided weapons throughout the operation, and deployed cyber and preemptive fire from fourth- and fifth-generation fighter jets to distract the Iranians from the real strike package.

B-2 stealth bombers are the only aircraft capable of carrying and deploying the GBU-57A/B Massive Ordnance Penetrator, an even more powerful version of a weapon that a decade earlier had been nicknamed the "mother of all bombs." Caine said that the bomb, which only America possessed, had been developed specifically for the mission at Fordow, and that the strike had been fifteen years in the making. At one point, he added, "we had so many PhDs working on the MOP program doing modeling and simulation that we were, quietly and in a secret way, the biggest users of supercomputer hours" in the US.

* * *

At 7:39 p.m. local time on June 23, 2025, Iran retaliated by firing around ten ballistic missiles at US Central Command's al-Udeid Air Base in Qatar. US forces launched a slew of interceptors to shoot down the threats, and explosions were heard over Doha, Qatar's capital. The US suffered no casualties.[128]

Al-Udeid is the forward headquarters for CENTCOM, accommodating as many as ten thousand US troops. Iran attacked it even though Qatar has been one of its key allies. Tehran did, however, warn Qatar and the US hours before the attack, allowing Qatar to close its airspace before the missiles arrived. Iran had been issuing constant threats and the US had seen it moving missile launchers into place, according to officials cited by *The Wall Street Journal*.[129]

In typical fashion, Iran claimed to have "destroyed the American air base," which had already been substantially evacuated. A Pentagon official stated that US air defenses in Qatar intercepted thirteen Iranian missiles, while another was allowed to crash harmlessly off target. That was not entirely accurate either. Satellite images from Planet Labs revealed noticeable damage to a radar dome at the air base, and a Pentagon spokesman later confirmed that a missile had struck the radar.[130]

But as a response to the devastating US strike on Iran's most valuable nuclear assets, a strategic defeat that the regime had tried to ward off for more than two decades, this was on the weak end of the spectrum. Trump would treat the ayatollah like a child, commenting that the Iranians had "gotten it all out of their 'system.'" The weakness of Iran's attack allowed Trump to claim victory and impose a ceasefire without the need to retaliate again against Iran. Contrary to so many of the predictions, the US was not dragged into another "forever war." Trump was able to limit the American engagement to a single operation.

In imposing a ceasefire, Trump was pushing on an open door. Iran badly needed out of the fight. It had lost much of its military power already, its nuclear program was in ruins, and it could see Israel toying with the idea of regime change. This was the time to cut its losses, while it still had some missiles left in case of future engagements.

From Israel's point of view, it had already accomplished all it had ever dreamed of and it now faced diminishing returns. As the IDF ran lower on missile interceptors, it also had to worry that Iran could seriously harm Israel with its remaining missile launchers. IDF chief Zamir was pressing Netanyahu and the cabinet for a ceasefire. Though Israel was talking tough up to the end, Dermer had already let the Trump team know that Jerusalem was interested in a ceasefire.

The deal came together rapidly via US and Qatari mediation, and a ceasefire began in somewhat confusing fashion on the morning of June 24. Trump had announced the previous evening that Iran would cease firing first, then Israel would stop twelve hours later, and twelve hours after that, the war would be considered over. Araghchi, Iran's foreign minister, responded that Tehran had not signed any deal, but that if Israel stopped firing, Iran would also stop "no later than 4:00 a.m. Tehran time." Israel continued to bomb Iranian targets right until the ceasefire time, increasing the pace of its bombing in some areas—a common tactic by both sides in Israel's wars. These last-chance attacks hit regime facilities and eliminated hundreds of Basij members and Iranian security forces. In reply, Iran fired two ballistic missiles at Israel a couple hours after the ceasefire had officially kicked in, around 10:25 a.m. in Israel.

Though Israel shot down both missiles, it viewed the Iranian firings as a blatant violation of the ceasefire and a precedent that could not be allowed to stand. If this is how the ceasefire started, IDF officials reasoned, how would it end?

Defense Minister Katz said the IDF would unleash an intense strike against regime targets in Tehran in response. Then, in a public press conference, Trump said, "I'm not happy with Israel. You know, when I say, 'OK now you have twelve hours,' you don't go out the first hour, just drop everything you have on them. So I'm not happy with them. I'm not happy with Iran either," he added. "We basically have two countries that have been fighting so long and so hard, that they don't know what the [f—] they're doing," he said. "I'm gonna see if I can stop it."

Speaking on the phone with Netanyahu, Trump made clear in extremely harsh terms, including threats, that the strike Israel was about to carry out against Iran's internal repression units could kill the ceasefire in its crib. The Trump team thought it foolish of Netanyahu to "overreact" to what it saw as "just one missile into a farm field."

Netanyahu was suitably chastened by the demand to "completely cancel the attack," but responded that a "strike is necessary," per a senior

Israeli official. As such, Israel bombed only a single site in Iran, a token attack that hit two minor radar platforms. The prime minister called back most of the aircraft without attacking.

The dispute was a reminder that some things in US–Israel relations do not change with presidential administrations. There is always an impulse to restrain Israel; the question is how much or how little. Former senior Israeli lawyer and diplomat Tal Becker once defined American exceptionalism to us in four words: "Ocean, ocean, Canada, Mexico." In America's neighborhood, there is little reason to overreact to small provocations. But the Middle East is not the Middle West, as the Israeli statesman Moshe Arens used to put it.

Israelis chafe at the restraint, but they sometimes benefit from it too. Obsessed with signaling their toughness to the region, they can fail to realize when the message has already been received. In Iran, Israel left little doubt.

As Netanyahu and Trump spoke, senior US officials relayed a message to Iran via Qatar: "No further provocations, cease all attacks." The Israel–Iran war that had changed the region in only twelve days was over as suddenly as it had begun.

* * *

The most important question following the war was how much the IDF, the Mossad, and US Air Force had succeeded at pushing off the Iranian nuclear threat. Top IDF sources told us that, despite some contrary estimates, Iran's nuclear program had been pushed back by at least a couple years, maybe longer. They also said the program still had remnants that survived, and had not been "obliterated," as Trump had claimed.

The issue is highly complex, but analysis often seemed to break down along partisan lines, as if nuclear science and satellite readings corresponded to presidential politics. Much of the media coverage was also misleading. For example, the discussion centered on speculation that the enriched uranium at Fordow had been moved by Iran before the war. A satellite image of dumpster trucks at Fordow went viral, even though they were likely used to seal off the facility's entrances, not to smuggle out sensitive nuclear material, which would have required different and far fewer vehicles.

Even several months removed from the attack, Iran had not shown the world a picture of a single "healthy" centrifuge. It also appeared that Iran had not extracted the enriched uranium from the deep rubble of its facilities. As we have seen, US strikes on Isfahan collapsed the entrances to the tunnel complex where enriched uranium may have been stockpiled. The IDF also knew for certain that it had destroyed thousands of Iranian nuclear centrifuges, with growing indications over time that this number could be closer to twenty thousand. That would be the largest setback for any nuclear program in history.

If Israel had struck only the three major sites of Fordow, Natanz, and Isfahan, maybe Iran could have rebuilt hundreds of centrifuges within several months or a year—assuming no Israeli or US interference. But Israel also destroyed almost all of Iran's sites for constructing centrifuges, including a facility in Karaj that almost no one was talking about. Israel hit many pieces of Iran's nuclear program, such as mills for producing uranium ore and uranium conversion facilities. The entire process had been set back.

Given the Mossad's success at penetrating Iran, including in hallowed places where top Iranian officials and nuclear scientists thought they were safe, it was unlikely that Iran could have moved a large amount of its most precious highly enriched uranium without Israel noticing, in the lead-up to the attack. Iran will need to spend several months merely trying to dig out what was not destroyed, and then spend more time building new facilities to use the material. Recall that one reason Israel became more worried about Iran's nuclear program in 2025 was that the regime had finally advanced in the weaponization process. It was converting enriched uranium to uranium metal and working on neutron reactions and hemispheres for a nuclear warhead—all aspects intricately connected to finalizing a nuclear bomb. According to top IDF officials, all or nearly all of Iran's weaponization activities just described were bombed.

* * *

The next most important question of the war was how much the IDF and the Mossad had damaged Tehran's ballistic-missile program. According to Zamir and other members of the IDF high command, by the time Israel attacked on June 13, Iran had two thousand five hundred ballistic missiles and was on the way to building a new facility to mass-produce more. The facility was far enough along that IDF intelligence estimated Iran would have six thousand ballistic missiles by 2026 and eight thousand eight hundred by August 2027. Advancing at that same rate, Iran would have reached over ten thousand ballistic missiles sometime in 2028. At that quantity, could Israel ever be safe?

The IDF judged Iran to have around four hundred ballistic-missile launchers—the essential platform for firing a missile—before the war. Postwar, some top IDF officials said Israel had destroyed around half of those launchers, while others pegged the figure closer to two-thirds. These Israeli attacks were part of what led to a drop in the volume of missiles in Iran's salvos against Israel over the course of the war. The number of missiles fired per barrage tumbled from two hundred to one hundred to seventy-five to fifty to thirty to twenty to around ten by the war's end. This left Israel some breathing room.

Given that with 550 missiles, Iran was able to kill twenty-eight Israelis during the war and cause serious property damage, imagine if Tehran could have fired several salvos of five hundred ballistic missiles at a time, getting the same 14 percent of them through, or likely more.

Imagine next that instead of thirty-six missiles hitting Israeli residential areas, four hundred or five hundred missiles got through out of three thousand fired. Suddenly, the death toll could have easily reached the level of several hundred or more that the IDF had expected before the war. Large portions of Tel Aviv and Haifa could have been reduced to rubble. It's a grim picture.

After Iran had launched more than one hundred ballistic missiles at Israel in April 2024 and more than two hundred in October 2024, Israel was not going to leave the ayatollah with the ability to keep attacking.

* * *

On June 25, 2025, Mossad chief Barnea sent a message to his agents about Iran. "We will be there, like we have been there," he said. The next day, Zamir and the IDF high command explained that Iran will likely try to make a nuclear comeback, but that Israel will always be ready to stop it again, if need be. In fact, Israel will be even more ready and willing to act in the future, given the confidence and experience gained from this war. The Trump administration has also talked tough about its willingness to strike again.

Witkoff, the president's envoy, thought in July 2025 that Iran would eventually allow IAEA inspectors back in, which could form the basis for a monitoring regime and lay the groundwork for a deal. Wherever the IAEA had electronic surveillance in the past, it had 24/7 surveillance. IAEA inspections have never been sufficient by themselves, but they are invaluable.

If Iran would not allow inspections to resume, Witkoff believed, it would pay the price in international sanctions and isolation, while the rest of the region would leave it in the dust. On September 28, 2025, the UN snapped back global sanctions on Iran due to Khamenei's refusal to engage in serious negotiations toward a new nuclear deal. Whether the sanctions would have a real impact was a developing story.

But the US envoy's ultimate goal was not merely to recover and destroy Iran's remaining nuclear material, but to nail down a twenty- to twenty-five-year plan for peace. That is a dream an American diplomat can afford to have. Israelis will look instead to keep acting in the shadows and the skies until the Iranian regime one day falls and the war ends for good—a dream of their own.

CHAPTER SEVENTEEN

GAZA ENDGAME

The relief and rejoicing about the successful war with Iran were short-lived. When the war's twelve days were up, the world's attention swung back to Gaza, where the news was grim. The suffering was growing worse, and there seemed to be no end in sight.

In June and July 2025, warnings of famine from the UN and other sources began to escalate. Such predictions had been offered at many points throughout the war, but the famine or mass starvation never seemed to materialize. This time, it was more serious.

Starvation in Gaza became headline news around the world. Viral photos of skin-and-bones children—often suffering from preexisting muscular disorders, though much of the media coverage left that part out—were placed on the front pages.[131] Hamas's Gaza Health Ministry claimed that more than 133 Gazans died of starvation or malnutrition in July 2025, as opposed to sixty-six such deaths during all the preceding months of the war combined.[132]

IDF officials held a series of emergency briefings to let reporters know that the military was going into overdrive to correct the situation before a famine hit for real. "It's bad," a US official working on the issue told us. In July 2025, the price of flour in Gaza reportedly reached eighty times its prewar level.[133] "We are days away from saying bye-bye to the GHF" aid mechanism and leaving Israel hanging, the US official said, if the situation and the headlines became any worse. "We don't need this gum on our shoe."

A senior Israeli official told us, "We [f—ed] up royally on the PR with the aid. Our policy was to prevent starvation. We know the second there's a humanitarian crisis, the goals of the war are at risk." That was right; the failure, which went beyond public relations, was now jeopardizing Israel's military objectives.

Israel complained that the UN had been leaving huge amounts of aid to rot in the Gaza sun, failing to distribute it even after Israel had let it into the Strip. A US official blamed the "my-way-or-the-highway approach" of the traditional aid groups, and those groups blamed Israeli stubbornness for limiting their routes, other restrictions, and Israel's extending the fighting, which made it less safe to travel through Gaza to deliver the aid.

"It's the distribution, stupid," Ophir Falk, Netanyahu's foreign-policy adviser, argued. UN data showed that from mid-May 2025 to early August, 87 percent of aid trucks sent by the UN and its partners were being looted in Gaza, either by mobs or "armed actors."[134] Eventually, most of it would be sold to civilians, but not to all of them, not in any orderly fashion, and at a substantial markup. This was the case especially in northern Gaza, where the Gaza Humanitarian Foundation had no sites and disputes between Israel and traditional aid groups were intense. That's where hunger was the worst.

Israel had to scramble, but it succeeded in heading off a true disaster. By mid-August 2025, the price of flour in Gaza had fallen 90 percent from its July 20 peak.[135] That's according to Hebrew University economist Yannay Spitzer, who tracked Gaza prices and whose warnings in July had helped convince Israelis that the problem was real this time. Around seventy-five trucks of aid per day in northern Gaza became two hundred to three hundred aid trucks per day.

This did not stop the UN's Integrated Food Security Phase Classification (IPC) system from declaring a famine in Gaza on August 22, 2025. Subsequent data would show that though food insecurity had substantially spiked to its most dangerous point of the war, a full-fledged famine failed to materialize, and there was strong evidence that the IPC had cherry-picked its data in August to reach a famine determination.[136] But Israel paid a major diplomatic price for having let the food-scarcity problem spiral in the first place. American Jews couldn't help but notice how the explosion of anti-Israel animus also manifested itself as protests against their own institutions and calls for their marginalization.

Then on July 24, 2025, President Emmanuel Macron announced that France would recognize a Palestinian state. "In doing so," he wrote to Palestinian Authority chief Mahmoud Abbas, "France will make a decisive contribution to peace in the Middle East." It was never clear how Macron's actions would bring peace any closer, but he was soon joined by the UK, Canada, Australia, and other nations. They all cited the need to end the Gaza war and improve the humanitarian situation. Spain and Belgium imposed sanctions on Israel. The European Commission proposed suspending the EU–Israel free-trade agreement. Even Germany, an important ally, suspended exports of offensive weapons to Israel that could be used in Gaza. A large number of those countries formally recognized a Palestinian state in September 2025 during the UN General Assembly proceedings. Other than with President Trump, Israel's diplomatic relations were in free fall.

All of this told Palestinians that Hamas's strategy was working and gave Hamas an incentive to continue rejecting US and Israeli ceasefire offers. Hamas hardened its demands in this period and then refused to rejoin negotiations. Why should it bail out Israel from the storm of international criticism?

At the end of July 2025, a majority of Democrats in the US Senate for the first time voted to block arms sales to Israel. This was not merely the party's left wing anymore. Though it was not enough to pass, the vote signaled a remarkable negative shift. Even more worrying was that the politicians were still lagging behind their voters. There is moderate Democratic support for Israel on some issues, but Gallup polling in July 2025 found that only 8 percent of Democrats approved of Israel's military action in Gaza.[137] Accusations of genocide had become mainstream among activists and younger supporters.

While the Republican Party continues to support Israel, the Pew Research Center found that the share of Republicans under fifty who view Israel negatively had jumped from 35 percent in 2022 to 50 percent in March 2025.[138] A new online ecosystem had also empowered a cadre of aggressively antisemitic influencers on the Right.

In an August 2025 cabinet meeting, Netanyahu would concede that his and IDF chief Zamir's plan since the end of the second ceasefire in March 2025 had failed. Israel was unable to force Hamas to release more hostages, and to avoid a calamity, Jerusalem had to give the terrorists what they wanted in the food-control wars. Israel buckled on aid before Hamas did, and a hostage deal had never seemed further off.

Netanyahu still insisted that Hamas could not rule a postwar Gaza. "Otherwise," he told Fox News's Bill Hemmer on August 7, "we will have many more kidnappings and many more hostages"—which means more wars. The prime minister now spoke of taking over all of Gaza, with a promise to hand it over to an Arab-led force at an unspecified later date. Most observers wondered when that date would ever come, especially if Netanyahu was unwilling to confront his right-wing coalition partners who wanted to continue the war as a matter of principle.

The idea of a new Israeli offensive was to deny Hamas any haven, infrastructure, or control over Gaza's people. But it was late in the day for an undertaking of this kind. Throughout the war, Israel had done the opposite, including pushing Gaza's civilians out of the areas in which it had fought and into Hamas-run areas. The IDF had wanted to avoid an occupation of Gaza that left it responsible for running the territory's civilian affairs. Governing two million Palestinians was a trap, the defense establishment believed.

Even General Eyal Zamir, Netanyahu's handpicked, aggressive new IDF chief and the hero of the war with Iran, drew a line in the sand. He told the prime minister that extending the fight into the remaining 25 percent of Gaza not under Israeli control would risk the lives of the hostages, not to mention Israel's diplomatic standing. The latter point was emphasized privately to Netanyahu by his foreign minister, Gideon Sa'ar.

"The damage from each day of the war is immeasurably greater than the achievements," he argued.

At critical points in the summer of 2024, the fall of 2024, and the spring of 2025, despite consistently growing domestic opposition, the prime minister had managed to carry a large enough segment of Israeli public opinion to continue the war. Now, he seemed nearly alone. Had he become the poker player who keeps doubling down on a fading hand instead of cutting his losses?

The month of June 2025, after Netanyahu's unambiguous win against Iran, could have been a moment to declare victory over the Iranian axis and end the war. By this point, no Israeli defense official believed Hamas could present a substantial threat for many years to come, and certainly not if Israel carried out periodic antiterror raids as it does in the West Bank.

Only time will tell whether the mix of what Israel achieved and lost between June and October 2025 was worth continuing the full-scale war. If Netanyahu's earlier decisions to continue the war were hotly debated, but could be justified to try to break Hamas's political control, the vast majority of the IDF high command thought Netanyahu's final decision was difficult to justify other than to keep his hard-right coalition partners from toppling him. IDF leaders now viewed the conflict between national security and politics as laid bare.

President Trump wanted Israel to finish Hamas and be done. He spoke often of the hostages, and put their families front and center, but this was not the key issue for him. As Trump would later tell *Time* magazine, "Israel was so intent on the hostages, I was actually surprised. You would have thought they would have sacrificed the hostages in order to keep going, right?" But, he found, "the people of Israel wanted the hostages more than they wanted anything else."[139]

Netanyahu led the Israeli cabinet in August 2025 to approve an offensive against Gaza City, where half the population resided, along with most of Gaza's remaining infrastructure, with the Strip's central camps area likely to follow. At the same time, Israel would facilitate a US-led humanitarian surge to Gaza. This would stem the harmful headlines, but

Hamas would still be getting a lot of what it wanted without having to give up any hostages. Though Israel was fighting on, it felt like Hamas had gained the upper hand.

* * *

What happened next was hard to follow even for Middle East experts. Just as Netanyahu's Gaza City invasion was about to start, Hamas unexpectedly accepted the old Witkoff framework for a partial hostage deal that it had previously resisted. Against the expert and even the IDF consensus, the Israeli threat to invade Gaza City seemed to have worked. "Hamas is scared [s—]less right now," a Netanyahu adviser told us at the time. "Before, they didn't believe that we'd do it. Now, they know."

Netanyahu had only to accept the deal for which he had been desperate a month before. But he refused. Instead, Netanyahu shifted the goalposts and, under pressure from his right-wing coalition partners, declared himself unwilling to agree to any more partial deals. It would be all or nothing.

By this point, more than 70 percent of Israelis were ready to end the war. A Netanyahu confidant told us even his own children serving in the IDF were asking why they continued to fight in Gaza. "It's been 20 months already," they told him, "If we're not going to push for victory, what are we doing? And if we are going to do it, then let's do it already."

Netanyahu had said too many times that Israel needed only one more push, in one more area of Gaza, to break Hamas at last. And he kept pushing, until Trump would later put up a bright red stop sign.

Netanyahu tried to replace the partial hostage deal on the table (or at least push it off by some months) with a blitz to get all the hostages back at once. Toward that end, on September 9, 2025, he ordered the IDF and the Shin Bet to assassinate the very Hamas leaders in Qatar with whom he was negotiating. The consequences of the Qatar strike reverberated around the world.

Trump had remained calm over the phone, asking practical questions when Netanyahu informed him that Israel was about to strike in Qatar. But according to White House Press Secretary Karoline Leavitt, Trump directed envoy Steve Witkoff to "inform the Qataris of the impending attack." This stunned the Israelis, as did the heat they took from the Trump team when the airstrike failed to eliminate the Hamas leaders, only some of their staffers. "If you're going to do it," a senior Trump administration official told us, "don't miss. If you'd hit them, we wouldn't have been so upset."

Netanyahu and his allies would later try to spin the attack as successful because it had caused Qatar to pressure Hamas into a deal. In the moment, however, they knew they had failed. Their thought was that it would now take the destruction of Gaza City to cause Hamas to bend. They were wrong; Qatar really was rattled by the attack, especially coming after the Iranian missile strike on Qatar's al-Udeid Air Base in June. These attacks, from both sides of the regional divide, threatened the Gulf monarchy not in any serious military way, but jeopardized its business model and identity. Stability was essential to Qatar's ability to deal and secure long-term investments. Qatar decided to act quickly to bring the disturbances, which flowed from Hamas's hostages, to an end.

Trump called the Israeli strike "terrible" and "a tactical mistake" on Netanyahu's part. "We felt a little betrayed," Witkoff added. "We had lost the confidence of the Qataris." But however misguided they viewed it, Trump himself observed that the Israeli attack gave him a unique window to end the war. "This was one of the things that brought us all together," Trump said. "It was so out of joint that it sort of got everybody to do what they have to do. If you took that away, we might not be talking about this subject right now," he told an interviewer. The subject was peace in Gaza.[140]

* * *

In a series of blitzkrieg moves on September 24, September 29, October 4, and October 9 that took everyone by surprise, including Netanyahu, Trump seized the moment to seal a deal to end the Gaza war. This was the Trump show.

September 24, 2025, was Trump's meeting with leading Arab and Muslim powers on the sidelines of the UN General Assembly. These included Egypt, Qatar, Saudi Arabia, Turkey, and the UAE, as well as Indonesia and Pakistan. The president was able to play on the nerves from Israel's strike on Qatar to rally these regional allies behind an emerging plan to pressure Israel and Hamas into a deal. The terms at this stage were vague on certain points, and the Muslim powers were pleasantly surprised. Though they did not yet know it, Trump had banked their support and would not let it go. They would prove crucial in pressuring Hamas to take the deal and in providing a political horizon for postwar Gaza.

September 29 was Trump's meeting with Netanyahu at the White House to secure his cooperation and corner Hamas. At this stage, and after meetings with US envoys Jared Kushner and Steve Witkoff on September 25 and September 28, Netanyahu secured changes to key terms. Most notable was to allow Israel to hold on to slightly more than half of Gaza's territory for an interim phase that could last indefinitely and to retain a large buffer zone even after that. Critically, this second withdrawal was now tied to progress in Hamas's disarmament—the terms of which were also strengthened.[141]

Here, the Israelis felt good about the terms of the twenty-point plan: "All hostages, alive and deceased, will be returned" in the first few days. "Hamas and other factions agree to not have any role in the governance of Gaza, directly, indirectly, or in any form."[142] Witkoff would also explain that the deal reflects Israel's key principles. This was the high point for Netanyahu. Trump announced the plan with Netanyahu by his side.

US intelligence predicted that Hamas would reject the deal, according to Witkoff.[143] But his own contacts atop the Qatari monarchy signaled otherwise. Hamas would strive for a positive reply, even if it had disagreements, they told him. In our view, both were right.

On October 4, Hamas responded to Trump's plan to end the war and structure postwar Gaza with what was commonly characterized in the press as a "yes, but." Yes, Hamas could release all the hostages, but not quite so fast, the group said. Yes, it could hand over power, but only to a group based on "Palestinian national consensus," in which

Hamas is the leading party. Disarmament, it implied, would run afoul of Palestinian "inalienable rights."[144]

In essence, as Netanyahu saw it, Hamas had said no. Hamas could accept the twenty points or not, and it had made clear that it didn't. At this point, Netanyahu would have continued Israel's offensive in Gaza City to get the terrorists to a simple "yes" with no qualifications.

Trump, however, had a different solution. He heard what he wanted to hear and bulldozed both sides. The president thanked Hamas for accepting the deal and instructed Netanyahu to stop the war immediately, over the prime minister's objections, as if Hamas had agreed to everything. In uniquely Trumpian style, he also threatened Hamas with "complete obliteration" if it did not play along. Only a few months after he had dropped around a dozen thirty-thousand-pound bombs on Iran's nuclear program, Hamas did not view this as mere talk. Its Qatari and Turkish patrons made sure of that.

Kushner, Trump's Orthodox Jewish son-in-law and first-term Middle East maven who was one of the main architects of the Abraham Accords, had also reentered the fray. Working with Witkoff since September 2025, Kushner led the final charge to a deal. Trusted by the president, he was another outsider untethered to much of the conventional wisdom on the Israeli–Palestinian conflict. Kushner was secure in his support for Israel and not afraid to clash with Netanyahu. Since the first Trump term, he had also amassed extensive business interests in the Middle East, managing billions of dollars in investments, including from Saudi Arabia, Qatar, and the UAE.

Regarding Netanyahu, Trump told *Time* magazine, "He would have just kept going. It could have gone on for years. It would have gone on for years. But I stopped him, and everybody came together when I stopped him.... 'Bibi, you can't fight the world,'" Trump said, recounting their conversation. "You can fight individual battles, but the world's against you."[145] When Netanyahu pushed back, explaining that Israel could not stop until Hamas actually agreed to the deal, Trump launched into a profanity-laced monologue cataloging all he had done for Israel.

The president made clear that he would no longer stand with Netanyahu if the prime minister stood in the way of his peace plan.

The IDF ceased fire for five days, from October 4 to October 9, to allow the Trump administration to finalize the deal. A summit was planned in Egypt's Sharm El Sheikh, but Kushner insisted that Hamas "pre-agree" to much of it before the meetings began. Otherwise, he said, the US delegation would not attend.[146] This, he believes, helped defuse some of the more complex issues beforehand, smoothing the way to an agreement in Egypt.

Nevertheless, on the last day, the Arab states requested some seventeen different revisions to the deal, according to one of Israel's negotiators. "We fought it off," he said. Israel made its deal with the US and the mediators, and Hamas did the same. The Israelis never saw Hamas's agreement to disarm, but Witkoff promised them that Hamas officials had agreed to it during their rare in-person meeting only hours before the ceasefire was inked on October 9. Hamas would always deny that it had agreed to disarm, yet at this stage, it did not matter. The deal was moving forward. Trump had formed and hoodwinked an Arab coalition, bludgeoned Israel, and, with the help of Qatar and Turkey, bludgeoned Hamas. This was what it took to get the deal signed and bring the war to a stop.

* * *

On October 13, 2025, Hamas returned the twenty living hostages all at once. It would do so at the start of a ceasefire deal, not its end, while the IDF remained in the eastern half of Gaza. It is hard to overstate how significant these two victories were for Netanyahu, the IDF, and Israel. Up to the moment Trump got Hamas to agree to these terms, and really, up to the moment the twenty living hostages were returned, no one in Israel—least of all in the defense establishment—had believed such an outcome was possible.

Defense officials had repeated as a mantra that Hamas would need to keep at least ten hostages, even at the end of any war, as a form of "life insurance" to ensure Israel would not kill its leaders. The entire IDF and

Shin Bet high command was also convinced that Hamas would not release all the hostages until the IDF was fully withdrawn from Gaza and publicly committed to ending the war.

A majority of Israelis viewed getting back the twenty remaining living hostages as the primary goal of the war. For the first time, they had some closure for the nightmare that began on October 7, 2023. Another portion of Israelis could point to holding onto half the Gaza Strip as a major strategic advantage. It left Israel in a much better position to fight Hamas and defend towns bordering Gaza. The Israeli presence also could be used as leverage over Hamas after the war. Ironically, the late and controversial IDF operations to conquer 75 percent of Gaza and then expand into Gaza City, presumed to doom a deal, gave Israel more bargaining chips with which to trade. The IDF could now withdraw from substantial territory in Gaza and still control more than half of it.

Netanyahu emphasized that he had received an official promise that Hamas would disarm, and while the terror group would try to evade that commitment, this also gave Israel some additional leverage. In their September 29 White House press conference, Trump said that Israel would have "full backing" from the US to "finish the job" of disarming and dismantling Hamas if others could not do it through the deal.

The price for these Hamas concessions was some reciprocal victories for Hamas. When Trump ordered Netanyahu to pause the war on October 4, 2025, it was before a single hostage was handed over. Ultimately, they were handed over nine days later—a period longer than the entire first ceasefire in November 2023. Netanyahu also effectively agreed to end the war without disarming Hamas.

In a wild twist, Witkoff and Netanyahu adviser Ophir Falk have argued that Hamas came to view the hostages as something of a liability.[147] So long as they remained in captivity, the war could never end. By getting rid of them, Hamas may have wagered, it could keep its arms, and therefore, remain at least the power behind the throne in Gaza.

Netanyahu also made two other politically painful concessions, both of which were necessary to keep a broad coalition of Muslim states behind the deal and pressure Hamas to accept it. These were to include the

Palestinian Authority and the idea of a Palestinian state in the agreement. Along with Hamas disarmament, these were some of the main issues that had led the prime minister to refuse to end the war in March 2025 and the summer of 2024.

The Trump plan for Gaza's governance was to establish an international stabilization force from supportive Arab and Muslim states to keep the peace, while a Trump-chaired Board of Peace would supervise a committee of Palestinian technocrats and international experts who would handle civil administration. That is, "until such time as the Palestinian Authority has completed its reform program"—a stringent set of reforms set out by Kushner in the first Trump term—"and can securely and effectively take back control of Gaza." Netanyahu believed this would never happen. But was it really so far-fetched? Who, after all, had the technocratic expertise in the Palestinian world? By allowing the PA into the deal, Netanyahu risked setting the stage for its return to govern Gaza.

Signing a deal that held up a Palestinian state as an ideal, despite many qualifications, may have been the toughest pill for Netanyahu to swallow.

Netanyahu was also forced to publicly apologize to Qatar and to compensate the regime for Israel's attack. Trump even promised to prevent any future Israeli attacks on Qatari soil. Via executive order, the president granted Qatar a personal security guarantee. The Hamas leadership in Qatar effectively gained immunity until the end of Trump's term. If Israel hoped to expose Qatar's double-dealing with Washington, it failed.

What really emerged from the Trump show was a series of trade-offs. Israel got all its hostages back, but Hamas first got an immediate pause in the war, initially for nothing, and then an end to the war. Israel got to keep its forces in half of Gaza, including the Philadelphi Corridor, yet Israel had to withdraw immediately from all areas where the Palestinian population was residing, giving Hamas control. Israel received promises about future efforts to replace and disarm Hamas, but there was no concrete timeline. Israel could use the territory it had not withdrawn from to pressure Hamas to make future concessions, and Hamas could use the lure of being replaced politically and some kind of partial disarmament to get Trump to pressure Israel to make further withdrawals from Gaza. In other words, while Israel was on top, Hamas was still very much in the game.

In truth, Israel needed a way out of the war. Two years of ugly urban warfare had pummeled its diplomatic standing, and it was not clear what a few additional months of fighting would accomplish. As Foreign Minister Sa'ar would tell us, "We are a small nation. We are standing against huge propaganda." At some point, even Netanyahu had to concede to that reality.

The end to the war would bring Israel some diplomatic relief. Twenty nations, including the US, Canada, Germany, Finland, France, and India, sent senior military representatives to Israel to hear the IDF's takeaways from the war. Morocco announced that it would establish a production facility for Israeli attack drones. Germany, Israel's top European ally, lifted its partial arms embargo on Israel and signed a $2.3 billion deal to buy Israeli-made Spike antitank missiles. Berlin also closed a deal to deploy the Israeli-made Arrow defense system, such that Israeli technology will now defend Germany from Russia.[148]

When it came time to submit the ceasefire deal for Israeli cabinet approval, however, Washington took no chances. Kushner and Witkoff sat in on the meeting to ensure a "yes" vote. They faced some dissent, especially from Netanyahu's hard-right coalition partner Itamar Ben-Gvir. "I'm sitting here looking at the list of terrorists being released—murderers of babies, rapists of women," Ben-Gvir said.[149] In exchange for twenty living hostages and twenty-eight dead, Israel would free one thousand seven hundred Gazans detained since the start of the war as well as 250 terrorists serving life sentences for killing Israelis. Five ministers would vote against the deal, but crucially, after all their threats over the preceding months and years, Netanyahu's coalition partners declined to bring down the government over it. Ben-Gvir announced that Netanyahu would get a chance to use the deal to dismantle Hamas. Trump had called these ministers' bluff.

* * *

As the ceasefire advanced from October to November 2025, a few things had become clear. First, Hamas was testing Israel. The terrorists had attempted some two dozen low-grade infiltrations into the Israeli half of Gaza. The IDF, in turn, was responding swiftly, killing the infiltrators. In three cases—two in which a couple of IDF soldiers were killed or wounded—the IDF also responded with dozens of airstrikes, some of them targeting senior Hamas commanders. Israel was not budging from its part of Gaza without Hamas disarmament. Yet the heavy Israeli counterattacks taxed the Trump administration's patience. Kushner and Witkoff complained that Israel was not being "proportional." The Netanyahu team complained in turn that the two US envoys wanted quiet at all costs.

A twist in Israel's favor was that before the ceasefire went into effect, Hamas failed to move more than one hundred fighters out of a portion of Rafah that would be under Israel's control. The IDF realized this in time, trapped the Hamas fighters, and was able to use them as leverage to force Hamas to return most of the remaining twenty-eight bodies of deceased hostages. Hamas had tried to pretend it had lost track of or was not able to reach half of them, and delayed returning them for weeks. Once the IDF had the Hamas fighters in Rafah cornered, suddenly the group managed to "find" missing hostage bodies and return them.

The international stabilization force (ISF) was supposed to deploy sometime in early 2026, but its fate and structure remained uncertain at the time of this writing. Troops from countries as diverse as Indonesia, Egypt, Turkey, Qatar, Azerbaijan, the UAE, and even the Palestinian Authority were all in consideration for the job of managing Gaza's internal security and borders. But would Hamas really let the ISF do anything substantial? Most of the countries being floated to join the ISF were plainly leaking that they would not allow their troops to face the direct dangers of gunfights with Hamas. Why should they? No Muslim state was going to kill Palestinians to keep Israelis safe.

In that case, would the ISF make any real difference? The risk was exemplified by the UN peacekeepers in Lebanon, who failed utterly to curb Hezbollah, but got in the way of Israel's attempts to do so. This was why the IDF's position within Gaza and its freedom of action against Hamas was crucial. If the IDF retained that capacity, then the ISF did not need to be as active. "The ISF will give way to the IDF," a senior Israeli official predicted to us. If the force could weaken Hamas's hold on the population along the way, that would be beneficial.

Hamas could make a tactical concession to a committee of Palestinian technocrats, giving up formal political leadership to secure foreign funding for the rebuilding of Gaza. Keeping its guns and intimidating other Gazans with public shows of force, however, are core to the group's identity and its hope to openly return to power at some later date.

As 2025 came to a close, Hamas had not disarmed. On the contrary, it had regrouped and reasserted control over the western half of Gaza. Immediately after the ceasefire, the terrorist group staged a series of public executions against rival clans and many of the more moderate Palestinians with whom Israel, the ISF, and the technocrats would have wanted to work. Clearly, Hamas had not been destroyed. This meant the fight would go on, even if the war had ended.

CONCLUSION

THE FUTURE OF THE MIDDLE EAST

The biggest mistake an analyst of this war can make is to think too small. "The Gaza war," we often hear it called, as if Israel has fought on only one front rather than seven. As if every one of those fronts were not part of a larger clash: Iran vs. Israel.

If the Gaza war mostly ended in October 2025 with the Trump deal, there were parts of the previous two years when it had already faded into the background behind intensified fighting with Iran, Hezbollah, or the remnants of the Syrian military.

When Prime Minister Netanyahu told us in December 2024 that "the campaign we carried out changed the Middle East," he didn't mean the initial blitz of Gaza City or the flattening of Rafah. He meant the rollback, the beatdown, the severing—he cannot stick to a metaphor—of the Iranian axis.

"We knocked down Hezbollah," Netanyahu said, "which was supposed to protect Iran. And Iran didn't protect Hezbollah either. And neither of them protected Assad. So, we just split that whole axis right down the middle." Contrary to Tehran's prewar planning, none of the proxies would lift a finger to help Iran in June 2025, when Israel bombed its nuclear and ballistic-missile programs along with its top military and intelligence officials.

During that Twelve-Day War with Iran, a video clip began to circulate among Israelis, reaching Iran experts both in the prime minister's office and the nation's taxi cabs. It was from a 2021 speech by the chief of Iran's joint military headquarters, who would be killed in Israel's first day of strikes.[150] He quoted Qassem Soleimani recounting his life's work for Iran soon before his death in 2020:

"I have assembled for you six armies outside Iran, and I have created a corridor 1,500 kilometers long and 1,000 kilometers wide, all the way to the shores of the Mediterranean," Soleimani told Iran's army chiefs. "Any enemy that decides to fight against the Islamic Revolution, and against the sacred regime of the Islamic Republic of Iran, will have to go through these six armies. It won't be able to do so," he pledged.

Yet Israel did. After the October 7 massacre, Israel fought through Hamas, Islamic Jihad, and Hezbollah, wiping out their leadership and slicing up their missile arsenals, leaving the Assad regime in Syria to crumble without support. Of Soleimani's six armies, only the Houthis and Iraq's Popular Mobilization Units, more distant from Israel, have escaped. Suddenly, Iran did not look so menacing.

For the first time, Israel could attack Iran's nuclear program and other capabilities without fear of incurring thousands of rockets a day from Iran's proxies—on top of Iran's own dangerous response. This was one war, and Israeli military achievements in Lebanon, Gaza, and Syria had paved the way to Tehran.

Israel's initial success against Iran then allowed President Trump and the US Air Force to enter the fight to remove all doubt. This part of the war, bearing down on Iran, was a full-spectrum strategic success, born of intelligence, military, and political-diplomatic accomplishments that surpassed even best-case predictions on October 8, 2023. In this most critical theater, Israel exceeded its war aims. Netanyahu, who has long seen Iran as the principal threat to Israel, even before that became the common view it is today, can claim a generational victory against Iran.

Gallant and Halevi planned and managed the military strategy of the October 2024 strikes that removed Iran's best air-defense systems, clearing the path. Gantz, as defense minister from 2020 to 2022, took Iran strike plans in a more practical direction, bringing them to life from back-office shelves and increasing training budgets to serious levels. This all took years, including some when Netanyahu was out of power. IDF chief Zamir and Mossad Director Barnea managed the incredible implementation of the years of planning in real time. But in the end, Netanyahu had to drive the preparations to the finish and take the risk to act.

Netanyahu is wary enough, however, to know that victories are rarely total, and that even overwhelming victories are not usually final. As someone who worked with Netanyahu for more than a decade put it to us, his ideal is to exchange one set of problems for a different, and slightly less bad, set of problems. Antiutopian to the extreme, Netanyahu does not believe that he finished off Iran in June 2025—or even any one of its individual proxy armies. Hamas hangs on. The Houthis stand proud. Hezbollah is reeling but doing all it can to rebuild its arsenal, and Assad is gone but was replaced by an enigmatic Islamist with Turkish backing. Iran was allowed to escape the war without terms being imposed on it and has not at all abandoned its desire to destroy Israel.

There is more work to be done on each front, but this should not obscure the big picture. Israel came back from the heavy defeat of October 7 to command a stronger military-strategic position than it has had in decades. Critics have called this the new age of Israeli "empire," not understanding that Jerusalem's forward-leaning defense strategy is not to seize strips of territory to subsume them, but to establish security buffers with its neighbors until they can be trusted not to conduct or allow new October 7–style invasions.

It was no coincidence that Hezbollah did not function as Iran's "insurance policy" in June 2025. It was unable to engulf Israel in fire in response to the IDF attack on Iran's nuclear program. That ability had been taken from it. Hamas had been militarily crushed and sent into hiding until the October 2025 ceasefire, able to poke out its head for only minutes at a time to attempt much more limited and disorganized guerrilla warfare. It can no longer set a match to the region. Syria changed from a crucial proxy of Iran to an opponent in the blink of an eye, costing Iran its transit hub and disrupting its land bridge to Beirut.

Multidecade Iranian investments went down the drain, tens of billions of dollars that Iran could hardly spare as it struggled to keep the lights on. The strategic concept of an axis of proxies that would assist one another, as well as their master, has been shattered. Israel broke out of the "ring of fire" that Iran had worked painstakingly to construct around it.

The Iranian regime was left with only bad options and felt it had to intervene to save its proxies. For years, Iran had sought to avoid such direct interventions until it would have the conventional, proxy, or nuclear strength to deter a real response by Israel. Now, it had to rush its plan. But when the Iranians did attack, in April 2024 and October 2024, they failed to make a substantial dent. Instead, they gave Israel openings to strike Iran directly, which the IDF did with ease, demonstrating aerial overmatch on offense and defense. This prepared Israel to do it again on a much grander scale in June 2025.

Israel's initial success against Iran and its nuclear program, the fruit of an arduous process of military planning and years of intelligence penetration and groundwork, served as the best argument for the US to join in and deliver a finishing blow. The US military was ready, having coordinated with Halevi well in advance—a byproduct of strong personal and military-to-military relationships. But Jerusalem needed to be daring enough to act first, so that the opportunity would be too good for President Trump to pass up.

When Netanyahu, Ron Dermer, and Barnea then convinced Trump to give the order, the first result was to set back Iran's nuclear program, and likely by longer than the estimates suggest. In the face of newly credible Israeli and US threats to strike again, Iran cannot easily resume nuclear work. The second result was to slash Iran's ballistic-missile arsenal, its strongest conventional military capability.

Even months after the twelve-day war, "satellite imagery indicates that Iran's uranium-enrichment program remains significantly set back," in the finding of veteran nuclear inspector David Albright of the Institute for Science and International Security. "At present, Iran does not appear able to enrich uranium in any significant manner or make gas centrifuges in significant numbers.... After five months, Iran appears to have made minimal progress on reconstituting its destroyed capabilities."[151]

Iran's power in the nuclear, conventional, and proxy arenas has diminished. The enormous resulting swing in the balance of power is to the advantage of Israel, the US, and their Sunni Arab allies, who have a rare opportunity to establish a new regional order before the jungle grows back. This change has reinforced Western diplomacy, and not only with Arab and Muslim states. The US and Europe joined together at last in the months following the attack to insist on an end to Iran's domestic enrichment capability and showed the determination necessary at the end of September 2025 to snap back global UN sanctions against Iran.

With Iran, unlike with Gaza, the West was quietly united behind Jerusalem. "Israel is doing the dirty work for all of us," German Chancellor Friedrich Merz acknowledged during the war in June 2025.[152] Everyone knew Iran had to be stopped from obtaining nuclear weapons, but no one wanted to do what it would take to stop it. This story is not over, and in halting short of regime change in Iran—which may not have been within its power at the time—Israel knows it could face a counterattack sometime down the road. But for now, Israel has succeeded in neutralizing an existential threat.

Instead of a rally-around-the-flag effect, the Iranian regime saw widespread domestic discontent over water and electricity crises, soaring inflation, and a plummeting currency. This book was finished in 2025, but in early 2026, Iran's government was beset by a massive protest wave and resorted to the largest massacre in its history to put it down. This brought on a confrontation with President Trump. which became two months of negotiations over the remainder of the nuclear program and the mostly rehabilitated ballistic-missile threat. But no deal was achieved. Ayatollah Khamenei insisted on retaining capabilities that would let Iran resume the pursuit of nuclear weapons at the date of his choosing, but after the beating Iran and its proxies had taken since October 7, 2023, he lacked leverage.

Working more closely than ever before, Israel and the US jointly unleashed on Iran the largest air attack of the war on February 28, 2026. Ayatollah Khamenei and nearly all of his top IRGC and military commanders, themselves replacements from June 2025, were killed in the opening hours. In the early days, Israel and the US were each striking around 500 Iranian targets per day, mostly to do with ballistic missiles and the IRGC, as well as drones, warships and other regime assets. The aim was to end the threat from the Iranian regime—and possibly end the regime itself, if luck held. Iran responded by firing over 1,000 missiles and 2,500 drones not only at Israel, but also at a dozen other Arab countries. Ostensibly targeting US bases, Iran aimed also at civilian targets and Arab oil and gas facilities. The regime even stopped traffic in the Strait of Hormuz, setting off a worldwide energy crisis. As of mid-March 2026, the regime had been shaken to its foundations and its forces had been substantially weakened, advancing Israeli and regional security and giving Iranian protesters a chance to topple the regime going forward. As the British-Iranian historian Ali M. Ansari told us, summarizing Hannah Arendt, "Revolutions are impossible before they happen and inevitable after they happen."

The Islamic Republic may well survive, given its support from the hard core, especially in the IRGC and the Basij, and its willingness to slaughter its own people. But Iran miscalculated. From the perspective of the Iranian regime, the result of the war with Israel is almost all negative—an unmitigated strategic disaster, a setback across theaters. In that, if nothing else, the leaders of Israel's war room can put aside their differences and take pride.

If Iran's regime survives, no one knows when or whether it will agree to a new nuclear deal with the West—and if it does, how long it will go before cheating. But after the recent military operations, the US and Israel have their best chance in decades to mitigate or upend the Iranian threat. No one should underestimate the resourcefulness, patience, and determination of this Iranian regime. Then again, after what they showed, no one should underestimate Israel and the US either.

* * *

Lebanon is another theater, as we look to the future, to help understand the impressive magnitude as well as the hard limits to Israel's achievement. It also offers one of the greatest gulfs between what was expected and what, in fact, occurred when Israel went to war.

In Gaza, if we told experts on October 8, 2023 that there would be a long, grinding war that destroyed the Strip and smashed Hamas's capabilities while it fought on at great cost to Palestinian civilians and Israeli political legitimacy, the experts would have said, "Sounds about right." But almost nothing about Israel's northern front followed that predictable pattern.

To start, Hezbollah was more cautious than many had anticipated. Given a once-in-a-lifetime chance to pile on Israel, it blinked. Israel also bided its time in its northern region, practicing "active defense" for eleven months while it focused on Gaza. This meant Israel was not overwhelmed in the early weeks after October 7. But as weeks turned to months, Hezbollah's strategy functionally shrank Israeli territory by moving the old buffer zone from southern Lebanon to northern Israel. For some sixty thousand to eighty thousand displaced northern Israelis, forced out of areas that the whole world recognizes as part of the Jewish state, this was intolerable.

Even as Jerusalem was winning on the tactical level of tit-for-tat, the Israeli north had been made a no-go zone. Would Israel ever be able to restore its sovereignty and security sufficient for the north to thrive? Even if Israel negotiated a ceasefire in Gaza and even if Hezbollah quieted down, could not Hassan Nasrallah restart the conflict any time he wanted? Would Israel ever be safe to live or invest in? In short, would Israel have a future?

All these questions were asked and more, because Israel seemed to be more afraid of Hezbollah than vice versa. Though the country had long claimed to be deterring the terrorists of Lebanon, at some point the equation had flipped. Hezbollah was deterring Israel. It could do so because everyone in Israel, from left-center politicians and right-wing generals to Netanyahu, Gantz, and Gallant, expected war with Hezbollah to be calamitous for Israel. Hezbollah might lead the IDF to bomb Lebanon back to the Stone Age, but it would also traumatize Israel forever, we were told.

That did not happen. The Israeli campaign that began in September 2024 and reached a crescendo with the exploding pagers and walkie-talkies and Nasrallah's assassination, dispensed with all conventional wisdom. Hezbollah, with its communications down and organization thoroughly penetrated by Israeli intelligence, was unable to get off large barrages of mid- and long-range rockets before Israel decimated its arsenal. When the big confrontation arrived, Hezbollah received knockout blow after blow while Israel was barely bruised.

As with Iran, Israel was prepared for this fight—and it showed. Even politically, Israel paid little cost abroad, as success spoke for itself. Israel killed Nasrallah and lost no international support, managing to move more swiftly and kill far fewer civilians than it had in Gaza.

Hezbollah is now working hard to recover its full strength, but it faces great challenges. First, even after the November 2024 ceasefire, Israel has not let down its northern guard. Over the next eight months, the IDF killed nearly five hundred Hezbollah fighters, mostly in one-off air strikes. In November 2025, Israel even killed Hezbollah's new military chief of staff in a targeted strike in Beirut. The old Israeli policy of exchanging "quiet for quiet" is no more. Months after Israel withdrew most of its forces from Lebanon in February 2025, the IDF still maintained five outposts just inside southern Lebanon. Israel claims no territory and is open to withdrawing these, but only in a different security reality, when Hezbollah is no longer a threat to invade northern Israel.

Second, the fall of the Assad regime in Syria has disrupted the weapons-smuggling pipeline that begins in Iran. "This makes the reconstitution of Hezbollah incomparably more difficult," General David Petraeus told us. "Then add what has been done to Iran. It's not clear that they have a lot left over to help Hezbollah."

Third, Hezbollah's weakness created a long-awaited opening for the Lebanese state to assert itself. After two years with no president, in part due to Hezbollah obstruction, the aftermath of Israel's operation saw the election of US- and Saudi-backed General Joseph Aoun. He pledged to disarm Hezbollah in his inaugural address and, under US pressure, tasked the Lebanese Armed Forces with doing so.

There is ample room for skepticism about whether that effort will succeed. After months of giving positive encouragement, Trump envoy Tom Barrack began to lose patience. "Should Beirut continue to hesitate, Israel may act unilaterally," he warned in October 2025. But the very fact that disarmament is being talked about reflects the weakening of Hezbollah and Iranian influence, which gives Lebanon its best chance in decades to pull itself together.

The result so far has been a restoration of security for Israel's northern residents. For now, Hezbollah has resigned itself to this. It has lost too many men, missiles, and leaders to do otherwise, and the organization does not trust itself to move without tipping off Israeli intelligence. The losses could set Hezbollah back years, even as it retains local Shia Muslim support[153] and remains a medium- and long-term threat to Israel. As Hezbollah does all it can to recover quietly, Israel's challenge is to continue to resist the complacency that it swore off after the October 7 attack.

* * *

After Israel's humiliation of Hezbollah in late 2024, the sharks of the region smelled blood in the water. They made quick work of Syria's Assad regime, which Hezbollah had propped up. Then, Israel showed it was not afraid to be one of those sharks. Destroying the strategic assets of the Syrian military and seizing the high ground on the border was a solid hedge against the uncertainty that remains.

The new Islamist regime of Ahmed al-Sharaa is not to Israel's liking. There is no precedent for a former al-Qaeda commander to lead a state to peace and prosperity. But Sharaa has thus far shown Israel considerable deference. He has even expressed openness to joining the Abraham

Accords or at least to signing a security deal with Israel, at the urging of President Trump. A formal peace is unlikely, but its discussion gives a sense of the radical change afoot in Syria.

Israel's main interest in the country is to keep Iran and its weapons smugglers out. So long as the Sharaa regime stays committed to doing that, Israel can find a way to work with it. In Iran, they share a common enemy.

Jerusalem clashed with Syria and even bombed Damascus in July 2025, however, after Sharaa's forces and some of their allies carried out a massacre against their own Syrian Druze minority. Israel may find itself tempted to play a larger role in Syria's sectarian politics, but this seems unlikely to end well.

The rise of Turkish influence in Syria is a concern, but one that can likely be balanced as Trump waives Assad-era sanctions and Syria enters the American orbit. For the first time, a Syrian president visited the White House, and for the first time, the US will have a seat at the table in shaping Syria's future. That is far better news on the Syrian front than Israel ever expected after seventy years of Syrian alignment with the Soviet and then Russian and Iranian camps. As Jerusalem proceeds with suspicion, it should not lose sight of the opportunity.

* * *

The toughest theater of all to assess and project is Gaza. This was where it started and ended, where Israel devoted its greatest focus and paid its highest price. This is the front that still hurts.

Begin with the numbers. Israel's ground invasion of Gaza cost 468 IDF soldiers their lives. A further 329 were killed in the October 7 battles inside Israel, along with fifty-eight police officers. Nearly twenty thousand Israeli soldiers have been wounded to different degrees over the course of the war. On the other side, more than twenty-two thousand Hamas fighters have been killed, according to Israel, and likely many more than that have been wounded, though no clear statistics are available. The new fighters recruited by Hamas have largely been teenagers, poorly armed and given little training. Hamas's entire top leadership has been killed, along with most of the replacements, leaving a power vacuum to be filled by third stringers whose names even well-informed Israelis have never heard.

Israel has brought back 168 hostages alive—160 of them through three ceasefire deals and eight through IDF rescue missions. That is likely more hostages saved than most would have predicted on October 8, 2023, but it took longer than expected, and far fewer than anticipated were sprung directly by force of arms. Certainly, the wait was excruciating and came to define much of the experience of the war for Israelis. They often felt powerless, even amid their extraordinary display of power.

Jerusalem also secured the return of all eighty-seven bodies of dead hostages, including a few taken captive before October 7. The bodies of around forty of those killed in the October 7 attack were taken hostage, and a similar number of other live hostages were killed by Hamas in Gaza. Eight were killed accidentally by the IDF. After two years, and the return of the last deceased hostage, Israel's painful weekly hostage rallies came to an end.

Almost a third of Gaza has been turned into an Israeli buffer in one form or another, which should make it very difficult for Hamas to mount another October 7–style attack. Israel has destroyed countless miles of Hamas tunnels, even as there are countless more left, and continues to act in the half of Gaza—east, north and south—that its troops control as of late 2025. In the south, Hamas's critical Egyptian supply route has been cut off by Israeli control of the Philadelphi Corridor.

Hamas remained in control of Western Gaza after the ceasefire. Israel had perversely encouraged the terrorists' control over the Strip's population, both by raiding and leaving neighborhoods and by evacuating Gazans from the areas the IDF held. "Hamas still has the most guys with the most guns," General Petraeus told us. "They're no longer a military, with combat-effective companies, battalions, brigades, and they certainly don't have the kind of rockets and missiles and other threats," he added, "but they are roughly the same size as they were before. They're just much less capable, the new members. There's no shortage of candidates for Hamas, given that there's no shortage of angry, young, unemployed, grievance-filled men."

Their grievances remain. In November 2025, Hamas's Gaza Health Ministry said more than 68,832 Gazans had been killed in the war and more than 170,690 injured, not distinguishing between civilians and combatants. The precise figures are disputed, but what is not in doubt is the enormous scale of the human tragedy.

How and when Gaza might recover is an open question. Even at a much earlier stage in the war, Benny Morris, one of Israel's leading historians, told us, "There was never destruction like what has happened in Gaza over the past five months in any of Israel's wars." In 1967, "Israel conquered the West Bank with almost no houses being destroyed," he said, "and the same applies in '56 in the Gaza Strip, and the same applies in '48. Israel didn't have the firepower to cause such devastation. This is totally new." Gaza City and portions of northern Gaza were hit hard. Khan Yunis has been largely flattened. Rafah is no more.

Will this new dynamic in the long-running conflict diminish the Palestinian will to resist over time or redouble it? Will it deter Israel's enemies or alienate its friends? Israel has legal defenses for its individual targeting choices, and much can be blamed on Hamas's abuse of civilian infrastructure. But it did not help that Israel fought again and again in the same neighborhoods. The resulting widespread destruction became a key driver of Israel's diminished global standing. Videos of Gazan neighborhoods turned to rubble, with nothing left intact for as far as they eye could see, told a story of their own.

After rolling out his February 2025 plan for mass Gazan emigration with aplomb, Trump ignored it for months and then downgraded any real efforts at resettling Gazans on a large scale with the October 2025 ceasefire deal. The overwhelming majority of Gaza's two million people will likely stay in the territory despite the devastation—or, more accurately, not have other countries agree to take them in. But the territory itself may be redefined. UNRWA, the UN's forever-refugee agency for Palestinians only, has subsidized Hamas's rule and sustained the conditions for war on Israel for seventy-five years. In January 2025, Israel effectively banned UNRWA from Gaza, and other UN agencies and groups have filled its role in delivering aid. Whether the ban will be implemented fully or reversed under the new authority managing Gaza will be a bellwether for the extent of the break from the Gaza Strip's miserable history.

In its system of governance and education and its population's permanent refugee status, modern Gaza has been geared toward perpetual war to destroy Israel. This was Gaza's unwritten constitution, and amending it will be essential to preventing wars in the future. But creating a new system of aid and governance is easier said than done. Excluded from the Trump peace plan, the Gaza Humanitarian Foundation officially ended operations in November 2025. Early failures sank it, even though it showed promise. At one point in the summer of 2025, shutting down the GHF topped Hamas's list of demands for a hostage deal.

* * *

For long months of the war—some say since early 2024—Netanyahu refused to take up recommendations by Biden, Gallant, Gantz, and Halevi to replace Hamas as Gaza's governing authority. This helped keep the terrorists in control of the population and allowed armed gangs to take advantage of the chaos. His refusal to move toward having an international stabilization force (ISF) ready to deploy also helped Hamas immediately reestablish control over much of Gaza within days of the October 2025 Trump ceasefire.

At the same time, the suggestion to replace Hamas with a hybrid of Arab authorities has always had obvious downsides. Would any of those Arab countries fight to prevent Hamas from reigniting its terror wave against Israel? Why assume that the PA, which failed from 2005 to 2007 to hold Hamas down in Gaza, would be able to do it this time, when it is weaker and less popular?

Gallant, who despises the PA, had a simple answer: There is no one else. "In Gaza, there are two identity cards, Hamas and the PA. You pick one or the other," he said. Gallant believed Israel needed to defeat Hamas militarily and then needed to put the least-bad option that was not Hamas in control of Gaza. He knew the PA's many flaws and harbored no illusions that it would succeed with flying colors. But he believed that just as the PA has, with significant Israeli help, kept general control of the West Bank despite Hamas's many takeover attempts, Israeli help could enable it to do the same in Gaza.

The Netanyahu team had become well-practiced at pushing off discussion of the day after the war. "First, kill the killers," Ron Dermer told us in March 2024. Political alternatives "are nonsense if there are 5,000 Hamas fighters around." Maybe then, that sufficed. But two years into the war, Trump made Netanyahu swallow these arguments. The war would end with Hamas holding its weapons—and refusing to give them up, despite Trump's internationally backed assurances. The deal would even raise a potential return of the PA to Gaza and keep alive the idea of Palestinian statehood, albeit both in a qualified fashion. Dermer was right that Hamas power would threaten the viability of any alternative government, but he and Netanyahu had little choice in the end other than to give one a try.

"There is no way we will leave Hamas intact," Netanyahu adviser Ophir Falk insisted to us in November 2025. An international stabilization force could help spare the IDF the unwanted burdens of military occupation, but Israel knows it is no substitute for dismantling Hamas. For that, the Israelis can only hope to rely on a Trump promise to let the IDF disarm Hamas if the deal's mechanisms cannot. Even then, however, it is not clear that the IDF can disarm Hamas by force. It tried for two years, and this deal was the best it could get.

We do not rule out escalations in Israeli air strikes, new raids, or even an IDF advance into parts of the western half of Gaza to pressure Hamas. But we do not sense a readiness or desire among Israeli reservists, IDF brass, or political leaders for a return to full-scale war in Gaza. Certainly, Trump and his team are attached to the peace they crafted and are determined not to let it collapse, if they can.

In the ceasefire's aftermath, Gallant's vision seemed more prescient about the future of Gaza, predicting that Israel would need to accept some place for Hamas in Gaza as well as a return of the PA in some form and the idea of Palestinian statehood. For his part, Netanyahu was correct that he could obtain better terms from Hamas than were on offer in the summer of 2024—receiving all hostages up front and remaining in half of Gaza under the Trump plan. The war was going to end looking something like this, but keeping it going allowed the IDF to squeeze Hamas, even after most thought the squeeze had stopped working.

Gaza's future, though, will depend on decisions to come. Netanyahu accepted Trump's peace plan, but what will happen if Hamas wants changes and Trump needs to referee? Will Israel retain eastern Gaza and the various conditions for which it fought on so long? Will the new Board of Peace fight to deradicalize the Gazan education system, and secure help from the United Arab Emirates in doing so? How adept will the Palestinian technocrats and other committees appointed to manage Gaza be? Looking further ahead, whatever arrangement emerges in Gaza, will a future Democratic Party president use it to force through Palestinian statehood?

Finally, who will be leading Israel after the mandatory 2026 election? Will it be Netanyahu, Naftali Bennett—who is the favorite as of late 2025—or some unforeseen player? The challenge for this next prime minister will be to carry forward the new Israeli consensus that Iran's jihadist proxies must be not merely deterred, but prevented from developing the capabilities to threaten Israel in the first place. Israel now maintains buffer zones on all the relevant fronts and, within diplomatic constraints, retains significant freedom of action to strike its enemies. Gaza is unlikely to see lasting peace while Hamas remains its leading power, but this new Israeli security doctrine hopes to stop the terrorist group from plunging Israel into damaging new wars.

* * *

Despite all the successes and theatrics Israel would pull off in Iran and Lebanon, October 7 remains the day of this war which has seared deepest into the Israeli mind. Hamas invaded from Gaza and packed an entire *intifada*'s worth of slaughter into a single day, setting everything else into motion. Even if the war that followed becomes enshrined in Palestinian memory as a story of pure victimization, the initial ecstasy expressed at the slaughter of Israeli civilians should not be forgotten.[154]

As we have seen, much of the international opposition to Israel's war effort sprung up soon after the October 7 attack. The UN General Assembly resisted condemning the Hamas attack until September 2025, and even then, only as part of a larger French diplomatic shot across Israel's bow. The UN Security Council still has never condemned the October 7 massacre.

The longer Israel fought, the more support for the war effort drained at home and abroad. The world wanted quiet, and for the Palestinians' suffering to end. Israelis wanted the hostages to come home, and most came to believe there was not much more the IDF could achieve to defeat Hamas.

Israel had opportunities to conclude the fighting at earlier junctures. In the summer of 2024, after the invasion of Rafah. In March 2025, extending the second hostage deal. In each case, the prime minister refused, deciding to fight on for better terms. Gallant, Gantz, and Halevi had reservations, but were willing to accept the terms of the deals on the table. Halevi believed that Netanyahu had not sufficiently invested in negotiations about the second phase of the January 2025 hostage deal, involving the shaping of postwar Gaza.

The rising diplomatic costs of the war were undeniable. But the costs of acceding to a new normal that yields another Gaza war a few years from now are equally daunting. The key for Israel, now that it has already paid the costs in blood, treasure, and diplomacy of a major war in Gaza, is to avoid having to do this all over again. This means preserving indefinitely a security perimeter and demilitarized zone around the outskirts of the Gaza Strip, as well as the option of Israeli raids against terror groups as needed, as currently exists in the West Bank. One test for the new Gaza is the West Bank test: How big a force do you need to get in and destroy a terrorist cell? If it only requires a small unit, then Israel can act quickly and often, keeping the terrorists on the defensive.

* * *

Hamas's October 7 gambit delayed the expansion of the Abraham Accords. But so far, it has failed to break them up, a sign they are built to last. Given that Bahrain, the UAE, and Morocco continued to stick with Israel through this long and bloody war, they are even more committed to the relationship than Israelis had thought. The process of normalizing relations with the Arab world, then, continues. It has not lost its beachhead.

Expansion is another story. The Saudis, long presumed to be the next domino to fall, have hesitated. In what seems like a new strategic judgment, Saudi leaders have turned more against Israel during the war. Perhaps they cannot be seen abandoning the Palestinians in their dire straits and must insist on real progress toward statehood. The Trump plan did include a Palestinian state, but only as a distant, highly contingent aspiration. That was the most leading Israeli politicians could sign on to after October 7. Even centrist officials who support the idea in the long term, view such a state as too politically dangerous to pursue in the short and medium terms. On October 7, the broad Israeli middle saw a version of Palestinian nationalism that shook it to its core. Israelis will need to see something different to change their minds.

Hamas succeeded in blocking the Israel–Saudi deal, and the Israel–Sunni alliance has taken a hit. But at the same time, those Sunni states saw what Israel did to Iran—and how it was able to bring in American power to help finish the job.

Given that stopping the Iranian nuclear program had been a major US priority for years, Israel also amply proved what it brings to the table as an American ally. Even as support for Israel declines sharply among Democrats and younger and isolationist Republicans, the realist, national-interest case for US support for Israel has never been stronger. What other US ally has the capability and the will to do what Israel just did to a dangerous US adversary? As the US seeks a way out of the conflicts of the Middle East, it will need regional partners to shoulder the burden. In short, it will need allies with a backbone like Israel.

At the same time, with military aid to Israel being scrutinized more seriously in the US than it has been in decades, Jerusalem must contend with the possibility that Washington will not always come to its aid with weapons deliveries. If the embargoes and delays during the war didn't make that clear, the new politics of US aid should. The most serious conversation in years is taking place within the Jewish state about how to achieve greater independence in a wide variety of weapons areas, even as Israel hopes to hold onto its military support from America for some years while it transitions.

* * *

For decades, Netanyahu promised to remove the Iranian nuclear threat. In June 2025, he kept that promise. The war room of Netanyahu, Gallant, and Gantz, the IDF high command, and the Mossad also promised to return Israel's northern residents to safety on the border with Hezbollah. Between the fall and winter of 2024, they kept that promise. Israel's decision-makers never said a word about Syria. But their actions over the course of the war helped transform Syria from a longtime strategic threat to a potential addition to the Abraham Accords.

Of course, Iran has not given up its nuclear or regional ambitions. Jerusalem and Washington will need to remain on guard. But the rollback of Iranian power establishes a new security baseline that Israelis will gladly accept.

The above successes, however, all came fairly late in the war. The first and foundational promises by Netanyahu, Gallant, and Gantz in October 2023 were to end the threat from Hamas and return the Israeli hostages it kidnapped. Both promises were kept in part, but not in full, given that the threat from Hamas has been substantially reduced, but not ended, and nearly all of the hostages were returned, but around forty were killed over the course of the war.

The failures of October 7, and of the previous sixteen years in which Hamas was allowed to cement its rule and pack Gaza with tunnels, left Israel with challenges that were very difficult to solve. Israel's two goals in Gaza, dismantling Hamas and returning the Israeli hostages, were complementary in the early phase of the war. In the war's middle phases, however, some IDF operations led to hostages being killed. Then, as 2025 went on, the goals were often in direct contradiction. Netanyahu's determination to keep fighting to achieve all his goals in Gaza eventually encountered the problem of dramatically diminishing returns.

Crucially, the war room never made a promise about the Jewish state's place in the world. Maybe it should have. If it had, for one, it certainly would not have blocked all new food aid to Gaza from March to May in 2025, precipitating a crisis. Perhaps Israel could have prevented the diplomatic cascade of that summer, when European allies recognized a Palestinian state while offering Israel nothing in return. Then again, if Israel really had treated preserving its international standing as a key objective, it would not have allowed its urban war in Gaza to drag on for two years. It would have shown more flexibility on postwar planning, signaling to the world that it was working to end the war, rather than sustain it indefinitely.

Critics will say the prime minister fought on only to keep power. Netanyahu would say that after October 7, Israel needed total victory to restore security and deterrence. The debate would then go on in endless circles about whether total victory was even possible, and whether the interest being pursued was national or personal.

For a time, pushing forward worked to Israel's advantage. Even against great pressure, Netanyahu prevailed to maintain the war to keep open the possibility of invading Rafah, defeating Hezbollah, and destroying the Iranian nuclear program and proxy axis should the right opportunities arise for him.

But continuing beyond that? The quest to end the fight in Gaza on a similarly convincing victory would drain Israel—and cost it severely on the world stage.

The war appears to have ended in October 2025. Yet even as distance from the war brings some diplomatic relief, its length and intensity mean that Israel now has to start from a much more hostile diplomatic baseline. In the US, this is something new and dangerous. A young generation's first impression of the Jewish state has been formed by the destruction of Gaza. Second impressions are less formative, but Israelis and fair-minded Americans will have to make the case anew for bipartisan support for Israel. Nothing, on either side of the aisle, can be taken for granted anymore.

For all the war room's dysfunction and small-minded rivalries, for large portions of the war, Netanyahu, Gallant, and Gantz balanced each other's views. This may have helped Israel avoid major errors and kept its relations with US Democrats and Western Europe from collapsing. Once Gantz quit and Netanyahu fired Gallant, the prime minister had no war room of substance to push back on his ideas—or those of his coalition partners. He did not think he would miss Gantz or Gallant, but on this, he did.

More than two years after the war started, it is less clear than ever whether the legacy of Israel's war room will be its military victories or its diplomatic fumbles. Which will last and which will prove ephemeral?

AUTHOR'S NOTE FROM YONAH JEREMY BOB

We are in an age of hyperpolarization, where few see bipartisan dialogue and actions as positively as they were once seen. In some cases, no one can even agree on the same basic set of facts of what happened. In addition to fulfilling its main goal: being an enticing behind-the-scenes account of the Middle East war of 2023–2025, I hope that this book can also be a small contribution to restoring some bipartisan dialogue.

Elliot Kaufman is a brilliant writer and thinker, and after I saw his blockbuster interview with Israeli Prime Minister Benjamin Netanyahu in *The Wall Street Journal* on December 20, 2024, I knew he was the coauthor I wanted for this book.

We have a long list of views in common, which I will not list here. And yet, with so much in common, we still have some significant differences. Some are smaller and have to do with phraseology, such as my preference for "judicial overhaul" and his preference for "judicial reform" to describe the internal Israeli battle over the powers of the Israeli legal establishment from 2023 to 2025; as a compromise, we alternated between the terms. Some have to do with our jobs: I write news and Elliot writes editorials. That means my writing on controversial political issues tends to be drier and inextricably linked to factual descriptions. Elliot's writing is equally concerned with the facts, but tends to be more colorful.

A few examples of my own personal views were watered down by our bipartisan process. I believe and said publicly as early as October

2023 that all Israeli leaders, including Netanyahu, Gallant, Gantz, and the many IDF and Shin Bet leaders who did in fact resign, should have resigned long before now for their joint roles in the failure to prevent Hamas's October 7 invasion. For me, this is bipartisan blame. I fully credit Netanyahu along with the Israeli defense establishment for historic accomplishments against Iran, Hezbollah, and Syria. However, I believe he made historic errors as the primary architect of Israel's policies from 2009 to 2023 in missing some peace negotiations opportunities (without opining on how much of the Israeli–Palestinian conflict would actually have been resolved) and in seeking to contain and deter Hamas. He also harmed Israel's name with US Democrats and other parts of the fair-minded West (Germany is another notable example) by continuing the war for too long (two IDF chiefs and the IDF high command also think so).

Whether the war should have ended in late summer 2024, early 2025 or summer 2025 is hotly debated within the Israeli defense establishment. But close to zero of the Israeli defense establishment supported continuing the war beyond that point, and beyond that point is where Israel's standing took the largest global walloping. Regarding US Democrats, I am not challenging the presumption that currently the US Republican Party is more supportive of Israel, only that, as *The Jerusalem Post* consistently holds, it is in Israel's interests to keep support for the Jewish state bipartisan, given that American politics is always a pendulum.

Similarly, in our complex world, one can compliment Netanyahu, and especially Trump, on finally arriving at a ceasefire deal while still being ready to critique both of them in other areas (for example, critiquing Trump for his lack of support for Ukraine over a period of several months).

I believe that critics of Netanyahu do not give him enough credit in believing that he is solely motivated by keeping his coalition alive and having additional power as prime minister to influence his public-corruption trial. He has serious and sophisticated ideological positions, and there were times during the war when he was right and Gallant and

Gantz were wrong. But I believe his supporters are disingenuous not to realize that the politics and trial do have a major negative impact on his decisions.

A word on the International Criminal Court and the alleged war crimes controversy: There is no question in my mind that for the vast majority of the war, Israel tried harder than most militaries would if invaded by a foreign terror army to focus its fire on Hamas and not on Palestinian civilians. Also, there is no question in my mind that Hamas did all it could to push its own civilian populace into harm's way in a cynical attempt to harm Israeli legitimacy. At the same time, given the tens of thousands of Palestinian noncombatants killed by Israel even according to IDF estimates (which reduce the sixty-nine thousand number down to somewhere in the thirty-five thousand to forty-five thousand range), I believe there are many times that Israel could have done better. Due to the unjustified ongoing ICC proceedings against Israel, I refrain, for now, from identifying specific incidents. I have, however, dropped hints in some of my *Jerusalem Post* reporting, and pressed for the IDF to rush out the results of its more than ninety criminal probes to set the record straight on Israel's narrative—both the extensive efforts to avoid civilian harm and regarding the many mistakes that Israel has admitted to.

I know there is plenty in the above with which Elliot would agree, but plenty that he would put differently. After all of the above, it has been an honor to work with Elliot. I have learned a lot from him and better understand a number of views that I did not properly understand beforehand. I hope that open-minded readers on the Right and Left of US and Israeli politics will find the same benefit by being confronted by a mix of ideas and the nuanced telling of the story that we achieved together.

One last note on what the book does not cover as much as we would like, though all issues are mentioned: the October 7 disaster and suffering of Israeli victims, the suffering of Israeli hostages, and the suffering of Palestinian civilians. The book does address all three, but more in passing since all three have already been extensively covered. This book's unique contribution is giving an in-depth insider account of the Israeli war room's decisions. In order to tell that long and complex story, these other critical topics could not be addressed in the same depth.

ENDNOTES

Chapter One

[1] Jake Sullivan, "The Sources of American Power," *Foreign Affairs* (November/December 2023); and "Notable & Quotable: Sullivan," *The Wall Street Journal*, October 26, 2023.
[2] Bob Woodward, *War* (Simon & Schuster, 2024), 206.
[3] Ibid.
[4] Ibid.
[5] Ibid.
[6] Nadav Eyal, "Gallant Describes the Drama of October 11 as 'The Largest Defense Missed Opportunity in Our History,'" *Yediot Ahronot*, February 8, 2025; and independently confirmed through interviews by the authors.
[7] Woodward, 206.

Chapter Two

[8] For two views, see: Benny Morris, *The Birth of the Palestinian Refugee Problem Revisited* (Cambridge University Press, 2003); and Efraim Karsh, *Palestine Betrayed* (Yale University Press, 2010).
[9] See: Adi Schwartz and Einat Wilf, *The War of Return: How Western Indulgence of the Palestinian Dream Has Obstructed the Path to Peace* (St. Martin's Griffin, 2020).
[10] Reuven Paz, "Higher Education and the Development of Palestinian Islamic Groups," *Middle East Review of International Affairs* 4, no. 2 (June 2000).
[11] Daniel Estrin and William Marx, "Who Was Hamas Leader Yahya Sinwar?" *NPR*, October 17, 2024.
[12] Ibid.
[13] "The Covenant of the Islamic Resistance Movement," *The Avalon Project at Yale Law School*, 1988; and "Hamas Leaders: Our Goal Is Establishment of Global

Islamic Caliphate, Not Just Liberation of Palestine," *Middle East Media Research Institute*, December 8, 2023.

14 Samia Nakhoul, "Yahya Sinwar: The Hamas Leader Committed to Eradicating Israel Is Dead," *Reuters*, October 18, 2024.

15 "Senior Hamas Official Ali Baraka: We Have Been Secretly Planning the Invasion for Two Years," interview on Russia Today TV, October 8, 2023, *Middle East Media Research Institute*, October 11, 2023.

16 "Hamas Leader Abroad Khaled Mashal Rejects Accusations of Transgressions Against Civilians on October 7 Attack," interview on Al-Arabiya Network, *Middle East Media Research Institute*, October 19, 2023.

17 "'Al-Aqsa Flood': Initiated by 70 Elite Fighters, Crafted by 5 Hamas Leaders," *Asharq Al-Awsat*, January 10, 2024.

18 Jonathan Foreman, "The Untold Story of How Israel Failed on October 7," *Commentary* (May 2025).

19 Ibid.

20 Marcus Walker and Summer Said, "Oct. 7 Attack Aimed to Derail Israeli Talks with Saudi Arabia," *The Wall Street Journal*, May 19, 2025.

21 Yigal Carmon, "Signs of Possible War in September-October," *Middle East Media Research Institute*, August 31, 2023.

22 Avi Jager, "The Transformation of the Israel Defense Forces," *Naval War College Review* 74, no. 2 (Spring 2021): 3-4; see also: Jacob Siegel, "Israel's Forgotten Army," *Tablet* (October 2025).

23 Lahav Harkov, "Netanyahu: Money to Hamas Part of Strategy to Keep Palestinians Divided," *The Jerusalem Post*, March 12, 2019.

Chapter Three

24 "SJP – Day of Resistance Toolkit," *The Investigative Project on Terrorism*, October 8, 2023, https://www.investigativeproject.org/document/1179-sjp-day-of-resistance-toolkit.

25 "Joint Statement by Harvard Palestine Solidarity Groups on the Situation in Palestine," *Birzeit University*, October 8, 2023, https://www.birzeit.edu/en/the-world-sides-with-gaza/joint-statement-harvard-palestine-solidarity-groups-situation-palestine; and "Columbia SJP and JVP 10/9 Open Letter," *Disruptnow.org*, October 9, 2023, https://disruptnow.org/wp-content/uploads/2025/05/Columbia-SJP-and-JVP-10_9-Open-Letter.pdf; and Sean Stevens and Nathan Honeycutt, "2024 Student Encampment Protests," *The Foundation for Individual Rights and Expression*, 2024.

26 Eado Hecht and Eitan Shamir, "Does Israel Need a Large Army If It Has Advanced Technology?" *The Begin-Sadat Center for Strategic Studies*, Perspectives Paper No. 2,277, May 29, 2024, 5.

27 Arthur Herman, "The Strategic Fruits of Israel's Military Victory," *Mosaic* (November 2025).

28 "Israel/OPT: Civilians on Both Sides Paying the Price of Unprecedented Escalation in Hostilities Between Israel and Gaza as Death Toll Mounts," *Amnesty International*, October 7, 2023; and "Damning Evidence of War Crimes as Israeli Attacks Wipe Out Entire Families in Gaza," *Amnesty International*, October 20, 2023; and "'You Feel Like You Are Subhuman': Israel's Genocide Against Palestinians in Gaza," *Amnesty International*, December 5, 2024.

29 Yoav Gallant and John Spencer, "Between Illusion and Imitation: The IDF and the West's War Dilemma," *The Defense Memo*, August 6, 2025.

Chapter Four

30 Qatari Ministry of Foreign Affairs, "Qatar Expresses Concern over the Developments in Gaza Strip and Calls for De-Escalation," October 7, 2023.

31 Raz Segal, "A Textbook Case of Genocide," *Jewish Currents*, October 13, 2023.

32 Ben Samuels, "Conditioning U.S. Military Aid to Israel Triggers Fierce Debate Among Democrats," *Haaretz*, November 28, 2023.

Chapter Five

33 Hecht and Shamir, 5; and Azar Gat, "Expanding Israel's Ground Forces or Prioritizing Technology?" *The Institute for National Security Studies*, March 24, 2024.

34 "Hamas Official Mousa Abu Marzouk: The Tunnels In Gaza Were Built to Protect Hamas Fighters, Not Civilians," interview on Russia Today TV, *Middle East Media Research Institute*, October 27, 2023.

35 Meir Ben Shabbat, "If Israel Wants a Decisive Win, It Must Renew the Blockade on Gaza," *Israel Hayom*, December 21, 2023.

36 Video shared by Mark Dubowitz (@mdubowitz), "Now with English subtitles. Is the Biden administration's pressure on Israel costing the lives of Israeli soldiers?" *X*, December 13, 2023. https://x.com/mdubowitz/status/1735061318703464841.

Chapter Six

37 John Spencer (@SpencerGuard), "The 2016-2017 Battle of Mosul was one battle, in one city against 3 to 5k militants with limited defenses," *X*, January 25, 2024. https://x.com/SpencerGuard/status/1750628148130054302; and Spencer, "The IDF have actually cleared urban terrain/tunnels at historic pace," *X*, January 28, 2024. https://x.com/SpencerGuard/status/1751629221049376847

38 Woodward, 269.

39 Ibid.

40 Ibid.

41 Ibid.

42 Jonathan Martin, "Forget No Labels. Biden's Third-Party Peril Is on the Left," *Politico*, February 4, 2024.

43 "Hostilities in the Gaza Strip and Israel - Reported Impact, 13 February 2024," *UN Office for the Coordination Humanitarian Affairs*, February 13, 2024.

44 Carol Lee, Jonathan Allen, Peter Nicholas, and Courtney Kube, "Biden Disparages Netanyahu in Private but Hasn't Significantly Changed US Policy Toward Israel in Gaza," *NBC News*, February 12, 2024.

45 Karen DeYoung, Susannah George, and Loveday Morris, "U.S., Arab Nations Plan for Postwar Gaza, Timeline for Palestinian State," *The Washington Post*, February 14, 2024; and Jacob Magid, "US Revives Policy Deeming Settlements Illegal, Pans Israel's Plan for 3,000 New Homes," *The Times of Israel*, February 23, 2024.

46 Rory Jones, Dov Lieber, Summer Said, and Anat Peled, "Israel Forced Sinwar From His Tunnels," *The Wall Street Journal*, October 21, 2024.

47 Woodward, 277.

48 "Gallant Left a War Cabinet Meeting – and Returned After an Hour," *Yediot Ahronot*, January 13, 2024; and independently confirmed by the authors through interviews.

Chapter Seven

49 David Adesnik and Mark Montgomery, "The Big Lies About Israel's Big Bombs," *Commentary* (April 2024).

50 See: Martin Kramer, "The Nazi Case for Hamas," *Sandbox Blog*, October 26, 2023.

51 "Gaza Humanitarian Aid Data," *Humanitarian Efforts Israel* (COGAT), accessed May 20, 2024; and Barak Ravid and Andrew Solender, "White House Says ICC Sanctions 'not the right answer,'" *Axios*, May 28, 2024.

Chapter Eight

52 Ben Samuels, "Nancy Pelosi Among 40 Democrats Urging Biden to Halt Pending Israel Arms Sales, Condition Aid," *Haaretz*, April 6, 2024; and Hannah Sarisohn and Tovah Lazoroff, "Democratic Congressional Calls to Halt Arms Sales to Israel Picks Up Steam," April 10, 2024; and Joe Gould, "Top Democrat Says He Needs More Answers Before Approving F-15 Sale to Israel," *Politico*, April 9, 2024.

53 Woodward, 281.

54 Louisa Loveluck, Heidi Levine, and Sufian Taha, "Israelis Recount Worry, Fear After Night of Iran Missile Interceptions," *The Washington Post*, April 14, 2024.

55 Yaghoub Fazeli, "IRGC Chief Spells 'New Equation' After First-Ever Iranian Strikes on Israel," *Al-Arabiya English*, April 14, 2024.

Chapter Nine

56 "Mohammed Deif," *Counter Extremism Project*, February 27, 2024.

57 Nidal Al-Mughrabi and Maayan Lubell, "Israeli Air Strike Kills Three Hamas Commanders in Gaza," *Reuters*, August 21, 2014.

58 Ronen Bergman and Patrick Kingsley, "Israel Targets Architect of Oct. 7 Attacks in Airstrike," *The New York Times*, July 13, 2024; and Lauren Irwin, "Israeli

strike Targeting Hamas Commanders Leaves More Than 70 Dead: Officials," *The Hill*, July 13, 2024; and independently confirmed by the authors in interviews.

[59] See: John Yoon, "After Haniyeh's Death, Who Are Hamas's Most Prominent Leaders?" *The New York Times*, July 31, 2024; and Samia Nakhoul and Stephen Farrell, "Who Was Ismail Haniyeh and Why Is His Assassination a Blow to Hamas?" *Reuters*, July 31, 2024; and Louisa Loveluck, Hajar Harb, Hazem Balousha, and Miriam Berger, "Where Does Hamas Go from Here?" *The Washington Post*, July 31, 2024.

[60] Matthew Levitt, "The Death of a Hezbollah Lifer," *The Washington Institute for Near East Policy*, July 31, 2024.

[61] Ibid.

[62] Sune Engel Rasmussen, Adam Chamseddine, and Carrie Keller-Lynn, "How Israel Killed a Ghost," *The Wall Street Journal*, August 18, 2024.

[63] Thomas Joscelyn, "State Department Offers Rewards for 2 Hezbollah Leaders," *Long War Journal*, October 10, 2017.

Chapter Ten

[64] Amichai Stein, "Behind the Scenes at the Pentagon on the Day Hezbollah's Pagers Exploded – Interview," *The Jerusalem Post*, March 13, 2025; and independently confirmed with sources by the authors.

[65] Ibid.

[66] Lior Ben Ari, "Arab World Mocks Hezbollah for Damaging Israeli Chicken Coop in Revenge Attack," *Ynet*, August 26, 2024.

[67] Mohanad Hage Ali, "Hezbollah Doesn't Want a War with Israel," *Foreign Affairs*, July 26, 2024.

[68] "Tens of thousands Rally in Tel Aviv to Demand Hostage Deal, Denounce Government," *The Times of Israel*, June 2, 2024.

[69] Lesley Stahl, Aliza Chasan, Shachar Bar-On, and Jinsol Jung, "Israel's Spy Agency, Mossad, Spent Years Orchestrating Hezbollah Walkie-Talkie, Pager Plots," *CBS News*, December 22, 2024.

[70] Ibid.

[71] Jonathan Yerushalmi and Dan Milmo, "Hezbollah Device Blasts: How Did Pagers and Walkie-Talkies Explode and What Do We Know About the Attacks," *The Guardian*, September 18, 2024; and Maya Gebeily and Laila Bassa, "How Hezbollah Used Pagers and Couriers to Counter Israel's High-Tech Surveillance," *Reuters*, July 9, 2024.

[72] Ibid.

[73] Ibid.

[74] Ibid.

[75] Ben Blanchard, "Gold Apollo says Budapest-Based BAC Produces Model of Pagers Used in Lebanon Blasts," *Reuters*, September 18, 2024.

[76] Tom Edgington, Joshua Cheetham, William Dahlgreen, and Daniele Palumbo, "What We Know About Firm Linked to Lebanon Pagers," *BBC*, September 19, 2024.

[77] Ibid.

[78] Ibid.

[79] Stahl, Chasan, Bar-On, and Jung; and Edgington, Cheetham, Dahlgreen, and Palumbo.

[80] Lazar Berman, "Mossad Chief Backs Netanyahu Over Decision to Hold Off on Lebanon offensive," *The Times of Israel*, February 26, 2025.

Chapter Eleven

[81] Ron Ben-Yishai, "In the Heart of Dahieh: The Daring Mossad Operation That Led to the Assassination of Nasrallah," *Yediot Ahronot*, September 21, 2025.

[82] Meir Ben Shabbat, "'Spider Web' Theory Unravels," *Israel Hayom*, September 30, 2024.

Chapter Twelve

[83] Tovah Lazaroff, "US deploys Anti-Ballistic System to Israel, Iran Says 'No Red Lines,'" *The Jerusalem Post*, October 12, 2024.

Chapter Thirteen

[84] Emanuel Fabian, "Army Pushes Back on Reported Fears Sinwar Fled to Sinai, as Battles Return to Gaza City," *The Times of Israel*, February 20, 2024.

[85] Uri Isaac, "IDF Assessment: 'At the End of the War, There Will Be Missing Persons like Ron Arad,'" *Yediot Ahronot*, July 30, 2024.

[86] Lazar Berman and Jessica Steinberg, "IDF Recovered Sinwar's DNA in Tunnel Complex Where 6 Hostages Were Executed," *The Times of Israel*, October 18, 2024.

[87] Anat Peled, Dov Lieber, Carrie Keller-Lynn, and Summer Said, "How Luck Ran Out for Hamas Leader," *The Wall Street Journal*, October 19, 2024.

[88] Ibid.

[89] TOI Staff and Agencies, "Abbas's PLO Mourns 'Martyrdom' of Hamas Chief Sinwar, a 'Great National Leader,'" *The Times of Israel*, October 19, 2024; and "Turkey's Erdogan Offers His Condolences for Killing of Hamas LEader Sinwar," *Associated Press Videos*, October 19, 2024.

[90] Mark Hookham, "British Lawyer Who Called for Netanyahu to Be Arrested over 'War Crimes' Denies Misconduct Following Harassment Claims," *The Daily Mail*, October 19, 2024; and Joshua Goodman and Molly Quell, "International Court Prosecutor Who Charged Netanyahu Faces Sexual Misconduct Accusation," *The Associated Press*, October 25, 2024; and Harry Davies and Robert Flummerfelt, "ICC Chief Prosecutor Facing Staff Calls for External Inquiry into Sexual Misconduct Claims," *The Guardian*, October 31, 2024.

[91] See: Kamala Harris, "The Constant Battle," *Atlantic*, September 10, 2025; and Jake Tapper and Alex Thompson, *Original Sin* (Penguin Press, 2025).

[92] "Poll Shows Israelis Massively Favor Trump over Harris in US Election," *The Times of Israel,* October 29, 2024.

[93] F. Brinley Bruton, Max Burman, and Yarden Segev, "Netanyahu Fires Gallant as Israel's Defense Minister," *NBC News*, November 5, 2024.

[94] Nava Freiberg and Emanuel Fabian "Netanyahu Taped Saying He Replaced Gallant, Halevi So Haredi Draft Exemption Bill Can Pass," *The Times of Israel*, June 4, 2025.

Chapter Fourteen

[95] Anshel Pfeffer, "Iran Has Saved Bashar Assad (for Now)," *Haaretz*, April 6, 2012.

[96] See: Nicole Grajewski, "Why Did Iran Allow Bashar al-Assad's Downfall?" *Diwan*, December 9, 2024.

[97] Antonio Giustozzi, "Russia and the Collapse of the Assad Regime," *The Russia Program at George Washington University*, February 18, 2025.

[98] "Eldest Son of Syria's President Assad Is Killed in Car Crash," *Associated Press*, January 22, 1994.

[99] Susan Sachs, "Bashar al-Assad: The Shy Young Doctor at Syria's Helm," *The New York Times*, June 14, 2000.

[100] See: Thomas Friedman, *From Beirut to Jerusalem* (Farrar, Straus & Giroux, 1989), ch. 4.

[101] Jay Solomon, "The North Korean-Israeli Shadow War," *The Washington Institute for Near East Policy*, September 19, 2019; and "Timeline: Crackdown on Protests in Syria," *Reuters*, February 24, 2012.

[102] Haid Haid, "Turkey's Gradual Efforts to Professionalize Syrian Allies," *Sada*, November 2, 2018.

[103] Fuad Shahbazov, "What Turkey Hopes to Gain from the HTS Offensive in Syria," *The Stimson Center*, December 5, 2024.

[104] Ben Hubbard, "Jihadist, Rebel, Statesman: The Many Faces of Syria's Leader," *The New York Times*, September 23, 2025.

[105] "Hay'at Tahrir al-Sham (HTS)," *Center for Strategic and International Studies*, October 4, 2018.

[106] Carlotta Gall, "Turkey Emerges as a Big Winner in the Wake of al-Assad's Ouster," *The New York Times*, December 13, 2024.

[107] "Israeli Airstrike in Syria Kills Senior Iranian Revolutionary Guards Member," *Reuters*, December 25, 2023; and "5 IRGC Officers, Including Syria Intel Chief, Killed in Damascus Strike Blamed on Israel," *The Times of Israel*, January 20, 2024.

[108] "Exclusive: Iran's Guards Pull Officers from Syria After Israeli Strikes," *Reuters*, February 1, 2024.

[109] Walid Al Nofal, "'Decades to Rebuild': Israel Grabs Land and Wipes Out Syria's Arsenal," *Syria Direct*, December 10, 2024.

Chapter Fifteen

110 Jane Prinsley, "BBC headlines 'three times more likely to hold Israel to account than Hamas,'" The Jewish Chronicle, November 23, 2025.

Chapter Sixteen

111 Francois Murphy, "IAEA Board Declares Iran in Breach of Non-Proliferation Obligations," *Reuters*, June 12, 2025; and David Albright, Sarah Burkhard, and Andrea Stricker, "Analysis of the IAEA's May 31, 2025, Comprehensive Iran NPT Safeguards Report," *Institute for Science and International Security*, June 6, 2025.

112 Vasco Cotovio and Brad Lendon, "Built Inside a Mountain and Hardened Against Bunker-Busting Bombs. Here's What We Know About Iran's Fordow Nuclear Site," *CNN*, June 18, 2025.

113 Tucker Carlson (@TuckerCarlson), "It's worth pointing out that a strike on the Iranian nuclear sites will almost certainly result," *X*, March 17, 2025, https://x.com/TuckerCarlson/status/1901761608449216890 ; and Carlson, "Mark Levin was at the White House today, lobbying for war with Iran," *X*, June 4, 2025, https://x.com/TuckerCarlson/status/1930430114602402183.

114 Jacob Magid and Agencies, "Witkoff Indicates US Seeks to Cap Iran Uranium Enrichment, Not Dismantle Nuclear Program," *The Times of Israel*, April 15, 2025.

115 "The Seven Deadly Sins of a Bad Iranian Nuclear Deal," *The Foundation for Defense of Democracies*, April 25, 2025.

116 "Risch, Ricketts Send Letter Backing President Trump's Call for Full Dismantlement of Iran's Nuclear Program," *Senate Foreign Relations Committee*, May 14, 2025.

117 Matthew Boyle, "Exclusive—Steve Witkoff Ahead of Round 4 of Talks: Iran Has Agreed 'They Don't Want' Nuclear Weapon," *Breitbart*, May 9, 2025.

118 "Read the Full Transcript of Donald Trump's '100 Days' Interview With TIME," *Time*, April 25, 2025.

119 "Iran FM Rules Out Negotiations over Enrichment, Says Khamenei Set Red Line," *Iran International*, May 20, 2025; and Somayeh Malekian, "Iran Leader Casts Doubt on US Nuclear Talks, Saying Tehran Won't Stop Enrichment," *ABC News*, May 20, 2025.

120 Jacob Magid, "Trump: I told Netanyahu Striking Iran Would Be 'Very Inappropriate' When Talks 'Very Close' to Solution," *The Times of Israel*, May 28, 2025.

121 Parisa Hafezi, Elwely Elwelly, and Jana Choukeir, "Iran's Khamenei Dismisses US Nuclear Proposal, Vows to Keep Enriching Uranium," *Reuters*, June 4, 2025.

122 Stephen Kalin, "Iranian Health Ministry Says 610 People Killed in Israeli War," *The Wall Street Journal*, June 24, 2025.

123 "Twelve Days Under Fire: A Comprehensive Report on the Iran-Israel War," *Human Rights Activists News Agency*, June 28, 2025.

[124] Mehul Srivastava, Neri Zilber, and John Paul Rathbone, "Israel's Secret War Inside Iran," *The Financial Times*, June 18, 2025; and independently confirmed with sources by the authors.
[125] Michael Doran and Zineb Riboua, "Predatory Sparrow Hacks Iran's Financial System," *The Wall Street Journal*, July 20, 2025.
[126] Itamar Eichner and Lior Ben Ari, "Report: Israel Used DNA, fake Phone Calls to Lure and Kill Top Iranian Generals," *Yediot Ahronot*, July 22, 2024.
[127] David Albright and Spencer Faragasso, "Post-Attack Assessment of the First 12 Days of Israeli and U.S. Strikes on Iranian Nuclear Facilities," *Institute for Science and International Security*, June 24, 2025.
[128] Jon Gambrell, "Iran's Attack on Qatar Air Base Hit Geodesic Dome Used for US Communications, Satellite Photos Show," *Associated Press*, July 12, 2025.
[129] Lara Seligman, "Iran Positions Missile Launchers for Potential Attack on U.S. Forces, U.S. Officials Say," *The Wall Street Journal*, June 23, 2025.
[130] Gambrell.

Chapter Seventeen

[131] Eitan Fischberger, "Gaza Starvation Photos Tell a Thousand Lies," *The Wall Street Journal*, July 31, 2025; and David Collier, "The Truth Behind the Viral Gazan Famine Photo," author's personal website, https://david-collier.com/the-truth-behind-the-viral-gaza-famine-photo/.
[132] Emanuel Fabian, "Israel Says Review Shows Hamas Inflating Gaza Hunger Data in 'Orchestrated Campaign,'" *The Times of Israel*, August 12, 2025.
[133] Amit Segal, "The Price of Flour Shows the Hunger Crisis in Gaza," *The Free Press*, July 24, 2025.
[134] "UN2720 Mechanism for Gaza," *UNOPS*, accessed August 5, 2025, https://app.un2720.org/tracking/collected.
[135] Yannay Spitzer (@YannayASpitzer), "The time has come for charts, based on data from the Gaza Chamber of Commerce and Industry," *X*, August 15, 2025, https://x.com/YannayASpitzer/status/1956420012161343682.
[136] Jeremy Sharon, "Updated Gaza Data Shows Famine Claims Likely Inflated by UN-Backed Monitor," *The Times of Israel*, November 20, 2025.
[137] Megan Brennan, "32% in U.S. Back Israel's Military Action in Gaza, a New Low," *Gallup*, July 29, 2025.
[138] Laura Silver, "How Americans View Israel and the Israel-Hamas War at the Start of Trump's Second Term," *Pew Research Center*, April 8, 2025.
[139] "Read the Full Transcript," *Time*; and "Jared Kushner and Steve Witkoff's Extended 60 Minutes interview," *CBS*, October 19, 2025.
[140] Ibid.
[141] See: Jacob Magid, "Netanyahu Secured Key Edits to Trump Plan, Slowing and Limiting IDF's Gaza Withdrawal," *The Times of Israel*, September 30, 2025.
[142] "Trump's 20-Point Gaza Peace Plan in Full," *BBC*, October 9, 2025.
[143] "Jared Kushner and Steve Witkoff's Extended 60 Minutes Interview," *CBS*.

[144] "Text of the Response by Hamas to Trump's Plan for Ending Gaza's War," *Reuters*, October 4, 2025.

[145] "Read the Full Transcript," *Time.*

[146] "Jared Kushner and Steve Witkoff's Extended 60 Minutes Interview," *CBS.*

[147] Ophir Falk, "Taking Hostages Turned Out to Be Hamas's Undoing," *The Wall Street Journal*, November 4, 2025.

[148] "Morocco to Open Production Facility for Tactical Attack Drones in Partnership with IAI," *The Jerusalem Post,* November 23, 2025; and Oded Yaron, "Germany Is Buying Israeli-Made Spike Anti-Tank Missiles in 2 Billion Euro Deal," Haaretz, October 21, 2025.

[149] "Ben Gvir to US Envoys: Would You Make a deal with Hitler?" *Arutz Sheva,* October 9, 2025.

Conclusion

[150] "IRGC General Gholamali Rashid: Hizbullah in Lebanon, Hamas and PIJ in Palestine, PMU in Iraq, and the Houthis in Yemen Are All Armies Ready to Defend the Iranian Regime," *Middle East Media Research Institute,* September 25, 2021.

[151] David Albright, Sarah Burkhard, and Spencer Faragasso, "Comprehensive Updated Assessment of Iranian Nuclear Sites Five Months After the 12-Day War," *Institute for Science and International Security*, November 21, 2025.

[152] Philissa Cramer, "Germany's Freidrich Merz Calls Iran Fight 'The Dirty Work Israel Is Doing for All of Us,'" *Jewish Telegraphic Agency*, June 17, 2025.

[153] David Daoud, "Don't Wait for Beirut to Tie Hezbollah's Hands," *The Wall Street Journal*, November 12, 2025.

[154] See: Shany Mor, "Ecstasy and Amnesia in the Gaza Strip," *Mosaic* (November 2023).

ACKNOWLEDGMENTS

From Both Authors

From the bottom of our hearts, we would like to thank everyone who agreed to be interviewed on the record, off the record, on deep background, and who otherwise contributed to this book. This includes top political and diplomatic officials, but also top military and intelligence officials who are more used to operating in the shadows, and for whom speaking about their experiences and views is difficult and complicated.

Our agents, Peter and Amy Bernstein, ably guided us through the many twists and turns we went through to bring this project to fruition during a dynamic and ever-changing war. Thank you for your insight and experience.

Working with Adam Bellow, Lauren Campbell, and the talented staff at Wicked Son has helped push us both to reach high standards. Adam's comments and profound understanding of the material elevated the book. Kate Post led the copyediting of this book with clarity and precision. Working on book proposal drafts, Richard Bernstein substantially contributed to the core narrative and structure of this book.

We hope the lessons coming out of this book can in some small way help achieve lasting peace and security in the region.

From Yonah

I would like to thank *Jerusalem Post* Editor-in-Chief Zvika Klein for his vision and support. I would also like to thank Bob Bender, who was my editor for *Target Tehran*, and who gave me critical advice just before he retired from Simon & Schuster about the direction of this book when my ideas were at the formation stage.

I would also like to thank my mother, Joan Bob; my father, Harold Bob of blessed memory; and my wife's parents, Martin and Ruth Lockshin. Significant aspects of what is worthwhile in this book are an outgrowth of my parents raising me to be dedicated to integrity, seeking truth, excellence, and dreaming big. I was blessed to marry into a family that shares similar principles; and my in-laws have been a tremendous source of support.

I would also like to thank my wife, Channa, and our children Natan, Shahar, and Ayala. Channa is not only my life partner, but her deep insights and incisive mind as well as her support and love during the sometimes incredibly intense process of writing and editing this book (and three prior books) were invaluable.

From Elliot

I would like to thank my wife, Sarah, first for our adorable baby, Lev, and second for her superb edits. Without your love and understanding, and your heavy lifting with our big-little guy, this book would not have been possible. My father, Allan, is owed special thanks for taking time off work to review the manuscript. I am also grateful to my mother and brother, Vicki and Harris, who put their careful eyes on this book. For years, my family placed the daily newspaper by my cereal bowl and discussed Middle East policy at the dinner table. It was the finest education I will ever receive.

The Wall Street Journal's Paul Gigot gave me the opportunity to cover this war for the best editorial page anywhere. Thank you for placing your trust in me and for all the work you do. It is a privilege to write for you and all our readers.

ABOUT THE AUTHORS

Yonah Jeremy Bob is the author of three books, including *Target Tehran* (Simon & Schuster, 2023), which told the story of the Mossad's secret war against Iran's nuclear program and its role in the Abraham Accords. *The Wall Street Journal* listed the book in its "Top 5 for Politics" and it won the Jewish Book Council's Natan Award. As the senior military analyst for *The Jerusalem Post*, Yonah has unparalleled access to top Israeli officials, including in the clandestine services, and has interviewed a wide range of current and former US defense and intelligence officials. Yonah graduated from Boston University Law School and Columbia University.

Elliot Kaufman is a *Wall Street Journal* editorial writer and editorial board member focusing on Israel and Iran. He has covered the Middle East war for the *WSJ* from October 7 onward, speaking regularly with top Israeli and US officials. He has also published major interviews with Israel's prime minister, defense minister, foreign minister, and leading historian. Elliot lives in New York with his wife and son and has worked for the *WSJ* since 2018. He graduated from Stanford University.